Frommer's®

Ottawa

4th Edition

by James Hale

Here's what the critics say about Frommer's:

"Amazingly easy to use. Very portable, very complete."
—**BOOKLIST**

"Detailed, accurate, and easy-to-read information
for all price ranges."
—**GLAMOUR MAGAZINE**

"Hotel information is close to encyclopedic."
—**DES MOINES SUNDAY REGISTER**

"Frommer's Guides have a way of giving you
a real feel for a place."
—**KNIGHT RIDDER NEWSPAPERS**

WILEY

John Wiley & Sons Canada, Ltd.

Published by:

JOHN WILEY & SONS CANADA, LTD.

6045 Freemont Blvd.
Mississauga, ON L5R 4J3

Library and Archives Canada Cataloguing in Publication Data
Hale, James, 1954–
    Frommer's Ottawa / James Hale. — 4th ed.

Includes index.
ISBN 978-0-470-15695-7

    1. Ottawa (Ont.)—Guidebooks. I. Title. II. Title: Ottawa.
FC3096.18.H338 2009   917.13'84045   C2008-907366-5

Editor: Gene Shannon
Project Manager: Elizabeth McCurdy
Project Editor: Lindsay Humphreys
Project Coordinator: Lynsey Stanford
Cartographer: Lohnes & Wright
Vice President, Publishing Services: Karen Bryan
Production by Wiley Indianapolis Composition Services

Front cover photo: The Royal Canadian Dragoons (with plumes) and the Royal
    Canadian Regiment parade at Parliament Hill in Ottawa
Back cover photo: The inside of the Museum of Civilization in Gatineau, Quebec

For reseller information, including discounts and premium sales, please call our sales department: Tel. 416-646-7992. For press review copies, author interviews, or other publicity information, please contact our publicity department: Tel. 416-646-4582; Fax: 416-236-4448.

Wiley also publishes its books in a variety of electronic formats. Some content that appears in print may not be available in electronic formats.

Manufactured in the United States

1 2 3 4 5 RRD 13 12 11 10 09

CONTENTS

OTTAWA

CONTENTS

8 CITY STROLLS 158

9 SHOPPING 167

10 OTTAWA AFTER DARK 185

11 SIDE TRIPS FROM OTTAWA 198

APPENDIX: FAST FACTS, TOLL-FREE NUMBERS & WEBSITES 216

INDEX 226

LIST OF MAPS

ABOUT THE AUTHOR

An Ottawa native, James Hale is a writer, editor and broadcaster with a keen interest in urban life around the world. He divides his time between providing communications counsel to government and corporate clients and writing about jazz for publications that include *DownBeat* and *Signal to Noise*. He is also Vice-President of the Jazz Journalists Association.

ACKNOWLEDGMENTS

My thanks to Sabrina Hale for giving up her summer vacation to work the phones, to Gene Shannon for advice and enthusiasm for the project, and to Ellen Henderson for her great eye for detail.

AN INVITATION TO THE READER

In researching this book, we discovered many wonderful places—hotels, restaurants, shops, and more. We're sure you'll find others. Please tell us about them, so we can share the information with your fellow travelers in upcoming editions. If you were disappointed with a recommendation, we'd love to know that, too. Please write to:

Frommer's Ottawa, 4th Edition
John Wiley & Sons Canada, Ltd. • 6045 Freemont Blvd. • Mississauga, ON L5R 4J3

AN ADDITIONAL NOTE

Please be advised that travel information is subject to change at any time—and this is especially true of prices. We therefore suggest that you write or call ahead for confirmation when making your travel plans. The authors, editors, and publisher cannot be held responsible for the experiences of readers while traveling. Your safety is important to us, however, so we encourage you to stay alert and be aware of your surroundings. Keep a close eye on cameras, purses, and wallets, all favorite targets of thieves and pickpockets.

Other Great Guides for Your Trip:

Frommer's Canada
Frommer's Toronto 2009
Frommer's Montreal & Quebec City 2009

FROMMER'S STAR RATINGS, ICONS & ABBREVIATIONS

Every hotel, restaurant, and attraction listing in this guide has been ranked for quality, value, service, amenities, and special features using a star-rating system. In country, state, and regional guides, we also rate towns and regions to help you narrow down your choices and budget your time accordingly. Hotels and restaurants are rated on a scale of zero (recommended) to three stars (exceptional). Attractions, shopping, nightlife, towns, and regions are rated according to the following scale: zero stars (recommended), one star (highly recommended), two stars (very highly recommended), and three stars (must-see).

In addition to the star-rating system, we also use seven feature icons that point you to the great deals, in-the-know advice, and unique experiences that separate travelers from tourists. Throughout the book, look for:

Finds	Special finds—those places only insiders know about
Fun Facts	Fun facts—details that make travelers more informed and their trips more fun
Kids	Best bets for kids, and advice for the whole family
Moments	Special moments—those experiences that memories are made of
Overrated	Places or experiences not worth your time or money
Tips	Insider tips—great ways to save time and money
Value	Great values—where to get the best deals

The following **abbreviations** are used for credit cards:

AE	American Express	DISC	Discover	V	Visa
DC	Diners Club	MC	MasterCard		

FROMMERS.COM

Now that you have this guidebook to help you plan a great trip, visit our website at www.frommers.com for additional travel information on more than 4,000 destinations. We update features regularly to give you instant access to the most current trip-planning information available. At **Frommers.com**, you'll find scoops on the best airfares, lodging rates, and car rental bargains. You can even book your travel online through our reliable travel booking partners. Other popular features include:

- Online updates of our most popular guidebooks
- Vacation sweepstakes and contest giveaways
- Newsletters highlighting the hottest travel trends
- Podcasts, interactive maps, and up-to-the-minute events listings
- Opinionated blog entries by Arthur Frommer himself
- Online travel message boards with featured travel discussions

What's New in Ottawa

A city with one of the fastest growing populations in Canada, Ottawa is a community of constant change. Since the publication of the last edition of *Frommer's Ottawa* in 2007, there have been a number of developments.

PLANNING YOUR TRIP Although the weakened U.S. dollar means that Canada is no longer the bargain it once was for travelers from south of the border, at least the taxes are slightly lower. The federal Goods and Services Tax (GST) is now 5% rather than 6%.

ACCOMMODATIONS One of the busiest corners in central Ottawa is now the location of Canada's first hotel in the Indigo chain. **Hotel Indigo,** 123 Metcalfe St. (© **866/246-3446** or 613/231-6555), is also the only local hotel retrofitted into a heritage building—a well-executed renovation that created a soaring lobby space and extremely attractive rooms. See p. 74.

Ottawa gained two new airport hotels in 2008, although both are located a distance from the main terminal and require a short taxi ride. **Hilton Garden Inn Ottawa Airport,** 2400 Alert Rd. (© **613/288-9001**), provides some amenities like HDTV, bedding options, and ergonomic desk chairs that you expect at pricier properties. See p. 87. **Holiday Inn Express Hotel & Suites,** 2881 Gibford Rd. (© **877/660-8550** or 613/738-0284), is more of a no-frills place, but does provide the option of some large executive-level suites with fireplaces and whirlpool tubs. See p. 87.

In the last edition of this guide, I picked the **Carmichael Inn & Spa** as the city's best B&B. Sadly, the owners have relocated and the business is closed.

DINING Nowhere in Ottawa has change been more widely felt than in the restaurant business. The summer of 2008 seemed like a citywide game of musical stoves, as a half-dozen of the leading chefs were on the move. Several of them have opened new restaurants—broadening the dining choices available and, in several cases, adding stiff competition for the top spots in town.

Derek Benitz has gathered more accolades for his work in the kitchen than most of his Ottawa peers, and the past 2 years have seen him open two new restaurants: **Benitz Bistro,** 327 Somerset St. W. (© **613/567-8100**), which specializes in classic bistro fare and menus that change with the season; and **b/Side,** 323 Somerset St. W. (© **613/567-8100**), an adjacent wine bar that features smaller portions and opened too late to be reviewed. See p. 96 for a review of Benitz Bistro.

Navarra, 93 Murray St. (© **613/241-5500**), is the latest adventure for chef René Rodriguez, and sees him returning to his Spanish roots for dishes native to the Basque Region. See p. 100.

Directly opposite Navarra—and contributing to Murray Street's new sobriquet as "Gastro Alley," is **Murray Street Kitchen, Wine & Charcuterie,** 110 Murray St. (© **613/562-7244**), which took over the space vacated by the popular Bistro 115. If 115 was one of your favorite Ottawa spots, don't worry; Chef Steve Mitton's adventurous ways with meat and cheese will help you forget. See p. 104.

Although it existed in 2007, **Absinthe,** 1208 Wellington St. (© **613/761-1138**), has moved into a terrific, new, Parisian-styled space, where Chef Patrick Garland is serving steak and other bistro standbys that have people talking. See p. 107.

A few blocks west, another young chef—Chris Deraiche—is making his charismatic presence felt at **Wellington Gastropub,**

1325 Wellington St. (✆ **613/729-1315**). Based on a European model, the restaurant combines a super-relaxed atmosphere with top-notch food from a menu that changes daily. See p. 108.

One of Ottawa's oldest restaurants—**Courtyard,** 21 George St. (✆ **613/241-1516**)—now has one of the youngest chefs. After an apprenticeship at Chicago's renowned Moto, Michael Hay has landed his first executive chef job, filling the big shoes left by his one-time boss, Marc Lepine. See p. 99.

As for Lepine, at press time he was still readying a revolutionary new dining room called **Atelier** on Rochester Street that will function without a stove.

Another new dining experience in 2009 will see the return to Ottawa of the vaunted Steve Vardy, who previously had people flocking to taste his food at Beckta Dining & Wine, Whalesbone Oyster House, and Par-fyum, which is now closed. Vardy will be at the helm of a newly reconstituted **Black Cat Café** in the heart of the Corso Italia.

ATTRACTIONS The renovations continue apace at the **Canadian Museum of Nature,** 240 McLeod St. (✆ **613/263-4433**), but one side of the gorgeous old castle it occupies is now finished. Included as part of the renovations was the restoration of Clarence Tillenius's renowned Canadian nature dioramas. With their colors restored and animal models refurbished, the dioramas are the centerpiece of the new mammal gallery. See p. 124.

The Bytown Museum (✆ **613/234-4570**), located beside the Ottawa Locks of the Rideau Canal, just below Parliament Hill on its eastern side, launched a new audio tour that allows visitors to hear the commentary in any of six languages. See p. 129.

The **Canadian Aviation Museum,** 11 Aviation Pkwy. (✆ **800/463-2038** or 613/993-2010), was scheduled to close for several months in late 2008 for substantial renovations and updating of its exhibits.

Ottawa's AAA baseball team—the Ottawa Lynx—departed for greener outfields after the 2007 season; their former stadium near Ottawa's train station was home field for the **Ottawa Rapidz** of the semipro CAN-AM league for a year until it folded.

The winter of 2007–08 came close to setting a new record for snowfall, and one result was serious erosion of the riverbanks along the Gatineau River north of Ottawa. This erosion undermined the tracks on which the popular **Wakefield Steam Train** runs, sidelining the attraction during 2008 and possibly forever. At press time, the business was for sale.

The **Hershey Chocolate Factory Tour** in Smiths Falls, another popular attraction in the area, fell victim to company-wide shutdowns and relocations.

SHOPPING Surrounded by farmland, Ottawans have been quick to embrace the local produce movement, something that can be witnessed in many of the new restaurants noted above. Another indication of this is the opening in 2007 of a new **Ottawa Farmers' Market,** Lansdowne Park, 1015 Bank St. (✆ **613/2239-4955**), which is held twice weekly between early May and late October. See p. 180.

The Wellington West neighborhood continues to undergo rapid change, and the arts scene is booming there. James Robinson's adventurous **Parkdale Gallery,** 229 Armstrong St. (✆ **613/614-4308**) is rapidly becoming the nexus of a lot of activity.

AFTER DARK Much of the rejuvenation activity in Wellington West has been sparked by the relocation of the **Great Canadian Theatre Company** to a new multipurpose building, the Irving Greenberg Theatre Centre, 1233 Wellington St. (✆ **613/236-5196**). See p. 190.

On other fronts, Ottawa's music scene continues to contract with the closure of **Rasputin's**—one of Canada's foremost folk music rooms—after a serious fire.

The Best of Ottawa

As a native of this city, I've seen Ottawa evolve over 5 decades—from a sleepy civil service town to a national capital that can proudly hold its own with any city of comparable size.

The official population is more than 800,000, but the central core is compact and its skyline relatively short. Most Ottawans live in suburban, or even rural, communities. The buses are packed twice a day with government workers who live in communities like Kanata, Nepean, Gloucester, and Orleans, which were individually incorporated cities until municipal amalgamation in 2001. Although there are a number of residential neighborhoods close to downtown, you won't find the kind of towering condominiums that line the downtown streets of Toronto or Vancouver. As a result, Ottawa is not the kind of city where the downtown sidewalks are bustling with people after dark, with the exception of the ByWard Market and Elgin Street.

One could make the case that Ottawa would be very dull indeed were it not for Queen Victoria's decision to anoint it capital of the newly minted Dominion of Canada. Thanks to her choice, tourists flock to the Parliament Buildings, five major national museums, a handful of government-funded festivals, and the Rideau Canal. Increasingly, tourists are spreading out beyond the well-established attractions to discover the burgeoning urban neighborhoods like Wellington West and the Glebe, and venturing into the nearby countryside.

For visitors, Ottawa is an ideal walking city. Most of the major attractions—and since this is a national capital, there are many—are within easy walking distance of the major hotels.

Size also expresses itself in the way people treat each other here. Although there is a typically central Canadian reserve to human relations, it's balanced by an openness that's characteristic of small communities. Community is important; neighborhood activities are well attended.

Ottawa is also a city connected to nature. The glacial deposits known as the Gatineau Hills sit just across the border with Quebec to the north. To the south and west, farmers' fields begin long before you hit the city limits. Ottawa's European heritage shows itself in the large number of green spaces in the urban core. And the city's clean—you'll hear that from other visitors, and probably pass the remark yourself. Although the air quality can be poor on humid summer days, fall and winter bring crystalline air, and the streets are remarkably free of litter. Graffiti is frowned upon and quickly erased.

Ottawa's other bond with nature is its rivers. The city's roots as a community lie in its proximity to three—the Ottawa, Rideau, and Gatineau rivers —and they, along with the history that flows from them, define Ottawa. Geographically, the city streets curve to follow the rivers, and having to cross the rivers is a daily fact of life. The Rideau Canal, a distinguishing feature of the city, was built to make the Rideau River navigable. In the winter, when the canal is transformed into the world's largest skating rink, you can see Ottawans and visitors alike celebrating winter even as they defy its bitter sting.

Aside from its history, natural beauty, and cleanliness, Ottawa is known as a great place to raise a family. I'll attest to that, both as a son and as a father. It has been, and continues to be, a wonderful place to live. Enjoy my city!

1 FROMMER'S FAVORITE OTTAWA EXPERIENCES

- **Celebrate Canada's Birthday:** Spend Canada Day (July 1) in the nation's capital—there's no experience quite like it. Head downtown and prepare for a full day of uniquely Canadian celebrations. Start the day with the ceremony of the Changing of the Guard. Watch the Canadian flag rise above the Peace Tower on Parliament Hill, chat with the friendly Mounties mingling with the crowds (don't forget to ask if they'll pose for a photo), and take in a free concert. Have your face painted or tattooed (temporarily) in red and white, wave a paper flag, and buy a hat or T-shirt with a Canadian symbol to blend in with the throngs wandering the streets. In the evening, cast your eyes skyward for the best fireworks display of the year. See "A Capital Is Born" in chapter 2.

- **Skate on the Rideau Canal:** Even if you live in a part of the country where ice skating is a winter activity, it likely takes place at a community rink, where you end up skating around . . . and around . . . and around. An hour or two of that is enough to make anyone hang up their blades for good. But in Ottawa, you can experience the world's ultimate skating rink—the Rideau Canal—which offers almost 8km (5 miles) of wide-open space and ever-changing scenery. Warm-up huts are stationed along the way, where you can sip a hot chocolate or munch on a BeaverTail pastry. Skate and sled rentals are available. See p. 142.

- **Enjoy the Waterways:** Ottawa's history and beauty are deeply tied to the waterways in the region, the scenic Ottawa River, Gatineau River, Rideau River, and Rideau Canal. You can watch the locks in operation; take a cruise on the

Ottawa River or the Rideau Canal; rent a paddleboat, canoe, or kayak on Dow's Lake; picnic on the city's riverbanks; sizzle on a sandy beach; or ride the white water of the Ottawa River northwest of the city. See chapter 7.

- **Marvel at the Museums:** At a minimum, set aside half a day to spend at the world-class **Canadian Museum of Civilization.** Life-size renderings of the social, cultural, and material history of Canada since the landing of the first Europeans in A.D. 1000 will captivate even the most reluctant museumgoer. The majestic Grand Hall displays more than 40 gigantic totem poles from the Pacific Northwest. A hands-on Children's Museum, which invites children to experience the fascinating cultural mosaic of the world we live in, is housed within the complex. See p. 119.

- **Play in the Snow at Winterlude:** This annual winter festival, held during the first three weekends of February, is a celebration of snow, ice, and outdoor activity. Downtown Ottawa and Gatineau are transformed into winter wonderlands filled with gigantic snow sculptures, glittering ice sculptures, and a Snowflake Kingdom especially for kids. The Snowbowl, a new outdoor entertainment venue, features a variety of performances including music, skating demonstrations, and more. Winterlude activities are based at three main sites: the Rideau Canal Skateway (major access points are Rideau St. downtown, Fifth Ave. and Lansdowne Park in the Glebe, and Dow's Lake), Confederation Park, and Jacques-Cartier Park in Gatineau. See p. 29.

- **View the Parliament Buildings and the Ottawa Skyline:** From the Alexandra Bridge, Jacques-Cartier Park in

Gatineau, and the pathways along the north shore of the Ottawa River, you'll get a breathtaking view of the Parliament Buildings and the Ottawa skyline. The view from the Capital Infocentre on Wellington Street facing toward the front of Parliament Hill is one of the most photographed in Ottawa, but the very best view of the Hill and its surroundings is from the little-used amphitheatre just behind the National Art Gallery. Watching the moon rise from the wooden benches can be spectacular—to say nothing of romantic.

- **Ride to the Top of the Peace Tower:** When you've taken in the grace and majesty of the exterior of the Parliament Buildings, hop in the elevator and ride up to the observation deck at the top of the Peace Tower. Built between 1919 and 1927, the 92m (302-ft.) tower is a memorial to the more than 60,000 Canadian soldiers who lost their lives during World War I. The glass-enclosed observation deck offers magnificent views in all directions. See p. 118.

- **Stroll the ByWard Market:** The ByWard Market district has something for everyone, from funky shops to upscale restaurants, outdoor cafes, and an authentic farmers' market with excellent-quality fresh produce and flowers. The place bustles with activity and bubbles with personality. See p. 133.

- **Shop in the Glebe:** This fashionable shopping district stretches along Bank Street between the Queensway and the Rideau Canal. Most retailers are independent and the merchandise is good quality. It's well worth spending a morning or afternoon strolling up one side of the street and down the other. See p. 168.

- **Tiptoe Through the Tulips:** Visit Ottawa in mid-May and you'll be dazzled by millions of tulips blooming throughout the capital region. Commissioners Park, alongside Dow's Lake, features an orchestrated display of tulip beds with more than 300,000 blooms. Many of the events of the Canadian Tulip Festival take place in Major's Hill Park, northeast of the Parliament Buildings and behind the Fairmont Château Laurier. Ottawa's festival of tulips began with a thank-you gift of several thousand bulbs from the Dutch royal family after World War II. Since then, the tulips of Ottawa have grown to represent international friendship and the arrival of spring in Canada. See p. 30.

- **Be Dazzled by the Autumn Leaves:** Gatineau Park, a wilderness area covering 361sq. km (139 sq. miles) in Quebec's Gatineau Hills, is a short drive from downtown Ottawa. It's beautiful in all seasons, but the abundance of deciduous trees makes it especially colorful in the fall. There are many hiking trails to suit a variety of ages and fitness levels. Maps are available. See p. 202.

2 BEST HOTEL BETS

- **Best Historic Hotel:** The elegant Edwardian **Fairmont Château Laurier,** 1 Rideau St. (© **800/441-1414** or 613/241-1414), is a most admirably preserved and maintained property, both inside and out. If you're looking for tradition, luxury, and attentive service, this is the place to stay. The extensive health club and pool area, added back in 1929, superbly demonstrate Art Deco design. See p. 80.

- **Best Business Hotel: Bostonian Executive Suites,** 341 MacLaren St. (© **866/320-4567** or 613/594-5757), has placed a real emphasis on business travelers, creating a business-focused atmosphere with Wi-Fi, a 24-hour business center, ergonomic desk chairs, and concierge service. See p. 76.

- **Best for Families:** With so many Ottawa hotels competing for the family leisure market, family packages and facilities for children abound at many downtown properties, so it's not easy to choose a single property as the best of the bunch. For many years, the **Delta Ottawa Hotel and Suites,** 361 Queen St. (☎ **800/268-1133** or 613/238-6000) has unofficially earned the title of tops for children in Ottawa, due not least to the popularity of its two-story indoor waterslide. See p. 71.

- **Best Luxury Hotel:** The breathtaking splendor of the **Hilton Lac-Leamy,** adjacent to Casino du Lac-Leamy, 3 boul. du Casino, Gatineau (☎ **866/488-7888** or 819/790-6444), set a new standard of luxury in Canada's capital region when it opened in 2001. The main lobby features a spectacular blown-glass sculpture. Public areas are adorned with ceramic and marble. Views of Lac Leamy, Lac de la Carrière with its trademark fountain, and the Ottawa skyline are stunning. Guest facilities include spa, indoor/outdoor pool, tennis courts, fitness center, and adjacent performance hall and award-winning fine-dining restaurant. See p. 88.

- **Best Budget Accommodation:** Between May and August, head to the **University of Ottawa,** 90 rue Université, (☎ **613/564-5400**). Its downtown, apartment-style residences are two-bedroom units with double beds, TV, kitchenette, and private bathroom. Up to four people can stay for a flat fee of C$99 per night. See p. 83.

- **Best Suite Hotel:** There's an abundance of good suite hotels in the city, as you'll see if you browse through chapter 5,

"Where to Stay." Sharing the top spot by a whisker are the **Albert at Bay Suite Hotel,** 435 Albert St. (☎ **800/331-3131** or 613/231-2020), and **Minto Suite Hotel,** 433 Laurier Ave. W. (☎ **800/267-6644** or 613/238-8858). Both have beautifully appointed, spacious suites with well-equipped kitchens. Their convenient downtown locations, stylish design, and courteous, friendly staff earn them top marks. See p. 74 and 78.

- **Best Location: The Lord Elgin,** 100 Elgin St. (☎ **800/267-4298** or 613/235-3333), could not be better located as a base for visitors to Ottawa. Directly across the street is Confederation Park, a small but pretty city park that's a leafy respite in summer and a glittering ice palace in winter (during the Winterlude festival). The National Arts Centre is across the street; Parliament Hill, the Rideau Canal, ByWard Market, and Rideau Shopping Centre are a 5-minute stroll away. If you venture south along Elgin Street, you'll find plenty of pleasant eateries, lively pubs, and shops. See p. 78.

- **Best Health Club:** With its great views of Parliament Hill, outdoor lounge chairs, and barbecue area, it's tough to find a better place to work out than the Westin Workout Powered by Reebok gym at the **Westin Ottawa**, 11 Colonel By Dr. (☎ **888/625-5144** or 613/560-7000). The stationary bikes and treadmills face floor-to-ceiling windows, and there's also an indoor pool, whirlpool, and squash courts. See p. 80.

- **Best Resort:** Leisure and recreational activities are outstanding at the **Brookstreet** in Ottawa's west end, the heart of Silicon Valley North, 525 Legget Dr. (☎ **888/826-2220** or 613/271-1800). Their 18-hole golf course, the Marshes, was the final father-and-son Robert Trent Jones design collaboration. There's a state-of-the-art health club and spa on-site. Guest rooms have a boutique-hotel feel. Perspectives restaurant features contemporary Canadian fine dining with an Asian influence. See p. 86. **Château Cartier Resort,** 1170 chemin Aylmer, Gatineau (✆ **800/807-1088** or 819/777-1088), just a short drive from Ottawa, features an 18-hole golf course. Activities abound here—guests can enjoy racquetball, squash, tennis, ice skating, cross-country skiing, and more. Relax in the luxurious spa. Most rooms here are junior suites, above average in amenities and decor. See p. 90.

- **Best B&B Period Decor:** You'll find many period details throughout the distinguished **Auberge "The King Edward" B&B,** 525 King Edward Ave. (✆ **800/841-8786** or 613/565-6700). The front parlor is a peaceful oasis of tropical plants, accented by a trickling fountain. Antiques are featured throughout the principal rooms. Original fireplaces, plaster moldings, pillars, and stained-glass windows complete the picture. During the Christmas season, a 3.6m (12-ft.) tall Christmas tree trimmed with Victorian decorations is a sight to behold. See p. 82.

3 BEST DINING BETS

- **Best Service:** For pure attentiveness and attention to detail, I'd put **Signatures,** 453 Laurier Ave. East (✆ **613/236-2499**), on a par with any restaurant I've tried in North America. That much service comes with a price, of course; at Signatures, it's upwards of C$300. See p. 99.
- **Best Wine List:** The name says it all at **Beckta Dining & Wine** (p. 95), 226 Nepean St. (✆ **613/238-7063**). While most restaurants are chef driven, owner Stephen Beckta made his reputation as a sommelier, and he's proud enough of his establishment's wine list to tout it in the brand. The selection has a nice balance of Old and New World labels, but it's constantly in flux. Beckta's also one of the few Ottawa restaurateurs to take advantage of the liberalized provincial liquor laws that allow diners to bring their own vintages in exchange for a corkage fee. See p. 95.
- **Best Fusion:** A lot of restaurants throw the term *fusion* around as shorthand for saying that their chef's recipes combine different flavors or preparation styles, but no one in Ottawa does fusion more creatively—or naturally—than Phoebe

and Warren Sutherland, the co-owner-chefs at **Sweetgrass,** 108 Murray St. (✆ **613/562-3683**). The combination of her Cree heritage and his Jamaican roots (to say nothing of his time at a New York City kosher restaurant) is unique. See p. 101.

- **Best Canadian:** The freshest available regional, seasonal, and often organic products are employed to create uniquely Canadian dishes such as pan-roasted Quebec foie gras, grilled Ontario-raised buffalo striploin, and wild BC red spring salmon, on the constantly changing menu at **John Taylor at Domus Café,** 87 Murray St. (✆ **613/241-007**). p. 100.
- **Best Asian:** Kinki, 41 York St. (✆ **613/789-7559**) is one of those restaurants that changes the way people perceive a city's culinary scene. Its arrival created a buzz for months, and Kinki has continued to experiment with its menu, combining both traditional sushi with unusual hot dishes, like its spicy coconut sauce and gnocchi combination. See p. 103.
- **Best Italian:** Housed in a heritage stone building, **Mamma Grazzi's Kitchen,** 25 George St. (✆ **613/241-8656**), is

especially pleasant in the summer, when you can dine alfresco in the cobblestone courtyard at the rear. I've been coming here for years and have never been disappointed with the food or the service. See p. 103.

- **Best Young Chef:** This is a tough call since Ottawa has more than its share of bold, young kitchen magicians just now, but the edge goes to **Chris Deraiche** at the **Wellington Gastropub,** 1325 Wellington St. (✆ **613/729-1315**). From fragile fish dishes to hearty wild boar ragu, Deraiche does everything well, and his excitement about what he's preparing is palpable at the table. See p. 108.

- **Best Ice Cream:** There are several good gelato places in Ottawa, but you can't beat the authenticity of **Pasticceria Gelateria Italiana,** 200 Preston St. (✆ **613/233-6199**). See p. 102. As with the old-fashioned baked goods here—represented in staggering amounts and variety—the gelato is served the same way it has been for decades, and you won't find wacky flavors like peanut butter crunch.

- **Best Pizza:** Pizzas almost fly from the oven onto tables and out the door at **Café Colonnade,** 280 Metcalfe St. (✆ **613/237-3179**). Their famous pizza has a thick crust with a sprinkling of cheese around the edge, a generous smear of tangy tomato sauce, and gooey mozzarella to hold the toppings in place. On warm summer days and evenings you can hang out on the outdoor terrace. Takeout is also available. See p. 97.

- **Best Seafood:** The local owners of the **Whalesbone Oyster House,** 430 Bank St. (✆ **613/231-8569**), have long supplied first-rate bivalves to several restaurants around town. In 2006, they opened their own place and proved they

can do other types of seafood well too. See p. 96.

- **Best Bistro:** Another hard choice, given the number of new restaurants that are specializing in informal, bistro-style cuisine, but I found myself reflecting most rapturously on my first meal at the new **Murray Street Kitchen, Wine & Charcuterie,** 110 Murray St. (✆ **613/562-7244**), which opened in the summer of 2008. The restaurant combines the rustic charm of wide-plank wooden floors and its charcuterie/cheese bar with some of the most over-the-top cooking you'll find in Canada. See p. 104.

- **Best Alfresco Dining:** All of the four restaurants that share historic, cobble-stoned Clarendon Court provide a great outdoor setting, but **Social,** 537 Sussex Dr. (✆ **613/789-7355**), has the best view of the square. See p. 101.

- **Best Hotel Dining: Brookstreet,** 525 Legget Dr. (✆ **613/271-1800**), does a lot of things well, so it's no surprise that its restaurant, **Perspectives,** offers not only the best hotel dining in the city, but is in the running for best restaurant, period. The winner of several awards, it also finds ways of making dining a participatory event, with evenings that include preparation of part of the meal, and special seatings at the chef's table by invitation. See p. 86.

- **Best Casual Dining:** The **Elgin Street Diner,** 374 Elgin St. (✆ **613/237-9700**), is a comfy, neighborhood kind of place where you can saunter in, flop into a chair, and hang out with a coffee while the kids slurp milk shakes and chomp peanut butter and jam sandwiches. There are plenty of satisfying old-fashioned dinners on the menu, including meat loaf, shepherd's pie, and liver and onions. See p. 98.

4 BEST ADVENTURES FOR KIDS

- **See Canadian History on the Hoof:** The **RCMP Musical Ride** is a uniquely Canadian experience that has been successfully exported around the world. The force's rehearsals let you get up close and personal with their mounts. See p. 126.

- **Get in Touch with Nature:** Ottawa's proximity to natural areas allows you get into the heart of a forest or natural bog in a matter of minutes from downtown. The best place to do this is the **Mer Bleue Conservation Area,** a favorite with school groups. See p. 137.

- **Burn Off Some Energy:** Okay, it's raining and your brood has had its fill of museums for the day. There's no better place to let them run wild than **Cosmic Adventures,** where kids 12 and under can explore a four-level play area.

- **Be Afraid, Be Very Afraid!:** A town with as much history as Ottawa has to have some ghosts, right? **Haunted Walks** offers several ghostly adventures, including a tour of the city's old jail, where Canada's last public hanging took place. See p. 144.

- **Roll On!:** Few cities in North America are as bike friendly as Ottawa, and the best way to see a lot of it is on Sunday in the summer, when 52km (32 miles) of paved parkways are restricted to bicycle—and skate—traffic, beginning at 6am. See p. 151 for details and p. 148 for bike rental information.

- **Winter Wonderland:** Ottawa is proud of its status as the world's second-coldest capital city. Snowbound activities aren't restricted to Winterlude, either; check out the tubing and snowboarding fun in the heart of the city at **Carlington Snowpark.** See p. 154.

- **Get Wet!:** In summer, the ski areas north of the city offer an alternative, wetter form of fun. With its vertical rise of 160m (525 ft.) **Mont Cascades'** water park offers a range of wet-and-wild fun, including tunnel slides, parallel racing, and splash areas for the younger ones. See p. 206.

- **Airborne Adventure:** The daredevils in your group can get it on by diving 60m (197 ft.) headfirst into a limestone quarry at **Great Canadian Bungee** or roaring down the 310m (1,017-ft.) RIPRIDE cable slide. See p. 207.

- **Go Up, or Down:** Located just a 30-minute drive from downtown, **LaFlèche Adventure** gives your kids a choice of aerial exploration—in the park's 82 suspension bridges—or going underground in a series of white marble caves. See p. 207.

- **Hit the White Water:** Rafting is immensely popular on the upper reaches of the Ottawa River, and **Owl Rafting** offers a half-day family float trip that will give you and yours a terrific overview of the mighty river that defines the city. See p. 214.

Ottawa in Depth

Built on high, rocky ground at the confluence of three rivers, Ottawa has always been a city that impresses with its natural beauty rather than its size or architecture. Like all federal capitals, it is above all a city of bureaucrats rather than entrepreneurs, so it has naturally attracted sobriquets that include "The Town That Fun Forgot," "Coma City" and "grey." While it's true that Ottawa is not a city dominated by forward-looking risk takers, the good-natured name-calling overlooks the region's tremendous natural beauty and doesn't reflect the influence of large numbers of university students, technology workers, and recent immigrants—all of whom help make Ottawa far more than the stodgy capital it once was.

Ottawa's role as Canada's capital also means that the city is the site of numerous national institutions—including six major museums and a performing arts center—and draws thousands of schoolchildren and others to tour the Parliament Buildings, watch the Changing of the Guard, or participate in national celebrations. As the home of many national associations and nongovernment organizations, the city is also the host of numerous conventions and smaller meetings.

All that means that the city does tourism well. In spring and summer, the ByWard Market, in the heart of downtown, buzzes with activity from morning until well past midnight, and the paths along the Rideau Canal are filled with joggers, cyclists, rollerbladers, and strollers. From January to March—when Ottawa proudly wears the title of the world's second-coldest capital city—the canal is chockablock with skaters; the steely sizzle of their blades can be heard late into the evening.

1 OTTAWA TODAY

Ottawa's modern era began in 2001 with the amalgamation of 12 communities—many of which were rural townships consisting of hamlets and large tracts of agricultural land. The new millennium also marked the sudden downturn in high technology, forcing a reevaluation of what many in the city had viewed as Ottawa's bright new future. Since amalgamation, the political landscape of the city has been dominated by tension between those who live or own businesses in the urban core, suburban dwellers, and citizens who live in rural areas. That seems appropriate, given that Ottawa is the rare national capital where one can drive from the national legislature to a ski hill, a secluded lake, or a dairy farm, within 30 minutes.

Make no mistake, politics—both municipal and federal—dominate life in Ottawa. Aside from the fact that many residents work for or with the federal public service, decisions made within the city are constantly fodder for the media. Over the years, Ottawans have developed something of an inferiority complex because of the scorn that is constantly aimed at the city by those in the far eastern or western Canadian provinces who must live by decisions made by federal politicians and bureaucrats. Even for those who have never visited the city, their Ottawa is a soulless place filled with overpaid apparatchiks and policy wonks. The national "concept" of Ottawa has come to overshadow the reality.

The real Ottawa began to change dramatically in the 1980s, when seeds planted 2 decades before started to bear fruit. As the site of the National Research Council, Ottawa became home to a number of bright, young scientists in the 1960s. Over time, a number of them left government to pursue their own interests with technology companies like Bell-Northern Research, MicroSytems International, Telesat Canada, and Mitel. By the '80s and early '90s, these companies had spun off yet more firms—including Cognos and Newbridge Networks—and the city's rising presence in the technology sector began to attract international players like Alcatel and Nortel Networks. At least one Ottawa-based company—JDS Uniphase—became a major international player. Those were heady times, when stock options and IPOs were on the lips of those who barely knew their definitions.

Anyone who played the market in 2000 knows what happened next. The bursting of the technology bubble left a lot of empty office space in Kanata—the techie exurb on Ottawa's western border—but as short-lived as the boom had been, it helped Ottawa turn a corner in terms of the number of good restaurants and its taste for a somewhat less-conservative lifestyle. Given a sample of free-spending boom times, it was difficult to turn back the clock.

For one thing, Ottawa had grown. Fueled in part by the technology boom, Ottawa's population increased by 132,000 between 1987 and 2002, and with amalgamation the city's population reached 850,000. The population is relatively young, with almost half under the age of 35. Twelve percent of the population is older than 65. Sixty percent of Ottawans consider English their mother tongue, while the remaining 40% is divided evenly between French and other languages. While still strongly Eurocentric in its ethnicity, Ottawa has attracted large numbers of immigrants from Lebanon, Pakistan, and other Middle Eastern countries, a significant number of Vietnamese refugees, and a growing influx of people from Somalia and other troubled African nations.

Over the years, Ottawa has remained an affluent city. Two of its communities—Rockcliffe Park and Manotick—have among the highest per capita incomes in the country, and the average family income across the city is $75,000. The average house price exceeds $300,000.

Much of Ottawa's growth has been in former green space to the east, south, and west, leading to fears of urban sprawl and protracted debates regarding public transit. The transit question—specifically what type of light-rail train to deploy and where to lay the tracks—dominated the municipal election of 2006. The incumbent, who supported one plan, was ousted, and a former technology executive—Larry O'Brien—was elected. His first significant act as mayor was to scrap the existing light-rail project, which the city council had adopted in 2006, reigniting the debate and drawing a $280-million lawsuit from the contracted supplier. By 2008, a new light-rail plan was on the table, but Mayor O'Brien was embroiled in a bigger controversy. In December 2007, O'Brien was charged with two criminal code violations related to his alleged attempt to pay a rival to drop out of the mayoral race and reward the rival with a federal government appointment. While the charges are not expected to be heard until 2009, O'Brien refused to either resign or take a leave of absence, and the question of his guilt has dominated his first term. If you want to strike up a conversation with an Ottawan, mentioning the mayor is a good opener.

Although there has been rising concern over the use of crack cocaine in the city—fears that have yet to be borne out by statistics—Ottawa remains a safe, highly insulated community. It's common to hear

Hey, I Didn't Know That About Ottawa!

- The name Ottawa is adapted from Outaouak, the name of the Algonquian people who settled and traded furs in the area.
- The world's largest gold depository is located in the Bank of Canada gold vaults, which lie under one of Ottawa's main streets, Wellington Street.
- Ottawa's official relationship with tulips began in 1945, when Queen Juliana of the Netherlands presented 100,000 bulbs to the city as a gift. They were given in appreciation of Canada's granting of a safe haven to the Dutch royal family during World War II and in recognition of the role that Canadian troops played in liberating the Netherlands. Half a century later, every May, three million tulips bloom in the city's parklands.
- The sport of basketball was invented by Dr. James Naismith, who hailed from Almonte, a small town just west of Ottawa.
- Canada's last public hanging took place at Ottawa's first jail. The building is now operated by Hostelling International, and guests can actually sleep behind bars in the cells.
- The Governor General's New Year's Day Levee at Rideau Hall originated from the French governor's practice of shaking hands and wishing a happy New Year to the citizens of Quebec City, a tradition begun in 1646.
- The grounds of Parliament Hill were laid out in 1873 by Calvert Vaux, the same landscape architect who co-designed New York's Central Park.
- The 7.8km (4³/₄-mile) Rideau Canal Skateway, the world's largest skating rink, is used by approximately 750,000 skaters each winter and has an average skating season of 64 days.
- The world's first international telephone call was made from Ottawa in 1927, when Canadian prime minister Mackenzie King called the British prime minister.
- North American entertainment stars Paul Anka and Rich Little were born in Ottawa and have streets named after them in the city's south end.
- Actor Dan Ackroyd was born in the region and attended Carleton University, and both rock star Bryan Adams and screen actor Tom Cruise attended high school briefly in Ottawa.
- The Stanley Cup was born in Ottawa. In 1892, Governor-General Lord Stanley Preston commissioned a silversmith in England to make a gold-lined silver bowl on an ebony base, which became the premier trophy of professional hockey in North America.

it compared to a small town, and the community pulls together quickly during times of distress, such as the ice storm of 1998, which devastated thousands of trees and left large numbers of residents without electricity for days. It is the mark of its relative innocence that Ottawa continues to react with shock when a murder or other serious crime occurs within its borders. Ottawans are anything but jaded;

they remain open, trusting people who will ensure that tourists get the best sense of the city.

Like all national capitals in the West, Ottawa has grown increasingly security conscious since the September 11, 2001, terrorist attacks in the United States. It's not unusual to experience sudden, unexpected road closures or traffic diversions along the length of Canada's Ceremonial Route

(Wellington and Rideau sts. between Western Pkwy. and Sussex Dr., and Sussex Dr. between Rideau St. and Rockcliffe Park) and particularly in front of the Parliament Buildings on Wellington Street. Security is especially tight and disruptive during official visits by the American president or the British prime minister.

2 LOOKING BACK AT OTTAWA

The heart of Ottawa's history is the grand Ottawa River, Canada's second-longest river at more than 1,100km (684 miles). Navigable between the St. Lawrence River and the many lakes in the region south of James Bay, the river had been used as a major transportation route by Native peoples for thousands of years prior to the arrival of the first Europeans in the early 1600s. Anxious to expand the fur trade, which was the basis of New France's economy, French governors encouraged exploration of the interior of the continent but did not give priority to establishing new settlements. Consequently, although many French explorers and fur traders paddled and portaged past the site of the future city of Ottawa, almost 200 years went by before the first settlers arrived there.

THE EARLY YEARS

The French explorer Samuel de Champlain, who had sent two Frenchmen on missions up the Ottawa River prior to his arrival in 1613, is often considered to be the first white man to visit the vicinity of present-day Ottawa and Gatineau. Champlain recorded detailed descriptions of Rideau Falls, Chaudière Falls, and the Native peoples in his diary. Legend has it that Champlain mounted the rocky cliffs on the south bank of the Ottawa, near the present site of the Parliament Buildings, to take his bearings from the stars, and lost his astrolabe there.

Champlain's journals drew European traders to the Ottawa River for the next 150 years, but the result was strictly transient traffic. Settlements finally began to be established in the Ottawa Valley toward the end of the 18th century, but it was Philemon Wright, a prosperous united empire loyalist from Massachusetts, who saw potential in the district. In 1800 he persuaded five homesteading families to join him, his wife, and six children to establish the first community in the area. Wright chose the north shore of the Ottawa River, and within 20 years

DATELINE

- **1610** Étienne Brûlé, by order of French explorer Samuel de Champlain, becomes the first white man to travel through the future site of Ottawa.
- **1613** Champlain records detailed descriptions of the Chaudière Falls and Rideau Falls while traveling up the Ottawa River.
- **1600s to 1900s** A large number of canoes travel the Ottawa River, trading goods for furs.
- **1763** The first Treaty of Paris ends French rule in Canada, and land is granted to the British.
- **1812** The War of 1812 between the United States and England, which employed Canada as a battleground, sparks British

military leaders to search for a more secure route between Montreal and Lake Ontario, to protect against a possible future invasion by the Americans.
- **1822** The first steamboat to travel up the Ottawa River, *Union of the Ottawa*, makes its inaugural journey.
- **1826** Lieutenant Colonel John By arrives on the south shore of the Ottawa River to

continues

Wrightsville became a thriving village of more than 700 residents. Wright's plan was to make the community self-sufficient, and with five mills, four stores, three schools, two hotels, two distilleries, a brewery, and agricultural endeavors, it seems he succeeded.

Wright was searching for additional income to boost the local economy, and timber was the obvious choice for an export commodity because of its quality and abundance. He established markets for the local lumber in Quebec and England, and the wood was transported down the Ottawa River.

At this time, about 1820, the south side of the Ottawa River was still covered in dense bush and swampland and only sparsely populated by settlers. What sparked the establishment of a larger community there was the need—during the War of 1812—for a more secure supply and transportation route than the St. Lawrence River between Kingston and Montreal. It was the British, who by that time were governors of Upper and Lower Canada and therefore had the responsibility of defending the territory, who pushed for a back door between Montreal and Lake Ontario as a security precaution in the event of an American invasion. They were unable to find any interested parties to share the cost of construction of a canal to

link Lake Ontario with the Ottawa River, and as a result, the canal project ended up to be a costly operation for the British. The advantage was that they had control over the building of the canal and its attendant settlement.

BYTOWN DAYS

In 1826, Lieutenant Colonel John By was assigned to oversee the construction of the Rideau Canal between the Ottawa and St. Lawrence rivers. By the end of that year, hundreds of people had arrived at the canal site in preparation for its construction. In the spring of the following year, the settlement was named Bytown.

The first buildings were an engineering office and a commissariat, constructed at the foot of the canal. At the head of the canal on the east side, civilian barracks were built in what would soon become known as "Lower Town." This area was an almost impenetrable swamp choked with cedars. As most of the land was uninhabitable, land purchasers were encouraged to buy or lease plots of land on the west side of the canal, then known as "Upper Town." Lieutenant Colonel By laid out a grid of streets on the higher ground.

The canal works yard was located in Lower Town, and as it expanded, settlers found it necessary to drain the surrounding swampland to free up more land. Most

oversee the construction of the Rideau Canal, a 202km (126-mile) waterway between Lake Ontario and the Ottawa River, designed to provide a safe transportation route between Kingston and Montreal.

- **1827** A settlement, population 1,000, is established on the south side of the Ottawa River and named Bytown.

- **1841** Work begins on Notre-Dame Cathedral Basilica on Sussex Drive.
- **1848** The population of Bytown reaches 6,000.
- **1855** Bytown becomes a city called Ottawa.
- **1857** Queen Victoria chooses Ottawa as the capital of the British Provinces of Upper and Lower Canada, ahead of Montreal, Toronto, Kingston, and Quebec City.

- **1860** Queen Victoria's son Edward, Prince of Wales, visits Ottawa and becomes the first member of the royal family to visit North America.
- **1866** The Parliament Buildings, modeled on the British Houses of Parliament, are completed.
- **1867** With Confederation, Ottawa becomes the capital of the new Dominion of

continues

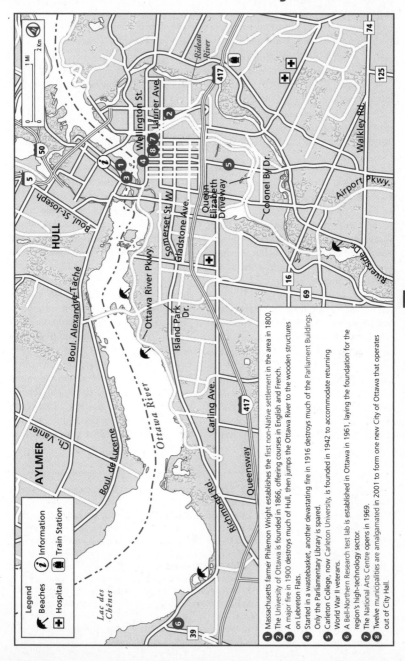

Legend

Beaches

ℹ Information

✚ Hospital

🚉 Train Station

1 Massachusetts farmer Philemon Wright establishes the first non-Native settlement in the area in 1800.

2 The University of Ottawa is founded in 1866, offering courses in English and French.

3 A major fire in 1900 destroys much of Hull, then jumps the Ottawa River to the wooden structures on Lebreton Flats.

4 Started in a wastebasket, another devastating fire in 1916 destroys much of the Parliament Buildings. Only the Parliamentary Library is spared.

5 Carleton College, now Carleton University, is founded in 1942 to accommodate returning World War II veterans.

6 A Bell-Northern Research test lab is established in Ottawa in 1961, laying the foundation for the region's high-technology sector.

7 The National Arts Centre opens in 1969.

8 Twelve municipalities are amalgamated in 2001 to form one new City of Ottawa that operates out of City Hall.

Local Wisdom

"Ottawa is a very civilized place." Violinist Pinchas Zukerman, musical director of the National Arts Centre Orchestra.

"There is not a surplus of nightlife in Ottawa. [The] name derives from the Algonquin *otta* ('open') and *wa* ('till six p.m.')." *Sports Illustrated* columnist Steve Rushin.

"Less a city than an abstraction." Travel writer Jan Morris.

of the new inhabitants of Lower Town were Irish and French laborers, thereby establishing the community as a predominantly Roman Catholic one; some of the poorest Irish immigrants lived in shanties along the edge of the canal construction site. Upper Town, which was not as densely populated, attracted more affluent and better-educated settlers, primarily English and Scottish Protestants.

The 202km (126-mile) Rideau Canal was completed in 1832. The enormous feat was all the more admirable for the fact that it comprised no fewer than 45 locks, manned by 24 lock stations; the locks allowed boats to ascend and descend the spine of the Precambrian Shield, an ancient rock formation that covers much of northern Canada and part of New York State. The highest point on the Rideau Waterway

is Upper Rideau Lake. At one end of the lake, water flows down to Lake Ontario, dropping a distance of 50m (164 ft.) in total. At the other end, water flows in the opposite direction down to the Ottawa River, dropping a distance of 83m (272 ft.), ending in the 30m-high (98-ft.) Rideau Falls.

The canal never did fulfill its original purpose as a military transportation route. For many years it operated as a commercial waterway before evolving into a recreational artery for boaters and tourists, which is a role it fulfills today.

Following completion of the canal, Bytown developed into a merchant-based community of retail shops and services that supported the growing timber trade. The native white pine, and to a lesser degree red pine and oak, were much in

Canada. The population is now 18,000.

- **1868** Canada's only political assassination to date occurs outside a rooming house on Ottawa's Sparks Street. Member of Parliament Thomas D'Arcy McGee is shot to death by Fenian loyalist Patrick Whelan.
- **1870** The capital's first streetcar service, Ottawa City Passenger Railway, begins operation.

- **1873** The grounds of Parliament Hill are laid out by Calvert Vaux, a landscape architect who also codesigned New York's Central Park.
- **1874** The city's municipal water supply is established.
- **1877** A new city hall is constructed of limestone on Elgin Street.
- **1879** Cartier Square Drill Hall, the oldest armory in

Canada still in use today, is built.

- **1880** A group of 26 prominent Canadian artists decide to found a national gallery. The gallery will have many temporary homes in future years.
- **1888** Lansdowne Park fairgrounds are built on the outskirts of town.
- **1891** The region's first strike takes place, as 2,400

demand by the British for shipbuilding during the mid–19th century. As a result of interference by Napoleon, Great Britain's supply of timber from the Baltic countries was temporarily halted, and for a time the British began to purchase a large amount of timber from Canada. By 1842, however, Britain was once again able to do business with the Baltic countries, and so the timber trade in the area around Bytown began to decline.

The Bytown of this period was a raw and dirty town, where most of the supplies for the lumber camps up and down the Ottawa River were purchased. Taverns, gaming houses, and brothels sprang up in response to demands from the rough, boisterous, lumber workers. Street brawls were common, with racial and religious strains running high, especially when fueled by drink. Tensions between the gentry of Upper Town and the laborers of Lower Town were rife, and in 1849 they erupted in a riot known as Stoney Monday. One young man died and dozens were injured in a hail of paving stones.

A CAPITAL IS BORN

The local lumber industry was launched into a new era of prosperity with the arrival of several U.S. entrepreneurs in the early 1850s. These men established sawmills to supply lumber to the United States. Around the same time, a branch railway was built between Bytown and Prescott to serve as a link with the main line between Montreal and Toronto. Although the railway turned out to be a financial disaster, its presence was an important influence in the choice of a capital city. As Bytown marched toward the future, it received a change in both name and status. On New Year's Day 1855, Bytown became a city called Ottawa (an English translation of the Algonquian term for "traders"). It was time to move forward and put the community's sordid reputation behind. The citizens were excited at the prospect of being considered for the title of capital of the Province of Canada.

There followed such bitter debate on the issue of a suitable location for the seat of government, however, that Parliament finally asked Queen Victoria to select the city. Montreal, Quebec, Kingston, and Toronto were Ottawa's rivals and worthy contenders. Though the myth has long persisted that the queen selected Ottawa by blindly pointing her finger at a map, the truth is far more prosaic. Factors in Ottawa's favor were its geographical position on the border of Upper and Lower Canada and its origins as a mixed English- and French-speaking settlement, in addition to the presence of the Rideau Canal and the

---

millworkers walk out in protest of wage cuts.
- **1899** The Ottawa Improvement Commission (later named the National Capital Commission, or NCC) is created to oversee city planning.
- **1901** The Alexandra Railway Bridge opens; its construction is at the forefront of engineering.

- **1908** The Royal Canadian Mint is established as a branch of the British Royal Mint.
- **1911** Ottawa's population is 87,000.
- **1914** World War I begins.
- **1916** The National Research Council is founded in Ottawa.
- **1927** A carillon of 53 bells is rung for the first time in the Peace Tower.

- **1931** Fire destroys Ottawa's city hall.
- **1930s** The Great Depression takes place; thousands are out of work.
- **1938** The federal government purchases the first lands of what would later become Gatineau Park following pressure from local citizens to protect the wilderness.

continues

new railway link. Queen Victoria duly appointed Ottawa as the capital of the Province of Canada in 1857. In the years immediately following, Ottawa enjoyed a period of strong growth. Within 6 years, several hundred stone buildings were erected and the population grew by 50%, reaching 14,000 by 1863. Shops lined Wellington and Bank streets, two hospitals improved medical service, and the city established a police commission. The commercial and professional classes grew, as did the number of industrial workers.

The construction of the government buildings took more than 5 years, and at the end of 1865 about 350 civil servants from Quebec City transferred to the new buildings. By the time Ottawa had a mere 18 months of experience as capital of the Province of Canada, it would take on the much larger role of capital of the new Dominion of Canada.

On July 1, 1867, there was a great celebration on Parliament Hill. The day was declared a public holiday. Viscount Monck was sworn in as governor-general of the Dominion of Canada at 10am, followed by a march of the troops. In the evening, revelers lit bonfires and watched a fireworks display. Since that first Dominion Day, Canadians have celebrated July 1 (now known as Canada Day) on Parliament Hill.

In the second half of the 19th century, Ottawa faced a number of conflicts: the lumber industry versus the government as economic influences; Catholics versus Protestants in terms of religious practices, culture, and education; and immigrants versus Canadian-born citizens, which often reflected differences in social class.

Despite the challenges faced by the growing city, growth in public and private enterprises surged ahead. A municipal water supply and electricity supply were established, and public transportation was improved with the installation of electric streetcars to replace horse-drawn trams. Many of Ottawa's recreational clubs were founded in the latter half of the 19th century. The Ottawa Field Naturalists Club, the Rowing Club, the Curling Club, the Cricket Club, the Tennis Club, the Aquatic Club, and the Golf Club all originated in the 1800s.

The urban landscape altered with the years. The Parliament Buildings dominated the skyline, while numerous mills crowded around Chaudière Falls. Stone and brick commercial and residential properties abounded in Upper Town, while the twin spires of the basilica and the more modest wooden houses of the inhabitants of the Market district marked Lower Town. In the 1890s, Prime Minister Wilfrid Laurier began to develop plans that

- **1939** The National War Memorial is unveiled in Confederation Square by King George VI; World War II begins.
- **1941** Ottawa's population reaches 155,000.
- **1945** Queen Juliana of the Netherlands presents a gift of thousands of tulip bulbs to the city in appreciation of Canada's granting a safe haven to the Dutch royal family during World War II.

- **1945** Igor Gouzenko, a clerk at the Soviet embassy in Ottawa, defects, revealing a spy network in North America and helping to ignite the cold war.
- **1950** French urban planner Jacques Gréber submits a plan to transform Ottawa's layout.
- **1951** Ottawa becomes the first major Canadian city to elect a female mayor, Charlotte Whitton.

- **1965** Canada gains its own flag, which is raised for the first time on the top of the Peace Tower on February 15.
- **1966** On August 10, one of North America's worst construction accidents kills nine and injures dozens when the Heron Road Bridge collapses.
- **1967** Prime minister Lester B. Pearson lights the Centennial Flame on Parliament Hill to commemorate 100 years of Confederation.

would help transform the still-dowdy city into what some referred to as "Washington of the North."

TRIAL BY FIRE

On April 26, 1900, a major fire swept through Hull (the former Wrightsville) and across the river to the Chaudière area of Ottawa. Seven people died, 15,000 were left homeless, and more than 3,000 buildings were destroyed. The cities recovered, thanks mainly to an international relief fund that raised $10 million, and to the resilience of Ottawa's citizens.

At the end of the 1800s, Ottawa's prosperity could be attributed to three major factors: the lumber industry, which was able to produce 500 million board feet of lumber annually by harnessing the power of Chaudière Falls; growth of the civil service; and the trade generated by the railways. Downtown Ottawa was a maze of tracks: four rail systems with nine different lines. In 1912, the imposing Union Station with its domed ceiling and huge stone pillars opened on the east bank of the Rideau Canal, bordered by Rideau Street. The same year saw the opening of one of Ottawa's most famous landmarks—the Château Laurier (now named the Fairmont Château Laurier and used as a convention center), which sits directly opposite the Union Station building. Built of granite and sandstone in a Loire Valley Renaissance style similar to that of the Château Frontenac Hotel in Quebec City, the building is topped with a copper roof, echoing the structure of the adjacent Parliament Buildings. Also in 1912, the Victoria Memorial Museum, now known as the Canadian Museum of Nature, was completed. Three hundred Scottish stonemasons contributed their expertise to the museum's intricately designed turreted stonework.

In 1916, fire again changed the face of Ottawa's landscape, destroying the Centre Block of the Parliament Buildings. Only the Parliamentary Library was saved, due to the actions of a quick-thinking employee who closed the steel fire doors against the advancing flames. The height of the drama occurred when the huge bell in the clock tower crashed to the ground on the last stroke of midnight. Rebuilding began a few months afterward, and the new Centre Block, taller and more distinctive than the original, was completed 6 years later. The central tower, named the Peace Tower, contains a memorial chamber dedicated to Canada's war dead, a 27.3m (90-ft.) belfry with a carillon of 53 bells, a four-faced clock, and an observation deck. Rising from the peak of the roof of the Peace Tower is a 10.5m (34-ft.) bronze flag mast proudly flying the Canadian flag.

OTTAWA IN DEPTH

2

LOOKING BACK AT OTTAWA

- **1970s** The NCC constructs the first section of a recreational pathway, marking the beginning of the "greening" of the city.
- **1970** The Ottawa portion of the Rideau Canal is opened to public skating; A few years later, Guinness World Records recognizes it as the largest naturally frozen ice rink in the world, equal to 90 Olympic-size rinks.
- **1971** Ottawa's population is 302,000.
- **1979** Ottawa's premier winter attraction, Winterlude, is launched by the NCC.
- **1980s** The growth of Ottawa's tech industry continues to strengthen and Silicon Valley North takes hold.
- **1988** A permanent location for the National Gallery of Canada opens at 380 Sussex Dr. Designed by Canadian architect Moshe Safdie, the structure is made of glass, steel, and concrete.
- **1989** Douglas Cardinal's spectacular Canadian Museum of Civilization opens in Hull (now part of the city of Gatineau).
- **1990s** Ottawa's high-tech industry explodes, bringing new jobs to the district and indirectly causing traffic congestion and a housing shortage.

continues

Overseas, the two world wars were Canada's proving ground as an independent nation. Sacrifices at Vimy Ridge in World War I and Dieppe and Normandy in World War II showed the world that Canada was no longer a mere outpost of the empire, but by the end of World War II, Ottawa remained a far cry from the beautiful green capital of today. Rail lines choked the city. More than 100 trains, with their associated smoke and soot, thundered into the city every day, and there were no fewer than 150 level crossings within city limits.

THE POSTWAR ERA

Much of the credit for the establishment of Ottawa's physical beauty goes to Jacques Gréber, a French urban planner, and then–prime minister William Lyon Mackenzie King. Prior to World War II, in the late 1930s, King had invited Gréber to Ottawa, initially as an adviser to plan the War Memorial and Confederation Square. World War II interrupted these plans, but following the war, Gréber returned to Ottawa and, in 1950, prepared a report with recommendations for extensive urban renewal. One of the most significant was the establishment of a wide swath of greenbelt around the city. Gréber also recommended eliminating slum areas, creating parks and pathways, purchasing land

in Quebec to further enhance Gatineau Park, and removing or relocating railway lines.

To implement Gréber's plan, the National Capital District was enlarged to 2,900sq. km (1,120 sq. miles), encompassing 72 municipalities in Ontario and Quebec, and the Federal District Commission (the official agency of capital planning) was restructured and renamed the National Capital Commission and given a full-time chairman. A powerful organization with sweeping responsibilities, the National Capital Commission today remains the region's largest landlord, and oversees many festivals and other cultural events.

Removing the vast network of railway lines dramatically changed the face of Ottawa. In their place, sweeping scenic drives were created for vehicular traffic, and pathways for walkers and cyclists were built alongside the waterways, lined with grass verges, shrubbery, and flowerbeds. To manage high volumes of through traffic, the multilane Queensway (Hwy. 417) was built on an old railway bed, providing a high-speed expressway from west to east.

In the mid-1900s, the number of diplomatic missions with embassies in Ottawa grew at an enormous pace. There are now more than 100 countries represented in Canada's capital, contributing vitality and diversity to the city's cultural and social life.

- **1992** Ottawa's National Hockey League franchise, the Ottawa Senators, begins play.
- **1999** Ottawa's population is now 324,000 in the city, and the surrounding communities continue to experience rapid population growth.
- **2000** Hull's Jacques-Cartier Park is designated "Mile 0" of the new Trans Canada Trail, a multiuse trail that

will eventually stretch from coast to coast.
- **2000** High-tech stocks begin to slide and Silicon Valley North, Ottawa's high-tech community, feels the pinch.
- **2001** Population of the newly amalgamated city is 800,000.
- **2002** Following in Ottawa's expansion footsteps, the new City of Gatineau is

created from five former municipalities—Aylmer, Buckingham, Gatineau, Hull, and Masson-Angers, with a combined population of 229,000.
- **2003** The new Ottawa airport passenger terminal building (PTB) opens in October, 6 months early, on budget, and without the help of government subsidies.

REJUVENATION

The 1960s brought radical changes to the capital. A building and rejuvenation boom accompanied Canada's centennial celebrations in 1967. With Ottawa playing host to heads of state from virtually every nation in the world, streets were resurfaced and public places beautified. A sleek, new performing arts center was opened on Confederation Square, adjacent to the Rideau Canal.

And the changes were more than physical. With the election of Pierre Trudeau as prime minister in 1968, the city took on a new, glamorous aura. Stars such as Barbra Streisand visited as swinging bachelor Trudeau's dates. Immigration from nontraditional sources such as Lebanon and Pakistan began to increase, changing the cultural face of the city. A new federal policy of French-English bilingualism increased the demand for French-language services in Ottawa.

Across the Ottawa River, many of Hull's remaining wooden structures fell to the wrecker's ball, replaced by government office complexes that still dominate the waterfront across from Parliament Hill and the Supreme Court of Canada.

The presence of blue-collar workers had dwindled in the years after the war, replaced by that of office workers to support the growing federal government and civil service. A second economic influence began to appear by the 1960s—one that was to become a major player in the region. The high-tech industry, with its emphasis on electronics and communications, soon thrived in Ottawa. The National Research Council, the Communications Research Council, the two universities, and private companies such as Bell-Northern Research were rich sources of research material and a highly skilled workforce. Demand for electronic equipment was increasing, and a ready customer, the federal government, was right on the doorstep. Other major markets, including Toronto, Montreal, the eastern seaboard of the United States, and Europe, were also within grasp.

The tech boom characterized the 1980s, when the more entrepreneurial of the research scientists began to start up their own companies, including international players such as Mitel, Corel, Cognos, Newbridge, and JDS Uniphase. Ottawa became known as Silicon Valley North and in the 1990s, millions of dollars changed hands in the hot tech sector. The injection of young, irreverent techies has brought new life to the city, spurring the growth of upscale bars and restaurants downtown and an array of service industries in the neighboring city of Kanata. The demand for easy access to other technology centers such as Boston, North Carolina, Texas, and California called for a major renovation to Ottawa's airport, which was completed in 2008.

- **2005** Ottawa celebrates its 150th anniversary as a city. On January 1, 1855, the town of Bytown became the City of Ottawa.
- **2005** The new Canadian War Museum, featuring 4,200sq. m (45,208 sq. ft.) of exhibition space, opens on Lebreton Flats, about 2km (1¼ miles) west of Parliament Hill.

- **2007** The Rideau Canal marks its 175th anniversary and is named a UNESCO World Heritage Site.

Only in Ottawa: Redcoats and Bearskin Hats

Between late June and late August, a colorful Canadian ceremony is held every morning (weather permitting) on Parliament Hill's lawn—the **Changing of the Guard.** Two historical regiments—the Governor General's Foot Guards and the Canadian Grenadier Guards—make up the Ceremonial Guard of the Armed Forces. The daily parade includes 125 soldiers in bearskin busbies and scarlet tunics. The guard assembles at Cartier Square Drill Hall, 2 Queen Elizabeth Dr. (near the corner of Laurier Ave. by the Rideau Canal) at 9:30am and marches north on Elgin Street, sweeping west along Wellington Street and timed to reach Parliament Hill at 10am. On arrival at the Hill, the Ceremonial Guard splits, with the old and new guard positioning themselves on opposite sides of the lawn. The dress and weaponry of both groups are inspected. The colors are then marched before the troops and saluted, and the guards present arms to one another. In true military fashion, sergeants major bark commands that prompt the soldiers to perform their synchronized maneuvers. The final symbolic act is the transfer of the guard-room key to the incoming guard commander. The relieved unit marches down Wellington Street and back to the Drill Hall to the beat of the military band.

3 OTTAWA IN POPULAR CULTURE: BOOKS, FILM & MUSIC

As Canada's capital and a popular tourist destination, Ottawa is the subject of numerous nonfiction books. Among the best is Phil Jenkins's *An Acre of Time,* which traces a single acre of land on Ottawa's Lebreton Flats from prehistoric times to today, and tells the city's story in the process.

Ottawa has been home to a number of internationally known authors, including Margaret Atwood, Elizabeth Smart, and poet Archibald Lampman. Among the recent novels that are set in Ottawa, one of the best is Elizabeth Hay's *Garbo Laughs,* a Canadian bestseller in 2004. For a comprehensive overview of how Ottawa has been represented by authors ranging from Jack London to Norman Levine, see *Ottawa: A Literary Portrait,* edited in 1990 by John Bell.

Some of the most striking images of the city can be found in *Ottawa and the National Capital Region* by Malak Karsh, who was to landscape photography what his brother Yousuf was to portraiture.

Unlike Montreal, Toronto, and Vancouver, Ottawa is only rarely the setting of major motion pictures. You can catch glimpses of the city in *Mr. & Mrs. Bridge,* a Merchant Ivory film that stars Paul Newman and Joanne Woodward.

Ottawa is the hometown of several well-known musicians, including Paul Anka, Kathleen Edwards, Bruce Cockburn, and Alanis Morissette, but the capital city seldom plays an explicit role in their music. You'll have to listen between the lines to learn that Anka's "Diana" refers to his onetime Ottawa babysitter, or that Morissette's angry "You Oughta Know" was inspired by a teenage romance in Ottawa. For songs about the background of Ottawa and the surrounding region, search out the work of the band Tamarack, a folk group that specialized in historical songs.

4 EATING & DRINKING IN OTTAWA

It has taken a while, but Ottawa now has a number of restaurants that can compete for innovation, quality, and consistency with the best of other capital cities.

Every longtime Ottawan recalls the dark ages of the 1970s, before a place called Daphne & Victor's landed in the ByWard Market and changed the dining landscape with adventurous main courses, homemade desserts, and a kitchen that stayed open past 9pm.

Still, it wasn't until the high-tech boom of the '90s—long after Daphne & Victor's had departed—that dining out became serious business in Ottawa. Suddenly, young, mobile, and moneyed patrons began demanding food on par with what they had discovered in San Francisco, Boston, New York City, and Vancouver. Local restaurant entrepreneurs responded by opening new establishments, and by recruiting exciting young chefs. Talented cooks and sommeliers like John Taylor of Domus, Stephen Beckta of Beckta Dining & Wine, and Warren Sutherland of Sweetgrass, brought experience learned in New York City and

other tough markets to town. As diners sat up and took notice, so did other restaurateurs, and the bar was raised across the city. Even old standbys, that had gotten by on decades-old menus and mediocre service, began to adjust their attitudes. The result has been good for everyone who lives in or visits Ottawa. Ottawa has always had a good selection of ethnic restaurants, with particularly strong representation from Italy, India, Lebanon, and Vietnam. The city's proximity to Gatineau has also put a large number of French-influenced restaurants on its doorstep.

Another indication that Ottawa's restaurant sector is maturing is the development of several key concentrations of above-average establishments. While restaurants fill every corner of the ByWard Market, certain blocks—such as Murray Street between Parent Avenue and Dalhousie Street—have come to dominate for fine dining. A much-newer neighborhood—Wellington Street West between Parkdale Avenue and Island Park Drive—began audaciously referring to itself as "Epicurean Row" a few years ago;

Local Fare

Celebrity chef Gordon Ramsay has a point when he says that Canada is too young a country to have developed a strong national cuisine, but a number of specialties stand out as you move among Ottawa's restaurants and takeout food stores:

- Beau's All-Natural beer
- Chip wagon chips and poutine
- Foie gras from Quebec
- Organic heirloom vegetables from Bryson Farms in the Pontiac region northwest of Ottawa
- Oysters imported by Whalesbone Sustainable Oyster & Fish Supply
- Sugar pie, made with Quebec maple syrup
- Wild mushrooms, especially chanterelles
- Wines from Prince Edward County

Frommer's Favorites

Every city has cuisine you won't find anywhere else, or restaurants that make something so tasty, so unique, that people can't get enough of it. Ottawa is no exception.

The egg roll has faded in popularity in favor of dumplings and other more authentic Chinese appetizers, but authenticity goes out the window when the egg rolls are as good as they are at **Golden Palace,** 2195 Carling Ave. (© **613/ 820-8444**). Fat, greasy, and bursting with flavor, these burnt-end-style egg rolls have fans around the world. Damn the diet!

New Yorkers and Montrealers often debate which city has the best bagels. After tasting them in both cities, I'll throw my vote behind the *Robb Report's* selection of those from **Ottawa Bagelshop and Deli,** 1321 Wellington St. (© **613/722-8753**). Rolled by hand and baked in a wood-burning oven, these kosher bagels are made using canola oil, contain no preservatives or salt, and fly out of the shop 7 days a week. They are available in a variety of styles, but the traditional poppy seed ones are best, and all can be found at grocery stores throughout Ottawa.

Another kosher product that stands among my favorite foods in the world is the light caraway rye bread from **Rideau Bakery,** 384 Rideau St. (© **613/789-1019**) and 1666 Bank St. (© **613/737-3355**). Baked by the Kardish family since 1930, this sweet-tasting bread is positively addictive—either fresh from the bag or toasted. It is available at grocery stores throughout Ottawa, but get it fresh.

Since they are unique to Ottawa, BeaverTails are a bit of a ringer in the best-of category, but so what? They taste best at one of the Rideau Canal outlets following a brisk skate on a cold day, but who can resist the combination of deep-fried dough and cinnamon anytime? You can get them at **BeaverTails,** 87 George St. (© **613/241-1230**).

Finally, a more recent find is the cold-pressed, extra-virgin olive oil from **Terra Foods** (© **613/225-2191**). Stavros Kalogerakos presses the oil within 24 hours of hand picking the olives from trees in his native village of Krokees, Sparta. Rich in vitamins and antioxidants, the oil is fruity and nicely peppery on the tongue. It is available either directly from Terra Foods, or at **Rainbow Natural Foods,** 1487 Richmond Rd. (© **613/726-9200**).

now, it's living up to the name. Farther west—on Richmond Road between McRae Avenue and Berkley Avenue—there are some interesting, if lower-key, developments. Even well-established dining areas—notably Preston Street between Carling Avenue and Somerset Street West—are growing denser and more diverse.

Perhaps the most significant sign that Ottawa's culinary scene has reached a new level is the growing prominence of the "star chef." Long a reality in cities as close to Ottawa as Toronto and Montreal, it is only in the past couple of years that local chefs have had the cachet to prompt bidding wars or be recruited by restaurant entrepreneurs to serve as the face of a new establishment. Since 2007, several important chefs—among them Derek Benitz of Social fame, Marc Lepine of Courtyard, and Steve Mitton, Benitz's replacement at Social—have switched kitchens.

3

Planning Your Trip to Ottawa

As a modern city in one of the world's most open democracies, Ottawa will hold few surprises—and no major challenges—to the seasoned traveler, but good planning can still ensure that you get the most out of your visit.

Travel anywhere in the post-9/11 era—with its increased security, sky-high fuel prices, and airline financial problems—demands patience and a good understanding of the pitfalls of poor scheduling or incomplete documentation. Once you're in Ottawa, the biggest decision affecting your planning may be to determine what kind of visit you want to have, and how much you can accomplish in your time here. As a capital city filled with Canada's national institutions and a major tourist destination for schoolchildren and adults alike, there is no shortage of things to see. Because Ottawa is a city with radical fluctuations in temperature between summer and winter—and a diverse range of seasonal activities and events—your planning will also be significantly affected by when you choose to be in Ottawa.

For additional help in planning your trip and for more on-the-ground resources in Ottawa, please turn to "Appendix: Fast Facts, Toll-Free Numbers & Websites," on p. 216.

1 VISITOR INFORMATION

FROM NORTH AMERICA

Within Canada, your starting point is the **Capital Infocentre,** 90 Wellington St., Ottawa (© **800/465-1867** or 613/239-5000; www.canadascapital.gc.ca), located directly across the street from the Parliament Buildings. The Capital Infocentre is administered by the **National Capital Commission (NCC)** and provides information on Ottawa and the surrounding region. During the main tourist season, from mid-May to Labour Day (first Mon in Sept), the Capital Infocentre is open daily 8:30am to 9pm. The rest of the year it's open daily 9am to 5pm. To receive printed material on Ottawa and the entire National Capital Region, write in advance to the Capital Infocentre's mailing address at 40 Elgin St., Room 202, Ottawa, ON K1P 1C7.

The **Ottawa Tourism and Convention Authority Inc. (OTCA),** 130 Albert St., Ste. 1800, Ottawa, ON K1P 5G4, maintains a comprehensive website with visitor information at www.ottawatourism.ca. The **OTCA** publishes an annual visitor guide, which includes maps and listings of cultural sites, things to see and do, accommodations, places to dine and shop, and services. You can obtain a free printed copy of the guide by phoning the **Capital Infocentre** (© **800/465-1867**). Allow 10 business days for delivery. Or you can pick up a copy at the **Capital Infocentre** when you arrive in the city.

Visitors to Canada from the U.S. can check out the Canadian federal government's Department of Foreign Affairs and International Trade website, **www.dfait-maeci. gc.ca/can-am,** which deals with issues pertaining to Canada-U.S. relations. Contact information for Canadian government offices in the U.S. is listed, as are links for tourism information. In addition to the Canadian Embassy, located in Washington, D.C., there are about a dozen Canadian consulate-general offices and several consulates located throughout the U.S.

FROM ABROAD

Visit the official travel site of the **Canadian Tourism Commission, www.travel canada.ca**, and click on your country of residence to access customized visitor information, including contact information for tour operators and travel agents in your country who specialize in Canada as a destination.

There are more than 300 government of Canada diplomatic and consular missions overseas that can provide information on traveling to Canada and direct you to the appropriate tourist information sources. If your country of residence is other than those listed below, you can access the full directory online at **www. dfait-maeci.gc.ca/world/embassies/ menu-en.asp**.

U.K.: The **Canadian High Commission,** 1 Grosvenor Sq., London W1K 4AB (② **0207/258-6600**).

Ireland: The **Canadian Embassy,** 65 St. Stephen's Green, Dublin 2 (② **01/417-4100**).

Australia: The **Canadian High Commission,** Commonwealth Ave., Canberra, ACT, 2600 (② **02/6270-4000**), or the Consulate General of Canada, Level 5, Quay West Building, 111 Harrington St., Sydney, NSW, 2000 (② **02/9364-3000**). There are also consulates in Perth and Melbourne.

New Zealand: The **Canadian High Commission,** Level 11, 125 The Terrace, PO Box 8047, Wellington, 6011 (② **04/473-9577**).

South Africa: The **Canadian High Commission,** 1103 Arcadia St., Hatfield, Pretoria (② **012/422-3000**). There is also a Canadian high commission in Capetown and a consulate in Durban.

TRAVEL BLOGS

To read a few blogs about other travelers' experiences visiting Ottawa, try **www.real travel.com/ottawa-ontario-travel-guide-d17389.html**, **http://.blogs.bootsnall. com/tags/Ottawa**, **www.travelpost.com/ NA/Canada/Ontario/Ottawa/logs/ 5386307**, or **www.travel-library.com**.

---

2 ENTRY REQUIREMENTS

PASSPORTS

For hassle-free travel, carefully follow these guidelines regarding entry documents. Security has been heightened at border crossings and other points of entry since September 11, 2001. Laws, restrictions, and entitlements that affect visitors are subject to change at any time. It's best to check requirements before you travel.

All visitors to Canada must show proof of citizenship. A valid passport is the preferred entry document, and is a requirement for most visitors. U.S. citizens

traveling by air are required to carry a valid passport or other valid travel document. U.S. permanent residents must also carry their Alien Registration Card (Green Card). As of June 1, 2009, U.S. citizens who travel by land or sea must also carry a valid passport, passport card, or valid document recognized under the Western Hemisphere Travel Initiative. If you plan to drive into Canada, be sure to bring your car's registration papers and insurance documents.

Traveling with Minors

If you are traveling with children, make sure they too have identification documents. Parents who share custody of their children should carry copies of the legal custody documents. If you are not the parent or legal guardian of the child traveling with you, you should carry a written statement from the parent or guardian, granting permission for the child to travel to Canada under your supervision.

VISAS

Citizens of most European countries, Commonwealth countries, and former British colonies, as well as certain other countries, do not need visas but must carry passports. Entry or transit visas are required for citizens of more than 140 countries. You must apply for and receive your visa from the Canadian embassy, high commission, or consulate in your home country. For a complete list of countries and territories whose citizens require visas in order to enter Canada as visitors, visit **www.cic.gc.ca**.

MEDICAL REQUIREMENTS

Canada does not require medical examinations for tourists who will be in the country for less than 6 months. If you plan to stay in Canada for longer, see the requirements listed at **www.cic.gc.ca/english/ information/medical/medexams-temp. asp**.

CUSTOMS
What You Can Bring into Canada

Generally, you are allowed to bring in goods for personal use during your trip to Canada, although there are restrictions and controls on the importation of firearms, ammunition, fireworks, meat and dairy products, animals, plants and plant products, firewood, fresh fruits and vegetables, and certain food and drug products. Outdoor sportsmen and sportswomen should note that fishing tackle can be brought into Canada, though the bearer must possess a nonresident license for the province where he or she plans to use it. However, there are severe restrictions on firearms and weapons, and visitors are strongly advised to contact the Canada Firearms Centre (© **800/731-4000** in Canada and the U.S.; 506/624-5380 from other countries) prior to travel.

If you meet the minimum age requirement of the province or territory through which you enter Canada (the age is 19 in Ontario), you can bring in, free of duty or taxes, no more than 1.1 liters of liquor, or 1.5 liters of wine, or 24 containers of beer (355ml each). Visitors entering Ontario who are age 19 or older can also bring up to 200 cigarettes, 50 cigars or cigarillos, 200 grams of manufactured tobacco, and 200 tobacco sticks duty free. Dogs and cats in good health can enter Canada from the U.S. with their owners, but you should bring with you a valid rabies vaccination certificate. Check with the Canadian Food Inspection Agency's Import Service Centre (© **800/835-4486**), if you wish to bring other kinds of animals from the U.S., or any animal from another country.

For more information on customs matters, contact your nearest Canadian embassy or consulate, or call the **Automated Customs Information Service** (© **204/983-3500** or 506/636-5064). Information is also available online at **www. cbsa-asfc.gc.ca**. Print publications can be ordered by calling © **800/959-2221**.

What You Can Take Home from Canada

Returning **U.S. citizens** who have been away for at least 48 hours are allowed to take back, once every 30 days, US$800 worth of merchandise duty free. You'll be charged a flat rate of duty on the next US$1,000 worth of purchases. Any dollar amount beyond that is dutiable at whatever rates apply. On mailed gifts, the duty-free limit is US$200. Be sure to have your receipts or purchases handy to expedite the declaration process. *Note:* If you owe duty, you are required to pay on your arrival in the United States, either by cash, personal check, government or traveler's check, money order, or in some locations, a Visa or MasterCard.

To avoid having to pay duty on foreign-made personal items you owned before you left on your trip, bring along a bill of sale, insurance policy, jeweler's appraisal, or receipt of purchase. Or, before you leave you can preregister with Customs any items that can be readily identified by a permanently affixed serial number or marking—such as laptop computers, cameras, and CD players. Take the items to the nearest Customs office or register them with Customs at the airport from which you're departing. You'll receive, at no cost, a certificate of registration, which allows duty-free entry for the life of the item.

With some exceptions, you cannot bring fresh fruits and vegetables into the United States. Nor can Cuban tobacco products purchased in Canada be brought into the United States.

U.S. Citizens: For specifics on what you can bring back and the corresponding fees, download the invaluable free pamphlet *Know Before You Go* from www.cbp.gov. (Click on "Travel," and then click "Know Before You Go"). Or contact the **U.S. Customs and Border Protection (CBP),** 1300 Pennsylvania Ave., NW, Washington, DC 20229 (© **202/354-1000**) and request the pamphlet.

U.K. Citizens: For information, contact **HM Customs and Excise** at © **0845/010-9000** (© 020/8929-0152 from outside the U.K.), or consult their website at **www.hmce.gov.uk**.

Australian Citizens: A helpful brochure available from Australian consulates or Customs offices is *Know Before You Go.* For more information, call the **Australian Customs Service** at © **1300/363-263,** or log on to **www.customs.gov.au**.

New Zealand Citizens: Most questions are answered in a free pamphlet available at New Zealand consulates and Customs offices: *New Zealand Customs Guide for Travellers, Notice no. 4.* For more information, contact **New Zealand Customs,** The Customhouse, 17–21 Whitmore St., Box 2218, Wellington (© **04/473-6099** or 0800/428-786; **www.customs.govt.nz**).

3 WHEN TO GO

THE CLIMATE

Spring in Ottawa runs from late March to mid-May (although some years there may be a snowfall as late as Apr); **summer** is mid-May to mid-September; **fall** is mid-September to mid-November; and **winter** is mid-November to late March. The average annual high is 50°F (10°C), and the average annual low is 32°F (0°C). In winter, fluctuations in temperature sometimes cause freezing rain, a serious hazard for drivers (and pedestrians).

Ottawa's Average Temperatures (°C/°F)

	Jan	Feb	Mar	Apr	May	June	July	Aug	Sept	Oct	Nov	Dec
High	–4/25	–6/21	3/37	9/48	17/63	20/68	23/73	22/72	18/64	12/54	5/41	–3/27
Low	–18/0	–18/0	–13/9	–1/34	8/46	14/57	17/63	15/59	11/52	2/36	–6/21	–15/5

Full House

Hotel rooms fill up quickly during the most popular events in Ottawa: Winterlude, a winter festival held during the first three weekends in February; the Canadian Tulip Festival, a 10-day event in mid-May; and Canada Day weekend, incorporating Canada Day on July 1. If you plan to visit during these times, reserve accommodations several weeks or even months ahead, and when comparing accommodations ask about special packages, which may include tickets or entrance fees to attractions.

HOLIDAYS

On most public holidays, banks, government offices, schools, and post offices are closed. Museums, retail stores, and restaurants vary widely in their policies for holiday openings and closings, so call before you go to avoid disappointment.

Note that most museums in Ottawa are closed on Monday between mid-October and late April. Ottawa celebrates the following holidays: New Year's Day (Jan 1), Good Friday and/or Easter Monday (Mar or Apr, varies each year), Victoria Day (Mon following the third weekend in May), Canada Day (July 1), Civic Holiday (first Mon in Aug), Labor Day (first Mon in Sept), Thanksgiving (second Mon in Oct), Remembrance Day (Nov 11), Christmas Day (Dec 25), and Boxing Day (Dec 26).

OTTAWA CALENDAR OF EVENTS

The following list of events will help you plan your visit to Ottawa. Contact the **Capital Infocentre** (© 800/465-1867; www.canadascapital.gc.ca) to confirm details if a particular event is a major reason for your vacation. Even the largest, most successful events sometimes retire, a few events are biennial, and dates may change from those listed here. In addition to the following events, numerous smaller community and cultural events take place throughout the year. **Lansdowne Park,** a multipurpose sports and entertainment facility, hosts many trade and consumer shows catering to special interests—call them at © 613/580-2429 for information on upcoming events. There are many websites listing annual events and festivals for Ottawa. Check out **www.canadascapital.gc.ca**, **www.ottawatourism.ca**, **www. ottawakiosk.ca**, and **www.ottawastart.com**.

For an exhaustive list of events beyond those listed here, check **http://events. frommers.com**, where you'll find a searchable, up-to-the-minute roster of what's happening in cities all over the world.

JANUARY

The Governor General's New Year's Day Levee, Rideau Hall. The public is invited to meet the governor-general (the queen's representative in Canada), visit the historic residence's public rooms, and enjoy entertainment and light refreshments. Note that in some years the date may be brought forward to December, depending upon the governor-general's official duties. For more information call © 866/842-4422 or visit www.gg.ca.

FEBRUARY

Winterlude, throughout Ottawa and Gatineau. In a city that gets as cold as Ottawa does, there are only two ways you can approach winter: hibernate or celebrate. Every year, the first three weekends of February are filled with family winter fun in the snow and ice. Sites on both sides of the Ottawa River are transformed into winter wonderlands filled with gigantic snow sculptures, glittering ice sculptures, and a Snowflake Kingdom especially for kids. Children's entertainment, craft workshops, horse-drawn sleigh rides, snowboarding demonstrations, dogsled rides, and more are on offer for little ones. A free shuttle bus operates between sites. For more information call © **800/465-1867** or visit www.canadascapital.gc.ca/winterlude.

Canadian Ski Marathon, Gatineau Park. The world's longest cross-country ski tour is a skier's paradise and offers some of the best wilderness trails anywhere. You can ski as little as 15km (9 miles) or as much as 160km (99 miles)—you set the pace. The marathon attracts 2,200 novice and veteran skiers from ages 5 to 85. For more information call © **819/770-6556** or visit www.csm-mcs.com.

Gatineau Loppet, Gatineau Park. Close to 3,000 skiers from more than a dozen countries gather to participate in Canada's biggest annual cross-country ski competition. Events include 50km (31-mile) and 25km (16-mile) classic and freestyle races. Kids under age 13 can ski, snowshoe, or walk the 2km (1.25-mile) Mini-Gazifere. For more information call © **800/465-1867** or 819/595-0114 or visit www.keskinada.com.

Ottawa Boat, Sportsmen's & Cottage Show, Lansdowne Park. Revel in the outdoors at this show for fishers, hunters, and weekend cottagers. Dozens of demos feature everything from tying a fly to paddling a canoe. For more information call © **613/580-2429.**

MARCH

The Ottawa-Gatineau International Auto Show, Ottawa Congress Centre. While not on the scale of shows in Detroit or New York, this display features the latest cars, minivans, pickups, and SUVs. For more information call © **613/563-1984** or visit www.ottawa-gatineauautoshow.com.

APRIL

Ottawa Eco-Stewardship Fair, RA Centre. A diverse range of speakers and exhibitors address issues of biodiversity and environmental stewardship. For more information call © **613/230-3292** or visit www.ottawaecofair.ca.

Ottawa International Writers Festival, Spring Edition, Library and Archives Canada, and other locations. A celebration of the finest new and established writing from Canadian and international creators. Highlights include authors reading from their published or forthcoming works, and panel discussions. For more information call © **613/562-1243** or visit www.writersfestival.org.

MAY

Jane's Walk, various sites. Named in honor of celebrated urban activist Jane Jacobs, the event features a number of walking tours that highlight various aspects of city life, architecture, heritage, and culture. For more information call © **613/563-4922** or visit www.janeswalk.net.

WaterCan Embassy Dinner, Aberdeen Pavilion, Lansdowne Park. Chefs from dozens of embassies and high commissions provide samples of their favorite dishes to raise funds for the WaterCan charity's projects abroad. For more information call © **613/230-5182** or visit www.watercan.com.

Canadian Tulip Festival, various sites. Ottawa blooms with millions of tulips every spring, courtesy of an annual gift of bulbs from the Netherlands, given in gratitude for Canada's sheltering of the Dutch royal family during World War II. Visitors can view the blooms at sites along a 15km (9-mile) Tulip Route, explore the Tulip Explosion floral design show, or catch concerts and a craft show in Major's Hill Park. For more information call © **800/66-TULIP** (668-8547) or 613/567-4447 or visit www.tulip festival.ca.

National Capital Race Weekend, downtown Ottawa. Thousands of runners, volunteers, spectators, and visitors gather for this world-class marathon. Several other races, ranging from 2km (1.2 miles) to 21km (13 miles), are held. Families, in-line skaters, and beginner runners are welcome. For more information call © **866/786-6882** or visit www.ncm.ca.

Odawa Annual Pow Wow, Ottawa Municipal Campground. This energetic and colorful event is designed to bring First Nations culture to Native and non-Native audiences through the sharing of music, dance, art, and food. For more information call © **613/722-3811** or visit www.odawa.on.ca.

JUNE

Annual Contemporary Art Fest & Fair, Gallery 101, 301½ Bank St. Top local artists display works based on a theme. Video screenings, musical acts, and performance art are also included. For more information call © **613/230-2799** or visit www.gallery101.org.

Doors Open Ottawa, across the city. Take a peek inside some of the region's most distinctive residences and official buildings that are normally closed to the public. For more information call © **613/580-9674** or visit www.ottawa. ca/doorsopen.

Ottawa International Children's Festival, across the city. This event brings the best of live theatrical arts to children at sites in and around the Canada Science and Technology Museum. Families will enjoy music, theater, crafts, and other kids' entertainment. Other performing arts events for children are staged throughout the year at various local venues. For more information call © **613/241-0999** or visit www.ottawa childrensfestival.ca.

Magnetic North Theatre Festival, National Arts Centre. Canada's national festival of contemporary English-language theater is staged in Ottawa during odd-numbered years. For more information call © **866/850-2787** or 613/947-7000 or visit www.magnetic northfestival.ca.

Gloucester Fair, Rideau Carleton Raceway. This old-fashioned fair offers agricultural displays, gymkhana and western horse shows, a demolition derby, a lumberjack show, midway rides, bubblegum-blowing contests, pony rides, face painting, and more. For more information call © **613/744-2671**.

Festival Franco-Ontarien, Ottawa City Hall. One of the largest celebrations of French culture in North America features a variety of musical and theatrical performances to entertain all ages. For more information call © **613/321-0102** or visit www.ffo.ca.

Ottawa Dragon Boat Race Festival, Rideau Canoe Club. This festival features dragon boat races, multicultural stage performances, exhibits, and activities for children. Admission is free. For more information call © **613/238-7711** or visit www.dragonboat.net.

Changing of the Guard, Parliament Hill. This half-hour ceremony is one of Ottawa's most popular and outstanding attractions. From late June to late August, the Ceremonial Guard parades from Cartier Square Drill Hall to Parliament Hill daily between 9:30 and

10am. The ceremony itself begins at 10am, weather permitting. An interpretation program starts 15 minutes earlier. For more information call ✆ **800/465-1867** or visit www.parl.gc.ca/vis.

ByWard Market Auto Classic, ByWard Market. On the first Sunday in June, this event showcases automotive history with more than 150 vintage, classic, and high-performance cars on display for fun and prizes. The event is free to the public. For more information call ✆ **613/562-3325** or visit www.bywardmarket.com.

Italian Week, Corso Italia (Preston St.). The commercial heart of Ottawa's Little Italy is the place to be in mid-June to celebrate the food, music, pageantry, and art that is Italy. For more information call ✆ **613/231-2815** or visit www.prestonstreet.com.

Carnival of Cultures, Astrolabe Theatre. A kaleidoscope of cultures comes together in this celebration of music, food, and dance from around the world. The dynamic entertainment includes international artists and Ottawa's top folk dancers, singers, and musicians. For more information call ✆ **613/742-6952** or visit www.carnivalofcultures.ca.

Westfest, Richmond Road, Westboro Village. Started in 2004, this neighborhood street festival has grown to become the largest free musical event in the city. Combining buskers, theater, dance, and pop music, past festivals have featured performers like Buffy Sainte-Marie, Holly McNarland, and local-girl-made-good Kathleen Edwards. For more information call ✆ **613/729-3565** or visit www.westfest.ca.

UniSong, National Arts Centre and other sites. More than 400 members of youth and children's choirs from across Canada perform 4 days of concerts. Enjoy a full program of Canadian music, including a mass performance

on Canada Day. For more information call ✆ **613/234-3360** or visit www.abc.ca.

Garden Party at Rideau Hall. The governor-general hosts the annual garden party in June (the date varies according to the governor-general's official duties). The first Changing of the Guard ceremony of the summer is held before the party, and then Her Excellency greets visitors on the upper terrace of the gardens. Guests can explore the residence's public rooms, gardens, and greenhouses, and children can enjoy many special activities on the grounds, including entertainment and crafts. Light refreshments are served. For more information call ✆ **866/842-4422** or 613/991-4422 or visit www.gg.ca.

Ottawa Fringe Festival, various sites. Enjoy a wide range of exciting and vibrant theater, dance, music, visual arts, video, and film on six stages in the heart of Ottawa's arts and theater district. More than 70 companies stage more than 300 shows. For more information call ✆ **613/232-6162** or visit www.ottawafringe.com.

TD Canada Trust Ottawa International Jazz Festival, citywide. Founded in 1981, this 10-day festival features international headliners and local musicians in both indoor and outdoor venues from noon until well after midnight. For more information call ✆ **888/226-4495** or 613/241-2633 or visit www.ottawajazzfestival.com.

July

Canada Day, various sites. Each July 1, hundreds of thousands of Canadians gather in Ottawa to celebrate Canada's birthday. Activities center around Parliament Hill, Majors Hill Park, and Jacques-Cartier Park in Hull. Shows, street performers, and concerts mark the event. Don't miss the spectacular nighttime fireworks display over the

Ottawa River. For more information call ✆ **800/465-1867** or visit www.canadascapital.gc.ca.

Sound and Light Show, Parliament Hill. This free, dynamic show illuminates Parliament Hill at dusk, weather permitting, from July to September. The music, narrative, and images projected on the face of the Parliament Buildings celebrate Canada's heritage. For more information call ✆ **800/465-1867** or 613/239-5000 or visit www.canadascapital.gc.ca/soundandlight.

HOPE Volleyball SummerFest, Mooney's Bay. HOPE, a nonprofit, charitable organization, holds the largest beach volleyball tournament in the world, with 1,000 teams playing on 79 courts. The tournament attracts more than 30,000 participants and spectators. For more information call ✆ **613/237-1433** or visit www.hopehelps.com.

International Youth Orchestra Festival, various sites. Held in Ottawa during odd-numbered years, the festival offers concerts, broadcasts, demonstrations, and a gala mass concert. For more information call ✆ **800/465-1867.**

The Ottawa International Chamber Music Festival, various sites. The world's largest chamber music festival showcases the finest musicians in some of the most beautiful churches in downtown Ottawa over 2 weeks in late July and early August. For more information call ✆ **613/234-8008** or visit www.chamberfest.com.

Cisco Ottawa Bluesfest, Lebreton Flats. One of North America's largest outdoor music festivals presents a diverse array of rock, blues, and roots performers. Headliners—who have included Bob Dylan, Van Morrison, and Sting—are usually announced by the end of April each year. For more information call ✆ **866/258-3748** or

613/247-1188 or visit www.ottawabluesfest.ca.

Children's Hospital of Eastern Ontario Teddy Bear Picnic, Rideau Hall. Bring your kids and their bears to this annual picnic, held on the second Saturday of July. Meet a Mountie, enjoy a pancake breakfast, visit the petting zoo, and watch live entertainment. For more information call ✆ **613/737-7600.**

AUGUST

Sound of Light, Casino du Lac-Leamy. Competitors from around the world light up the night with displays of fireworks. For more information call ✆ **819/771-3389** or visit www.feux.qc.ca.

Lumière Festival, Stanley Park. Residents of the posh New Edinburgh neighborhood light up historic Stanley Park for neighbors and visitors. Family-oriented activities include lantern-making workshops and other handcrafts. For more information call ✆ **613/745-2742** or visit www.lumiereottawa.com.

Glengarry Highland Games, Maxville Fairgrounds. The clans gather on the first weekend of August to celebrate their Scottish heritage with traditional sports events, more than 200 dancers, and 60 pipe bands. For more information call ✆ **888/298-1666** or visit www.glengarryhighlandgames.com.

Buskerfest, Sparks Street Mall. Jugglers, comedians, storytellers, fire-eaters, mimes, musicians, and magicians entertain audiences of all ages. For more information call ✆ **613/230-0984** or visit www.sparksstreetmall.com.

Ottawa Folk Festival, Lakeside Gardens in Britannia Park. This 3-day gathering celebrates Canada's rich folk traditions with music, dance, storytelling, and crafts. Some of the world's finest acoustic musicians perform evening concerts on the main stage, and afternoon musical stages feature such themes as songwriting, Ottawa Valley fiddling and step-dancing, Celtic music, and vocal harmonics. The setting is one of the most scenic in the region. For more information call ℂ 613/230-8234 or visit www.ottawafolk.org.

Capital Pride Festival, various sites. The Ottawa area highlights its gay, lesbian, bisexual, and transgender community with a week of events including the annual Pride Parade. For more information call ℂ 613/421-5387 or visit www.prideottawa.com.

SuperEx: Central Canada Exhibition, Lansdowne Park. This is wholesome family entertainment at a great price. "The Ex" combines interactive theme exhibits, agricultural programs, entertainment, and a large midway with more than 60 rides, including a roller coaster. For more information call ℂ 613/237-7222 or visit www.ottawa superex.com.

SEPTEMBER

Feast of Fields, Vincent Massey Park. Some of the region's top chefs prepare meals using local produce supplied by members of Canadian Organic Gardeners. For more information call ℂ 613/244-4000 or visit www.cog.ca/ottawa.

Gatineau Hot Air Balloon Festival, La Baie Park. Some 150 balloons take to the skies at Canada's largest balloon festival, held on Labor Day weekend. There are plenty of concerts and child-oriented activities, fairground rides, and a dazzling fireworks display. For more information call ℂ 800/668-8383 or 819/243-2330 or visit www.balloon gatineau.com.

La Vendemmia: Italian Harvest Festival, Corso Italia (Preston St.). Celebrate the harvest with grape-stomping contests, wine seminars, wine-making demonstrations, and children's entertainers.

For more information call ℂ 613/231-2815 or visit www.prestonstreet.com.

Ottawa International Animation Festival, various sites. Held in even-numbered years, this is North America's largest animation festival, featuring showcase screenings of new animated films from around the world and discussions of the art form. For more information call ℂ 613/232-8769 or visit www.awn.com/ottawa.

International Student Animation Festival of Ottawa, various sites. Alternating with the Ottawa International Animation Festival in odd-numbered years, this event is devoted to students and first-time animators. Competitions, workshops, recruiting, and a trade fair are part of the event. For more information call ℂ 613/232-8769 or visit www.awn.com/ottawa.

Ladyfest, various sites. Top female performers from various musical genres entertain. For more information visit www.ladyfestottawa.com.

Fall Rhapsody, Gatineau Park. Workshops, guided tours, nature interpretation programs, and other outdoor activities take place against a spectacular backdrop of colorful fall leaves. Kids can watch and participate in games and crafts. The towns and villages surrounding Gatineau Park celebrate autumn with exhibits of arts and crafts and activities for the whole family. For more information call ℂ 800/465-1867 or 819/827-2020 or visit www.canadas capital.gc.ca/gatineau.

OCTOBER

Great Pumpkin Weigh-off, ByWard Market. On the first Saturday in October, growers from Ontario, Quebec, and the northeastern United States bring their entries to compete for the title of Great Pumpkin. Some of the monsters weigh in at 450 kilograms (992 pounds). Expert carvers are on hand to produce jack-o'-lanterns. For more information call ☏ 613/562-3325 or visit www.byward-market.com.

Ottawa International Writers Festival, Fall Edition, Library and Archives Canada, and other locations. A celebration of the finest new and established writing from Canadian and international creators. Highlights include authors reading from their published or forthcoming works, and panel discussions. For more information call ☏ **613/562-1243** or visit www.writersfestival.org.

Ottawa Senators, Scotiabank Place. Ottawa's entry in the National Hockey League faces off against their rivals. The regular season runs to April. For more information call ☏ **613/599-0250** or visit www.ottawasenators.com.

NOVEMBER

Ottawa Wine and Food Show, Ottawa Congress Centre. Thousands flock to this annual event to sample fine wines, beers, and spirits from around the world, taste the delicious food, be entertained by celebrity chefs, or attend wine seminars. Limited to ages 19 and over. For more information call ☏ **613/563-1984** or visit www.playerexpo.com.

Ottawa Storytelling Festival, Library and Archives Canada. Features the best storytellers from around the region and across Canada. For more information call ☏ **613/722-2606** or visit www. ottawastorytellers.ca.

Lebanorama, various sites. Ottawa's large Lebanese community celebrates its heritage with performing artists and displays. For more information call ☏ 613/742-6952 or visit www.al-arz.ca.

Vintage Clothing Sale, Fairmont Château Laurier. More than 40 exhibitors display antique dresses, linens, accessories, and jewelry. For more information call ☏ **613/730-8785.**

Help Santa Toy Parade, downtown Ottawa. On the third or fourth weekend in November, the annual Santa Claus Parade winds its way through the city. Floats, bands, and clowns entertain the crowds lining the streets. The Professional Firefighters' Association collects toys along the parade route and distributes them to less fortunate children in the Ottawa area. For more information call ☏ **613/526-2706** or visit www.toyparade.org.

DECEMBER

Christmas Lights Across Canada, Confederation Boulevard and Parliament Hill. On December 1, more than 300,000 color-coordinated lights are illuminated to mark the beginning of the holiday season. For more information call ☏ **800/465-1867** or 613/239-5000 or visit www.canadascapital.gc.ca.

Christmas Carollers, ByWard Market. Leading up to Christmas, local choirs sing Christmas carols, and visitors can enjoy free horse-drawn carriage rides while listening to the music. For more information call ☏ **613/562-3325** or visit www.byward-market.com.

Deck the Halls, Parliament Hill. The public is welcomed into the Centre Block to view the holiday decorations. Visitors can view the two houses of Parliament through open doors, and take the elevator to the observation deck of the Peace Tower for a view of the Christmas lights in the city below. For more information call ☏ **613/239-5000** or 613/996-0896 or visit www. parl.gc.ca.

Ottawa International Hockey Festival: The **Bell Capital Cup,** various hockey arenas. More than 400 junior teams from Canada, the U.S., and Europe compete. For more information call ☏ **613/599-0241** or visit www. oihf.net.

GETTING TO OTTAWA
By Plane

The **Ottawa Macdonald-Cartier International Airport (YOW; www.ottawa-airport.com)** is Ottawa's only public airport, located about 15 minutes by car from the downtown core. The airport is open 24 hours daily.

Although the Ottawa airport has been significantly expanded in recent years (some renovations were ongoing at press time), the city is not considered a hub and getting a direct, nonstop flight can be challenging, particularly from many regions of the U.S., and from Europe or Asia. Note that, in airline parlance, the term *direct flight* may include an en route stop but not an aircraft change.

WITHIN CANADA **Air Canada** (see "Toll-Free Numbers & Websites," p. 222, for a list of airline contact information), which also operates under the "Jazz" logo, offers nonstop flights to Ottawa from Vancouver, Edmonton, Calgary, Saskatoon, Winnipeg, Thunder Bay, London, Hamilton, Toronto (Lester B. Pearson Airport), Montreal, Quebec City, Moncton, Halifax, Charlottetown, and St. John's. **WestJet** flies nonstop from Vancouver, Calgary, Winnipeg, Toronto (Pearson), and Halifax. **Porter** flies nonstop from Toronto (City Center) and Halifax. **Bearskin Airlines** flies nonstop from Sudbury and Waterloo, and has direct flights from Thunder Bay and Sault Ste. Marie. **Canadian North** flies nonstop from Iqaluit and direct from Rankin Inlet and Yellowknife. Ottawa-based **First Air** flies nonstop from Iqaluit.

FROM THE U.S. **Air Canada** operates year-round, nonstop flights from Las Vegas; Chicago; New York (LaGuardia); Washington, D.C. (Dulles and Reagan); and Boston, and seasonal nonstop flights from Fort Lauderdale and Orlando. **American Airlines** and **United Express (Shuttle America)** fly nonstop to Ottawa from Chicago. **ASA-Delta Connection** operates nonstop flights from Atlanta. **Continental Express** flies nonstop from Cleveland and Newark (Liberty). **Northwest Airlink** offers nonstop service from Detroit. **US Airways** operates nonstop flights from Philadelphia. From November to May, **WestJet** flies nonstop from Tampa and Orlando.

FROM ABROAD **Air Canada** flies year-round nonstop to Ottawa from London (Heathrow) and Frankfurt, and seasonally from Cancun and Montego Bay.

Getting into Town from the Airport

Yow Airporter shuttle service (✆ **613/260-2359**; www.yowshuttle.com) departs for major hotels from Arrivals Level 1, Post 13 every half-hour from 5:35am to 12:05am. The return fare is C$24. Children under 8 travel free. An airport limo can be summoned by calling ✆ **613/523-1560**. You can also hop into a regular cab; the fare will be around C$25 to downtown. If you wish to use the public transit system, OC Transpo provides high-frequency rapid service along the scenic Transitway, a roadway built specifically for buses. Rte. 97 departs the terminal at the curb outside the arrivals area. Adult cash fare (exact change only) is C$3. Tickets are available at the Ground Transportation Desk located on Level 1 of the terminal building. Two tickets, at a cost of C$1 each, are required for one adult to travel downtown.

Avis, Budget, Enterprise, Hertz, and National Alamo each have kiosks at the airport, located on the ground floor of the Parkade adjacent to the arrivals area. If you are renting from Thrifty, a representative will meet you at the Ground Transportation kiosk on Level 1 and transport you to the company's off-site location. If you decide to rent a car during the high season, try to make arrangements well in advance to ensure the vehicle you want will be available. If you are traveling from outside Canada, you may obtain a reasonable discount by booking before you leave home. The rental fee depends on the type of car. For a compact or midsize vehicle, the fee can range from C$30 to C$50 a day, plus taxes. These prices do not include insurance, but some credit cards offer automatic coverage if you charge the full amount of the car rental to the card (check with your credit card issuer before you travel). Be sure to read the fine print of the agreement and complete a thorough visual check for damage before accepting the vehicle. Some companies add conditions that will boost your bill if you don't fulfill certain obligations, such as filling the gas tank before returning the car.

Note: If you're under age 25 or over 70, tell the rental company when you book—most companies have a minimum age policy, and some have implemented a maximum age as well.

For listings of the major car rental agencies in Ottawa, please see "Toll-Free Numbers & Websites," p. 222.

If you're driving from the airport to the downtown core, follow the Airport Parkway until it becomes Bronson Avenue, then follow Bronson north to Queen Street. There are no hotels on the airport property.

Long-Haul Flights: How to Stay Comfortable

- Your choice of airline and airplane will definitely affect your leg room. Find more details about U.S. airlines at **www.seatguru.com**. For international airlines, the research firm Skytrax has posted a list of average seat pitches at **www.airlinequality.com**.

- Emergency exit seats and bulkhead seats typically have the most legroom. Emergency exit seats are usually left unassigned until the day of a flight (to ensure that able-bodied people fill the seats); it's worth checking in online at home (if the airline offers that option) or getting to the ticket counter early to snag one of these spots for a long flight. Many passengers find that bulkhead seating offers more legroom, but keep in mind that bulkhead seats have no storage space on the floor in front of you.

- To have two seats for yourself in a three-seat row, try for an aisle seat in a center section toward the back of coach. If you're traveling with a companion, book an aisle and a window seat. Middle seats are usually booked last, so chances are good you'll end up with three seats to yourselves. And in the event that a third passenger is assigned the middle seat, he or she will probably be more than happy to trade for a window or an aisle.

- To sleep, avoid the last row of any section or the row in front of an emergency exit, as these seats are the least likely to recline. Avoid seats near highly trafficked toilet areas. Avoid seats in the back of many jets—these can be narrower than those in the rest of coach. Or reserve a window seat so you can rest your head and avoid being bumped in the aisle.

- Get up, walk around, and stretch every 60 to 90 minutes to keep your blood flowing. This helps avoid **deep vein thrombosis,** or "economy-class syndrome." See the box "Avoiding 'Economy-Class Syndrome,'" p. 49.

- Drink water before, during, and after your flight to combat the lack of humidity in airplane cabins. Avoid caffeine and alcohol, which will dehydrate you.

By Car

With the completion several years ago of Hwy. 416, which serves as a direct link between Hwy. 401 and Ottawa, the approach from the south and west of Canada's capital is a smooth and easy drive. Unless you're headed for the west end of the city, take exit 57 from Hwy. 416—look for the sign that reads BANK-FIELD ROAD (COUNTY ROAD 8)/AIRPORT/SCENIC ROUTE. Follow County Road 8 east to Hwy. 73 north through the countryside until you reach Hunt Club Road on the southern edge of the city. From here, you can take one of several routes downtown—Prince of Wales Drive and Riverside Drive are the most pleasant. The Airport Parkway/Bronson Avenue is the most direct route downtown, and Bank Street will take you past the most shops. From Montreal and Eastern Canada, travel west along Hwy. 417 and follow the signs for downtown. Keep an eye out in local stores for the handy, easy-to-read MapArt plasticized folding road map, which has a map of the region, a city map, and a large-print map of downtown that includes one-way streets, churches, major attractions, and some hotels. *Warning:* Be alert to the possibility of deer suddenly appearing in the roadway in rural forested areas, particularly on Hwy. 416, most often at night.

If you're arriving from south of the border, there are several convenient crossing points. From Vermont, enter Canada via I-89 or 91, travel toward Montreal, and pick up the westerly route (Hwy. 417). In New York State, I-81 crosses at Hill Island to Hwy. 401; you can also take Rte. 37 and enter at Ogdensburg-Johnstown or Rooseveltown-Cornwall. On I-87 in New York State, cross into Quebec, travel toward Montreal, and keep to the west of the city, heading onto Hwy. 417. If you're driving from Michigan, you'll enter Ontario at Detroit-Windsor (via I-75 and the Ambassador Bridge or tunnel) or Port Huron-Sarnia (via I-94 and the Bluewater Bridge).

Here are some approximate driving distances to Ottawa: from Montreal, 200km (124 miles); from Toronto, 450km (280 miles); from Quebec City, 475km (295 miles); from Boston, 749km (465 miles); from Buffalo, 539km (335 miles); from Chicago, 1,287km (800 miles); from Detroit, 845km (525 miles); from New York City, 749km (465 miles); from Washington, D.C., 933km (580 miles).

Be sure to carry your driver's license, car registration, and insurance documents if you plan to drive your own vehicle. If you are a member of the American Automobile Association (AAA), the **Canadian Automobile Association (CAA)** North and East Ontario branch provides emergency roadside assistance (© **800/222-4357** or 613/820-1400 within the City of Ottawa area).

By Train

Ottawa is part of VIA Rail's Quebec City–Windsor Corridor, and is linked directly to Montreal (and points east) and Toronto (and points west). Several trains make the Ottawa-Montreal (2 hr.) and Ottawa-Toronto (5 hr.) runs every day, with departures primarily aimed at business travelers in the early morning and late afternoon. Both coach and VIA-1 (first-class) cars with reserved seating, Wi-Fi connectivity, and food and beverage service are available on most trains. **Ottawa Station** is located in the southeast part of Ottawa, about 5 minutes by car from the downtown core. The station is well served by taxis. If you are arriving by train from west of Ottawa, and staying in the western part of the city, you may find it more practical to leave the train at the **Fallowfield Station,** which is about 15 minutes by car from the downtown core.

By Bus

The **Ottawa Bus Terminal** (© **613/238-5900**) is located at 265 Catherine St., near the Kent Street exit from Hwy. 417, on the edge of the downtown core. **Greyhound**

Canada (© **800/661-8747**) provides coast-to-coast service with connections to Ottawa from most cities and Montreal's Pierre Trudeau International Airport. Book online or obtain schedule and fare information at www.greyhound.ca. **Greyhound Lines, Inc.** (© **800/229-9424;** www.greyhound.com) provides bus service between the U.S. and Canada.

Investigate offers such as unlimited-travel passes and discount fares. It's tough to quote typical fares because bus companies, like airlines, are adopting yield-management strategies, resulting in frequent price changes depending on demand.

GETTING AROUND

Ottawa is a walker's paradise. Its compact size, relatively flat setting, and numerous parks make it easy to get around, and with most of the major national sites in the downtown core, you can leave the car in the hotel parking lot for most of your visit. You can readily find your way around the city without a car, using one only if you have time for a few day trips to outlying attractions.

As the national capital of an officially bilingual country, and the close neighbor of one of Quebec's largest cities, Ottawa operates fluently in both English and French. As you stroll around the city, you are as likely to hear French spoken as English (and often in the same conversation, as bilingual Canadians switch back and forth between languages with ease). But don't despair if you don't speak French. The people you will meet as a visitor to Canada's capital—hotel staff, restaurant servers, museum and attractions employees—are usually fluent in both official languages.

For those used to cities laid out on a grid, Ottawa's layout does require some adjustment. Like all cities that are defined by its waterways—and Ottawa is defined by three rivers and a canal—the streets can seem to follow illogical courses, and matters are

made worse by the number of one-way streets in the downtown core, and by so-called traffic calming, which is achieved by creating cul-de-sacs where you least expect them.

Like all northern cities, Ottawa is also defined by its climate. In the summer, the weather can be hot and humid for days at a time, while in January and February the temperature can plunge to well below the freezing point, and northern winds can make it seem much colder than it actually is.

Orienting yourself in Ottawa is as simple as remembering which side of the Rideau Canal you are on, since many things in the city follow the age-old division between the "upper" (west) and "lower" (east) parts of the city core. With the Ottawa River as its northern boundary, the city can easily be viewed as two roughly equal halves.

The Ottawa River—Canada's second longest at more than 1,100km (684 miles)—sweeps around the northern edge of the city. Most of the major attractions are clustered in the downtown area on the south bank of the river. The **Rideau Canal** takes center stage, curving through the city and dividing the downtown area in two: **west of the canal** (often called **Centretown**), and **east of the canal** (often called **Lowertown**).

In the downtown area west of the canal you'll find **Parliament Hill**, the **Supreme Court,** the **Canadian War Museum,** and the **Canadian Museum of Nature** (a few blocks south). Situated on the east side of the **Ottawa Locks** where the Rideau Canal meets the Ottawa River is the majestic **Fairmont Château Laurier,** Ottawa's most elegant hotel, with the **Canadian Museum of Contemporary Photography** nestled along its west wall. Continuing east, the **ByWard Market** district hosts dozens of restaurants, boutiques, bars, and clubs. Along **Sussex Drive** (which follows the south bank of the Ottawa River), you'll find the **National Gallery of Canada,** the **Royal Canadian Mint,** and the **prime minister's residence.** Crossing the Rideau River heading east on Sussex Drive you pass by the gates of many embassies and their official residences. **Rideau Hall, Rockcliffe Park,** the **Canada Aviation Museum,** and the **RCMP Musical Ride Centre (Rockcliffe Stables)** are all east of the Rideau River. The area south of the Queensway (Hwy. 417), west to Bronson Avenue, and east to the canal is known as **the Glebe** and offers boutique shopping and trendy cafes along **Bank Street.** North across the river, in the **province of Quebec,** lies the city of **Gatineau,** connected to the east end of Ottawa by the Macdonald-Cartier and Alexandra bridges and to the west by the Portage and Chaudière bridges. At the north end of the Alexandra Bridge stands the architecturally stunning **Canadian Museum of Civilization.** The **Casino du Lac-Leamy,** with its theater, convention center, and luxury hotel, is situated on Lake Leamy in Gatineau. North and west of Gatineau stretches breathtaking **Gatineau Park,** 361sq. km (139 sq. miles) of wilderness managed by the National Capital Commission.

Finding your way around town by car in Ottawa can be a challenge, since some streets halt abruptly and then reappear a few blocks farther on, one-way streets are common in the downtown core, and some streets change names several times. Traffic-calming measures—including chicanes (a series of tight curves), speed bumps, and cul-de-sacs—are common in many residential neighborhoods.

By Car

The scale of Ottawa makes driving your vehicle unnecessary for most sightseeing, although it will come in handy if you want to visit outlying attractions such as the Canada Aviation Museum, the Diefenbunker, or Gatineau Park.

As a rule, traffic is not heavy in Ottawa; even during the peak hours before and

after work, traffic does not build up excessively, except during heavy snowfalls. All of the major arteries feed into the downtown core, where most of the visitor accommodations are located. These main arteries are well marked for visitors, including special signage for national tourist attractions such as Parliament Hill and the major museums.

If you do decide to drive, be prepared for one-way streets that don't follow any predictable pattern. Keep an eye out, as well, for traffic blocks designed to prevent vehicles from using residential streets as thoroughfares. Some streets change names several times along their length, and others stop abruptly, only to continue a few blocks over. Needless to say, a map is essential if you're driving in city areas and will give you the added convenience of being able to locate major tourist attractions, parking lots, and other useful destinations.

When parking downtown, you have a choice of meters or lots. Parking meters are color-coded: Meters with a 1-hour time limit have gray domes, those with a 2-hour limit have green domes, and those for tour-bus parking only have yellow domes. Meters accept quarters, loonies, toonies, and City of Ottawa parking cards that are available at most banks. Increasingly, the city is introducing centralized meters, which dispense short-term permits for display on your dashboard.

Always read the signs posted near parking meters to find out if there are any parking restrictions. One of the most common restrictions is a ban on parking weekdays between 3:30 and 5:30pm on certain streets, to improve traffic flow during the evening rush hour. Generally, short-term parking rates downtown are C$.50 for 12 minutes. Your best bet is to use a municipal parking lot, marked with a large white "P" in a green circle. On weekends, parking is free in city lots and at meters in the area bounded by Elgin Street and Bronson Avenue, and by Wellington and Catherine streets. If you must leave your vehicle on a

(Fun Facts   A Town by Any Other Name

The sharp geographical division between the area immediately south of Parliament Hill and the area that runs east from the Hill to the Rideau River was historically a class division, as well. Prior to Confederation, the higher ground was known as Upper Town, and was home to the (primarily English) professional class, military officers, and politicians. The lower ground—which naturally became known as Lower Town, spelled as two words—housed the Irish and French working class, their taverns, and shops. Sometime after Confederation, as the Glebe and other neighborhoods grew, the term *Upper Town* was replaced by *Centretown* and *Lower Town* took on the contemporary single-word spelling. To complicate matters further, *Lowertown* is used by many native Ottawans to denote a specific neighborhood between King Edward Avenue—the eastern border of the ByWard Market—and the Rideau River. If you encounter Ottawans born prior to World War II, you may face yet another anomaly of nomenclature; many older people call the central business core of the city "Uptown."

city street overnight, ask hotel staff or your B&B host whether there are parking restrictions.

From November 15 to April 1 there are parking restrictions on city streets between 1 and 7am when an accumulation of 7 centimeters of snow or more is forecast. Call the Environment Canada weather line at © **613/998-3439** for a detailed forecast. Motorists should be aware that snow-removal crews may be working to remove snow from recent storms at any time; signs informing the public are placed in snowbanks several hours before removal begins. If your car is there when the snow-removal crew arrives it will be ticketed for a C$50 fine and towed to a nearby street that has already been cleared.

In Ontario, a right turn on a red light is permitted after coming to a complete stop unless the intersection is posted otherwise, provided you yield to oncoming traffic and pedestrians. Be aware that once you cross the Ottawa River you enter the province of Quebec, where the rules are different, and vary from municipality to municipality. In Gatineau, you can turn right on a red light when it is safe to do so, and only if there is no signage indicating that right-hand turns on a red light are not allowed. Throughout Quebec, some street signs prohibit right turns on a red during specific periods. Wearing your seat belt is compulsory; fines for riding without a seat belt are substantial. Speed limits are posted and must be obeyed at all times. Always stop when pedestrians are using the crosswalks, but also be careful of pedestrians crossing against the lights—Ottawans seem to have a mild disregard for pedestrian-crossing signals in the downtown core. Beware, as well, of drivers running red lights. Always check that an intersection is clear before advancing when the light turns green, especially if your vehicle is going to be the first one through. Eight major intersections throughout the city are equipped with red-light cameras to dissuade drivers from running red lights and enforce penalties.

If you're visiting from abroad and plan to rent a car in Canada, keep in mind that foreign driver's licenses are usually recognized, but you should get an international one if your home license is not in English.

Check out **Breezenet.com**, which offers domestic car-rental discounts with some of the most competitive rates around. Also worth visiting are Orbitz.com, Hotwire. com, Travelocity.com, and Priceline.com, all of which offer competitive online car-rental rates. For additional car rental agencies, see "Toll-Free Numbers & Websites," p. 222.

By Bus

Public transit in Ottawa is provided by **OC Transpo.** This is an economical and efficient way to get around, since buses can bypass rush-hour traffic through the Transitway, a rapid-transit system of roadways reserved exclusively for buses. Routes 94, 95, 96, 97, 101, and 102 are the main Transitway routes, operating 22 hours a day. All OC Transpo bus routes travel along parts of the Transitway or connect at one of the stations. OC Transpo stations, many of which are located next to major shopping or employment centers, offer convenient transfer points with heated waiting areas, information displays, and pay phones. Many have bike racks and vendor kiosks. For transit information call ✆ 613/741-4390 or visit www.octranspo.com. There are four sales and information centers in the city—one in the Rideau Centre shopping mall in downtown Ottawa, and three more at transit stations: Lincoln Fields Station in west Ottawa, and St. Laurent Station and Place d'Orléans Station in the east.

The regular exact-cash fare is C$3 for an adult and C$1.50 for a child. It's cheaper to use tickets, at C$1 each, since the adult fare is two tickets and the child fare (ages 6–11) is one ticket. The exception is during weekday rush hours, when some express routes charge C$4 or a three-ticket fare. Day passes are a good buy at C$6.50 in advance at a vendor or C$7.25 on the bus for unlimited rides. The Family Day Pass is a real bargain. Just one day pass will entitle a family of up to two adults and four children ages 11 and under to unlimited same-day travel on Sunday and statutory holidays. You can buy bus passes and tickets at more than 300 vendor locations across the city. Day passes can

also be purchased at the National Capital Infocentre at 90 Wellington St. in front of the Parliament Buildings and at many downtown hotels.

The number of buses that are fully accessible to **people with disabilities** has increased dramatically in recent years. More than half of the bus fleet currently has fully accessible low floors, although some trips each day may use nonaccessible buses so it's best to check before starting out on a trip, by calling ✆ 613/560-1000. A telephone hot line has been set up to help customers find out more about accessible services on conventional transit (✆ 613/842-3625, Mon–Fri 9am–5pm). For information on designated accessible bus routes, call the main OC Transpo phone line at ✆ 613/741-4390. Fully accessible buses, marked on the front by a blue and white wheelchair symbol, have low floors to provide access for seniors, people with limited mobility, people using wheelchairs, and parents with small children or strollers. Drivers lower the buses to the curb so that there are no stairs to climb, and can extend a ramp to accommodate wheelchairs. In addition, these buses are equipped with air-conditioning, cloth seats, yellow grab rails and pull cords, and easy-to-reach stop-request buttons.

For persons with permanent or short-term disabilities who are unable to walk to or board regular transit, there's **Para Transpo.** Both visitors and residents can use this service, but you must register, and the application form must be signed by an appropriate health professional. Reservations must be made 1 day before your trip. Call ✆ 613/244-1289 for information and registration, or ✆ 613/244-7272 for reservations (the reservations office is open daily 9am–5pm).

Public transit throughout the city of **Gatineau** and the **Outaouais region** on the Quebec side of the Ottawa River is provided by **Société de transport de**

l'Outaouais (STO; ✆ 819/770-3242; www.sto.ca). An information office is located at 111 Jean-Proulx St. in Gatineau (Hull Sector), and open Monday to Friday 8:30am to 5:30pm and Saturday 10:30am to 5pm.

By Train

A limited light-rail pilot project was launched in October 2001. Designed to go where the Transitway doesn't, the O-Train uses an 8km (5-mile) stretch of existing Canadian Pacific rail line running between Greenboro Transitway Station in the south end and Bayview Station in the north end of the city, close to downtown. Greenboro Station has parking for more than 600 vehicles and connects to Ottawa International Airport via bus route 97. Confederation Station is close to Vincent Massey Park. Carleton Station serves students and staff of Carleton University. Carling Station is conveniently close to Dow's Lake and Little Italy. Bayview Station is minutes from downtown, with a high-frequency bus service. Each state-of-the-art train, built by the Canadian company Bombardier, consists of three air-conditioned cars, accommodating 135 seated and 150 standing passengers. The front and rear diesel-powered units allow the train to travel in either direction on the track without having to turn around. A low-floor design ensures easy access for passengers and a quiet, comfortable ride.

Operating hours are Monday to Saturday 6:30am to midnight, and Sunday and holidays 7:30am to 11pm. The fare is C$2.25. Children 11 and under ride free on the O-Train. Tickets can be purchased, using exact change, from the vending machines on the station platform. You may transfer to an OC Transpo bus at no extra charge, except on rush-hour routes, which require a top-up of a single bus ticket or C$1. Children ages 6 to 11 who transfer to a bus must pay the child's bus fare.

The current rail line is the first step toward citywide light-rail transit. After numerous delays—and what has seemed like interminable political wrangling—a new plan calls for a transit tunnel to be excavated under the city's central core, with train lines running to key junction points east and west.

By Taxi

You can hail a taxi on the street, but you'll find one more readily at taxi stands in front of most hotels, many government buildings, and some museums. You can also summon a taxi by phone. The drop charge for Ottawa taxis is C$3.20, and the mileage charge is C$.16 for every 93m (305 ft.). In the Ottawa area, 24-hour cab companies include **Blue Line** (✆ 613/238-1111), with a fleet of more than 600 cabs, and **Capital Taxi** (✆ 613/744-3333). **West-Way Taxi** (✆ 613/727-0101) has drivers who have been trained to transport people with disabilities.

By Tour Bus

There are so many interesting buildings, monuments, attractions, and views in Ottawa that hopping on a tour bus is a great idea, especially if it's your first visit to Canada's capital. Tours are fully narrated so that you don't miss anything while you're cruising around town. On-and-off privileges allow you to take a break to stretch your legs, or, if you see someplace you'd like to visit, you can just hop off the bus and join it again later.

Choose an open-top double-decker bus or a vintage trolley bus operated by **Gray Line Sightseeing Tours** for a 2-hour tour. Step on or off the bus at any of the 15 designated stops as many times as you wish as you pass the following major tourist attractions: Parliament Hill, the Canadian Museum of Civilization, Notre-Dame Cathedral Basilica, Rideau Hall, RCMP Musical Ride Centre and Stables, the Canada Aviation Museum, and the

ByWard Market. The tours officially start at the corner of Sparks and Metcalfe streets. Tickets are valid for 2 days, and the tour buses run in a continuous circle between 10am and 3pm. Tours operate from May 1 to October 31. A family of four can get a 2-day, on/off-privilege ticket for C$81; a child single ticket is C$19; an adult single ticket is C$29. For departure times and other information, call **Gray Line** at ℰ **800/297-6422** or 613/565-5463 or visit www.grayline.ca.

By Bicycle

A great way to get around in Ottawa is by bicycle. Ottawa and the surrounding regions offer a comprehensive network of pathways and parkways where people can bike and in-line skate through beautiful natural scenery. A number of city streets also have designated bike lanes. For maps of the pathways and more information, drop in at the **Capital Infocentre,** opposite Parliament Hill at 90 Wellington St. (ℰ **800/465-1867;** www.canadascapital. gc.ca). If you find your planned bike route overly ambitious, hop on the bus: **OC Transpo** has installed **bike racks** on more

than 200 buses, including all articulated buses, and on routes 2, 85, 95, 96, 97, 101, 118 and 145. Each rack holds two bikes, and loading and unloading is quick and easy. There's no additional cost to use the rack. The program runs from mid-April to November.

If you didn't bring your own equipment, numerous places in Ottawa rent out bicycles and in-line skates. See chapter 7, "Exploring Ottawa," for a list of rental outfits.

Some specific rules apply to cyclists. All cyclists under age 18 must wear a bicycle **helmet.** Cyclists cannot ride on the sidewalk and must not exceed speeds of 20kmph (12 mph) on multiuse pathways. Be considerate of other road or pathway users, and keep to the right. Pass only when it is safe to do so, and use your bell or voice to let others know you're about to pass.

If you're in the vicinity of the Rideau Centre and the ByWard Market, you can **park** your bike at a supervised lot. Located at Rideau and William streets, the facility operates daily 8:30am to 5:30pm, from Victoria Day until Labor Day weekend (third Sat in May to first Mon in Sept).

5 MONEY & COSTS

CURRENCY

The currency of Canada is the Canadian **dollar**, made up of 100 **cents.** Since 2007, the Canadian and U.S. dollars have been hovering near par—a noteworthy shift from the not-too-distant years when the Canadian dollar was worth about 65¢. The British pound has been sitting at around

C$1.95, a little lower than in recent years, but still translates into excellent value for visitors from the U.K. (Visit a website such as **www.oanda.com** for up-to-the-minute exchange rate information.)

Be aware that sales taxes are high in Canada (13% tax is added to retail goods purchased in Ontario, with taxes for

---

Fun Facts **Crazy Money**

The common name for the C$1 coin is the "loonie" because of the loon on the reverse side. When the bimetallic C$2 coin was subsequently introduced into circulation, it was instantly dubbed the "toonie."

The prices in this guide are given in Canadian dollars, on the assumption that it will remain at or near par with the U.S. dollar for the foreseeable future. Amounts over $10 have been rounded to the nearest dollar. The U.K. pound is included here for your reference, with C$1 worth about 52p. Note that exchange rates are subject to fluctuation, and you should always check currency rates when preparing for your trip. Here's a quick table of equivalents:

C$	UK£	UK£	C$
1.00	0.52	1.00	1.95
5.00	2.60	5.00	9.75
10.00	5.20	10.00	19.50
50.00	26.00	50.00	97.50
80.00	41.60	80.00	156.00
100.00	52.00	100.00	195.00

restaurant meals even higher). Paper currency comes in $5, $10, $20, $50, and $100 denominations. Coins come in C$.01 (penny), C$.05 (nickel), C$.10 (dime), and C$.25 (quarter) and C$1 and C$2 denominations.

Most businesses in Ottawa will accept U.S. cash at par, but to avoid having it refused, change your funds into Canadian currency. In the U.S., before leaving on your trip you can exchange money at your local American Express or Thomas Cook office. Banks in Ottawa generally offer currency-exchange services. If you're far from a bank that has such a service, American Express (📞 **800/673-3782;** www.americanexpress.com) offers traveler's checks and foreign currency for a US$15 order fee and additional shipping costs.

ATMS

The easiest and best way to get cash when away from home is through an ATM (automated teller machine), sometimes referred to as a "cash machine," or a "cashpoint." ATMs are as plentiful in Ottawa as they are in any U.S. city. The **Cirrus** (📞 **800/424-7787;** www.mastercard.com) and **PLUS** (📞 **800/843-7587;** www.visa. com) networks span the globe; look at the back of your bank card to see which network you're on, then call or check online for ATM locations at your destination. Be sure you know your personal identification number (PIN) and daily withdrawal limit before you depart. *Note:* Remember that many banks impose a fee every time you use your card at another bank's ATM, and that fee can be higher for international transactions (up to C$5 or more) than for domestic ones (where they're rarely more than C$2). In addition, the bank from which you withdraw cash may charge its own fee. For international withdrawal fees, ask your bank.

CREDIT CARDS

Credit cards are another safe way to carry money. They also provide a convenient record of all your expenses, and generally offer relatively good exchange rates. You can withdraw cash advances from your credit cards at banks or ATMs, provided you know your PIN. Keep in mind that you'll pay interest from the moment of your withdrawal, even if you pay your monthly bills on time. Also, many banks now assess a 1% to 3% "transaction fee" on all charges you incur abroad (whether you're using the local currency or your native currency). Visa, MasterCard, and American Express cards are all widely accepted in Ottawa. The Diners Club card is not as widely accepted as it is in many U.S. cities, particularly among Ottawa's newer restaurants.

TRAVELER'S CHECKS

You can buy traveler's checks at most banks, and they are readily accepted throughout Ottawa, provided you have personal ID, such as a driver's license or passport. Traveler's checks are offered in denominations of C$20, C$50, C$100, C$500, and sometimes C$1,000. Generally, you'll pay a service charge ranging from 1% to 4%.

The most popular traveler's checks are offered by **American Express** (✆ 800/ **807-6233** or 221-7282; this number accepts collect calls from cardholders, offers service in several foreign languages, and exempts Amex gold and platinum cardholders from the 1% fee); **Visa** (✆ 800/ **732-1322;** AAA members can obtain Visa checks up to C$1,500 for a C$9.95 fee at most AAA offices or by calling ✆ **866/ 339-3378**); and **MasterCard** (✆ 800/ **223-9920**).

American Express, Thomas Cook, Visa, and **MasterCard** offer **foreign currency traveler's checks,** which are useful if you're traveling only to Canada; they're accepted at locations where checks in U.S. dollar denominations may not be.

If you carry traveler's checks, keep a record of their serial numbers separate from your checks in the event that they are stolen or lost. You'll get a refund faster if you know the numbers.

What Things Cost in Ottawa

Although it is a primary Canadian tourist destination and a world capital, Ottawa is not as expensive a city to visit as Vancouver, Toronto, or Montreal for large-ticket items such as food or accommodations. That stated, some necessities, like taxis and public transit, cost more in Ottawa than in cities of comparable or larger size. The following chart outlines some common tourist expenses:

Taxi from the airport to downtown (15 min.)	C$25
A night in a moderately priced hotel	C$150
A three-course dinner for one, without alcohol	C$40
A bottle of Canadian beer	C$6
A glass of California pinot noir	C$9
A toasted bagel with cream cheese	C$3.25
A cup of regular coffee	C$1.95
Bus fare	C$3
Museum entrance fee	C$6

Tips   Easy Money

You'll avoid lines at airport ATMs by exchanging at least some money—just enough to cover airport incidentals and transportation to your hotel—before you leave home.

When you change money, be sure to ask for some small bills or loose change. Petty cash will come in handy for tipping and for using public transportation. Consider keeping the change separate, so that it's accessible, and your larger bills tucked away, making you less of a target for theft.

6   HEALTH

STAYING HEALTHY

Contact the **International Association for Medical Assistance to Travellers** (IAMAT; ✆ 416/652-0137 in Canada; 716/754-4883 in the U.S.; www.iamat. org) for tips on travel and health concerns in Canada, and lists of local doctors. The **United States Centers for Disease Control and Prevention** (✆ 800/311-3435; www.cdc.gov) provides up-to-date information on health hazards by region or country and offers tips on food safety.

General Availability of Health Care

All common over-the-counter medicines are readily available, and each major chain pharmacy sells generic equivalents.

If you suffer from a chronic illness, consult your doctor before your departure. For conditions such as epilepsy, diabetes, or heart problems, wear a **MedicAlert identification tag** (✆ 800/668-1507 in Canada; 888/633-4298 in the U.S.; www. medicalert.ca or www.medicalert.org), which will immediately alert doctors and give them access to your records through MedicAlert's 24-hour hot line.

Pack **prescription medications** in your carry-on luggage, in their original containers with pharmacy labels—otherwise, they may not make it through airport security. Also bring along copies of your prescriptions in case you lose your pills or run out, and carry the generic name of your prescription medicines in case a local pharmacist is unfamiliar with the brand name. Don't forget an extra pair of contact lenses or prescription glasses.

As noted in "Medical Requirements" above, a medical examination is not required for tourists who will be in Canada for less than 6 months.

COMMON AILMENTS

BUGS, BITES & OTHER WILDLIFE CONCERNS   Mosquitoes are a nuisance in low-lying and rural areas during Ottawa's hot and humid summer months. While there have been no reports of the West Nile Virus among humans in the region, the disease was found in dead crows in 2008. Visitors are advised to use insect repellant if they are likely to be in areas where they may encounter mosquitoes. The city's close proximity to rural, wooded areas can bring visitors into contact with wildlife that may include black bears, coyotes, foxes, and skunks. You are advised to stick to well-traveled areas and exercise common sense. See "What Should I Do If I Meet a Bear?" on p. 202.

RESPIRATORY ILLNESSES   Colds and flu are not unusual during Ottawa's damp, cold months, and physicians advise elderly people with a weakened immune system to receive the flu vaccine if there is a possibility that they will be exposed to infection. The hot, humid weather during summer is frequently accompanied by warnings about the city's air quality. During these warnings, people are advised to curtail strenuous outdoor activity.

EXTREME COLD EXPOSURE Ottawa has earned its reputation as the world's second-coldest capital city. Each winter brings several days when prolonged skin exposure can cause frostbite. Visitors are warned to dress warmly and protect exposed skin if they plan to be outside for prolonged periods, and particularly if they plan to engage in outdoor activities like skating or skiing.

WHAT TO DO IF YOU GET SICK AWAY FROM HOME

For non-life-threatening emergencies that require a physician consultation, go to a **walk-in clinic.** These clinics operate just as the name implies—you walk in and wait your turn to see a doctor. Look in the Yellow Pages for a local clinic or ask your hotel to recommend one. Payment procedures and operating hours vary among clinics, so call ahead and ask about their billing policy for nonresidents of Ontario or Canada. Most clinics will accept health cards from other provinces, although Quebec residents may be required to pay cash and later obtain reimbursement from their provincial government. Out-of-country

patients may be required to pay cash—checks or credit cards may not be accepted. Some doctors will make house calls to your hotel.

If you are suffering from a serious medical problem and are unable to wait to be seen at a walk-in clinic, visit the nearest hospital emergency room. Emergency rooms operate on a triage system, where patients are assessed upon arrival and those who need care the most urgently are seen first. There are emergency services available at several hospitals in the Ottawa area. For adults, **Ottawa Hospital** offers emergency care at two sites: the **General Campus** at 501 Smyth Rd. ((©) **613/737-8000**), and the **Civic Campus** at 1053 Carling Ave. ((©) **613/761-4621**). In addition, the **Children's Hospital of Eastern Ontario (CHEO)** is a large pediatric teaching hospital with emergency care services, located at 401 Smyth Rd. ((©) **613/737-7600**). Ontario emergency rooms are extremely busy and wait times for nonurgent cases are typically several hours. If at all possible, use the walk-in clinics. For minor health problems, consult a **pharmacist.** These professionals are trained in health consultation and will recommend whether you should see a doctor about your particular condition. Many pharmacies are open evenings and weekends and advertise their hours in the Yellow Pages. **Shopper's**

Dear Visa: I'm Off to Ottawa!

Some credit card companies recommend that you notify them of any impending trip abroad so that they don't become suspicious, when the card is used numerous times in a foreign destination, and block your access. Even if you don't call your credit card company in advance, you can always call the card's toll-free emergency number (see "Credit Cards" above, or "Toll-Free Numbers & Websites," p. 222) if a charge is refused—a good reason to carry the phone number with you. It's also a good idea to carry more than one card on your trip; a particular card might not work for any number of reasons, so having a backup is the smart way to go.

Avoiding "Economy-Class Syndrome"

Deep vein thrombosis, or as it's known in the world of flying, "economy-class syndrome," is a blood clot that develops in a deep vein. It's a potentially deadly condition that can be caused by sitting in cramped conditions—such as an airplane cabin—for too long. During a flight (especially a long-haul flight), get up, walk around, and stretch your legs every 60 to 90 minutes to keep your blood flowing. Other preventative measures include frequent flexing of the legs while sitting, drinking lots of water, and avoiding alcohol and sleeping pills. If you have a history of deep vein thrombosis, heart disease, or another condition that puts you at high risk, some experts recommend wearing compression stockings or taking anticoagulants when you fly; always ask your physician about the best course for you. Symptoms of deep vein thrombosis include leg pain or swelling, or even shortness of breath.

Drug Mart has three **24-hour drugstores** in the Ottawa area; the closest location to downtown Ottawa is in the Westgate Shopping Mall, 1309 Carling Ave. (© **613/ 722-4277**).

We list **additional emergency numbers** in the appendix, p. 216.

7 SAFETY

STAYING SAFE

As large cities go, Ottawa is generally safe, but be vigilant and use common sense, particularly at night. Sadly, in recent years the number of homeless people and panhandlers has increased, but they are not generally aggressive by nature. The liveliest and rowdiest areas tend to be around the bars in the ByWard Market and Elgin Street neighborhoods, especially late at night. Two specific places to avoid after dark are the pedestrian underpass on the south side of Confederation Square just west of the Rideau Centre and the main east-west ByWard Market streets between Dalhousie and King Edward streets.

8 SPECIALIZED TRAVEL RESOURCES

TRAVELERS WITH DISABILITIES

Most disabilities shouldn't stop you from traveling. There are more options and resources out there than ever before. To find out which attractions, accommodations, and restaurants in Ottawa are accessible to people with disabilities, refer to the *Ottawa Visitor Guide,* available from the **Capital Infocentre** (© **800/465-1867**).

The guide includes symbols next to each listing to indicate whether the entry and bathrooms are accessible. **Full accessibility** is defined as independently accessible to people using wheelchairs or with limited upper-body strength. Services should include automatic front doors, ramps, sufficient turning space for a wheelchair in the rooms or bathrooms, and wider doorways (84cm). **Basic accessibility** indicates that people using wheelchairs may require assistance to use the services within the establishment. The owners and managers of each establishment determine whether their property is accessible. For more information, contact **Disabled Persons Community Resources (DPCR),** 1150 Morrison Dr., Ste. 100, Ottawa ((C) **613/724-5886;** www.dpcr.ca). This nonprofit organization publishes *Accessibility Guide,* which can be ordered online and covers cinemas and theaters, financial institutions, hotels and motels, medical facilities, museums and tourist attractions, parks, religious facilities, restaurants, shopping malls, retail stores, and transportation. **OC Transpo,** which provides **public transit** in Ottawa, is committed to accessible public transit. Call their hot line at (C) **613/842-3625,** Monday to Friday, 9am to 5pm, to find out more about accessible services on conventional transit. *Note:* if you use a wheelchair, scooter, or walker, you can ride for free the conventional transit service and the ground-level, light-rail **O-Train,** which runs from Greenboro Station in the south to Bayview Station close to downtown and has seating for 135 (and standing room for another 150). The low-floor trains and stations are fully accessible, but you must be able to get to and from the station. Additionally, there are more than 60 designated accessible bus routes that use fully accessible buses. These buses have low floors and no stairs to climb, providing easier access for seniors, passengers with limited mobility, people using wheelchairs, and parents with small children or strollers. The buses lower themselves to the curb and have an extendable ramp for wheelchair users. You can spot low-floor buses by the blue and white wheelchair symbol on the upper corner of the front of the vehicle. Call (C) **613/741-4390** for more information on these routes. Blind and visually impaired travelers can obtain information on how to make the most of their trip to Ottawa by

calling the **Canadian National Institute for the Blind (CNIB)** Information Centre at (C) **613/563-4021.**

For persons with permanent or short-term disabilities who are unable to walk to, or board, conventional transit, **Para Transpo** is available. Both visitors and residents can use this service, but you must register and book a reservation a day in advance. You must also have your application form signed by an appropriate health professional and submit it in advance to the Para Transpo office. Application forms can be downloaded from www.octranspo.com/acc_menue.htm. Para Transpo uses a large fleet of modern, air-conditioned cars and lift-equipped vans. Call (C) **613/244-1289** Monday to Friday, 9am to 5pm, for information and registration and call (C) **613/244-7272** for reservations.

Many travel agencies offer customized tours and itineraries for travelers with disabilities. Among them are **Flying Wheels Travel** ((C) **507/451-5005;** www.flyingwheelstravel.com); **Access-Able Travel Source** ((C) **303/232-2979;** www.access-able.com); and **Accessible Journeys** ((C) **800/846-4537** or 610/521-0339; www.disabilitytravel.com). **Avis Rent A Car** has an "Avis Access" program that offers such services as a dedicated 24-hour toll-free number ((C) **888/879-4273**) for customers with special travel needs and added car features, such as swivel seats, panoramic mirrors, and hand controls. In Ottawa, reservations for vehicles with special access features require 48 hours notice.

Organizations that offer assistance to disabled travelers include **MossRehab** (www.mossresourcenet.org); the **American Foundation for the Blind (AFB)** ((C) **800/232-5463;** www.afb.org); and **SATH (Society for Accessible Travel & Hospitality)** ((C) **212/447-7284;** www.sath.org). **AirAmbulanceCard.com** is now partnered with SATH and allows you to preselect top-notch hospitals in case of an emergency.

The community website **iCan** (www.icanonline.net/channels/travel) has destination guides and several regular columns on accessible travel. Also check out *Open World* magazine, published by SATH, and the quarterly magazine *Emerging Horizons* (www.emerginghorizons.com).

For more on organizations that offer resources to disabled travelers, go to www.frommers.com/planning.

GAY & LESBIAN TRAVELERS

Ottawa is considered a relatively gay- and lesbian-friendly city, and the communities are exceptionally well integrated. The city's annual Capital Pride Festival—held each August—includes a parade that is well attended by both gay and straight citizens. Although both the city government and merchants have been reluctant to officially name it, a gay village is clustered around Bank Street in the vicinity of Frank Street, Somerset Street West, and Lisgar Street. There are also several bars and clubs in the ByWard Market district (see chapter 10, "Ottawa After Dark").

To find out what's happening in Ottawa that's of interest to gays and lesbians, pick up a copy of *Capital Xtra!*, a monthly newspaper distributed widely throughout the Ottawa area, Eastern Ontario, and Montreal. News, arts, culture, entertainment, and local events are covered. To receive a copy in advance of your visit, write to Capital Xtra!, 251 Bank St., Ste. 503, Ottawa, ON K2P 1X3. Alternatively, you can call (C) **613/237-7133** or visit www.xtra.ca.

Other resources that cater to Ottawa's gay and lesbian population include: **Gay-Ottawa** (www.gayottawa.com), **Out Ottawa** (www.outottawa.com), and **Out in Ottawa** (www.outinottawa.com).

For more gay and lesbian travel resources visit www.frommers.com/planning.

SENIOR TRAVEL

Many city attractions grant senior discounts—usually around 10%—and some hotels offer special rates. Carry a form of photo ID that includes your birth date.

Resources that cater to Ottawa's seniors include: **Ottawa Seniors** (www.ottawaseniors.com), the **Council on Aging of Ottawa** ((C) **613/789-3577;** www.coaottawa.ca), and the **City of Ottawa's Services for Seniors** (www.ottawa.ca/residents/seniors).

Becoming a member of a seniors' organization may earn you a discount on travel arrangements. Consider joining the **Canadian Association of Retired Persons (CARP),** 27 Queen St. E., Ste. 1304, Toronto, ON M5C 2M6 ((C) **416/363-8748;** www.carp.ca). The website has a comprehensive travel section for members that features hotels, packages, transportation, and travel insurance.

Members of **AARP** (formerly known as the American Association of Retired Persons), 601 E. St. NW, Washington, DC 20049 ((C) **888/687-2277;** www.aarp.org), get discounts on hotels, airfares, and car rentals. AARP offers members a wide range of benefits, including *AARP The Magazine* and a monthly newsletter. Anyone over 50 can join.

For more information and resources on travel for seniors, see www.frommers.com/planning.

FAMILY TRAVEL

Luckily for visitors with kids in tow, Ottawa has a good selection of suite hotels that are equipped with kitchenettes or full kitchens and one or two bedrooms; some have two bathrooms. Prices are usually comparable to the cost of two hotel rooms (sometimes cheaper), but you get the advantage of food preparation facilities and accommodations for the entire family in one unit, which are important considerations when you have young children with you. Suite hotels often encourage families, offering children's programs, play centers, or indoor pools. When booking your accommodations, always ask if family packages are available.

When you're deciding which time of year to visit, try to schedule your trip during school vacation periods, which in Ontario run for 2 weeks during Christmas/New Year, 1 week in mid-March, and the months of July and August. Special events and festivals aimed particularly at families are held at various museums and other locations during school holidays. Many of Ottawa's attractions are clustered downtown within walking distance of one another, so it's possible to enjoy Ottawa without the need for a vehicle.

To locate those accommodations, restaurants, and attractions that are particularly kid friendly, refer to the "Kids" icon throughout this guide.

See chapter 1, "The Best of Ottawa," for a number of recommendations for age-appropriate activities and attractions.

For a list of more family-friendly travel resources, visit www.frommers.com/planning.

STUDENT TRAVEL

Check out the **International Student Travel Confederation (ISTC)** (www.istc.org) website for comprehensive travel services information and details on how to get an **International Student Identity Card (ISIC),** which qualifies students for substantial savings on rail passes, plane tickets, entrance fees, and more. It also provides students with basic health and life insurance and a 24-hour help line. The card is valid for a maximum of 18 months. You can apply for the card online or in person at **STA Travel** (✆ **800/781-4040** in North America; 132 782 in Australia; 0871/2300040 in the U.K.; www.statravel.com), the biggest student travel agency in the world; check out the website to locate STA Travel offices worldwide. If you're no longer a student but are still under 26, you can get an **International Youth Travel Card (IYTC)** from STA Travel, which entitles you to some discounts. **Travel CUTS** (✆ **800/592-2887;** www.travelcuts.com) offers similar services for both Canadians and U.S. residents. Irish students may prefer to turn to **USIT** (✆ **01/602-1904;** www.usit.ie), an Ireland-based specialist in student, youth, and independent travel. Students who would like to attend lectures, seminars, concerts, and other events can contact **Carleton University,** 1125 Colonel By Dr. (✆ **613/520-7400;** www.carleton.ca) or the **University of Ottawa,** 550 Cumberland St. (✆ **613/562-5700;** www. uottawa.ca).

TRAVELING WITH PETS

Like most large North American cities, Ottawa offers a number of challenges to visitors who are traveling with pets. See chapter 5, "Where to Stay," for details on hotels that allow pets. For more resources about traveling with pets, go to www. frommers.com/planning.

9 SUSTAINABLE TOURISM

Sustainable tourism is conscientious travel. It means being careful with the environments you explore, and respecting the communities you visit. Two overlapping components of sustainable travel are **eco-tourism** and **ethical tourism.** The **International Ecotourism Society** (TIES) defines eco-tourism as responsible travel to natural areas that conserves the environment and improves the well-being of local people. TIES suggests that eco-tourists follow these principles:

Tips **It's Easy Being Green**

Here are a few simple ways you can help conserve fuel and energy when you travel:

- Each time you take a flight or drive a car, greenhouse gases release into the atmosphere. You can help neutralize this danger to the planet through "carbon offsetting"—paying someone to invest your money in programs that reduce your greenhouse gas emissions by the same amount you've added. Before buying carbon offset credits, just make sure that you're using a reputable company, one with a proven program that invests in renewable energy. Reliable carbon offset companies include **Carbonfund** (www.carbonfund.org), **TerraPass** (www.terrapass.org), and **Carbon Neutral** (www.carbonneutral.org).

- Whenever possible, choose nonstop flights; they generally require less fuel than indirect flights that stop and take off again. Try to fly during the day—some scientists estimate that nighttime flights are twice as harmful to the environment. And pack light—each 15 pounds of luggage on a 8,047km (5,000-mile) flight adds up to 50 pounds of carbon dioxide emitted.

- Where you stay during your travels can have a major environmental impact. To determine the green credentials of a property, ask about trash disposal and recycling, water conservation, and energy use; also question if sustainable materials were used in the construction of the property. The website **www.greenhotels.com** recommends green-rated member hotels around the world that fulfill the company's stringent environmental requirements. Also consult **www.environmentallyfriendlyhotels.com** for more accommodations that are environmentally friendly.

- At hotels, request that your sheets and towels not be changed daily. (Many hotels already have programs like this in place.) Turn off the lights and air-conditioner (or heater) when you leave your room.

- Use public transport where possible—trains, buses, and even taxis are more energy-efficient forms of transport than driving. Even better is to walk or cycle; you'll produce zero emissions and stay fit and healthy on your travels.

- If renting a car is necessary, ask the rental agent for a hybrid, or rent the most fuel-efficient car available. You'll use less gas and save money at the tank.

- Eat at locally owned and operated restaurants that use produce grown in the area. This contributes to the local economy and cuts down on greenhouse gas emissions by supporting restaurants where the food is not flown or trucked in across long distances. Visit the website **Sustain Lane** (www.sustainlane.org) to find sustainable eating and drinking choices around the U.S.; also check out **www.eatwellguide.org** for tips on eating sustainably in Canada.

- Minimize environmental impact.
- Build environmental and cultural awareness and respect.
- Provide positive experiences for both visitors and hosts.
- Provide direct financial benefits for conservation and for local people.
- Raise sensitivity to host countries' political, environmental, and social climates.
- Support international human rights and labor agreements.

You can find some eco-friendly travel tips and statistics, as well as touring companies and associations—listed by destination under "Travel Choice"—at the **TIES** website, www.ecotourism.org. Also check out **Ecotravel.com,** which lets you search for sustainable touring companies in several categories (water based, land based, spiritually oriented, and so on).

While much of the focus of eco-tourism is about reducing impacts on the natural environment, ethical tourism concentrates on ways to preserve and enhance local economies and communities, regardless of location. You can embrace ethical tourism by staying at a locally owned hotel or shopping at a store that employs local workers and sells locally produced goods.

Ottawa has generally lagged behind other cities in North America in many areas related to sustainability—particularly related to political wrangling over public transit, household and business recycling, and solar energy. That said, there is a sizable community of residents who support the concepts of sustainability, and a growing number of restaurants that actively promote the use of local produce. A number of these are highlighted in chapter 6, "Dining."

Responsible Travel (www.responsibletravel.com) is a great source of sustainable travel ideas; the site is run by a spokesperson for ethical tourism in the travel industry. **Sustainable Travel International** (www.sustainabletravelinternational.org) promotes ethical tourism practices, and manages an extensive directory of sustainable

---

Frommers.com: The Complete Travel Resource

Planning a trip or did you just return from one? Head to **Frommers.com,** voted Best Travel Site by *PC Magazine*. We think you'll find our site indispensable before, during, and after your travels—with expert advice and tips; independent reviews of hotels, restaurants, attractions, and preferred shopping and nightlife venues; vacation giveaways; and an online booking tool. We publish the complete contents of over 135 travel guides in our **Destinations** section, covering over 4,000 places worldwide. Each weekday, we publish original articles that report on **Deals and News** via our free **Frommers.com Newsletters.** What's more, **Arthur Frommer** himself blogs 5 days a week, with cutting opinions about the state of travel in the modern world. We're betting you'll find our **Events** listings an invaluable resource; it's an up-to-the-minute roster of what's happening in cities everywhere—including concerts, festivals, lectures, and more. We've also added weekly **podcasts, interactive maps,** and hundreds of new images across the site. Finally, don't forget to visit our **Message Boards,** where you can join in conversations with thousands of fellow Frommer's travelers and post a report about your trip once you return.

properties and tour operators around the world.

In the U.K., **Tourism Concern** (www.tourismconcern.org.uk) works to reduce social and environmental problems connected to tourism. The **Association of Independent Tour Operators (AITO;** www.aito.co.uk) is a group of specialist operators leading the field in making holidays sustainable.

Volunteer travel has become increasingly popular among those who want to venture beyond the standard group-tour experience to learn languages, interact with locals, and make a positive difference while on vacation. Volunteer travel usually doesn't require special skills—just a willingness to work hard—and programs vary

in length from a few days to a number of weeks. Some programs provide free housing and food, but many require volunteers to pay for travel expenses, which can add up quickly.

For general info on volunteer travel, visit **www.volunteerabroad.org** and **www.idealist.org**.

Before you commit to a volunteer program, it's important to make sure any money you're giving is truly going back to the local community, and that the work you'll be doing will be a good fit for you. **Volunteer International** (www.volunteerinternational.org) has a helpful list of questions to ask to determine the intentions and the nature of a volunteer program.

10 PACKAGES FOR THE INDEPENDENT TRAVELER

Package tours are simply a way to buy airfare, accommodations, and other elements of your trip (such as car rentals, airport transfers, and sometimes even activities) at the same time and often at discounted prices.

One good source of package deals is the airlines themselves. Most major airlines offer air/land packages, including **American Airlines Vacations** (© **800/321-2121;** www.aavacations.com), **Delta Vacations** (© **800/221-6666;** www.deltavacations.com), **Continental Airlines Vacations** (© **800/301-3800;** www.covacations.com), and **United Vacations**

(© **888/854-3899;** www.unitedvacations.com). Several big **online travel agencies**—Expedia, Travelocity, Orbitz, Site59, and Lastminute.com—also do a brisk business in packages.

Travel packages are also listed in the travel section of your local Sunday newspaper. Or check ads in the national travel magazines such as *Arthur Frommer's Budget Travel Magazine, Travel & Leisure, National Geographic Traveler,* and *Condé Nast Traveler.*

For more information on package tours and for tips on booking your trip, see www.frommers.com/planning.

11 SPECIAL-INTEREST TRIPS

ADVENTURE TRIPS

Ottawa's close proximity to nature provides a number of year-round options for adventure-minded visitors—ranging from world-class cross-country skiing to cycling, whitewater rafting, canoeing, and kayaking,

hiking, and sailing. So popular are these types of activities that a thriving group of outfitter stores have blossomed in the city's Westboro neighborhood (see chapter 9, "Shopping").

Trailhead (© 613/722-4229; www.trailhead.ca) is Ottawa's primary source for information about adventure trips. In addition to renting and selling a wide range of equipment, maps, and clothing, its website serves as a clearinghouse for information about activities organized by various clubs and commercial operators.

While not based in Ottawa, **Black Feather** (© 888/849-7668; www.blackfeather.com) operates a wide assortment of adventure trips in the wilderness northwest of the city, including whitewater canoeing and dog sledding.

Another good source for information about local adventure activities is ***Ottawa Outdoors*** magazine (© 888/228-2918; www.ottawaoutdoors.ca). The publication can be found at most sports and fitness stores in Ottawa, and digital copies of back issues are available on its website.

12 STAYING CONNECTED

TELEPHONES

Telephone service in Canada is consistently rated among the world's most advanced, and has been undergoing progressive deregulation since 1992. Long distance services are offered by a number of carriers—including, in Ottawa, Bell Canada, Telus, Rogers, and Primus—and several carriers now offer alternative local competition to Bell Canada, the former monopoly. While limited pay phone competition has been introduced, most pay phones in Ottawa belong to the Bell Canada network. The number of pay phones has been steadily declining with the rise of cellphone use, and finding one in some parts of Ottawa can be a challenge.

Canada's long distance rates are among the lowest in the world, so it is not generally necessary to purchase a long distance calling card from your own carrier for use in Ottawa, unless the card provides access through your discounted subscription plan. Phone cards issued by Canada's long distance carriers are readily available at convenience stores, electronics shops, and other outlets. To make an overseas call, dial © 011, followed by the country, the city code, and the local number.

Local calls from pay phones cost C$.50. All local calls must include the area code. The area code for Ottawa is **613;** numbers in Gatineau and other parts of western Quebec are in the **819** area code.

To reach local assistance, dial © **411.** For long distance assistance, dial © **800/555-1212.**

As in most locations in North America, hotels in Ottawa charge a premium for long distance calls from your room, although many provide free local calling. To avoid any unwelcome surprises at checkout, always inquire at the front desk about telecommunications pricing before making calls from your room.

CELLPHONES

While changes are afoot, cellphone use remains tightly regulated in Canada, with services offered by three national carriers (Bell Mobility, Rogers Wireless, and Telus Mobility). Among western countries, Canada has one of the lowest per capita cellphone usage rates. That stated, coverage areas are extensive, and it is rare to be unable to connect to any of the three networks in the area immediately adjacent to Ottawa.

If your cellphone is on a GSM system, and you have a world-capable multiband phone, such as many Sony Ericsson, Motorola, or Samsung models, you can make and receive calls across civilized areas on much of the globe. Just call your wireless operator and ask for "international

> ## (Tips) Hey, Google, Did You Get My Text Message?
>
> It's bound to happen: The day you leave this guidebook back at the hotel for an unencumbered stroll, you'll forget the address of the lunch spot you had earmarked. If you're traveling with a mobile device, send a text message to © **46645** (GOOGL) for a lightning-fast response. For instance, type "national art gallery ottawa" and within 10 seconds you'll receive a text message with the address and phone number. This nifty trick works in a range of search categories: Look up weather ("weather ottawa"), language translations ("translate goodbye in french"), currency conversions ("10 usd in canadian dollars"), movie times ("harry potter 60605"), and more. If your search results are off, be more specific ("the abbey gay bar west hollywood"). For more tips and search options, go to www.google.com/intl/en_us/mobile/sms/. Regular text message charges apply.

roaming" to be activated on your account. Unfortunately, per-minute charges can be high.

For many, **renting** a phone is a good idea. Federal telecommunications regulations make renting a phone in Canada more difficult than renting one in many other countries, but one outlet in Ottawa is **Hello Anywhere** (© 613/569-4355; www.helloanywhere.com). Some car rental agencies also rent cellphones to customers. Nevertheless, we suggest renting a phone before you leave home. North Americans can rent reliable phones from **Cellular Abroad** (© 800/287-5072; www.cellular abroad.com), **InTouch USA** (© 800/ 872-7626; www.intouchglobal.com), or **RoadPost** (© 888/290-1606 or 905/272-5665; www.roadpost.com). InTouch will also advise you, for free, on whether your existing phone will work in Ottawa; simply call © 703/222-7161 between 9am and 4pm EST, or go to **http://intouch-global.com/travel.htm**.

Buying a phone may be your most economically attractive option, depending on the amount of time you'll be away and the type of calling you require. Canada's three cellular suppliers each offer prepaid phone systems. Once you arrive in Ottawa, stop by a local cellphone shop and get the cheapest package; you'll probably pay less

than C$100 for a phone and a starter calling card. Local calls on these types of services cost about C$.32 per minute, and incoming calls are usually free.

VOICE-OVER INTERNET PROTOCOL (VOIP)

If you have Web access while traveling, consider a broadband-based telephone service (in technical terms, **voice-over Internet protocol,** or **VoIP**) such as Skype (www.skype.com) or Vonage (www.vonage.com), which allow you to make free international calls from your laptop or in a cybercafe. Neither service requires the people you're calling to also have that service (though there are fees if they do not). Check the websites for details.

INTERNET & E-MAIL
With Your Own Computer

Ottawa has more than 80 Wi-Fi public wireless hot spots—most operated on the Boingo network or by one of Canada's mobile phone carriers—but no general public wireless network. Connectivity can be expensive for those not already a subscriber. To find public Wi-Fi hot spots in Ottawa, go to **www.jiwire.com**; its Hotspot Finder holds the world's largest directory of public wireless hotspots.

Online Traveler's Toolbox

Veteran travelers usually carry some essential items to make their trips easier. Following is a selection of handy online tools to bookmark and use.

- **Airplane food** (www.airlinemeals.net)
- **Airplane seating** (www.seatguru.com; www.airlinequality.com)
- **Concert tickets** (www.ticketmaster.ca; www.capitaltickets.ca)
- **Entertainment listings** (www.ottawaxpress.ca)
- **Foreign languages for travelers** (www.travlang.com)
- **Hockey tickets** (www.capitaltickets.ca)
- **Maps** (www.mapquest.com)
- **Movie listings and times** (www.film-can.com)
- **Restaurant reviews** (www.ottawafoodies.com; www.restaurantthing.com/ca/on/ottawa)
- **Time and date** (www.timeanddate.com)
- **Tourist information** (www.ottawatourism.ca)
- **Travel warnings** (http://travel.state.gov; www.fco.gov.uk/travel; www.voyage.gc.ca; www.smartraveller.gov.au)
- **Universal currency converter** (www.oanda.com)
- **Weather** (www.intellicast.com; www.weather.com)

One reliable source of free Wi-Fi connectivity in Ottawa is the **Bridgehead Coffee House chain** (**www.bridgehead.ca**), which has nine locations (p. 106).

Most hotels provide either dataports or Wi-Fi, or both (see chapter 5, "Where to Stay").

Without Your Own Computer

To find cybercafes in Ottawa, check **www.cybercaptive.com** and **www.cybercafe.com**. You'll find most of the city's cybercafes along Bank Street in the downtown core.

Aside from formal cybercafes, most **youth hostels** and **public libraries** have Internet access. Avoid **hotel business centers** unless you're willing to pay exorbitant rates.

Ottawa Macdonald-Cartier International Airport also has **Internet kiosks** scattered amid its gates. These give you basic Web access for a per-minute fee that's usually higher than cybercafe prices.

Suggested Ottawa Itineraries

The compact size of Ottawa's downtown and the concentration of many national institutions make it relatively easy to see the city's high spots without the use of public transit or a rental vehicle. Still, the scope of the major museums and public buildings means allotting more than 1 day. The 1-, 2-, and 3-day itineraries provided below allow you to cover the top attractions without suffering museum burnout and still have enough time for some extended explorations of the capital's distinctive historical traits. During the winter months, when even the locals will admit that the climate is less than ideal, you can substitute more indoor activities for outdoor ones.

1 THE NEIGHBORHOODS IN BRIEF

In addition to the influx of French- and English-speaking European settlers, waves of immigration that parallel world history have marked Ottawa's evolution. A large number of Italians flooded in during the early decades of the 20th century, followed by numerous Lebanese families in the 1950s. Ottawa became home to many Vietnamese refugees in the 1970s, and more recently Somalis have arrived, escaping poverty and warfare in their African homeland. The various business and residential areas each have their own mix of shops, cuisine, architecture, sights, and sounds, representing different cultures and traditions from around the globe. Strolling through the various neighborhoods will give you an appreciation of the city's heart and soul—its people.

DOWNTOWN WEST OF THE CANAL

Ottawa's downtown business district (also referred to as Centretown) is a maze of office towers in an area stretching several blocks to the south of Parliament Hill. ARC The. Hotel, an upscale boutique hotel, and a number of worldwide chains including Delta, Marriott, and Sheraton are located here. There are many excellent restaurants and shops tucked in and around the office buildings. The Sparks Street Mall, Canada's first pedestrian shopping street, runs between Elgin Street in the east and Lyon Street in the west, one block south of Parliament Hill. The streets tend to be quiet in the evenings, with the notable exception of Elgin Street, which attracts young revelers with its many bars and restaurants.

THE GOLDEN TRIANGLE

Situated to the east of Elgin Street, between Somerset Street West and the Queensway, this area is where the original gentry of the area built their homes. While many of the large dwellings were subsequently subdivided, the neighborhood remains rich in Victorian architecture, and offers a pleasant area for strolling.

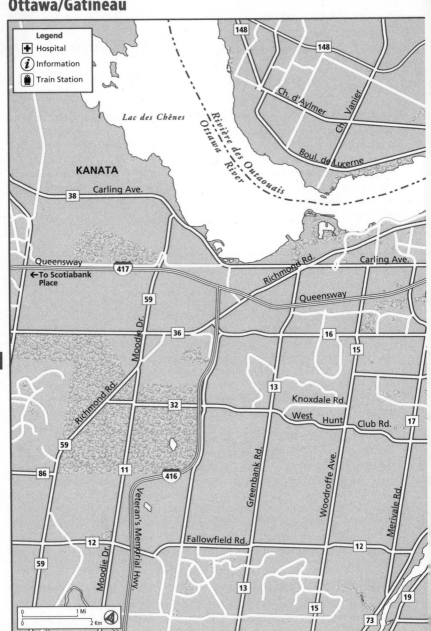

Legend
- ✚ Hospital
- ⓘ Information
- 🚉 Train Station

Lac des Chênes

Rivière des Outaouais
Ottawa River

Ch. d'Aylmer

Ch. Vanier

Boul. de Lucerne

KANATA

Carling Ave.

Queensway

← To Scotiabank Place

Richmond Rd.

Carling Ave.

Queensway

Moodie Dr.

Richmond Rd.

Knoxdale Rd.

West Hunt Club Rd.

Greenbank Rd.

Woodroffe Ave.

Merivale Rd.

Veteran's Memorial Hwy.

Moodie Dr.

Fallowfield Rd.

0   1 Mi
0   2 Km

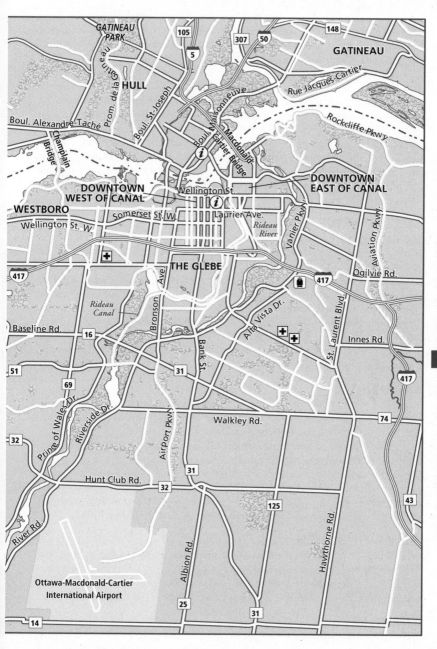

DOWNTOWN EAST OF THE CANAL

Situated northeast of the Parliament Buildings, on the east side of the Rideau Canal and bordered to the east by the Rideau River, this historic neighborhood is the oldest section of Ottawa. Originally, downtown east of the canal (also known as Lowertown) was an uninhabitable cedar swamp. During the construction of the Rideau Canal, the land was drained and a mix of settlers soon moved in, including canal workers, shantymen, rivermen, and their families. The area was populated by poor Irish immigrants and French Canadians, and a reputation for general rowdiness and unlawfulness soon took hold. The building of the farmers' market in the mid–19th century helped to boost the local economy. Today the ByWard Market district, with its eclectic mix of boutiques, cafes, and bars, is a prosperous, attractive city neighborhood with a vibrant personality. This is a great place to shop in one-of-a-kind boutiques, enjoy a drink or two in a pub or bar, or stroll around checking out restaurant menus to decide where to dine. Several major hotels are right on the doorstep, including the Fairmont Château Laurier, Les Suites Ottawa, Novotel, and the Westin.

SUSSEX DRIVE

Winding along the south shore of the Ottawa River, historic Sussex Drive is a grand boulevard featuring many well-known landmarks. The National Gallery of Canada, the Royal Canadian Mint, the Notre-Dame Cathedral Basilica, the U.S. Embassy, the French Embassy, the residence of the prime minister of Canada (24 Sussex Dr.), and Rideau Hall (home of the governor-general) are all found on this route. Also on Sussex Drive are the scenic Rideau Falls and the imposing Lester B. Pearson Building, home of the federal Department of Foreign Affairs. Earnscliffe, the residence of the British high commissioner, was originally the home of Canada's first prime minister, Sir John A. Macdonald. It sits high on a cliff overlooking the Ottawa River. This area can be explored on foot, by bicycle, or as part of a scenic drive.

SANDY HILL

Sitting east of the canal between Rideau Street and Mann Avenue is a large, historic, and attractive neighborhood that should not be ignored, even though it holds few high-profile visitor attractions. The University of Ottawa—the city's bilingual postsecondary institution—dominates, and the university's influence can be felt in the many cafes, pubs, and inexpensive restaurants situated here. Like the Golden Triangle on the opposite bank of the canal, this area too is filled with many grand, old homes—particularly along Daly, Stewart, and Wilbrod streets, and Laurier Avenue East. The neighborhood's far eastern parameter is particularly notable for the stately embassies and official residences on Range Road, and beautiful Strathcona Park, which abuts the Rideau River.

NEW EDINBURGH

Sandwiched between the Rideau River and the expansive grounds of Rideau Hall, New Edinburgh is one of Ottawa's toniest neighborhoods, and one of its prettiest. The commercial heart of the area—the short strip of Beechwood Avenue between the Rideau River and Springfield Road—offers several options for refreshment if you're exploring the area.

THE GLEBE

Just south of downtown, between the Queensway and Lansdowne Park, lies Ottawa's first suburb. In the 1870s, residential development began to encroach on farmland south of the city. The construction of exhibition grounds at Lansdowne Park and of a streetcar link between the Glebe and the city fueled the growth of this neighborhood. Middle-class families settled here in large numbers. Today, the Glebe is an upscale middle-class enclave served by a stretch of trendy, high-end stores, services, and eateries on Bank Street. It's well worth spending a morning or afternoon strolling up one side of the street and down the other. If you begin at the north end, take a break near the canal before making your return journey. Brown's Inlet and Park are tucked a block or two west of Bank Street, north of Queen Elizabeth Drive. If you start at the canal end, rest in Central Park, which straddles Bank Street in the vicinity of Powell and Clemow avenues. For winter strolling, take refuge in the atrium at Fifth Avenue Court, about midway down this section of Bank Street, or in one of the many cafes along the way.

OTTAWA SOUTH

If you venture farther south past the Glebe—crossing the canal via the Bank Street Bridge—you'll reach one of the city's most low-key and pleasant shopping areas, and the home of many of Ottawa's antiques shops. Once the poor cousin to the Glebe, Ottawa South can now hold its own, with several attractive pubs and coffee shops.

WELLINGTON STREET WEST

What's the hottest neighborhood in the city? There's no question it's the strip of Wellington Street that runs east and west between Bayswater Avenue and Island Park Drive. Long a hodgepodge of small stores established to serve the large residential population to its north and south, this section of Wellington Street is changing so quickly that even the locals can't keep up. Among the catalysts: the Parkdale Market, which has been one of the area's best-kept secrets for years; the conversion of warehouse space north of Wellington into condos, art galleries, and commercial space; and the opening of the Great Canadian Theatre Company—Ottawa's longest-running theater—in 2007. The section east of Parkdale Avenue is staunchly working class—and proud of it—but has been welcoming to artists and students who have brought new vigor to the community.

WESTBORO

Continuing west, the next commercial district is Westboro. Originally a small, incorporated village on the outskirts of the city, Westboro has retained its friendly small-town atmosphere. This traditional city neighborhood west of downtown has enjoyed a revitalization that began in the late 1990s. The catalyst here was the decision of several outfitter shops to locate in close proximity to the well-established, locally owned Trailhead. Other retailers followed, and more recently, a number of upscale shops, cafes, and restaurants have moved in. The western extension of Wellington Street, which becomes Richmond Road just east of Island Park Drive, is the commercial heart of this area.

CHINATOWN

It's a cultural misnomer to relate the hilly section of Somerset Street West between Preston Street and Bronson Avenue to China alone, but the name has stuck. In reality, the neighborhood is an Asian and South Asian mix, with large representations from Vietnam, Cambodia, Indonesia, Thailand, Hong Kong, mainland China, and Taiwan. Intriguing markets sell a variety of Asian produce, crafts, traditional Chinese medicinal ingredients, hand-painted silk garments, and many more fascinating treasures. Local residents own and frequent the stores and restaurants, which therefore offer an authentic ethnic neighborhood experience.

CORSO ITALIA (PRESTON ST.)

The heart of Ottawa's Italian immigrant population is Preston Street, also fondly known as Corso Italia (both names appear on the official street signs). The area serves as the commercial and cultural center of Little Italy. Every June, the street comes alive with the festivities of Italian Week, culminating in a street party stretching over 3 evenings. While the neighborhood continues to be dominated by Italian cafes and restaurants, there is a growing number of other types of cuisine represented. Grab a cab and head out here 1 evening for a memorable meal.

2 THE BEST OF OTTAWA IN 1 DAY

National capitals are a window onto their entire country, so this itinerary is designed to provide an overview of Canada's history, as well as Ottawa's transformation from grimy lumber town to glittering world capital. Because both country and city are defined by the yin and yang of English and French cultures, it's appropriate that this downtown tour encompasses sites on both sides of the Ottawa River. During the winter months you can substitute a cab for your feet to make the short trek across the Alexandra Bridge. *Start: National War Memorial.*

❶ National War Memorial

Historians like to say that Canada came into its own on the battlefield. The large granite arch topped by a winged figure, unveiled by King George VI in May 1939, is one of the country's most visible historic icons. In addition to serving as a constant reminder of Canada's losses in the two world wars and Korea, the cenotaph is an ideal downtown rendezvous point. See p. 161.

❷ Parliament Hill ★★★

No visit to Ottawa is complete without a trip to the Peace Tower's observation deck, which provides a good perspective on the city's layout. The Centre Block tour provides a quick peek at the two chambers of Canada's government and an interior view of Ottawa's most spectacular building: the recently restored Parliamentary Library, the only structure on the Hill to survive the devastating fire of 1916. On nice days between mid-May and late August, you'll want to time your arrival to witness the Changing of the Guard ceremony at 10am. If you're visiting in summer and are averse to lineups, save the Centre Block

tour for one of the evening sessions. See p. 133.

❸ Fairmont Château Laurier ★★★

If you're not staying at this imposing hotel, you'll want to make a point of cutting through the public areas to get a feel for the grandeur of life at the top of Ottawa's social and political scene. Built in 1912 as one of a series of railroad hotels across the country, the Château has been witness to more political intrigue and glamorous hobnobbing than anyplace else in Ottawa. For years, renowned portrait photographer Yousuf Karsh kept a studio here, and the deal to patriate Canada's constitution was cooked up between political leaders on the infamous "Night of the Long Knives" in one of the hotel's backrooms. See p. 80.

❹ The ByWard Market ★

Today, it's more of a late-night playground for college kids and high-tech executives, but Ottawa's central market is one place where age-old customs—and architecture—rub up comfortably against contemporary additions like the U.S. Embassy and the Rideau Centre. Local farmers and craftspeople still hawk their wares at outdoor stalls along the expanse of the main market building, while retailers like Irving Rivers (p. 181) and Lapointe's Fish operate out of the same locations they've had for decades. Be sure to stroll through the Tin House Court just east of Sussex Drive between York and Clarence streets to get an idea of how early Ottawa was patterned after European cities. See p. 133.

---

⑤ EMPIRE GRILL

How cool is the **Empire Grill**? Cool enough to attract the Rolling Stones, who filmed a video here in the summer of 2005. The place has one of the best patios for people-watching, and a cozy interior for cooler weather. Share a European-style Empire Platter for two, or try one of the steaks—the restaurant's mainstay. The wine list is extensive, including about 20 vintages by the glass. **47 Clarence St.** ✆ **613/241-1343.**

---

⑥ Canadian Museum of Civilization ★★★

One of several exceptional pieces of architecture added to the capital region in the 1980s, Douglas Cardinal's swooping design houses almost four million artifacts that capture the scope of human life on what the First Peoples called Turtle Island. If you're traveling with children, the Children's

Museum will be a must, but don't miss the Native heritage section on the lower level. The West Coast totem pole collection is one of the nation's treasures. See p. 119.

---

⑥ CANADIAN MUSEUM OF CIVILIZATION CAFETERIA

The museum's cafeteria is better than average for an institution, and the view of the river and Parliament Hill is so spectacular that it once graced the back of a Canadian bank note. If the weather is nice, take your food to the adjacent picnic area in Jacques-Cartier Park.

---

⑦ The Ottawa River ★

Ottawa is defined by its rivers. The Ottawa, which flows from Northern Ontario to the St. Lawrence River, delivered the explorer Samuel de Champlain here in 1613; logs were floated down the Ottawa and Gatineau to fuel America's early building boom; and the Rideau provided a (never used) supply route during the War of 1812. The best way to see Ottawa is from the deck of the *Paula D,* which departs four times a day from the dock adjacent to the Canadian Museum of Civilization. If you're in town before Labor Day, schedule your tour for the 7pm departure, which provides lovely twilight views. See p. 145.

---

3 THE BEST OF OTTAWA IN 2 DAYS

With a good idea of the city's heritage under your belt, it's time to visit a couple of Canada's other national institutions and shake off any museum-induced torpor with some walking and shopping. This tour will take you into three of Ottawa's oldest neighborhoods. ***Start:*** *Sussex Drive and St. Patrick Street.*

---

① National Gallery of Canada ★★

Like the Canadian Museum of Civilization, the new, glass-encased National Gallery revitalized Ottawa's architectural landscape in the 1980s, and provided a showcase for the work of a Canadian

architect: Moshe Safdie. The collection includes all the names you expect to see in a major national institution, but don't let the small highlights by Picasso and Chagall distract you from spending some quality time in front of works by Tom Thomson and Canada's famous Group of Seven, or from exploring the significant collection of Inuit art. See p. 123.

❷ Lowertown ★

A working-class neighborhood during Ottawa's years as ramshackle Bytown, Lowertown has since been gentrified, but many of the original houses remain, and whether you choose to wander down St. Patrick, Guiges, Bruyere, or Cathcart streets you'll get a flavor of what life was like before Queen Victoria proclaimed Ottawa the capital.

> **☕ I DEAL COFFEE**
> The north end of Dalhousie Street was once a no-go zone for visitors, but it's now a burgeoning hub of funky boutiques. **i deal coffee** roasts and grinds fair-trade coffee on-site and serves fresh baked goods. **176 Dalhousie St.** ☎ **613/562-1775.**

❹ Canadian Museum of Nature ★★

Now that you're suitably caffeinated, take a quick cab ride to Ottawa's favorite—and only—castle. Built in 1910, the museum is always a hit with kids, although an extensive renovation scheduled to conclude in 2010 has curtailed the number of exhibits. Despite the ongoing construction, visitors can take in an impressive new fossil gallery, including the always-popular dinosaurs, which delivers a powerful message about the importance of our environment. See p. 124.

❺ The Golden Triangle ★★

While Bytown's working class hunkered down in Lowertown, the gentry occupied some impressive digs on higher ground. Some of the Victorian mansions have since been subdivided, but you can still find impressive examples of how the other half lived on the streets that run between Elgin Street and the Rideau Canal.

> **☕ THE WORKS GOURMET BURGER BISTRO**
> Hungry? That's good, because **The Works Gourmet Burger Bistro** features more than 60 varieties of burger, topped with everything from peanut butter to blue cheese. Management calls the decor "factory meets Ikea." You'll call it fun. The Bank Street location is one of five in Ottawa. **580 Bank St.** ☎ **613/235-0406.**

❼ The Glebe ★★

Developed in the 1870s, this expansive neighborhood of gracious homes has long been Ottawa's most sought-after residential location. The pace here is noticeably slower than in downtown, but there is no shortage of great shopping, eating, and drinking along Bank Street between Pretoria Avenue in the north and Holmwood Avenue in the south. You'll find the most impressive houses on Monkland, Linden, and Clemow avenues in the area around Central Park. If your lunch didn't kill your appetite—you *shared* that order of Fajita Poutine, didn't you?—linger into the evening in the chill atmosphere of **InFusion** (p. 107) or over beer at the **Arrow & Loon** (p. 194).

4 THE BEST OF OTTAWA IN 3 DAYS

There are still more museums to see, but today's a day to spend more time outside than in, and to exercise your options in exploring one of Ottawa's most prominent man-made features. ***Start:*** *Confederation Square.*

DAY ONE ●🍵

1 National War Memorial
2 Parliament Hill
3 Fairmont Chateau Laurier
4 Byward Market
5 Empire Grill
6 Canadian Museum of Civilization
7 Ottawa River Tour

DAY TWO ●●🍵

1 National Gallery of Canada
2 Lowertown
3 i deal coffee
4 Canadian Museum of Nature
5 The Golden Triangle
6 The Works
7 The Glebe

DAY THREE ○🍵

1 The Rideau Canal
2 Bytown Museum
3 Richtree Market Restaurant
4 Canadian War Museum
5 Little Italy
6 The Arboretum

❶ The Rideau Canal ★★★

How you travel the downtown portion of the 177-year-old man-made waterway depends on the season and your fitness level. If it's winter—there's no excuse if you didn't bring your own skates, just rent some (p. 152)—strap on the blades and enjoy the world's longest skating rink. There are even more options if the canal's not frozen: Rent a bike (p. 148) or some in-line skates (p. 148), or even a canoe (p. 148); or climb aboard one of **Paul's Boat Line's** vessels. Can you picture Dow's Lake as a malarial swamp that killed dozens of canal builders? What a difference 177 years make. See p. 139.

❷ The Bytown Museum ★

This small museum is housed in one of the city's oldest buildings, and though the collection is not extensive, it offers an interesting audio tour in six languages and some period Victorian clothing and dolls. The third floor features some fascinating scale models of Ottawa through its history. See p. 129.

---

❸ RICHTREE MARKET RESTAURANT
The food court of the Rideau Centre offers numerous refreshment options, but your best bet is the **Richtree Market Restaurant,** where a wide range of choices—including Vietnamese soups, Indonesian stir-fries, and fresh pasta—are available in one place. **50 Rideau St.** ✆ **613/569-4934.**

---

❹ Canadian War Museum ★★

Nestled into the landscape of Lebreton Flats—once a thriving working-class neighborhood—Canada's newest national museum has won both praise, for its radical design, and criticism, for ignoring the country's longstanding peace movement. But, if the best museums are meant to spur reaction, then this extensive collection of military weaponry, memorabilia, and art does its job. See p. 122.

❺ Little Italy ★

The Corso Italia (or Preston St.) isn't much to look at, but next to the ByWard Market it is home to Ottawa's most eclectic selection of eateries. Though Italian specialties still dominate, the latest arrivals have brought more flavors of the world, so whether your taste at this point in the day runs to gelato, curry, or microbrews, Little Italy can provide something to hit the spot. See p. 64.

❻ The Arboretum ★★★

Okay, I'll admit I'm biased since I contemplated holding my wedding here, but to me this nicely treed oasis in the center of the city is Ottawa's most romantic spot. Adjacent to the Central Experimental Farm, the Arboretum offers pleasant walks beside the locks of the Rideau Canal from April to November, and exceptional sledding after the snow arrives. See p. 127.

Where to Stay

Although the accommodations in other cities are leaning toward luxury high-rises with an eye to contemporary design and Euro-style boutique hotels in heritage buildings, Ottawa hasn't embraced either of these trends. Instead, what characterizes the city's hotel scene are the unusually high percentage of suite hotels— a reflection of the number of expense-conscious people who come to town on long-term government business—and B&Bs, which cater to the large number of summer tourists on a budget. You can find some very chic rooms at Ottawa's top hotels—particularly at Brookstreet, Hilton Lac-Leamy, and ARC The.Hotel—but this is not a city that aims to wow you with over-the-top accommodations. Neither is it a city that has attracted the kind of hoteliers who have turned older buildings in Montreal, Toronto, and San Francisco into distinctive tourist accommodations.

What you will find in Ottawa are some great views—especially from higher, north-facing rooms at the Fairmont Château Laurier, the Westin Hotel, and the Delta Ottawa Hotel & Suites—and hotels that are within walking distance to all the major downtown attractions. If you're used to paying in excess of C$200 a night in large cities, you may be pleasantly surprised at Ottawa's hotel rates; it's quite possible to find comfortable accommodations for much less than you'll pay in other cities of comparable size and interest— another byproduct of the type of clientele that dominates in the capital.

PARKING   If you have a vehicle with you, remember to factor in parking charges when estimating the cost of your chosen accommodations. Hotel parking rates vary from C$4 to C$29 per night in the downtown area. Most lots are underground and a few do not allow in-and-out privileges, which restricts your flexibility. Overnight street parking is allowed where signs are posted. From November 15 to April 1, a city bylaw prohibits overnight on-street parking from 1 to 7am if a snowfall of 7 centimeters or more is forecast (including ranges such as 5–10cm). When the parking ban is in effect, the information is available through the local media. These bans are actively enforced, and those who fail to comply could find their vehicle ticketed and towed. Call the Snowline at © **613/580-2460** to obtain current information about parking restrictions.

A NOTE TO SMOKERS   Most hotels in Ottawa are almost completely non-smoking, partly due to a reduced demand for smoking rooms and partly due to tough provincial laws that prohibit smoking in public places. Typically, about 5% of the rooms in any given hotel are reserved for smokers. However, people who want a smoke-free environment should always make that clear when reserving a room. Finding a room where smoking is permitted is usually a bit easier in Quebec, where nonsmoking legislation is more recent, and smoking is more prevalent.

BED & BREAKFASTS   As noted, Ottawa has an abundance of gracious older homes that have been transformed into B&Bs. For the most part, B&Bs in Ottawa are located in quiet residential neighborhoods with tree-lined streets. If you're traveling solo or as a couple, then a B&B presents an economical and delightful alternative to a hotel room; however, families will usually need to rent two rooms in order to secure enough sleeping area, and that must be taken into account when estimating costs. Also, be aware that B&Bs and inns are usually geared to adult visitors, and some don't allow children at all. Many homes have expensive antiques on display and guests are expecting a quiet, restful stay. If you have children with you and they're young, boisterous, or both, then you're better off in a downtown suite hotel with a pool.

Two organizations in the city can help you choose a B&B. The Ottawa Tourism and Convention Authority (OTCA), 130 Albert St., Ste. 1800, Ottawa, ON K1P 5G4 (✆ **800/465-1867** or 613/239-5000; www.ottawatourism.ca), has around 18 member B&Bs and inns. OTCA also operates a walk-in accommodations reservation desk at the Capital Infocentre, 90 Wellington St. (across from Parliament Hill), Ottawa, ON (✆ **800/465-1867** or 613/239-5000). Online, visit **BBCanada. com** and have a look at more than 75 properties in the city and around the region that offer bed-and-breakfast accommodations. The **Association of Ottawa Bed and Breakfasts** represents a group of about a dozen BBCanada members who operate B&Bs in distinctive historical properties.

CAMPING Across the Ottawa River in Quebec, Gatineau Park's 36,000 hectares (88,958 acres) of woodlands and lakes has two campgrounds. Philippe Lake Family Campground has around 300 sites, and La Pêche Lake has a limited number of canoe

camping sites. For details on these and other camping facilities, contact the Gatineau Park Visitor Centre, 318 Meech Lake Rd., Old Chelsea, PQ J0X 1N0 (✆ **819/827-2020**), or call the National Capital Commission at ✆ **800/465-1867.**

IMPORTANT NOTES ON PRICES
The prices quoted in this chapter are generally a range from the cheapest low-season rate up to the highest, undiscounted price for a room—what is known in the industry as the rack rate. In each listing, the prices are for two adults sharing a room. Discounts can result in a dramatic drop from the rack rate, anywhere from 10% to 50%. The rule of thumb in booking a hotel room is this: Always ask for a deal. Corporate discounts, club memberships (CAA, AAA, and others), and discounts linked to credit cards or a hotel's own loyalty card are just a few of the ways you can get a lower price. In Ottawa, hotels are especially eager to boost their occupancy rates with families on weekends, when their corporate and government clients desert them. Weekend rates and family packages are often available. Even though Winterlude, March break, the Canadian Tulip Festival, and the summer months are all peak tourist times, many hotels offer packages that may include complimentary museum passes, restaurant vouchers, or other money-saving deals. Hotel rooms in Ottawa are subject to a 5% accommodations tax and a 5% Goods and Services Tax (GST).

1 DOWNTOWN (WEST OF THE CANAL)

East side, west side—it makes little difference in Ottawa because the scale of the downtown is small enough that everything is within walking distance. The west side of the Rideau Canal will put you a bit closer to the Parliament Buildings, the Canadian War Museum, and the Canadian Museum of Nature, but the hotels are farther from the concentration of restaurants and bars in the ByWard Market.

VERY EXPENSIVE
Crowne Plaza Ottawa ★ If you're looking for contemporary luxury in a traditional hotel, this is a fine place to stay. The public areas reflect a sophisticated Art Deco style,

with clean lines, expanses of wood, and a rich, earthy color scheme. The upscale decor continues into the hallways and guest rooms, which have been refurbished with new carpets, draperies, wall coverings, furniture, and redesigned bathrooms. An underground shopping arcade, open primarily during weekday office hours, is accessible from inside the hotel. The extensive health club features a large fitness center, basketball court, outdoor terrace, and saunas. The indoor pool area, nicely set in a light-filled space, has patio doors leading onto a courtyard. The staff is attentive, courteous, and efficient. International cuisine is served in the sophisticated atmosphere of 101 Café.

101 Lyon St., Ottawa, ON K1R 5T9. (℄ **800/227-6963** or 613/237-3600. Fax 613/237-2351. www.crowne ottawa.ca. 411 units. C$170–C$240 double; C$315–C$450 suite. Weekend packages available. Children 17 and under stay free in parent's room. AE, DC, DISC, MC, V. Valet parking C$23; self-parking C$15. Pets accepted. **Amenities:** Restaurant; lounge; indoor pool; health club; sauna; children's play area; concierge; business center; shopping arcade; 24-hour room service; babysitting; laundry service; dry-cleaning; executive floors. *In room*: A/C, TV w/pay movies, dataport, fridge (in some), coffeemaker, hair dryer, iron/ ironing board.

Delta Ottawa Hotel and Suites ★ (Kids)

While it isn't the bargain that it once was, one of Ottawa's largest hotels continues to be a hit with vacationing families who flock here on weekends, during March break, and over the summer. The giant two-story indoor water slide is a major hit with kids. In addition to standard guest rooms, the hotel offers studios with kitchenettes (fridge, microwave, sink, and utensils) and one- and two-bedroom suites with balconies and kitchenettes. Two on-site dining facilities provide above-average fare.

361 Queen St., Ottawa, ON K1R 7S9. (℄ **800/268-1133** or 613/238-6000. Fax 613/238-2290. www.delta hotels.com. 328 units. C$209 double; C$235 studio; C$260 1-bedroom suite. Children under 18 stay free in parent's room. AE, DC, DISC, MC, V. Valet parking C$27; self-parking C$19. Small domestic pets C$50 flat fee. **Amenities:** 2 restaurants; lounge; indoor pool with water slide; exercise room; Jacuzzi; sauna; children's center; seasonal children's program; concierge; business center; salon; limited room service; massage; babysitting; same-day laundry service and dry-cleaning; washers and dryers; executive floor. *In room*: A/C, TV w/pay movies, dataport, kitchenette (in some), coffeemaker, hair dryer, iron.

Marriott Residence Inn Ottawa ★

The units in this all-suites hotel are at least 50% larger than those in standard hotels. If you're staying in town longer than a night or two, it's nice to be able to spread out a little in comfort. If you have kids with you, splurge if you can on a two-bedroom suite, which boasts a well-equipped kitchen, two full bathrooms, and three TVs. It's well worth the money—and if it's going to push you over budget, take advantage of the grocery service and cook meals in the suite. The pool has a uniform 1.1m (3^1/$_2$-ft.) depth. Expect cheerful faces and friendly greetings from staff whenever you cross paths. Two one-bedroom suites are equipped for guests with disabilities.

161 Laurier Ave. W., Ottawa, ON K1P 5J2. (℄ **800/331-3131** or 613/231-2020. Fax 613/231-2090. www. residenceinn.com. 171 units. C$205 studio; C$325 2-bedroom suite. Rates include breakfast and snacks. AE, DC, DISC, MC, V. Parking C$15. Pets C$150 flat fee. **Amenities:** Lounge; indoor pool; exercise room; spa next door; hot tub; sauna; business center; same-day laundry service and dry-cleaning; laundry room. *In room*: A/C, TV w/pay movies, dataport, kitchen (including dishwasher in larger rooms), coffee-maker, hair dryer, iron/ironing board, washer/dryer (in some).

Ottawa Marriott ★ (Kids)

While furnished with the chain's usual dark-wood armoires and ergonomic desk-and-chair sets, Ottawa's downtown Marriott has the distinction of having the only rooftop revolving restaurant in the region, where diners can gaze at an ever-changing view of the nation's capital while enjoying global cuisine highlighted with Canadian products. While revolving restaurants are routinely viewed as somewhat

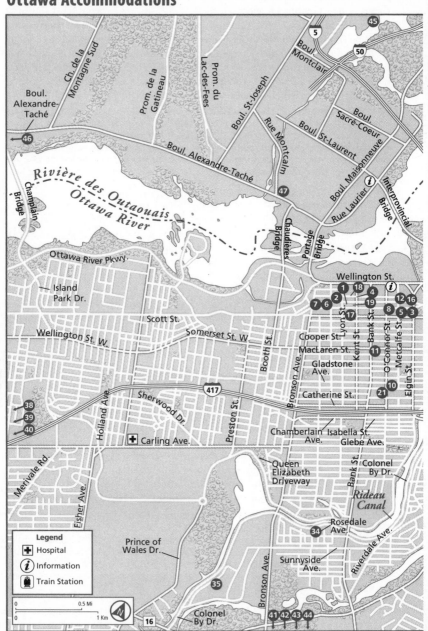

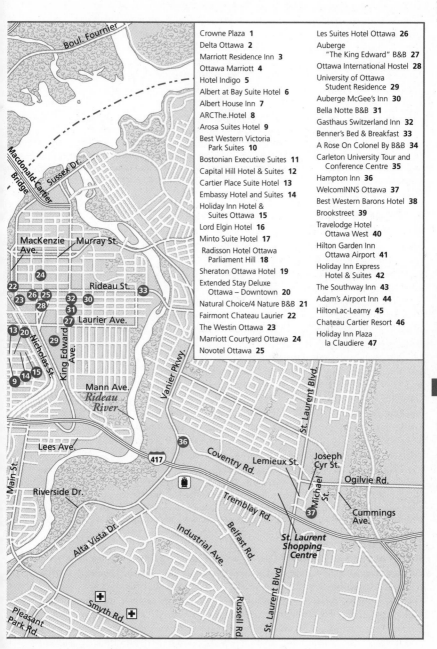

Crowne Plaza **1**
Delta Ottawa **2**
Marriott Residence Inn **3**
Ottawa Marriott **4**
Hotel Indigo **5**
Albert at Bay Suite Hotel **6**
Albert House Inn **7**
ARCThe.Hotel **8**
Arosa Suites Hotel **9**
Best Western Victoria
    Park Suites **10**
Bostonian Executive Suites **11**
Capital Hill Hotel & Suites **12**
Cartier Place Suite Hotel **13**
Embassy Hotel and Suites **14**
Holiday Inn Hotel &
    Suites Ottawa **15**
Lord Elgin Hotel **16**
Minto Suite Hotel **17**
Radisson Hotel Ottawa
    Parliament Hill **18**
Sheraton Ottawa Hotel **19**
Extended Stay Deluxe
    Ottawa – Downtown **20**
Natural Choice/4 Nature B&B **21**
Fairmont Chateau Laurier **22**
The Westin Ottawa **23**
Marriott Courtyard Ottawa **24**
Novotel Ottawa **25**

Les Suites Hotel Ottawa **26**
Auberge
    "The King Edward" B&B **27**
Ottawa International Hostel **28**
University of Ottawa
    Student Residence **29**
Auberge McGee's Inn **30**
Bella Notte B&B **31**
Gasthaus Switzerland Inn **32**
Benner's Bed & Breakfast **33**
A Rose On Colonel By B&B **34**
Carleton University Tour and
    Conference Centre **35**
Hampton Inn **36**
WelcomINNS Ottawa **37**
Best Western Barons Hotel **38**
Brookstreet **39**
Travelodge Hotel
    Ottawa West **40**
Hilton Garden Inn
    Ottawa Airport **41**
Holiday Inn Express
    Hotel & Suites **42**
The Southway Inn **43**
Adam's Airport Inn **44**
HiltonLac-Leamy **45**
Chateau Cartier Resort **46**
Holiday Inn Plaza
    la Claudiere **47**

kitschy, the Merlot Rooftop Grill offers one of the most-extensive wine lists in the city. With the aim of attracting families on weekends and during school holidays, the hotel has expanded its facilities for children, including an activity and craft center, a games room for teens, minigolf, half-court basketball, and big-screen movies. The screens in the guest rooms are large, too; the 94-centimeter flatscreens that are standard issue are the largest in the city. Down comforters, duvets, and fluffier-than-average pillows are standard fare as at all Marriotts. The hotel's guest rooms are slated for a top-to-bottom renovation in 2009.

100 Kent St., Ottawa, ON K1P 5R7. (✆ **800/853-8463** Canada or 613/238-1122. www.ottawamarriott. com. 480 units. C$230 double; C$350–C$450 1- and 2-bedroom suites. Children 18 and under stay free in parent's room. AE, DC, DISC, MC, V. Valet parking C$25; self-parking C$15. Pets accepted. **Amenities:** 2 restaurants; cafe; indoor pool; health club; Jacuzzi; sauna; children's center; games room; concierge; business center; shopping arcade; limited room service; babysitting; same-day laundry service and drycleaning; washers and dryers; executive floors. *In room:* A/C, TV w/pay movies, dataport, coffeemaker, hair dryer, iron/ironing board.

EXPENSIVE

Hotel Indigo ★   The boutique hotel chain's first Canadian property occupies one of Ottawa's busiest street corners and is the only downtown hotel to be retrofitted into a heritage building. The renovation was of major proportions—opening the center of the structure into a spectacular atrium. The light that floods the lobby and exposed upper corridors is symbolic of the chain's emphasis on nature and renewal. The corporate philosophy of the Indigo chain—which espouses belief in the power of Fibonacci numbers to define everything in nature—can seem a bit cultish, but look past the hotel's branding mumbo jumbo and you'll find a restful hotel with some pleasant designer touches. The beds are large and sumptuous, and the dark hardwood flooring is a welcome change from ubiquitous industrial-strength broadloom, as are the operational windows. Thirteen of the hotel's rooms have Jacuzzis, and all are equipped with ergonomically pleasing glass-and-tile shower stalls. Spa-quality Aveda products abound. The in-room electronics—including CD/MP3 players and flatscreen TVs—are contemporary, but the nature of the building means that Wi-Fi is only accessible in the lobby; the wired Internet service in the rooms is complimentary. Indigo prides itself on exceptional service, but there are some compromises in this location: While the fitness center is open 24/365, room service operates only during the hours of the in-house restaurant, Phi.

123 Metcalfe St., Ottawa, ON K1P 5L9. (✆ **866/246-3446** or 613/231-6555. Fax 613/231-7555. www.ottawa downtownhotel.com. 106 units. C$189–C$219 double; C$209 deluxe double; C$229 1-bedroom suite. AE, DC, DISC, MC, V. Valet parking C$24; self-parking C$17. **Amenities:** Restaurant; indoor pool; 24-hour fitness room; sauna; whirlpool; business center; limited room service; executive suites. *In-room:* A/C, LCD flatscreen TV w/pay movies, CD/MP3 player, dataport, coffeemaker, hair dryer, iron/ironing board.

MODERATE

Albert at Bay Suite Hotel ★ Ⓚids Ⓥalue   Boasting the largest suites in the city, the Albert at Bay seems more like a luxury condominium than a hotel. The lobby is richly appointed in marble and Art Deco–revival black accents, and the staff is low-key yet friendly. Upstairs, the suites are homey, too, with full-size kitchen appliances, dining tables, and comfortable furnishings. Same-day grocery delivery is available if you want to prepare your own meals. Many of the suites have two TVs and some feature a second bathroom. The hotel welcomes families and even goes so far as to provide a free children's program during July and August. The kids' club offers a wide variety of supervised activities for children ages 3 to 12, daily from 9am to noon and 1 to 5pm in July and

August. A bright and sunny exercise room with an adjacent rooftop patio provides a 75 refuge for parents who want to sneak away and relax while the children are busy at the kids' club. The downtown location is a great base for visitors traveling without children as well. You're within strolling distance of Parliament Hill (3 blocks), the National Arts Centre (7 blocks), and the Rideau Centre (8 blocks). A 5-minute walk will take you right down to the pathway along the banks of the Ottawa River.

435 Albert St., Ottawa, ON K1R 7X4. © 800/267-6644 or 613/238-8858. Fax 613/238-1433. www.albert atbay.com. 197 units. C$129–C$159 1-bedroom suite; C$179–C$299 2-bedroom suite. Children 16 and under stay free in parent's room. AE, DC, DISC, MC, V. Parking C$16. **Amenities:** Restaurant; bar; exercise room; sauna; seasonal children's program; business center; limited room service; laundry service; dry-cleaning; washers and dryers; executive suites. *In room:* A/C, TV w/pay movies, Wi-Fi, kitchen, coffee-maker, iron/ironing board, safe.

Albert House Inn   This gracious Victorian building has operated as an inn for the past 24 years. It was designed and built by Thomas Seaton Scott, a renowned architect whose work includes the Cartier Drill Hall, the Langevin Block (home of the prime minister's offices), and many other federal buildings. The furnishings and decor enhance the historical atmosphere. Its convenient downtown location is only a short walk from the Parliament Buildings and beautiful pathways for walking and biking along the Ottawa River. A secure storage room for bicycles is provided. The environment is adult oriented, but older children are welcome.

478 Albert St., Ottawa, ON K1R 5B5. © 800/267-1982 or 613/236-4479. Fax 613/237-9079. www.albert inn.com. 17 units. C$108–C$138 double; C$178 double with Jacuzzi. Rates include breakfast. AE, DC, MC, V. Parking C$10. **Amenities:** Business center; limited room service; washers and dryers. *In room:* A/C, TV, dataport, Wi-Fi, hair dryer.

ARC The.Hotel ★★ (Value)   Aiming to blend efficiency with luxury, ARC The.Hotel is one of the few properties in Ottawa to have adopted the boutique approach. Popular amenities include down-filled duvets, oversize pillows, cotton sheets, Frette bathrobes, Gilchrist & Soames toiletries (guests with allergies can request nonallergenic bedding and toiletries) and a nightly turn-down service that includes cold spring water, Belgian chocolates, and a fresh Granny Smith apple—the hotel's trademark. Six of the pricier rooms feature extra-large tubs and fresh-cut flowers. You can borrow from the hotel's collection of 3,000 CDs to enjoy in your room, sip a complimentary glass of sparkling wine (served after 3pm daily), browse the original artwork by local artists, or catch up on your reading in the attractive library just off the lobby. If you wish to customize your return visit, make your preferences known to the front desk staff and on your next trip you'll feel even more at home. The ARC lounge serves signature martinis at the cocktail hour, and the fine-dining restaurant features the best hotel dining in the city's core. Chef Jason Duffy is a proponent of buying local meats and produce. Based on a muted palette of black and white, the rooms are uniformly sized, and scheduled for rotating makeovers in 2009.

140 Slater St., Ottawa, ON K1P 5H6. © 800/699-2516 or 613/238-2888. Fax 613/235-8421. www.arcthe hotel.com. 112 units. C$125–C$305 double; C$310 junior suite; C$425 executive 1-bedroom suite. Children under 16 stay free in parent's room. AE, DC, DISC, MC, V. Valet parking C$20. **Amenities:** Restaurant/lounge; exercise room; concierge; business center; 24-hour room service; massage; babysitting; same-day laundry service and dry-cleaning; executive suites. *In room:* A/C, TV w/pay movies, CD player, data-port, minibar, coffeemaker, hair dryer, safe, umbrella, suit presser in executive suites.

Arosa Suites Hotel (Value)   If your budget is tight, consider the Arosa Suites for simple, no-frills accommodations. A maximum of four occupants plus one baby in a crib

WHERE TO STAY

5

DOWNTOWN (WEST OF THE CANAL)

is the limit in each one-bedroom suite. Some hotel guests, many of them corporate or government employees, are longer-stay occupants, but in the summer you'll see more families and other tourists around. Parking is cheap, but be warned: The parking lot doesn't have room for every vehicle—it's first-come, first-served. A kitchen is in every suite, but only some have a dishwasher, and all units but three have a private balcony. High-speed Internet access is provided in all guest rooms.

163 MacLaren St., Ottawa, ON K2P 2G4. ☎ **613/238-6783**. Fax 613/238-5080. www.arosahotel.com. 60 units. C$104 1-bedroom suite with 2 adults; C$109 1-bedroom suite with 4 adults. Children 16 and under stay free in parent's room. AE, DC, DISC, MC, V. Limited parking C$4. **Amenities:** Exercise room; washers and dryers. *In room:* A/C, TV, dataport, kitchen, dishwasher (in some), coffeemaker.

Best Western Victoria Park Suites

This hotel has comfortable and spacious studios and one-bedroom suites, all with kitchenettes, and—thanks to its location at the extreme south edge of the downtown core—ready access to the Rideau Canal, the Canadian Museum of Nature, and the Glebe. A deluxe continental breakfast can be enjoyed on the pretty treed patio in the warmer months. A penthouse fitness center overlooks downtown Ottawa, so you can work out with a view. All suites have complimentary high-speed wireless Internet. When the kids' club is running during July and August at the Albert at Bay Suite Hotel (a sister hotel), you can take your children there for free, supervised fun and games. A cut above the standard Best Western in its design and trim, the hotel is a good alternative for those who don't like being surrounded by high-rise buildings.

377 O'Connor St., Ottawa, ON K2P 2M2. ☎ **800/465-7275** or 613/567-7275. Fax 613/567-1161. www.victoriapark.com. 123 units. C$119–$C209 studio; C$129–C$239 1-bedroom suite. Children 16 and under stay free in parent's room. AE, DC, DISC, MC, V. Parking C$14. **Amenities:** Breakfast room; exercise room; sauna; free children's program off-site; business services; laundry service; dry-cleaning; washers and dryers; executive suites. *In room:* A/C, TV w/pay movies, fax machine, dataport, Wi-Fi, kitchenette, fridge, coffeemaker, hair dryer, iron/ironing board, safe.

Bostonian Executive Suites ★

The Bostonian is an all-suite property, converted from an existing high-rise building. Opened in 2001, the suites have full kitchens and a choice of studio or one-bedroom models. High-speed wireless Internet access, voice mail, 24-hour business support services, ergonomic seating, and long-stay options make the Bostonian an ideal base for business travelers. Families will enjoy the convenience of laundry facilities, grocery delivery, a microwave, and a dishwasher.

341 MacLaren St., Ottawa ON K2P 2E2. ☎ **866/320-4567** or 613/594-5757. Fax 613/594-3221. www.thebostonian.ca. 116 units. C$109–C$159 studio; C$139–C$229 1-bedroom suite. Children under 17 stay free in parent's room. Rollaway/crib free for children under 16, C$10 for guests 16 and over. AE, MC, V. Parking C$12. Some pets accepted. **Amenities:** Exercise room; concierge; business services; same-day dry-cleaning; washers and dryers. *In room:* A/C, TV w/pay movies, dataport, kitchen, coffeemaker, hair dryer, iron/ironing board.

Capital Hill Hotel & Suites (Value)

This comfortable but plain hotel offers good value and the advantage of a downtown location. About one-third of the guest rooms are equipped with a kitchenette, including a stove or microwave, a small fridge, dishes, and utensils, but none have dishwashers. The room size is average and bathrooms tend to be small. The price is the same for a double room with or without kitchenette, so if you'd like to do some self-catering, this represents good value. A penthouse suite featuring a fireplace, Jacuzzi, sauna, and kitchen is an exceptional value at C$250 per night. The entire hotel is being refreshed several floors at a time with a bright, neutral decor. Yuk Yuk's Comedy Club is just next door.

88 Albert St., Ottawa, ON K1P 5E9. ✆ **800/463-7705** or 613/235-1413. Fax 613/235-6047. www.capital hill.com. 150 units. C$125 double with or without kitchenette; C$159 1-bedroom suite. AE, DC, DISC, MC, V. Parking C$12. Pets accepted. **Amenities:** Restaurant; exercise room; business services; same-day laundry service and dry-cleaning; executive suites. *In room:* A/C, TV w/pay movies, dataport, kitchenette (in some), coffeemaker, hair dryer, iron/ironing board.

Cartier Place Suite Hotel ★ (Kids)

This suite hotel has wonderful amenities for children, making it an attractive choice for families. In addition to the indoor pool, bathed in natural light streaming through glass doors (which are thrown open in the summer and lead onto a sun deck), there is a well-equipped children's playroom and even a preschool-size play structure in the pool area. An outdoor courtyard features a climbing gym and children's play equipment in summer. Redecoration and replacement of kitchen appliances has been ongoing for the past few years, a couple of floors at a time, so many of the suites are fresh and bright. All units are suites with full kitchens and private balconies with garden chairs.

180 Cooper St., Ottawa, ON K2P 2L5. ✆ **800/236-8399** or 613/236-5000. Fax 613/238-3842. www.suite dreams.com. 250 units. C$119–C$169 1-bedroom suite; C$189–C$250 2-bedroom suite. Children 16 and under stay free in parent's room. AE, DC, MC, V. Parking C$15. Small pets C$15 per night. **Amenities:** Restaurant/lounge; indoor pool; exercise room; Jacuzzi; sauna; children's playroom; outdoor playground; games room; business center; limited room service; babysitting; same-day laundry service and dry-cleaning; washers and dryers. *In room:* A/C, TV w/pay movies, dataport, kitchen, coffeemaker, hair dryer, iron/ironing board.

Embassy Hotel and Suites

All units in this hotel have a full kitchen with full-size appliances (minus dishwasher). The bathrooms and bedrooms tend to be small, but there is plenty of seating in the living rooms of the suites; the two-bedroom executive suites are quite spacious at 90sq. m (969 sq. ft.). The on-site Nook restaurant/coffee shop serves breakfast and lunch only. The Study Lounge provides dinner service. The hotel is geared toward families as well as long-stay business travelers, and there's a children's lending library that stocks movies, books, and games.

25 Cartier St., Ottawa, ON K2P 1J2. ✆ **800/661-5495** or 613/237-2111. Fax 613/563-1353. www.embassy hotelottawa.com. 130 units. C$105 studio; C$109–C$125 1-bedroom suite; C$205–C$260 2-bedroom suite. Children under 16 stay free in parent's room. AE, DC, DISC, MC, V. Parking C$9. Pets C$10 per night. **Amenities:** Cafe; lounge (weekdays); exercise room; sauna; business center; limited room service; babysitting; same-day laundry service and dry-cleaning; washers and dryers. *In room:* A/C, TV, Wi-Fi, kitchen, coffeemaker, hair dryer, iron/ironing board.

Holiday Inn Hotel & Suites Ottawa (Kids)

The property is situated at the quiet end of Cooper Street, just steps from the banks of the Rideau Canal and a few blocks west of the shops and restaurants of Elgin Street. One-bedroom suites are equipped with a full kitchen, and a small number have a connecting door to a single room, effectively creating a two-bedroom suite. Some guest rooms include a kitchenette or fridge and microwave. Three luxury Jacuzzi suites are available. A special family guest room featuring a children's play area with a SpongeBob SquarePants theme has been added; maximum occupancy is two adults and two children.

111 Cooper St., Ottawa, ON K2P 2E3. ✆ **613/238-1331.** Fax 613/230-2179. www.hiottawa.ca. 229 units. C$138–C$142 double; C$165–C$240 1-bedroom suite. Children under 18 stay free in parent's room. AE, DC, DISC, MC, V. Parking C$10. Pets accepted. **Amenities:** Restaurant; exercise room; business center; limited room service; massage; babysitting; same-day laundry service and dry-cleaning; washers and dryers; executive rooms. *In room:* A/C, TV w/pay movies, dataport, kitchen or kitchenette (in some), coffeemaker, hair dryer, iron/ironing board.

 **Pool Safety**

Hotels do not usually provide lifeguards or other supervisory personnel at the pool. It is parents' responsibility to closely supervise their own children in the pool area. Exercise extra caution when the pool is crowded. Enjoy your swim and always follow pool safety rules.

Lord Elgin Hotel ★ (Value) This established, independent hotel, one of Ottawa's landmark properties, has 355 rooms in an elegant, château-inspired building that has been preserved and restored with attention to 1940s interior detail. The location could not be better as a base for visitors to Ottawa. Directly across the street is Confederation Park, a small but pretty city park that provides a peaceful respite from the dense metropolis of skyscrapers crowding the business district behind the hotel. Two new guest-room wings have been seamlessly added to the property, and all of the hotel's original rooms were renovated in the past 5 years. The massive renovation and expansion included upgrades to the health club and a new indoor lap pool. Room sizes vary, with the units in the new wings larger. Bathrooms have been fitted with dark granite countertops and polished nickel accents. Executive rooms on the top two floors have upgraded amenities from Gilchrist & Soames, in-room safes, bathrobes and slippers, and complimentary high-speed Internet and phone calls. The premium for these upgraded rooms is only C$30. Rooms at the back are quieter, but you lose the view of the park. One nice architectural feature is that all of the windows open. The staff is formal, courteous, and efficient.

100 Elgin St., Ottawa, ON K1P 5K8. (✆) **800/267-4298** or 613/235-3333. Fax 613/235-3223. www.lordelgin.ca. 355 units. C$140–C$199 double; C$152–C$275 executive double on upper floor. Children 17 and under stay free in parent's room. AE, DC, DISC, MC, V. Valet parking C$22. Pets accepted. **Amenities:** Restaurant; lounge; Starbucks coffeeshop; indoor pool; health club; hot tub; sauna; bicycle rental nearby; concierge; spa/hair salon next door; business center; limited room service; babysitting; same-day laundry service and dry-cleaning; executive floors. *In room:* A/C, TV w/pay movies, dataport, fridge (in most), coffeemaker, hair dryer, iron/ironing board.

Minto Suite Hotel ★★ (Value) Beautifully appointed, spacious suites with kitchenettes or full kitchens make the Minto one of Ottawa's best places to stay. Adding to its appeal is direct access to an indoor shopping concourse with a bank, food court, pharmacy, wine store, and 24-hour grocery store. The 19.5m (64-ft.) long indoor pool, lit by skylights, is a uniform 1.2m (4 ft.) deep, and uses an environmentally advanced saltwater system. A sundeck leads off the pool area. Staff members are courteous, pleasant, and experienced in helping visitors make the most of their stay in Ottawa.

185 Lyon St. N., Ottawa, ON K1R 7Y4. (✆) **800/267-3377** or 613/232-2200. Fax 613/232-6962. www.mintosuitehotel.com. 417 units. C$185 studio; C$217 1-bedroom suite; C$230 2-bedroom suite. Children 18 and under stay free in parent's room. AE, DC, DISC, MC, V. Parking C$15 Mon–Thurs; C$4 Fri–Sun. **Amenities:** Restaurant; bar; indoor pool; fitness center; Jacuzzi; sauna; business center; shopping arcade; hair salon; limited room service; massage; babysitting; same-day laundry service and dry-cleaning; washers and dryers. *In room:* A/C, TV w/pay movies, dataport, kitchen or kitchenette, coffeemaker, hair dryer, iron/ironing board, safe.

Radisson Hotel Ottawa Parliament Hill Stylish and contemporary, this hotel offers some nice views of Gatineau Hills and downtown from its upper north-facing

Tips **Room with a View**

If you're visiting on Canada Day, July 1, request a higher-floor room or suite at the **Delta Ottawa,** overlooking the Ottawa River. You'll get a prime seat for the spectacular fireworks display that is set off behind the Parliament Buildings.

floors. Better yet, the windows open, giving you the option of letting in some fresh air. Comfort is stressed with Radisson's adjustable beds, down comforters, and pillows. If you're traveling on business, you'll appreciate the ergonomic office chair, two-line phone, and large desk. Free high-speed Internet service is available, although the hotel doesn't offer Wi-Fi. The small, but bright, fitness room is open 24 hours. I find this kind of property somewhat faceless, but the hotel redeems itself with its close proximity to the Ottawa River and the scenic Western Parkway.

402 Queen St., Ottawa, ON K1R 5A7. ℭ **888/201-1718** or 613/236-1133. Fax 613/236-2317. www.radisson. com/hotels/onottawa. 176 units. C$145–C$175 double; C$250 suite. AE, DC, DISC, MC, V. Parking C$20. **Amenities:** Restaurant; bar; 24-hr. exercise room; whirlpool; business center. *In room:* A/C, TV w/pay movies, CD player, dataport, coffeemaker, hair dryer, iron/ironing board.

Sheraton Ottawa Hotel ★   This 236-unit Sheraton is an elegant hotel, symbolized by its impeccably dressed doorman and spiral staircase in the lobby. Its Carleton Grill restaurant is polished as well, furnished with rich, dark wood, gleaming brass, and sparkling chandeliers. Rooms are spacious, with upgraded vanities and ceramic tiles in the bathrooms. The spotless indoor pool complex features a bank of windows at one end to allow natural light to flood the space. If luxurious surroundings are a priority on your vacation, you won't be disappointed here.

150 Albert St., Ottawa, ON K1P 5G2. ℭ **800/489-8333** or 613/238-1500. Fax 613/235-2723. www. sheraton.com/ottawa. 236 units. C$139–C$260 double; C$350–C$575 executive suite. Children 18 and under stay free in parent's room. AE, DC, DISC, MC, V. Valet parking C$20. Small pets accepted. **Amenities:** Restaurant; lounge; Starbucks kiosk; indoor pool; exercise room; sauna; concierge; 24-hour business center; room service; babysitting; same-day laundry service and dry-cleaning; executive floor. *In room:* A/C, TV w/pay movies, dataport, coffeemaker, hair dryer, iron/ironing board.

INEXPENSIVE

Extended Stay Deluxe Ottawa—Downtown   With a full kitchen in every unit, this long-stay hotel guarantees self-sufficient accommodations. Be prepared to roll up your sleeves, though, because there are no dishwashers. Located in a quieter downtown district, away from the office-block bustle, it's still within walking distance of many downtown attractions—and a short stroll from the banks of the Rideau Canal, which is great for walkers. The bedrooms and living room are a decent size, but the kitchens are a bit short on elbowroom. An Italian restaurant on the main floor serves breakfast, lunch, and dinner daily. You can have groceries delivered to your suite to save you the trouble of shopping.

141 Cooper St., Ottawa, ON K2P 0E8. ℭ **800/563-5634** or 613/236-7500. Fax 613/563-2836. www. extendedstayhotels.com. 216 units. C$125–C$142 1-bedroom suite; C$147–C$187 2-bedroom suite. Pets C$75 flat fee. Children 18 and under stay free in parent's room. AE, DC, DISC, MC, V. Parking C$11. **Amenities:** Restaurant; bar; exercise room; Jacuzzi; sauna; business center; limited room service; laundry service; dry-cleaning; washers and dryers; executive floor. *In room:* A/C, TV w/pay movies, Wi-Fi, kitchen, coffeemaker, hair dryer, iron/ironing board.

Natural Choice/4 Nature B&B   If you take a nuts-and-granola kind of approach to life, you'll feel right at home in this vegetarian, nonsmoking B&B facing the Canadian Museum of Nature. The bedrooms are fresh and bright and decorated with original artwork, in keeping with the relaxed, friendly atmosphere. The hosts provide services ranging from massage to yoga classes and weddings. Their flourishing garden has a picnic table for guests' use, as well as a room on the second floor where children can play when meditation and yoga are not in session. Besides the green space outside the Museum of Nature, there's a park within walking distance with a children's playground and wading pool. For even more physical activity, get a day pass to the facilities at the YMCA across the street. Breakfasts are vegetarian, made with organic ingredients as much as possible.

263 McLeod St., Ottawa, ON K2P 1A1. ℂ **888/346-9642** or 613/563-4399. www.vegybnb.com. 3 units. C$85–C$120 double; C$150–C$175 per family occupying 2 rooms. Rates include breakfast. MC, V. Limited free parking. Pets C$15 per night. **Amenities:** Massage, yoga classes. *In room:* Ceiling fan, no phone.

2 DOWNTOWN (EAST OF THE CANAL)

Bedding down east of the canal puts you squarely in the heart of the downtown action, just steps from the ByWard Market, the National Gallery of Canada, and the canal itself. It's a bit of a hike uphill to the Parliament Buildings, the National War Memorial, and other historic sites, but the distances are so short that price, amenities, and availability should really be your determining factors.

VERY EXPENSIVE

Fairmont Château Laurier ★★★   One of Ottawa's premier landmarks, this grand hotel, built in 1912 in the same Loire Valley Renaissance style as Quebec City's Château Frontenac, has an imposing stone facade and a copper-paneled roof. If you're looking for luxury, tradition, and attentive service, this is the place to stay—royalty and celebrities have always been attracted to the Château Laurier's graceful beauty. You'll pay for the pleasure, but the surroundings are exceptional. The spacious public areas display the grandeur of another era, having been refurnished with the hotel's original furniture, rescued from a storeroom and meticulously restored. The less-expensive rooms are rather small but just as elegant as the larger rooms and suites; nine rooms are equipped for guests with disabilities. The upper floors offer impressive views over the Ottawa River toward the Gatineau Hills. The extensive health club and pool area, built in 1929 in Art Deco style, has been admirably preserved. The two dining rooms, Wilfrid's and Zoë's—named for former prime minister Sir Wilfrid Laurier and his wife, who were the first guests at the hotel—offer a sumptuous dining experience. This is a world-class hotel in every detail.

1 Rideau St., Ottawa, ON K1N 8S7. ℂ **800/441-1414** or 613/241-1414. Fax 613/562-7032. www.fairmont. com. 429 units. Low season C$219–C$289 double, C$469 suite; high season C$300–C$420 double, C$550 suite. Children 17 and under stay free in parent's room. AE, DC, DISC, MC, V. Valet parking C$29; self-parking C$23. Pets C$30 per night. **Amenities:** Restaurant; outdoor terrace; bar/tearoom; large indoor pool; exercise room; sauna; games room; concierge; business center; shopping arcade; 24-hr. room service; massage; babysitting; same-day laundry service and dry-cleaning; executive floor. *In room:* A/C, TV w/pay movies, dataport, minibar, coffeemaker, hair dryer, iron/ironing board, safe (in some).

The Westin Ottawa ★   A contemporary alternative to the Fairmont Château Laurier, the Westin Ottawa is attractively perched by the canal. All rooms feature floor-to-ceiling windows to provide the best possible views of the city, and canal views are available for a premium. As with any hotel in this price range, you can expect a full array of amenities, including 24-hour room service, in-room safes, and high-speed Internet access, and of course the Westin chain is renowned for the quality of its bedding and bath accessories. When you're ready for exercise, go for a challenging game of squash on one of the three international standard courts or take a dip in the indoor pool, which has an adjacent outdoor sun deck. The exercise facilities are contained in a branded "Westin Workout Powered by Reebok" gym, and the plate-glass windows offer great views. For those who live to shop, the third floor of the hotel provides direct access to the stores and services of the Rideau Centre. Indoor access is also available to the Congress Centre. While the Westin Ottawa was a bright addition to the city in the 1980s, it's in need of some refreshing, which is currently underway.

11 Colonel By Dr., Ottawa, ON K1N 9H4. ℂ **888/625-5144** or 613/560-7000. Fax 613/560-2707. www. starwoodhotels.com. 487 units. C$200–C$425 double; C$325–C$400 suite. Children 18 and under stay free in parent's room. AE, DC, DISC, MC, V. Valet parking C$25; self-parking C$14. Pets accepted. **Amenities:** Restaurant; 2 bars; indoor pool; health club; spa; hot tub; sauna; concierge; shopping arcade; 24-hr. room service; massage; same-day laundry service and dry-cleaning; executive floors. *In room:* A/C, TV w/ pay movies, dataport, minibar, coffeemaker, hair dryer, iron/ironing board, safe.

EXPENSIVE

Marriott Courtyard Ottawa   The only hotel situated in the heart of the ByWard Market, the Marriott Courtyard Ottawa has something of an old motor hotel air to it—largely due to its cramped grounds and small lobby—but the rooms and amenities will suit anyone who wants to be in the center of the action without the hefty prices of the closest competition. The rooms offer 32-inch flatscreens, free Wi-Fi, and complimentary coffee and tea, and while the furnishings won't win any design awards, they are comfortable and modern. The restaurant doesn't try to compete with the multitude of dining choices surrounding it for dinner, but it features a first-rate buffet breakfast for C$15 that includes an omelet station. The indoor pool is small, but opens onto—no surprise—a courtyard, which creates more of a spalike feeling during warm months. A fitness center is currently being relocated to integrate into the pool area.

350 Dalhousie St., Ottawa, ON K1N 7E9. ℂ **800/341-2210** or 613/241-1000. Fax 613/241-4804. www. marriottcourtyardottawa.com. 183 units. C$169–C$209 double; C$229 executive suite. AE, DC, DISC, MC, V. Self-parking C$16. No pets. **Amenities:** Buffet breakfast restaurant; bar; indoor pool; gym; same-day dry-cleaning. *In room:* A/C, LCD TV w/pay movies, Wi-Fi, coffeemaker, hair dryer, iron/ironing board.

Novotel Ottawa   Tucked away between the Rideau Centre and Sandy Hill, just a short walk from the ByWard Market, this is an attractive, contemporary styled property. Public areas and many of the rooms are decorated in Mediterranean hues of blue, orange, and yellow. The result is striking and sunny. The styling of the guest rooms is very European contemporary, with light wood, glass-topped tables, and chrome accents. Two floors have been refitted as business class; the decor here is neutral earth tones. Upgraded amenities include duvets, in-room safes, and 32-inch, wall-mounted LCD televisions. Guests can choose from a variety of pillow types, and the windows open. The staff is cheerful and attentive.

33 Nicholas St., Ottawa, ON K1N 9M7. ℂ **800/668-6835** or 613/230-3033. Fax 613/760-4766. www. novotelottawa.com. 281 units. C$149–C$169 double; C$179–C$209 junior suite. Children under 16 stay free in parent's room. AE, DC, DISC, MC, V. Parking C$14. Pets accepted. **Amenities:** Restaurant; cafe; bar; indoor pool; health club; hot tub; sauna; business services; limited room service; massage; babysitting; same-day laundry service and dry-cleaning; executive floors. *In room:* A/C, TV w/pay movies, MP3 player, dataport, minibar, coffeemaker, hair dryer, iron/ironing board.

MODERATE

Les Suites Hotel Ottawa ★ (Value   An all-suite property, Les Suites was originally built as a condominium complex in 1989. As a result, the one- and two-bedroom suites are spacious and well equipped, with a full kitchen and washer/dryer in each. Elevators are situated away from the rooms, and bedrooms are located at the back of the suites, away from potential hallway noise. For an even quieter environment, ask for a suite overlooking the garden courtyard. The 24-hour health club and indoor pool on the fifth floor have a panoramic city view and are shared with guests of Novotel Ottawa. The Rideau Centre and the ByWard Market area are on the hotel's doorstep. Many rooms have private balconies, and the windows can be opened.

130 Besserer St., Ottawa, ON K1N 9M9. ℂ **800/267-1989** or 613/232-2000. Fax 613/232-1242. www. les-suites.com. 242 units. C$149–C$179 1-bedroom suite; C$185–C$229 2-bedroom suite. Children under 18 stay free in parent's room. AE, DC, DISC, MC, V. Parking C$16. Pets accepted. **Amenities:** Restaurant; indoor pool; 24-hr. health club; hot tub; sauna; concierge; business services; shopping arcade; limited room service; massage; babysitting; same-day dry-cleaning; washers and dryers; executive suites. *In room:* A/C, TV w/pay movies, Wi-Fi, kitchen, coffeemaker, hair dryer, iron/ironing board.

INEXPENSIVE

Auberge "The King Edward" B&B   Conveniently situated close to the Rideau Canal and within walking distance of the ByWard Market, the Rideau Centre, and many downtown attractions, the King Edward is a distinguished Victorian home. The front parlor has been turned into a peaceful oasis of tropical plants, accented by a trickling fountain. A second sitting room offers comfortable chairs and sofas, suitable for reading or listening to music. Throughout the home you'll find many period details, including fireplaces, plaster moldings, pillars, and stained-glass windows. The elegant bedrooms, with Edwardian-era furnishings, are generously proportioned. One room is large enough to accommodate a cot, and two other rooms have private balconies. At Christmas, a 3.6m-high (12-ft.) tree trimmed with Victorian decorations is a sight to behold, and the owner also displays his extensive collection of Christmas village pieces on the main floor of the property. Children are welcome at the discretion of the owner.

525 King Edward Ave., Ottawa, ON K1N 7N3. ℂ **800/841-8786** or 613/565-6700. www.bbcanada.com/ kingedward. 3 units. C$90–C$120 double. Rates include breakfast. MC, V. Free parking. *In room:* A/C, TV, no phone.

Ottawa International Hostel (Moments (Kids   Before becoming a hostel, this building was the Carleton County Gaol (1862–1972). Guided tours of the former prison are available through Haunted Walks Inc. (see chapter 7, "Exploring Ottawa," p. 144). Your bed for the night is a bunk in a jail cell or one of the dorms. Enjoy a quiet night's sleep behind bars—if the ghost of the last prisoner to be publicly hanged in Canada doesn't disturb you. If you are a Hostelling International member, you'll receive a discounted room rate. The cozy TV lounge has leather couches and a big-screen TV. The communal kitchen recently received new appliances, tables, and chairs. Lockers for storing food are available for guests. The dining room is housed in the former prison chapel, and in the summer guests may use the barbecue in the garden. Washroom facilities, with washbasins, toilets, and showers, are unisex (except in single-sex dorm areas). Families may opt for a private room with bunk beds, which accommodates up to five people, but most likely your kids will want to sleep in the jail cells. Although the space is cramped and the beds are narrow, the experience will be authentic.

75 Nicholas St., Ottawa, ON K1N 7B9. ℂ **866/299-1478** or 613/235-2595. Fax 613/235-9202. www.hi hostels.ca. 154 units. Dormitory C$28 Hostel Association members, C$33 nonmembers; private room

(max. 5 people) C$71 members, C$81 nonmembers. Children 9 and under free. AE, MC, V. Parking C$5. **Amenities:** Games room; washers and dryers. *In room:* Tabletop fan, no phone.

University of Ottawa Student Residence (**Value**) Although availability is limited to May through August, this is prime tourist time, so for many visitors staying here will work out just fine. Rooms are available in a variety of student residences, but the one I recommend is the building at 90 rue Université, a recently built, all-suite residence. Each unit has two bedrooms with double beds, a kitchenette with fridge, microwave, sink, and storage, and an en suite bathroom. The location is perfect for visiting downtown attractions.

90 rue Université, Ottawa, ON K1N 1H3. (**C**) 613/564-5400. Fax 613/654-6530. www.uottawa.ca. 1,200 units. C$16–C$60 double with shared bathroom; C$99 2-bedroom suite (4 people max.). MC, V. Parking C$10. **Amenities:** Pool (for a fee); exercise room (for a fee); games room; washers and dryers. *In room:* A/C, TV, dataport, kitchenette.

3 SANDY HILL

Just southeast of the main downtown core, Sandy Hill offers several options if you prefer the atmosphere of a small inn or B&B, and staying in the area will give you a real taste of what Ottawa looked like a century ago.

MODERATE

Auberge McGee's Inn ★ (**Finds**)
Nestled on a quiet tree-lined avenue, the inn was built in 1886 as a residence for influential politician John J. McGee, and the current owners have furnished the inn with some nice touches, including a 1901 player piano and an antique telephone collection. The guest rooms are individually decorated and amenities vary. Some rooms have fireplaces; others have private balconies. There are two suites designed for romantic couples: the Egyptian Room and the Victorian Roses Suite, both with fireplaces and double Jacuzzis. The Windsor Room was renovated in 2008 to include a double Jacuzzi, and a steam shower body spa that includes a TV and hands-free phone. The second floor has a laundry room, ironing board and iron, and kitchenette with small stove and microwave for guest use. Wireless high-speed Internet is complimentary. In-room coffeemaker supplied on request. The entire inn is nonsmoking. Special packages are often available; check the website or call for details.

185 Daly Ave., Ottawa, ON K1N 6E8. (**C**) 800/262-4337 or 613/237-6089. Fax 613/237-6201. www.mcgeesinn.com. 14 units. C$118–C$184 double; C$198 romantic suite. Rates include breakfast. Children under 12 stay free in parent's room. AE, MC, V. Free parking. **Amenities:** Business services. *In room:* A/C, TV, Wi-Fi, fridge, hair dryer.

Bella Notte B&B
The hosts of this B&B, located in the historical residential Sandy Hill district just east of the Rideau Canal, are charming and welcoming. The Victorian property, built in 1868, was originally the home of Sir Alexander Campbell, one of Canada's Fathers of Confederation. Amenities are basic, but the hospitality of the owners and the care and attention given to the preparation and presentation of breakfast are worth experiencing. Bella Notte is well situated for reaching downtown on foot.

108 Daly Ave., Ottawa, ON K1N 6E7. (**C**) 613/565-0497. www.bellanottebb.com. 3 units. C$128–C$148 double. Rates include breakfast. Limited street parking. *In room:* No phone.

Gasthaus Switzerland Inn
A restored heritage property constructed of limestone in 1872 and expanded in 2006, this family owned and operated inn features Swiss-style

beds with cozy duvets and Swiss buffet breakfasts. Each room is individually decorated and amenities vary. The two specialty suites are popular with couples. Each suite has a poster canopy bed, double Jacuzzi, fireplace, CD stereo player, and en suite bathroom. Efforts have been made to reduce allergens—windows can be opened, hardwood flooring has been used where possible, and nonallergenic duvets can be arranged if requested when making your reservation. The entire building is nonsmoking. The property is best suited for adults and children over age 12.

89 Daly Ave., Ottawa, ON K1N 6E6. (*C*) **888/663-0000** or 613/237-0335. Fax 613/594-3327. www.ottawa inn.com. 22 units. C$118–C$168 large double; C$178–C$268 suite. Rates include breakfast. AE, DC, MC, V. Limited free parking. **Amenities:** Business services; same-day laundry service and dry-cleaning; meeting room. *In room:* A/C, TV, Wi-Fi, dataport, coffeemaker, hair dryer.

INEXPENSIVE

Benner's Bed & Breakfast   A comfortable stroll from the ByWard Market, University of Ottawa, and downtown shopping, Benner's B&B is an elegant Edwardian brownstone house in the historical residential district of Sandy Hill. Guest rooms have been decorated with simple, clean lines and restful colors. This property is best suited to adults; well-behaved children 9 years and older are welcome. Next door, a second B&B operated by the owners' daughter features contemporary decor and a spacious loft suite.

541 Besserer St., Ottawa, ON K1N 6P6. (*C*) **877-891-5485** or 613/789-8320. Fax 613/789-9563. www. bennersbedandbreakfast.com. 3 units. C$95–C$130 double. Rates include breakfast. MC, V. Free parking. *In room:* A/C, TV, no phone (in some).

4 THE GLEBE

The Glebe is a trendy, upper-middle-class family neighborhood lined with early 20th-century redbrick homes and a number of larger, elegant houses. Although the district's main street, Bank Street, has wonderful restaurants and shops, hotels and motels are scarce. But some of the nicest B&Bs are to be found here, and many people prefer to be on a quiet back street than in the high-rises of downtown.

MODERATE

A Rose On Colonel By B&B ★ (Finds)   This cozy Edwardian-style home, built in 1925, is just steps from the Rideau Canal on a quiet residential street. Before becoming a B&B, the property was leased for many years by the American and French embassies as a diplomatic residence. The atmosphere is warm and friendly. The breakfast room is decorated with a collection of blue glass, strikingly displayed along the windowsills to catch the sunlight. The two bathrooms are shared among three guest rooms, and bathrobes have been thoughtfully supplied. A comfy lounge on the second floor is equipped with a fridge, microwave, coffeemaker, and phone. A short walk away is Brewer Park, bordered on its southern edge by the scenic Rideau River. Children are very welcome; the owner of the B&B will even supply you and your children with crusts of bread to feed the ducks and swans on Brewer Pond.

9 Rosedale Ave., Ottawa, ON K1S 4T2. (*C*) **613/291-7831.** www.rosebandb.com. 3 units. C$124 double. Rate includes breakfast. AE, MC, V. Free parking. **Amenities:** Washer and dryer. *In room:* Ceiling fan, dataport, no phone.

INEXPENSIVE

Carleton University Tour and Conference Centre   The student residences at Carleton are available between early May and late August. There are about 2,000 beds available in several residence buildings. Most bedrooms are either single or double (two single beds) occupancy with shared bathrooms, and it's recommended that you bring sandals to wear in the shower areas. The newer buildings offer two- and four-bedroom suites, all with double beds and one or two bathrooms per suite; each suite also has a fridge and sink; some units have microwaves. Rates include an all-you-can-eat breakfast in the large cafeteria. Athletic and recreational facilities on campus, available for an additional charge, include an indoor pool, squash and tennis courts, a fitness center with sauna and whirlpool, and a games room and video arcade. You can walk, bike, or in-line skate all the way downtown on canal-side pathways. At nearby Dow's Lake you can rent canoes, kayaks, and bicycles.

1125 Colonel By Dr., Ottawa ON K1S 5B6. *(C)* **613/520-5611.** www.carleton.ca/housing/tourandconf. 2,000 units. C$28–C$70 per person in dorm-style room; C$70–C$90 per person in newer suite bldg. Rates include breakfast. MC, V. Parking C$8 per day Mon–Fri; free Sat–Sun. **Amenities:** Cafeteria; fast-food outlet; food court; indoor pool; health club; tennis courts; hot tub; sauna; games room; video arcade; washers and dryers. *In room:* A/C (in most).

---

5 NEAR THE TRAIN STATION

If you plan to concentrate your visit on east-end attractions like the Canadian Science & Technology Museum and the Canada Aviation Museum, or you just like to avoid the congestion of downtown, the area surrounding Ottawa's train station offers one solid option.

EXPENSIVE

Hampton Inn   This hotel, built in 2000, has larger than average guest rooms with high-quality furnishings and oversize bathrooms. Each room is equipped with a kitchenette that includes a microwave, sink, and small fridge (dishes and utensils are supplied on request). The indoor pool area is spotless and spacious. A complimentary continental breakfast is served in the lobby lounge.

100 Coventry Rd., Ottawa, ON K1K 4S3. *(C)* **877/701-1281** or 613/741-2300. Fax 613/741-8689. www. hamptoninnottawa.com. 179 units. C$160 studio. Rate includes breakfast. Children 17 and under stay free in parent's room. AE, DC, DISC, MC, V. Free parking. **Amenities:** Breakfast room/lounge; indoor pool; exercise room; hot tub; business services; babysitting; same-day laundry services and dry-cleaning; washers and dryers. *In room:* A/C, TV, dataport, kitchenette, coffeemaker, hair dryer, iron/ironing board.

MODERATE

WelcomINNS Ottawa   Newly renovated, this hotel is popular with both business groups and travelers who want to avoid the hassle of downtown traffic. The facility offers three floors of standard rooms, with a higher than average number of double rooms—popular with group bookings and senior couples—and several king rooms with Jacuzzis and upgraded furnishings. Wi-Fi is available on the lower floors. The lobby is large and comfortable, featuring a fireplace and a business center, and there is an exercise room and conference area.

1220 Michael St., Ottawa, ON K1J 7T1. *(C)* **800/387-4381** or 613/748-7800. Fax 613/748-0499. www. welcominns.com. 109 units. C$99–C$150 double. Rates include breakfast. AE, DC, DISC, MC, V. Free parking.

Amenities: Exercise room; business center; dry-cleaning; washers and dryers. *In room:* A/C, TV w/pay movies, PlayStation, DVD player, dataport, fridge, coffeemaker, iron/ironing board.

6 OTTAWA WEST

If your Ottawa plans include a rock concert or a Senators hockey game at Scotiabank Place, you're in town on high-tech business, or you just want to stay apart from the traffic and noise of downtown, the west end of the city offers several options for accommodations, including one of Eastern Ontario's most modern hotels, Brookstreet.

EXPENSIVE

Brookstreet ★★★   Built with high-tech money to service the adjacent high-tech community, Brookstreet exudes contemporary luxury at every turn. Signature guest-room colors are raspberry and gray, and a minimalist approach gives a boutique-hotel feel to rooms and suites. Although surrounded by low-rise office buildings, Brookstreet nestles on the edge of green space, overlooking the award-winning Marshes Golf Club, as well as cycling and walking paths and cross-country ski trails. With a full spa on-site, indoor and outdoor swimming pools, children's wading pool, skating rink, putting green, and 9-hole, par 3 MarchWood golf course in addition to the 18-hole championship course, you will never wonder what to do with your time. The dining facilities are top class; Brookstreet's restaurant, Perspectives, has been awarded accolades for its cuisine, and features Food & Wine Raves on the first Friday of each month, allowing guests to participate in preparing and discussing the meal and wine selections. Options bar has live music on Thursday, Friday, and Saturday. Check the website for packages, ranging from romantic getaways to golf and spa weekends.

525 Legget Dr., Ottawa ON K2K 2W2. ✆ **888/826-2220** or 613/271-1800. Fax 613/271-1850. www.brook street.ca. 276 units. C$189–C$219 double; C$250 junior suite; C$299–C$499 master suite. Children 17 and under stay free in parent's room. AE, DC, DISC, MC, V. Free parking above ground; C$10 underground. Pets C$25 per night. **Amenities:** Restaurant; bar/lounge; championship 18-hole golf course; 9-hole golf course; putting green; health club; spa; Jacuzzi; steam room; concierge; car-rental desk; courtesy car; business center; shopping arcade; 24-hr. room service; massage; same-day laundry service and dry-cleaning. *In room:* A/C, TV w/pay movies, dataport, kitchenette (in some), minibar, coffeemaker, hair dryer, iron/ironing board, safe.

MODERATE

Best Western Barons Hotel   Although the location is a little way from downtown, the family-friendly nature of this hotel makes it a worthwhile option. Its proximity to the Queensway means you can drive in to the city in 15 minutes. A large regional shopping mall, Bayshore, is 5 minutes away (great if you have teenagers in tow), and Scotiabank Place is only a 10-minute drive west. Families will enjoy the clean, bright indoor pool. In the summer, a patio and grassy courtyard out back are popular with guests, who are welcome to use the two barbecues or enjoy a picnic under the trees. Rooms are larger than average, and 30 rooms in the back wing have received new granite-lined showers and countertops. Families will find the one-bedroom suites convenient, since they include a sink, microwave, and small fridge (utensils are available on request). High-speed wireless Internet access is complimentary.

3700 Richmond Rd., Ottawa ON K2H 5B8. ✆ **866/214-1239** or 613/828-2741. Fax 613/596-4742. www. bestwestern.com/ca/baronshotel. 83 units. C$115–C$135 double; C$180–C$275 suite. Children 17 and under stay free in parent's room. AE, DC, DISC, MC, V. Free parking. Pets C$10 per night; must be caged if left alone in room. **Amenities:** Restaurant; indoor pool; exercise room; hot tub; sauna; business services; limited room service; same-day laundry service and dry-cleaning; washers and dryers. *In room:* A/C, TV w/pay movies, dataport, kitchenette (in some), coffeemaker, hair dryer, iron/ironing board.

Travelodge Hotel Ottawa West (Kids)   This hotel is a huge magnet for families and traveling sports teams due to its indoor water park, featuring a wave pool, slide, whirlpool, and children's wading pool. Popular packages include pool-view rooms with balcony, complimentary continental breakfast, pizza coupon, and access to the water park. A leafy courtyard with a tranquil garden provides a haven from the mayhem; surrounding this quieter section of the hotel are the business-grade and longer-stay rooms.

1376 Carling Ave., Ottawa, ON K1Z 7L5. (C) **800/267-4166** or 613/722-7600. Fax 613/722-2226. www. travelodgeottawa.com. 196 units. C$109–C$190 double. Children under 18 stay free in parent's room. AE, DISC, MC, V. Free parking. Small pets C$50 flat fee may apply. **Amenities:** Restaurant; lounge; indoor water park; exercise room; games room; business center; limited room service; babysitting; same-day laundry service and dry-cleaning; executive floor. *In room:* A/C, TV w/pay movies, dataport, fridge, coffeemaker, hair dryer, iron/ironing board.

---

7 NEAR THE AIRPORT

None of these are actually located on the airport's property, but all are within a 5- or 10-minute drive.

EXPENSIVE

Hilton Garden Inn Ottawa Airport   One of two new airport-area hotels opened in 2008, Ottawa's first Hilton Garden Inn specializes in convenience, with a 24-hour convenience store and complimentary exercise room. The guest rooms are outfitted with a number of amenities that are standard at pricier properties, such as ergonomic desk chairs and large work surfaces, HDTV, a choice of pillow type, and upgraded shower facilities. Oddly, for a hotel that caters to air travelers, check-in isn't until 4pm.

2400 Alert Rd., Ottawa, ON K1V 1S1. (C) **613/288-9001.** Fax 613/249-8729. www.hiltongardeninn.com. 167 units. C$179–C$209 double. AE, DISC, MC, V. Valet parking C$10; self-parking C$6. **Amenities:** Restaurant; bar; indoor pool; whirlpool; exercise room; business center; evening room service. *In room:* A/C, HDTV w/pay movies, Wi-Fi, dataport, minibar, microwave, coffeemaker, hair dryer, iron/ironing board.

Holiday Inn Express Hotel & Suites   The second new hotel to open near Ottawa's Macdonald-Cartier International Airport, is a relatively no-frills facility with a few upgraded options. While the standard room is fairly bare bones, a limited number of executive-level king suites come equipped with a fireplace and whirlpool tub. All guest rooms feature 32-inch flatscreen TVs, microwaves, and refrigerators.

2881 Gibford Dr., Ottawa, ON K1V 2L9. (C) **877/660-8550** or 613/738-0284. Fax 613/491-0120. 91 units. C$136–C$170 double; C$250 suite. AE, DC, MC, V. Free parking. **Amenities:** Restaurant; business center; executive rooms. *In room:* A/C, flatscreen TV, dataport, microwave, fridge, hair dryer, iron/ironing board.

MODERATE

The Southway Inn   If you're seeking accommodations far from the high-rise hub, this property in the south end of the city will suit. Nearby there are chain restaurants and services, including a bank and drugstore, and if you avoid traveling during rush hour it's only a 15-minute drive from the action of downtown Ottawa. The airport is only 5 to 10 minutes away by car. The indoor pool is bright and pleasant. Recent expansion included the introduction of 15 new suites with full kitchens. High-speed Internet access is available in all guest rooms.

2431 Bank St. S., Ottawa, ON K1V 8R9. ☎ **877/688-4929** or 613/737-0811. Fax 613/737-3207. www.southway. com. 170 units. C$138–C$195 double; C$265 suite. AE, DC, DISC, MC, V. Free parking. Pets C$20 per night. **Amenities:** Restaurant/bar; indoor pool; exercise room; hot tub; sauna; business services; limited room service; same-day laundry service and dry-cleaning; washers and dryers; executive rooms. *In room:* A/C, TV, dataport, kitchen (in suites), fridge, coffeemaker, hair dryer, iron/ironing board, safe (in some).

INEXPENSIVE

Adam's Airport Inn (Value)   A 7-minute drive from the airport, this hotel is a good bet for a night's rest at either end of your vacation if you're traveling by air, especially if you have a late arrival or early-morning start. The rates are spot-on for what's on offer, which is a clean and comfortable bed, friendly desk staff, and free parking. Just the basics, nicely delivered. Although the building is set back a little way from busy Bank Street, ask for a room at the back overlooking the quiet residential neighborhood. A complimentary continental breakfast and 24-hour coffee are available in the lobby.

2721 Bank St., Ottawa, ON K1T 1M8. ☎ **800/261-5835** or 613/738-3838. Fax 613/736-8211. www.adams airportinn.com. 62 units. C$94 double; C$135 suite. Rates include complimentary continental breakfast and coffee 24 hr. AE, DC, MC, V. Free parking. Pets C$20 per night. **Amenities:** Exercise room; washers and dryers. *In room:* A/C, TV, dataport, fridge, hair dryer.

---

8 GATINEAU

If the casino, the Canadian Museum of Civilization, or the ski hills are your primary destination, you might want to consider staying on the Quebec side of the Ottawa River.

VERY EXPENSIVE

Hilton Lac-Leamy ★★★   To say that the Hilton Lac-Leamy is the closest the Ottawa area comes to Las Vegas is to refer to more than its close proximity to a luxury casino; it's really a case of doing so much more than any other area hotel, and doing it all well. There is a sense of whimsy about this place—which begins with the spectacular blown-glass sculptures that hang in the lobby—that makes it easy to forgive how over the top the place can seem when stacked up against any of its competitors. Little wonder, then, that Celine Dion and her husband once took the his-and-hers luxury suites on the top floor; I'm sure she felt that she'd never left the Nevada desert. Of course, not every guest room in the hotel has a grand piano and full-service butler's pantry, but the spectacular views of Lac Leamy and Lac de la Carrière are shared throughout. The 349 rooms are all larger than standard and every bathroom features extensive marble and woodwork, huge soaker tubs, large glass shower enclosures, and an array of bath products. The 24-hour gym and spa facilities are substantial, and a three-floor executive area—which houses 35 large guest rooms, 6 suites, and the aforementioned "presidential" apartments—has a private lounge where a buffet breakfast is served. In addition, there is the Arôme Seafood and Grill restaurant, which has a terrific 100-seat heated patio, the Bacchus bar and cigar lounge, and a poolside cocktail terrace. Beyond the sense of effortlessness the staff exudes and the plethora of first-class amenities, what makes Hilton Lac-Leamy so different is its setting: on one side the wilderness of the Gatineau Hills, on the other the capital city—somehow it manages to sum up Canadian history perfectly.

Family-Friendly Accommodations

Whether it's to see the national museums and Parliament Hill, skate on the canal, play in a hockey tournament, or catch a Senators game, families flock to Ottawa year-round, and the city's hoteliers have responded. Consequently, you'll find more family-oriented hotels and other types of accommodations than any place this side of Orlando.

Albert at Bay Suite Hotel (p. 74)   A free children's program during the summer months and March break keeps kids 3 to 12 occupied, giving them a chance to run off some steam, and you a chance to enjoy your own vacation. Great proximity to Parliament Hill, the Canadian War Museum, and the Canadian Museum of Civilization.

Cartier Place Suite Hotel (p. 77)   If your kids are feeling cramped from sitting in the car all day, or listless after too much museum walking, turn them loose on the play structure and climbing gym. There's also a terrific indoor pool that opens to the outdoors in the summer months.

Delta Ottawa Hotel and Suites (p. 71)   Let's see—is it the two-story waterslide, the children's center, the close proximity to everything, or just the kid-friendly attitude that Delta staff exudes? Whatever it is, it keeps families coming back year after year to this hive of activity.

Holiday Inn Hotel & Suites Ottawa (p. 77)   If you're traveling with very young children, this out-of-the-way suite hotel will please with its small children's play area with a SpongeBob SquarePants theme.

Ottawa International Hostel (p. 82)   For an adventure they won't soon forget, spend one night in the cells of the former county jailhouse (don't worry, the locks don't work). A working jail as recently as 1972, and the site of Canada's last public hanging, the hostel is surprisingly well-appointed, but there are enough remnants around to remind you of the building's former purpose. Don't be surprised if you encounter the ghost of Patrick Whelan—who's said to haunt the halls seeking to avenge his wrongful hanging for Canada's only political assassination.

Ottawa Marriott (p. 71)   Whether your kids are teens or younger, there's something here that will keep them occupied. Teens especially will enjoy the games room, minigolf, and half-court basketball area. For younger ones, there's also the novelty of Ottawa's only revolving restaurant—still a favorite memory from my childhood.

Travelodge Hotel Ottawa West (p. 87)   One of Ottawa's older west-end hotel properties, the Travelodge has been spruced up to cater to kids on the road with a wave pool, water slide, and wading pool. Why would they ever want to leave?

3 boulevard du Casino, Gatineau, QC J8Y 6X4. ✆ **866/488-7888** or 819/790-6444. Fax 819/790-6408. www.hiltonlacleamy.com. 349 units. C$260–C$330 double; C$370–C$5,000 suite. Children 18 and under stay free in parent's room. AE, DC, DISC, MC, V. Valet parking C$15; self-parking free. **Amenities:** Restaurant; bar; indoor and outdoor pools; tennis courts; health club; spa; Jacuzzi; sauna; bike/in-line skate rental nearby; children's center; theater; concierge; business center; 24-hr. room service; babysitting; same-day laundry service and dry-cleaning; executive floors. *In room*: A/C, flatscreen LCD TV w/pay movies, CD player, MP3 player, dataport, minibar, coffeemaker, hair dryer, iron/ironing board, safe.

EXPENSIVE

Château Cartier Resort ★★   A luxuriously comfortable resort set amid 62 hectares (153 acres) of rolling countryside on the north shore of the Ottawa River, just a 10-minute drive from downtown Ottawa. The majority of the guest rooms are junior suites, with a comfortable sitting room and separate bedroom with French doors. A number of guest rooms have been recently upgraded as part of a "boutique" offering, and feature hardwood floors and two wall-hung 42-inch LCD TVs. Leisure and recreational facilities are outstanding. There's an 18-hole golf course on the property, with teaching professionals on hand. Two outdoor tennis courts, indoor racquetball and squash courts, a fitness center with top-quality equipment, and a full-service spa are just some of the facilities available for guests. In the winter, there's a skating rink, tobogganing, tubing, cross-country skiing, snowshoeing, and horse-drawn sleigh rides. Downhill skiing is nearby and seasonal packages range from golf getaways to ski weekends. Public areas and guest rooms are extremely well-appointed and furnished.

1170 chemin Aylmer, Gatineau, QC J9H 5E1. ✆ **800/807-1088** or 819/777-1088. Fax 819/777-7161. www.chateaucartier.com. 129 units. C$230 double; C$260 suite; C$400 boutique suite. Children under 18 stay free in parent's room. AE, DC, DISC, MC, V. Free parking. **Amenities:** Restaurant/lounge; indoor pool; golf course; 2 tennis courts; health club; spa; Jacuzzi; sauna; bike rental; sports equipment rental; seasonal children's programs; business center; limited room service; massage; babysitting; same-day laundry service and dry-cleaning; executive suites. *In room*: A/C, TV w/pay movies, dataport, fridge, coffeemaker, hair dryer, iron/ironing board.

Holiday Inn Plaza la Chaudière   A convenient and pretty location opposite a city park where the Théâtre de l'Île performs in the summer. A couple of minutes' stroll will link you up with bike and walking pathways along the Ottawa River, and you're only a short drive or bike ride away from the entrance to Gatineau Park. Guest rooms offer nothing exceptional, but the place is bright and offers a convenient option if you're focusing your time on the Quebec side of the Ottawa River.

2 rue Montcalm, Gatineau, QC J8X 4B4. ✆ **800/567-1962** in Canada or 819/778-3880. Fax 819/778-3309. www.rosdevhotels.com. 232 units. C$120–C$160 double; C$242 1-bedroom suite. Children under 17 stay free in parent's room. AE, DC, DISC, MC, V. Parking C$11. Pets accepted. **Amenities:** Restaurant; lounge; indoor pool; exercise room; Jacuzzi; sauna; bike/in-line skate rental; games room; business center; hair salon next door; limited room service; babysitting; same-day dry-cleaning; executive floors. *In room*: A/C, TV w/pay movies, dataport, minibar, coffeemaker, hair dryer, iron/ironing board, safe.

Dining

In recent years, Ottawa's restaurant scene has been characterized—and greatly enlivened—by the arrival of a number of very good, young chefs. Following the example of local mainstays Richard Nigro (of Juniper Kitchen & Wine Bar) and John Taylor (of John Taylor at Domus) these young chefs have embraced the local produce movement, pushing Ottawa into the forefront of this trend.

Following the influx of high-tech workers in the late '90s, there was an increased demand for interesting restaurants and more money to invest in them.

Ottawans—and visitors—have been the beneficiaries of these two occurrences.

All this activity on the local restaurant scene reached some sort of critical mass in 2008, when suddenly half a dozen of the city's most interesting chefs were on the move, starting new restaurants or spicing up the menus and food presentation at existing places.

In addition to pushing local produce and meats (with its close proximity to farmland, Ottawa is ideally suited for this), a number of these young chefs have designed their menus to cater to contemporary tastes, with smaller plates that lend themselves to trying more dishes and flavor, and custom pairings with wine. Tasting menus—a great chance to sample a wide variety of a chef's offerings at a reasonable price—are popular at a number of the leading spots.

The following are by no means the only places to enjoy good food in the Ottawa area, but these listings will give you a sampling of the broad range of excellent cuisine that awaits you here.

DINING NOTES Though a few restaurants are edging toward the C$50 plateau for their highest-priced mains, dining out in Ottawa does not have to be an expensive venture; however, be aware that taxes are high. Meals are subject to 8% provincial sales tax and 5% GST, so when you factor in an average tip, a whopping 30% is added to the bill. Wine prices in restaurants are quite high—don't be surprised to find your favorite vintage at double the price you'd pay at the liquor store. Note that a 10% liquor tax is added to alcoholic beverage purchases.

All restaurants in Ottawa are entirely nonsmoking.

NOTES ON THE REVIEWS Restaurants are grouped by neighborhood and listed alphabetically according to the following top prices for main courses (not counting tax and tip): very expensive, above C$40; expensive, C$30 to C$40; moderate, C$10 to C$30; inexpensive, under C$10.

1 RESTAURANTS BY CUISINE

Aboriginal
Sweetgrass ★★★ (downtown east of the canal, $$$, p. 101).

Asian
Four Cuisine Bistro (Corso Italia, $$, p. 111).

Key to Abbreviations: $$$$ = Very Expensive $$$ = Expensive $$ = Moderate $ = Inexpensive

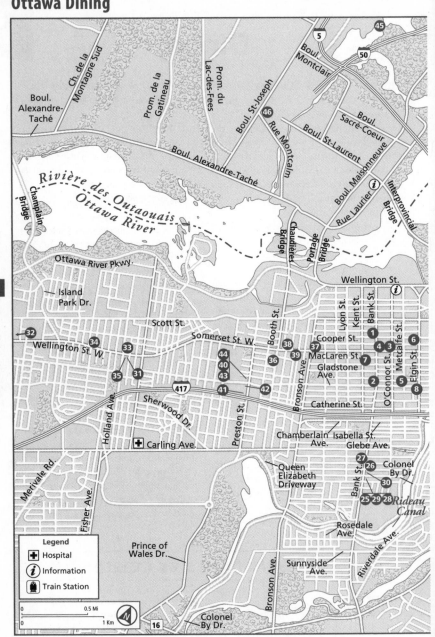

DINING

6

RESTAURANTS BY CUISINE

Legend
+ Hospital
(i) Information
🚆 Train Station

0   0.5 Mi
0   1 Km

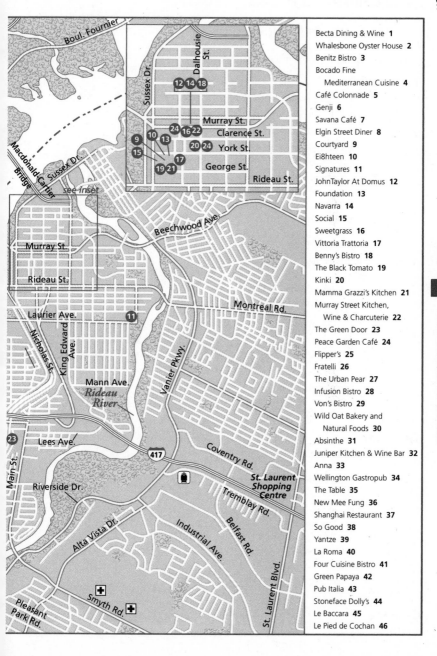

Becta Dining & Wine **1**
Whalesbone Oyster House **2**
Benitz Bistro **3**
Bocado Fine
  Mediterranean Cuisine **4**
Café Colonnade **5**
Genji **6**
Savana Café **7**
Elgin Street Diner **8**
Courtyard **9**
Ei8hteen **10**
Signatures **11**
JohnTaylor At Domus **12**
Foundation **13**
Navarra **14**
Social **15**
Sweetgrass **16**
Vittoria Trattoria **17**
Benny's Bistro **18**
The Black Tomato **19**
Kinki **20**
Mamma Grazzi's Kitchen **21**
Murray Street Kitchen,
  Wine & Charcuterie **22**
The Green Door **23**
Peace Garden Café **24**
Flipper's **25**
Fratelli **26**
The Urban Pear **27**
Infusion Bistro **28**
Von's Bistro **29**
Wild Oat Bakery and
  Natural Foods **30**
Absinthe **31**
Juniper Kitchen & Wine Bar **32**
Anna **33**
Wellington Gastropub **34**
The Table **35**
New Mee Fung **36**
Shanghai Restaurant **37**
So Good **38**
Yantze **39**
La Roma **40**
Four Cuisine Bistro **41**
Green Papaya **42**
Pub Italia **43**
Stoneface Dolly's **44**
Le Baccara **45**
Le Pied de Cochan **46**

Kinki ★ (downtown east of the canal, $$, p. 103).

Shanghai Restaurant ★ (Chinatown, $$, p. 109).

So Good (Chinatown, $$, p. 110).

Bakery

Wild Oat Bakery and Natural Foods (the Glebe, $, p. 107).

Bistro

Absinthe ★★ (Wellington St. West/Westboro, $$$, p. 107).

Benitz Bistro ★ (downtown west of the canal, $$, p. 96).

Benny's Bistro ★★ (downtown east of the canal, $$, p. 102).

The Black Tomato ★ (downtown east of the canal, $$, p. 103).

E18hteen ★ (downtown east of the canal, $$$$, p. 99).

Murray Street Kitchen, Wine & Charcuterie ★★ (downtown east of the canal, $$, p. 104).

Social ★ (downtown east of the canal, $$$, p. 101).

Stoneface Dolly's (Corso Italia, $$, p. 111).

Von's Bistro (the Glebe, $$, p. 107).

Wellington Gastropub ★★ (Wellington St. West/Westboro, $$, p. 108).

Canadian

Beckta Dining & Wine ★★★ (downtown west of the canal, $$$, p. 95).

Courtyard ★ (downtown east of the canal, $$$$, p. 99).

John Taylor at Domus ★★★ (downtown east of the canal, $$$, p. 100).

Juniper Kitchen & Wine Bar ★★ (Wellington St. West/Westboro, $$$, p. 108).

The Urban Pear ★★ (the Glebe, $$$, p. 105).

Chinese

Yangtze (Chinatown, $$, p. 110).

Diner

Elgin Street Diner (downtown west of the canal, $, p. 98).

French

Le Baccara ★★★ (Gatineau, $$$$, p. 112).

Le Pied de Cochon ★ (Gatineau, $$, p. 112).

Signatures ★★★ (downtown east of the canal, $$$$, p. 99).

Fusion

Foundation (downtown east of the canal, $$$, p. 100).

InFusion Bistro (the Glebe, $$, p. 107).

Savana Café (downtown west of the canal, $$, p. 98).

Italian

Fratelli (the Glebe, $$$, p. 105).

La Roma ★ (Corso Italia, $$$$, p. 110).

Mamma Grazzi's Kitchen ★ (downtown east of the canal, $$, p. 103).

Pub Italia (Corso Italia, $$, p. 111).

Vittoria Trattoria (downtown east of the canal, $$$, p. 102).

Japanese

Genji ★ (downtown west of the canal, $$, p. 97).

Mediterranean

Bocado Fine Mediterranean Cuisine (downtown west of the canal, $$, p. 96).

Pizza

Café Colonnade (downtown west of the canal, $$, p. 97).

Seafood

Flippers (the Glebe, $$, p. 105).

Whalesbone Oyster House ★ (downtown west of the canal, $$$, p. 96).

Spanish

Navarra ★★ (downtown east of the canal, $$$, p. 100).

Thai

Anna ★ (Wellington St. West/ Westboro, $$, p. 108).

Green Papaya (Corso Italia, $$, p. 111).

Vegetarian

The Green Door (downtown east of the canal, $, p. 104).

Peace Garden Café (downtown east of the canal, $, p. 104).

The Table (Wellington St. West/ Westboro, $, p. 109).

Vietnamese

New Mee Fung ★ (Chinatown, $$, p. 109).

---

2 DOWNTOWN (WEST OF THE CANAL)

Dominated by office buildings, this part of the city doesn't appear to hold much appeal for the hungry visitor, but you can find a number of interesting restaurants tucked in among the side streets and the high-rise buildings, as well as along busy Elgin Street. Office workers fill these eateries at lunchtime on weekdays, but if you arrive before noon you not only beat the crowd and get the best table, but you also get your order into the kitchen before the hungry hordes descend. Parking can be a challenge in the downtown core around noon on weekdays as vehicles circle around hunting for the perfect spot, so allow extra time. Public parking is free in this sector of downtown weekdays after 5:30pm, and on Saturday and Sunday.

EXPENSIVE

Beckta Dining & Wine ★★★ CANADIAN   No Ottawa restaurant has ever garnered as much press as Beckta has since opening in 2003 (much of which is posted in the front hall of its heritage house). Owner Stephen Beckta—who serves as the restaurant's sommelier—swept back into his hometown from New York City's Café Boulud as something of a savior to the capital's stale cuisine. So, is the hype deserved? We considered that question as we marveled at the tenderness and flavor of my wife's pan-roasted chicken breast, served with black truffles and lemon thyme on a cloud of chanterelle and corn risotto. The bird's skin alone was a thing of beauty—succulent and lightly crisped. My charred leg of lamb was perfectly cooked, and its full, rich flavor played against the maitake mushrooms and piquant jus. The organic string beans and small potatoes were exceptionally fresh. The waitstaff knowledgeably handled questions about Beckta's extensive and distinctive wine list. While Beckta has gone through several chefs since its debut, subsequent visits have shown no slippage in quality or imagination. Mark us down as believers: Beckta is a gem. For those who want to venture further than the mains, the restaurant offers a tasting menu, which can be paired with cheese- and wine-tasting selections, as well. On Sunday and Monday, diners may bring their own bottles of wine for a C$20 corkage fee. Stephen Beckta recently signed the lease on a heritage building on Sussex Drive for a second restaurant he's calling "play Food & Wine" that, beginning in 2009, will offer smaller plates to diners in the ByWard Market.

226 Nepean St. ℮ **613/238-7063.** www.beckta.com. Reservations recommended. Main courses C$27–C$38; tasting menus (5–6 courses) C$79–C$94; wine selection C$35. AE, DC, MC, V. Daily 5:30–9:45pm.

Whalesbone Oyster House ★ (Finds SEAFOOD   Don't let the funky neighborhood put you off; this tiny hole in the wall with the picnic table in the window serves up the city's most creative seafood dishes and the region's best selection of oysters. After opening in 2005, Whalesbone established itself with Ottawa's foody insiders, and while it has quickly gone through a number of personnel changes, the exceptionally well-sourced seafood remains at its heart. The service can be a bit quirky, but what seems to be inattention is merely a reflection of the place's laid-back atmosphere. With a plate of fresh bivalves (the featured selection varies by availability) and a Guinness in front of you, time takes on new meaning here. Whalesbone invites you to venture beyond the standard hot sauce additives for the oysters, offering up alternatives such as Scotch, or a house-specialty orange-infused seafood sauce. If mollusks leave you cold, and a little slimy perhaps, there are alternatives such as succulent shortribs, honey roasted and spiced up with a horseradish jus.

430 Bank St. ℂ **613/231-8569**. www.thewhalesbone.com. Reservations recommended. Main courses C$27–C$34. AE, MC, V. Sun–Wed 5–10pm; Thurs–Sat 5–11pm.

MODERATE

Benitz Bistro ★ BISTRO   Chef Derek Benitz is one of Ottawa's kitchen stars, and he was one of the first to step out with a place bearing his own name. The move worked so well that he expanded next door into a place called b/Side that specializes in "small plates," and it had just opened at press time. Located in a heritage house, the restaurant feels like it has one too many tables; there are some awkward seating arrangements, and the elevated area at the back of the room puts diners on display like a reinactment of the Last Supper. The service seemed a bit awkward, too; ill-timed for a place with such a strong food reputation. Despite those drawbacks, Benitz shows the solid-if-unspectacular kitchen skills that made his name. Pan-fried local perch had a nicely crisped exterior, and was well accented with fresh vegetables and fingerling potatoes. My squash bisque was a hearty preview of Benitz's fall menu. The chef's daily specials include a small tasting menu that provides a full range of his talents. Is Benitz Bistro a bit distracted by the boss's expansion? Perhaps. I'd give it another try; the food definitely warrants it.

327 Somerset St. W. ℂ **613/567-8100**. www.benitzbistro.com. Reservations recommended. Main courses C$21–C$28. AE, DC, MC, V. Mon–Fri 11:30am–2:30pm and 5:30–10pm; Sat 10am–3pm and 5:30–10pm; Sun 10am–3pm.

Bocado Fine Mediterranean Cuisine MEDITERRANEAN   Set in one of the elegant Victorian houses in historic Somerset Village, Bocado offers a variety of southern European and North African cuisines—ranging from seafood paella to Sicilian-style chicken breasts—as rendered by Polish chef and co-owner Tomasz Gurzynski. While redolent of the Old World, the restaurant has embraced the Western revival of small plates, and features 14 options on its "tapas" menu. While I didn't find much to distinguish my zucchini fritters from the fried zucchini at my local bar, the grilled sausage and fennel had a winning combination of flavors. Moroccan-style lamb brochettes were well spiced, and a wild mushroom risotto with mascarpone cheese was very good. You can also leave yourself in Gurzynski's hands with his daily chef's menu, which gives you the option of seafood, meat, or pasta.

343 Somerset St. W. ℂ **613/233-1536.** www.bocado.ca. Reservations recommended. Main courses C$18–C$27; table d'hôte C$26–C$40. AE, MC, V. Mon–Fri 11:30am–2pm and 5–11pm; Sat 5–11pm.

Take It Away!

Whether you're planning a picnic in one of Ottawa's many parks or just want an alternative to hotel room service, you'll find a number of tried-and-true establishments that provide great takeout.

Fresh pasta and sauces top the bill at **Fettucine's,** 280C Elgin St. (© **613/230-4723**). The four-cheese cappelletti topped with tomato-vodka sauce is a perennial favorite, as are the spinach and cheese ravioli, chicken parmigiana, and basil pesto. Everything is made on the premises.

Another terrific Italian takeout place is **Parma Ravioli,** 1314 Wellington St. W. (© **613/722-6003**). In addition to buying fresh pasta, you can stock up on bread, rolls, focaccia, and desserts.

One of the city's best caterers, **Thyme & Again,** 1255 Wellington St. W. (© **613/722-6277**), also offers a wide selection of items for takeout. The menu changes constantly, but expect to find seasonal soups, salads, and a variety of main courses that would be at home in any fine-dining restaurant.

Luciano's, 106 Preston St. (© **613/232-1675**), is a mainstay on Corso Italia, and a great place to get oven-ready portions of lasagna or cannelloni, as well as a large selection of fresh pasta and homemade sauces.

If you plan to picnic in New Edinburgh Park or you're headed across the Ottawa River to enjoy the fall colors, make a stop at **Epicuria Fine Food Store and Catering,** 419 Mackay St. (© **613/745-7356**). You can fill your basket with delicious soups, side dishes, or main courses.

Café Colonnade PIZZA   In the era of international pizza chains and frozen pizza that tastes like takeout, it is easy to forget—or even know—that pizzas were once made to order, by hand. Situated just a block west of Elgin Street's busy bar strip, Café Colonnade is a popular throwback to an earlier era. You can still watch the chefs knead, stretch, and roll the dough, and slide the pies in and out of the giant ovens. The restaurant continues to buck the trend toward deep dish, thin crust, and gourmet toppings, sticking to the tried-and-true pizzas that Canadians fell in love with in the '60s. Although you really should go for the pizza, the menu also offers pasta, veal, chicken, manicotti, cannelloni, and other Italian-Canadian dishes. Other fare, including sandwiches and burgers, is also listed. The dining room is spacious and plainly furnished—the focus is clearly on the food. An outdoor terrace stretches along one side of the building, providing a place to hang out on warm summer days and evenings.

280 Metcalfe St. © **613/237-3179.** Main courses C$7–C$11; pizza C$7–C$19. AE, DC, MC, V. Mon–Thurs 11am–10pm; Fri–Sat 11am–11pm; Sun 11am–9pm.

Genji ★ JAPANESE   Miles Davis's "So What" was playing softly the first time I dined here, and that has always seemed like the ideal Zen-like greeting to Genji's blond-wood-clad tranquility. Since opening in 2006, Genji has established a terrific reputation among the city's food cognoscenti, and has become one of my go-to places for a casual lunch. I'm clearly not alone; the place is always packed. What makes Genji work? While the menu is not as extensive as that of rival Kinki, which in recent years has been regarded as offering Ottawa's best sushi, what Genji does well—their house appetizer, sweet potato sushi, and *unagi maki* (freshwater eel roll)—it does very well. The prices are reasonable, and the restaurant also features takeout for those craving an alternative to room service.

175 Lisgar St. ✆ 613/236-2880. www.genji.ca. Main courses C$16–C$20; appetizers C$4–C$12; sushi C$4–C$14. MC, V. Mon–Wed 11:30am–10pm; Thurs–Fri 11:30am–10:30pm; Sat 4:30–10:30pm.

Savana Café FUSION   Savana bills itself as Ottawa's original fusion restaurant, and indeed, it has been serving original combinations of Caribbean-based dishes since 1987. For lunch, sweet basil shrimp flavored with oyster sauce, soya, orange juice, and Thai basil is a great choice. Or, for dinner, try the exceptional Cubana Chicken, stuffed with bananas and cream cheese, and served with an orange-jalapeño cream sauce and coconut rice. Servers are enthusiastic and knowledgeable. Don't be shy to ask for the ingredients of a particular dish or request to have the heat turned down if you're not a fan of spicy food. Savana is a popular spot and fills up quickly on weekdays at lunchtime. A small terrace out front in the shade of mature trees is pleasant in the summer.

431 Gilmour St. ✆ **613/233-9159.** www.savanacafe.com. Reservations recommended. Main courses C$15–C$25. AE, DC, MC, V. Mon–Fri 11:30am–3pm and 5–10pm; Sat 5–10pm.

INEXPENSIVE

Elgin Street Diner DINER   Make no mistake, Ottawa is a far cry from New York City. That said, there are those who do party—or work—late into the night, and the Elgin Street Diner meets their needs for a place that never closes. This is an unpretentious, neighborhood kind of place, and if home-style comfort food is your thing, this will be heaven for you. I have a friend who comes here just for the club sandwiches, made with grilled chicken at C$9.95, and another who thinks the poutine—a distinctive French-Canadian dish made with fried potatoes, cheese curds, and gravy—is the best anywhere. You can also cure what ails you with the Hangover Breakfast of two eggs, poutine, and baked beans for C$8.50 or make like it's the 1950s with the homemade macaroni and cheese for C$9.95. For those who like fewer carbs in their diet, there are eight different salads, a veggie burger, and a grilled vegetable club.

374 Elgin St. ✆ **613/237-9700.** www.elginstreetdiner.com. Most items under C$10. AE, DC, MC, V. Daily 24 hr.

3 DOWNTOWN (EAST OF THE CANAL)

By far the greatest concentration of restaurants and food shops in Ottawa is in the ByWard Market district—bordered by Sussex Drive, St. Patrick Street, King Edward Avenue, and Rideau Street. Late at night, the bar crowd makes its presence known here (see chapter 10, "Ottawa After Dark"), but the rowdiest action is concentrated east of Parent Avenue, while most of the finer restaurants are located on the west side—with the notable exception of Murray Street, which is chockablock with exceptional dining choices between Parent Avenue and Dalhousie Street. Parking is plentiful, but because of the popularity of the dining and shopping here, metered spaces are scarce. If you don't luck out on the first or second pass, bite the bullet and park in one of the open-air or underground lots. The most economical lots are the City of Ottawa–operated facility on Murray just east of Dalhousie, and the underground lot on the west side of Sussex Drive just north of Rideau Street. The latter is a particular bargain after 6pm, when the flat fee is C$6.

Courtyard ★ CANADIAN   Located in one of Ottawa's oldest buildings, and sharing a gorgeous stone-lined square with the Black Tomato, Social, and Mamma Grazzi's Kitchen, Courtyard has been a local landmark for years, but don't think it merely rests on its laurels. Under chef Marc Lepine, it vaulted into the front ranks of adventurous Ottawa dining. Lepine has moved on (his new venture is set to open in late 2008) and his former assistant, Michael Hay, has stepped up to assume his first executive chef's position, following his latest apprenticeship at Chicago's celebrated Moto. Hay is committed to sourcing local products and promoting food sustainability, so you can expect to find traditional items like burdock, nettle, and dandelion employed creatively in his dishes. My wife and I found his offerings a bit tame during a visit early in his tenure. My five pork medallions were beautifully cooked, but seemed a little naked sitting in a row with a small mound of squash and a moat of apple compote. Joanne's saddle of lamb, which sat on a large bed of lentils, would make a hearty winter dish, but seemed out of step with the warm summer night. Hay stepped out more effectively with a fascinating lobster vichyssoise topped with a spoonful of ice cream, and seems to really hit his stride with the dessert menu, which includes an exceptionally flavorful vanilla crème brûlée and Chef Lepine's superb gorgonzola cheesecake in phyllo—held over by popular demand with Lepine's blessing. Hay holds promise, and he has a great canvas to work on.

21 George St. ✆ **613/241-1516.** www.courtyardrestaurant.com. Main courses C$19–C$43. AE, DC, MC, V. Mon–Sat 11am–2pm and 5:30–9:30pm; Sun 11am–2pm and 5–9pm.

E18hteen ★ BISTRO   Save for its location in a stone heritage building, this is the Ottawa restaurant most likely to be mistaken for a set from *Sex and the City*. From the extensive cocktail menu to the open sightlines that invite young singles to see and be seen, E18hteen strives to be more than simply a place to eat. There's a large, comfortable lounge area on the upper level, a broad selection of cheeses and bar snacks, and DJs spin tunes until late on Friday and Saturday. But Chef Matthew Carmichael has the goods to make you come for the food, too. He specializes in rich, fragrant sauces and some exotic meats like ostrich, and isn't beyond a bit of food architecture, although he's more Moshe Safdie than Frank Gehry on the plate. I enjoyed the simplicity of my salad, which combined yellow and red beets with apple slices, some nicely aged cheddar, and candied walnuts, while my daughter feasted on a combination of crab cake and an entire soft shell crab that had been prepared tempura style—Carmichael seems to enjoy twinning ingredients. An adopted Nova Scotian, my daughter was disappointed in the quality of the lobster tail that topped her surf-and-turf main, but the piece of tenderloin was a joy. I opted for slices of rare tuna seared with a sesame coating and served with baby bok choy and shiitake mushrooms in an emulsion of sesame. The tuna was silky and firm, and chef hit just the right balance of spice and sweetness with the emulsion. Given its location and the quality of its ingredients, E18hteen might rank higher, but little things—like the texture of that lobster and a watery pull of espresso that ended our evening on a flat note—keep it out of the ranks of Ottawa's front-running eateries.

18 York St. ✆ **613/244-1188.** www.restaurant18.com. Reservations recommended. Main courses C$28–C$45. AE, DC, MC, V. Daily 5–11pm.

Signatures ★★★ (Moments) FRENCH   If you enjoy classic French cuisine and formal service, Signatures is a must. The only Le Cordon Bleu restaurant in North America, it is located in an exceptional 1874 mansion in historic Sandy Hill, which also houses the Le Cordon Bleu Paris Ottawa Culinary Arts Institute. We previewed the fall degustation

DINING

6

DOWNTOWN (EAST OF THE CANAL)

tasting menu—six courses that require a minimum of 4 hours to serve and consume. From delicate cured ham—carved at the table—served with fresh figs, through poached Pacific halibut with green olive tapenade and pistachio oil, to fork-tender venison with potato and porcini purée, the menu and service were flawless. The wine choices were also first-rate, and I'd recommend going with their selection, which is an important part of the overall experience. The formality might not be to everyone's taste, but Signatures represents the best of this kind of Old World style.

453 Laurier Ave. E. *C* 613/236-2499. www.restaurantsignatures.com. Reservations required. Main courses C$36–C$46; table d'hôte (3-7 courses) C$64–C$110; wine selection C$33–C$57. AE, DC, MC, V. Tues–Sat 5:30–10pm.

EXPENSIVE

Foundation FUSION   Despite its impressive setting, which subtly mirrors the glass and stone of the nearby National Gallery of Canada, Foundation somehow seems as programmed as the restaurant equivalent of a theme park. Consider the gaggle of beautiful, young women at the hostess station, the relentless electronic dance music, and the house magician who moves among the tables. As heavily conceived and impersonal as this seems, the food is quite good, ranging toward the tapaslike offerings preferred by the young, well-heeled clientele Foundation attracts. Tasting plates of appetizers and fondues encourage sharing. Among the mains, a honey-glazed spiral of salmon was mild and moist, sitting atop a delicate herb risotto, while an Angus striploin from the kitchen's grill was a nice cut, perfectly cooked. As long as you're not hoping for quiet conversation or attentive, informed service, Foundation could provide an entertaining night out.

18B York St. *C* 613/562-9331. www.foundationrestaurant.com. Reservations recommended. Main courses C$19–C$34. AE, DC, MC, V. Tues–Wed 4–10pm; Thurs–Sat 4–11pm.

John Taylor at Domus Café ★★★ CANADIAN   Recently renamed to reflect the growing fame of co-owner and chef John Taylor, the restaurant exudes freshness, from the butter-yellow walls and high ceilings to the locally grown produce that Taylor uses extensively on his all-Canadian menu. An Ottawa favorite for many years, the restaurant is an ideal place to dine if you want to sample the country's diversity of cuisine and wine. The selection changes frequently, but main courses often include quail, Arctic char, and venison. On our most recent visit we enjoyed a summery risotto with chanterelle mushrooms and peas, and a surprisingly piquant corn bisque. A warm salad featured more fresh, local corn, crisped prosciutto, and a sunny-side-up quail's egg. Sommelier Sylvia Taylor's specialty is finding distinctive Canadian wines that are perfect matches for her husband's creations, and the restaurant works directly with a number of the leading wineries in Ontario's Niagara region to find distinctive new offerings. Service is friendly and efficient.

87 Murray St. *C* 613/241-6007. www.domuscafe.ca. Main courses C$29–C$32. AE, MC, V. Mon–Sat 11:30am–2pm and 5:30–10pm; Sun 10:30am–2:30pm. Closed Sun during summer.

Navarra ★★ SPANISH   The narrow wooden house in the center of Murray Street's "Gastro Alley" is one of the oldest in Ottawa, and over the past decade it has established the reputation as housing one of the city's best kitchens. Ottawa native René Rodriguez has been responsible for that twice, now; first as chef—for 3 years—of the Black Cat Café, and currently at the helm of his own Basque-influenced restaurant. The beautiful back courtyard remains after the extensive renovations of 2008, and that's where we found ourselves on a warm August evening, 6 weeks after Navarra's debut. Fresh from a recent trip to Spain's Basque Country, we were anxious to try Rodriguez's interpretation of its distinctive cuisine. My cracked lobster "pil pil" (which denotes an oil-based sauce used to cook seafood in concert with garlic and peppers) was exceptional—combining small chunks of lobster, chorizo, and peas, topped with milk froth. The mascarpone risotto—featuring local mushrooms and generous shavings of manchego—was earthy and piquant. We were also impressed with the carefully selected, if small, wine list, and were delighted with our server's recommendation of an albariño from western Spain. There is much to explore on Rodriguez's menu—including some great small plates that showcase Spanish specialties.

93 Murray St. ℂ **613/241-5500.** www.navarrarestaurant.com. Reservations recommended. Main courses C$22–C$34. MC, V. Mon–Fri 11:30am–2pm and 5:30–10pm; Sat 5:30–10pm.

Social ★ BISTRO   One of a handful of new restaurants that brightened up the Ottawa dining scene in the early 2000s, Social has one of the best locations in the ByWard Market—with large windows facing chic, busy Sussex Drive and a back patio in the gorgeous Clarendon Court. Inside, the decor is restrained yet contemporary, with rich red velvet contrasting against the dominant black and gray. The food is somewhat restrained, too, avoiding vertical structures and exotic flavor fusions in favor of well-cooked, elegant fare—the trademark of chef Matthew Carmichael, who also supervises the kitchen at E18hteen. Mains include a terrifically rich duck leg confit with a pickled cranberry glaze, slow-roasted lamb in a pungent jus, and seared yellow fin tuna with rarely seen (in these parts, anyway) Jerusalem artichokes, but the main courses tell only part of the tale at Social. The restaurant has become a mecca for late-afternoon and late-night snacking, too, and offers an extensive range of small plates, cheeses, charcuterie, and antipasti.

537 Sussex Dr. ℂ **613/789-7355.** www.social.ca. Reservations recommended. Main courses C$21–C$33. AE, MC, V. Mon–Wed 11:45am–1am; Thurs–Sat 11:45am–2am; Sun 11:45am–midnight. Closed for lunch during winter.

Sweetgrass ★★★ (Finds) ABORIGINAL   Among bistros that tout "fusion" cuisine few offer blends as unique as those served up by Phoebe Sutherland, a James Bay Cree, and her husband Warren, who's Jamaican by birth. Since opening in the ByWard Market area in late 2003, this 57-seat restaurant has attracted a growing number of devotees to its serene atmosphere and the chefs' clever interpretations of Native American cuisine. Earth tones dominate the main room of the small heritage house, and the walls display a changing assortment of aboriginal art. The menus shift with the seasons in keeping with Native tradition, but game dishes are always plentiful. My favorites on the spring menu are the grilled *tatonka* (buffalo) in the house's special reduction, and the crispy leg of duck, which is accompanied by spicy corn crepes stuffed with a variety of spring beans and drizzled with a garlic-ginger sauce. Grilled caribou from Canada's Nunavut territory nestles on a bed of spinach with a side of mushroom-potato ragout. Arctic char is spiced mildly with a cucumber-cilantro sauce. Vegetarians aren't forgotten, with at least one main and a variety of salads that feature original dressings. Appetizers include smoked British Columbia salmon with peppered crème fraîche and pan-fried rabbit dumplings topped with a honey-mustard sauce. Sweetgrass excels at the small touches that create a memorable experience, like the wide variety of Native teas on offer, the understated, attentive service, and the warmth that exudes from Phoebe and Warren in their welcoming, open kitchen.

108 Murray St. ℂ **613/562-3683.** www.sweetgrassbistro.ca. Reservations recommended. Main courses C$29–C$36. MC, V. Mon–Fri 11:30am–2pm and 5:30–10pm; Sat–Sun 5:30–10pm.

Sweet Temptations

Whether you associate dessert with warming yourself on a cold winter night or eating alfresco under a starry sky, Ottawa has numerous options that will satisfy your sweet tooth.

With more than 30 cakes on offer at any given time, **Oh So Good Desserts & Coffee House,** 25 York St. (© **613/241-8028**), can likely supply anything you crave—from gooey chocolate cakes to tart lemon meringue torte. Expect to find a crowd late in the evenings.

When traditional Italian desserts are what you seek, there's no destination better than **Pasticceria Gelateria Italiana,** 200 Preston St. (© **613/233-6199**). From simple biscotti to extravagant chocolate concoctions, this neighborhood favorite has it all. On summer nights, expect a line for the huge selection of homemade gelato.

Speaking of gelato, the downtown core offers a couple of choices. On the Elgin Street bar strip, a young crowd favors **Pure Gelato,** 350 Elgin St. (© **613/ 237-3799**), with its wide selection of novel flavors, including ginger, mango, and chestnut. In the ByWard Market, it's **Piccolo Grande,** 55 Murray St. (© **613/241-2909**). Here, the variety is almost infinite—the staff will endeavor to make a gelato to order if you give 48 hours notice. The regular selection is pretty extensive, too, running from traditional flavors like amaretto to wacky concoctions like banana–peanut butter.

Vittoria Trattoria ITALIAN   A perennial winner in the readers poll conducted by the *Ottawa Xpress* newspaper for best Italian restaurant, I go here mainly for the wine list, although the pasta is just fine, too. With almost 30 wines available by the glass, and another couple of dozen offered as half bottles, the restaurant opens its wine selection up to just about any budget. Overall, the thick wine menu contains about 500 choices, offering a range of New and Old World options and prices that reach C$3,000 a bottle. The variety of pasta sauces and preparations is almost as deep, and I was pleased with my smoked salmon and fettuccine, which was accompanied by a mixture of arugula and fennel, and topped with a piquant cream sauce that used a lemoncello base and was spiked with peppercorns. Also recommended is the pan-seared halibut fillet and its vermouth sauce. Given the expansive size of the restaurant and the amount of food the kitchen turns out, the quality is quite consistent. If choice is what you're looking for, Vittoria Trattoria is a solid option in the ByWard Market.

35 William St. © 613/789-8959. www.vittoriatrattoria.com. Reservations recommended. Main courses C$13–C$36. AE, MC, V. Mon–Fri 11:30am–10pm; Sat–Sun 10am–10pm.

MODERATE

Benny's Bistro ★★ (Finds BISTRO   Tucked away down a narrow hallway behind a French bakery and open only for breakfast and lunch, this unpretentious little jewel is easy to miss. Build it into your agenda along with a tour of the ByWard Market or the National Gallery of Canada and you won't be disappointed. Maged Kamal's design—combining primary colors on the walls; a checkered floor; a high-pressed, tin ceiling; and open kitchen—is simple but creative, and chef Scott Adams' menu follows that lead. What he does with duck is a perfect example. The slices of duck breast are straightforward enough—tender, moist, and perfectly pan-fried—but to this Adams adds his version of French toast, served with roasted rhubarb from his garden and a vanilla bean compote. Or, consider his risotto, which is actually made from pearl barley and served with delicious wild mushrooms and grilled asparagus with a salad of radicchio and baby arugula. For smaller lunchtime appetites, Adams also has a daily sandwich and green salad combination for C$13. Needless to say, the bread from the front of the house is oven fresh.

119 Murray St. ✆ **613/789-6797.** www.bennysbistro.ca. Main courses C$13–C$18. AE, MC, V. Daily 8am–2:30pm.

The Black Tomato ★ BISTRO   Open since 1995, this unique restaurant is also an eclectic CD shop, and you can check out the music at the listening post before making a buying decision. The menu also covers a lot of bases, leaning heavily on southern influences with dishes such as jerk pork and jambalaya, and featuring a large selection of soups, salads, and sandwiches, which can provide a memorable dining experience for well under C$20. Among the mains, I like their smoked salmon filet, which is marinated in maple syrup and served with a crisp potato cake. A butternut squash agnolotti is served in a fresh sage cream sauce and topped with padano and asiago cheeses. In the warm months, the restaurant shares historic Clarendon Court with Social, Courtyard, and Mamma Grazzi's Kitchen. The Black Tomato's only drawback is that it doesn't accept reservations for fewer than eight people, and with a restaurant as popular as this, that can mean long waits or disappointment.

11 George St. ✆ **613/789-8123.** Reservations accepted for 8 or more. Main courses C$15–C$28. AE, DC, MC, V. Daily 11:30am–10pm.

Kinki ★ ASIAN   Along with Social and Beckta, Kinki has been touted as reviving Ottawa's moribund restaurant landscape. There's no question that the place introduced some new style into the dining scene, with its aggressive fusion of Asian and European food, its stylish approach to food and entertainment, and its suggestively sexy advertising. Sandwiched into one of the less-attractive corners of the ByWard Market, it nonetheless makes the most of its brick-lined space, with an inviting bar and sushi kitchen, and extensive use of mirrors. It invites beautiful people to preen, and they seem to flock to the place. And the food? It's hard to fault the presentation, and the array of choices on the menu is almost overwhelming. My Kontiki Gnocchi—traditional gnocchi and tiger shrimp in chili-spiked coconut sauce, with a side of very spicy blackened scallops—from the "hot kitchen" reflected well on Kinki's idea of East meets West. Items from the maki menu are fresh and tasty. The restaurant also offers tapas combination plates, and the fried smelts were delicious when dipped in wasabi mayonnaise.

41 York St. ✆ **613/789-7559.** www.kinki.ca. Main courses C$16–$22; sushi and maki C$5–C$16. AE, MC, V. Mon–Thurs 11:45am–11pm; Fri 11:45am–2am; Sat 10am–2am; Sun 9am–11pm.

Mamma Grazzi's Kitchen ★ ITALIAN   Mamma Grazzi's is one of those rare places that serves up consistently good food in a knockout location. I've been coming here for years and have never been disappointed. Whether you eat on either of the inside levels or outside on the stone courtyard (shared with the Black Tomato, Courtyard, and Social) the atmosphere is low-key, somewhat rustic, and always friendly. Several things set it apart immediately from standard Italian fare, including stout wine tumblers in place of stemware, and spicy grilled calamari instead of the ubiquitous battered variety. The menu features more than 30 pasta dishes, in cream, tomato, or olive oil sauces, and I have trouble deciding between the Siciliana with anchovies, capers, and olives, and the piquant Odessa with grilled chicken, mushrooms, roasted red peppers, and chiles.

25 George St. ✆ **613/241-8656.** www.mammagrazzis.com. Main courses C$9.50–C$17. AE, DC, MC, V. Daily 11:30am–10pm.

Murray Street Kitchen, Wine & Charcuterie ★★ (Value) BISTRO   One of several new restaurants opened in 2008, the creation of high-profile Ottawa restaurateurs Steve Mitton and Paddy Whelan addresses what they see as the need for high-quality Canadian comfort food. Their idea of comfort comes in the form of top-notch meats and cheeses, and a small, but select menu of Old and New World wines. At the bar, you can sample hand-cut slices of meats and a few pates, or you can take a table and tuck into something more substantial. An appetizer of poutine made with sheep-yogurt spaetzle— substituting for French fries—and shredded duck confit and gravy might be deemed almost too much comfort; it redefines the phrase *over the top,* but is so good! Chef Mitton's braised shortrib is beyond tender—the result of 2 days' processing in its red wine reduction. Despite the obvious care taken in dishes like this, Murray Street exudes a rustic air—a feeling that's reflected in the rough-hewn wooden floors, the artisan bread that arrives at your table in a small brown bag, and the casual grace of the serving staff. Set in an old house—the former site of the much-beloved Bistro 115—Murray Street is a deceptively large place with an inviting patio in the back.

110 Murray St. ✆ **613/562-7244.** www.murraystreet.ca. Main courses C$18–C$25. AE, MC, V. Daily 11:30am–midnight.

INEXPENSIVE

The Green Door VEGETARIAN   This casual eatery has tables set up cafeteria style and a U-shaped buffet with a dessert station in the middle. Grab a tray and wander past hot vegetable stir-fries, tofu dishes, pastas, salads, breads, fresh fruits, cakes, and pies—all exceptionally fresh when I've visited. A lot of the offerings are certified organic. Pricing is easy—just hand your plate to the cashier and you'll be charged by weight. With prices set at C$18 a kilogram, your stomach will be full before your wallet is empty. If you're heading out to a park, put together a picnic lunch. Servers will supply takeout containers and paper bags.

198 Main St. ✆ **613/234-9597.** C$18 per kg. AE, DC, MC, V. Tues–Sun 11am–9pm.

Peace Garden Café VEGETARIAN   A tiny oasis in the leafy inner court of the Times Square Building, Peace Garden is a great place to retreat when you feel the need to escape from noisy city streets. There are a few small tables in the courtyard next to a tinkling fountain and a counter with stools. If you're hungry, soup, salads, sandwiches, and a variety of Indian, Malaysian, Italian, and Greek specialties will fit the bill. It's also a great place just to sip a spicy Indian chai tea or a cool, fresh mango *lassi* (yogurt drink). To boost your energy after a day of sightseeing, ask the server to recommend one of their power juices. Closing hours vary seasonally.

47 Clarence St. ✆ **613/562-2434.** Most items under C$10. AE, MC, V. Thurs–Tues 9am–8pm; Wed 9am– 6:30pm.

4 THE GLEBE

Running north to south between the Queensway and the Bank Street Bridge, which separates the Glebe from Ottawa South, and bordered by the Rideau Canal in the east and Bronson Avenue in the west, here is one of the city's oldest neighborhoods. Bank Street bisects the residential areas, and is stuffed with boutiques, pubs, and eating places. Parking for more than an hour can be a challenge between 7am and 7pm, but it's an ideal area for strolling, so consider leaving the car behind. If you must drive, check out the 2-hour, metered spots on Third Avenue just east of Bank Street, or one of several City of Ottawa lots in the area.

EXPENSIVE

Flipper's SEAFOOD   Find the discreet doorway at 819 Bank Street, next to Von's Bistro (see below), and climb the steep stairs to a fresh fish restaurant that has been serving Ottawans since 1980—a long time in the fickle restaurant business. Flipper's has the relaxed, unpretentious feel of a place that's been around for more than 25 years, too. The wooden floors have a rustic appearance, and the nautical look—expressed through aged wainscoting and sea-themed art—doesn't seem like it came straight out of a box. The food also has a tried-and-true approach; you won't find the kind of edgy touches that you will at Whalesbone Oyster House, for example. Seafood-restaurant staples (bay scallops, salmon, shrimp, and mussels) are treated with respect and prepared with style. Specials include Alaskan king crab legs, Arctic char, and bouillabaisse. For the less adventurous, the menu includes English-style fish and chips, grilled Atlantic salmon, and pasta. Reservations are only accepted for large parties, but ask if it's possible to get one of the window tables, which provide a terrific view of the street life in the busy Glebe.

819 Bank St. (Fifth Ave. Court). © **613/232-2703.** www.819bank.com. Reservations accepted for 6 or more. Main courses C$17–C$34 and up. AE, MC, V. Mon 5–10pm; Tues–Fri 11:30am–2pm and 5–10pm; Sat 5–10pm; Sun 5–9pm.

Fratelli ITALIAN   Verging on chain status now that they've expanded to four locations, brothers Riccardo and Roberto Valente strive to be faithful to the Italian dining experience without specializing in any particular region of the country. All the ingredients are as fresh as possible, and the mains represent a good cross-section of traditional favorites, including osso buco, veal scaloppini, and chicken parmigiana. There are also 14 pasta dishes on the dinner menu, and four varieties of pizza. This is one of my favorite meeting places in the Glebe, and the food is uniformly good. The only drawback is that the restaurant has a lot of hard surfaces without much to buffer sound, and the volume of noise can make quiet conversation difficult.

749 Bank St. © **613/237-1658.** www.fratelli.ca. Reservations recommended. Main courses C$12–C$36. AE, MC, V. Mon–Fri 11:30am–10pm; Sat 11:30am–11pm; Sun 11:30am–9:30pm. Also at 309 Richmond Rd. © 613/722-6772; 499 Terry Fox Dr. © 613/592-0225; and 7 Springfield Rd. © 613/749-3369.

The Urban Pear ★★ CANADIAN   Quality trumps location at the Urban Pear, which is tucked away on a quiet side street in the Glebe. While the views are mostly of parking lots, the long, bright room—which features exhibitions of original artwork—quickly makes you forget the external environment. Owner-chef Ben Baird brings so much passion for food to the game that people come to this place in droves. A graduate of the Stratford Chefs School, Baird believes in using only fresh, local, seasonal ingredients. He also believes in staying in touch with his community, and frequently hosts 40

Coffee Break

Like all major cities, Ottawa's street corners are dotted with chain coffee shops—not just the ubiquitous **Starbucks,** but also homegrown franchises **Second Cup** and **Tim Horton's.** Look a bit further, though, and you can discover some alternatives that are more distinctively Ottawan.

With a growing number of locations around town, **Bridgehead** is one of Ottawa's best business success stories. Dealing only in fair-traded coffees, tea, and chocolate, the local chain has managed to compete successfully with the big boys in many of its locations. Expect to find friendly staff, a good selection of sandwiches made on the premises, and a range of baked goods to tempt you. Free Wi-Fi is offered, so you can also expect to find a large number of people with laptops.

Located in Clarendon Lanes in the ByWard Market, **Planet Coffee,** 24A York St. (✆ **613/789-6261**), provides a friendly oasis in the midst of the city's busiest shopping district. In the warm months, take advantage of the outdoor tables in the pleasant courtyard.

There was a time when no one ventured north of St. Patrick Street on Dalhousie, but the neighborhood has evolved into one of the city's more interesting shopping strips, and the service sector is finally catching up to the change. One of the newest Bridgehead locations is here, and so is **i deal Coffee,** 176 Dalhousie St. (✆ **613/562-1775**), which roasts and grinds fair-trade coffee on-site and serves fresh baked goods. The **Roasted Cherry Coffee House,** 93 O'Connor St. (✆ **613/236-1656**), isn't in a high-traffic area, but it's definitely worth seeking out if you crave a well-pulled shot of espresso or a sandwich and a muffin in pleasant surroundings.

If your sightseeing takes you into Gatineau, you may want to build in a pit stop at **Café La Brûlerie,** 152 rue Montcalm (✆ **819/778-0109**). It offers more than 36 types of coffee beans and blends, as well as a wide selection of soups, sandwiches, and salads.

For a unique, late-afternoon diversion, stop for tea at Zoë's Lounge in the **Fairmont Château Laurier,** 1 Rideau St. (✆ **613/241-1414**). You can choose among traditional English tea, Canadian high tea, or champagne tea, each with its own accompaniment of finger sandwiches, fruit, and cakes. The experience doesn't come cheap, though; prices range from C$24 to C$40.

people at a time at special dinners, to showcase new recipes and wine pairings. Often he invites an estate owner along, as well, to discuss the finer points of his or her wines. An ideal spot for lunch if you're perusing the Glebe's shopping options, the restaurant has a menu that changes daily. My last visit yielded an exceptionally light-yet-bold frittata, spiked with organic oyster mushrooms, chard, goat cheese, and fingerling potatoes. Baird's menus also frequently feature at least one fowl and beef main, pasta, and often a concoction based around a stuffed, open-face apple or Anjou pear. Freshness and variety rule here.

151 Second Ave. (✆ **613/569-9305**. www.theurbanpear.com. Reservations recommended. Main courses C$23–C$32. AE, DC, MC, V. Mon–Fri 11:30am–2pm and 5:30–9pm; Sat 5:30–9pm; Sun 11am–2pm and 5:30–9pm.

MODERATE

InFusion Bistro FUSION   The name says it all; bold tastes—particularly in unusual combinations—rule here. Dishes include portobello, shiitake, and oyster mushroom strudel with Gruyère and fresh herb cream sauce, grilled lamb and baby spinach salad, and house-made Jamaican jerk pork tenderloin. The atmosphere is extremely comfortable, with low-key electronic music enticing you to linger over another glass of wine.

825 Bank St. (✆ **613/234-2412.** Reservations recommended. Main courses C$10–C$25. AE, DC, MC, V. Mon 5–9pm; Tues–Thurs 11:30am–10pm; Fri 11:30am–11pm; Sat 10am–11:30pm; Sun 10am–9pm.

Von's Bistro BISTRO   Local residents are fond patrons of this centrally located Glebe eatery. The subdued, neutral decor with caramel walls, bisque tablecloths, and an abundance of dark wood is accented with chalkboard-covered pillars adorned with amusing and thought-provoking quotations. Lunch fare is light and quick—bagels, wraps, pasta, quiches, and omelettes. In the evening, the menu offers classic bistro fare, anchored by a larger-than-average steak frites (C$25) that features hand-cut Yukon Gold fries.

819 Bank St. (✆ **613/233-3277.** www.819bank.com. Reservations accepted for 6 or more; reservations not accepted for weekend brunch. Main courses C$18–C$29. AE, MC, V. Mon–Fri 11:30am–2pm and 5–10pm; Sat 8:30am–2pm and 5–10pm; Sun 8:30am–2pm.

INEXPENSIVE

Wild Oat Bakery and Natural Foods BAKERY   If you're into whole foods, health foods, or anything in between, you must drop in here if you're in the Glebe. The bakery, grocery shelves, and takeout sections are in the original location on the corner of Bank Street, and a casual, funky healthy eating restaurant has opened in the space next door, with a connecting doorway between the two. Ready-to-eat small pizzas, samosas, soups, crepes, or chili make a good light lunch, and you can follow them with brownies, squares, or one of the large cookies showcased in wicker baskets on the counter. Wheat-free, yeast-free, and naturally sweetened baked goods are available. Browse the shelves for organic pasta, 100%-organic fresh produce, and other healthy food items.

817 Bank St. (✆ **613/232-6232.** Most items under C$10. Cash or debit card only. Mon–Fri 8am–8pm (9pm in summer); Sat–Sun 8am–6pm.

5 WELLINGTON STREET WEST/WESTBORO

Stretching from Parkdale Avenue in the east to Island Park Drive in the west, Wellington Street West is a neighborhood in rapid transition. In the past decade, a number of new shops, galleries, and restaurants have sprung up. At Island Park, the more-established neighborhood of Westboro begins, offering slightly fewer dining options but still the occasional gem. Parking is plentiful, but be mindful of the 1-hour parking restrictions. Be aware that Wellington Street and Richmond Road are names of the same east-west thoroughfare; the name changes just east of Island Park Drive.

EXPENSIVE

Absinthe ★★ BISTRO   Directly across Wellington Street from the Irving Greenberg Theatre Centre, Absinthe—which moved into this location from around the corner in 2007—aims to evoke a hip, casual mood set in a Parisian bistro of the mind. While there's little mistaking this for the real Paris, chef-owner Patrick Garland does a good job at creating a faux-French experience—right down to the noisy atmosphere and the slightly arrogant stance of refusing to cook his signature hanger steak beyond medium rare. That suits me okay; in fact, I lean the other way and it's just fine—nicely marinated and with the edges perfectly seared. A pricier cut of Black Angus is just so, as well, as is pork tenderloin that's stuffed with apple and topped with a combination of cauliflower, goat cheese, and cranberries. With its sponged pumpkin-colored walls, extensive use of mirrors, and bare wooden floor, Absinthe is a beautiful room, and Garland's waitstaff strikes just the right note of knowledge about the menu and cheeky playfulness. On Friday and Saturday, a DJ takes over after the food service ends, and the place stays open well past midnight.

1208 Wellington St. ℂ **613/761-1138.** www.absinthecafe.ca. Reservations recommended. Main courses C$18–C$35. AE, MC, V. Mon–Fri 11am–2pm and 5:30–10pm; Sat–Sun 5:30–10pm.

Juniper Kitchen & Wine Bar ★★ CANADIAN   Richard Nigro was one of the first Ottawa chefs to gain quasi-celebrity status, back when he worked at the original Domus. Now, in partnership with chef Norm Aitken, he is a strong proponent of fresh, local produce and distinctive new Canadian cuisine. Juniper specializes in unusual combinations of flavors, which was evident in my exceptionally tender piece of Angus tenderloin with its jus of port and figs. We also sampled a lamb shank rubbed with Indonesian spices, which was complemented by a tomato-mint chutney and a sweet and spicy coconut sauce, and served with corn cakes. At C$30, a chunk of wild salmon seemed a bargain—and tasty, too, topped with a gooseberry and red pepper vinaigrette. In keeping with its Canadian focus, Juniper has a good selection of domestic wines from boutique wineries.

245 Richmond Rd. ℂ **613/728-0220.** www.juniperdining.ca. Reservations recommended. Main courses C$27–C$39. AE, MC, V. Mon–Thurs 11:30am–2pm and 5:30–10pm; Fri 11:30am–2pm and 5:30–11pm; Sat 5:30–11pm; Sun 5:30–10pm.

MODERATE

Anna ★ THAI   Located on a stretch of busy Holland Avenue that has a string of interesting restaurants, Anna combines contemporary elegant design and traditional Thai fare. Opened by chef Art Akarapanich in 2003, Anna offers eight different curries, with varying degrees of heat, a half dozen noodle and rice dishes, and many vegetarian selections. Among my favorites are the Pad Bai Gra Prow—sautéed shrimp with chile and basil—and Nua Tod—crispy beef with lemongrass and Thai herbs. Unlike many Thai restaurants, Anna pays close attention to its wine list, and also offers a good selection of imported beers to cool your mouth.

91 Holland Ave. ℂ **613/759-8472.** www.thaitaste.ca/anna. Reservations recommended. Main courses C$9.25–C$16. AE, MC, V. Mon–Fri 11:30am–2pm and 5:30–10pm; Sat 5:30–10pm; Sun 5:30–9pm.

Wellington Gastropub ★★ (Value) BISTRO   Up one flight of stairs from a small courtyard on busy Wellington Street, this restaurant is divided into two rooms that flank a small bar. The jean-clad, bearded, and tattooed waiters might make you think you've mistakenly entered a diner, but this is a place that mixes first-rate, big-flavored food with a casual atmosphere. A larger-than-average by-the-glass wine list and several local microbrews are welcome, as is the attractive offering of artisan breads. A sucker for risotto, I couldn't resist one that was filled with a variety of mushrooms, and I was rewarded with a large portion and expertly balanced flavors. I cadged a sizeable forkful of my companion's Arctic char, and immediately wished I'd forsaken my Italian rice fixation for the night; it was one of the best pieces of fish I've tasted. Equally fine was a creamy vanilla crème brûlée embedded with fresh blueberries and one succulent strawberry. Chef Chris Deraiche changes his menu daily.

INEXPENSIVE

The Table ⟨Value⟩ VEGETARIAN   In a large, bright cafeteria-style dining room with a generous number of country kitchen pine tables and chairs, you can eat for health and still enjoy the food. The Table has a wide selection of tasty vegetarian dishes arranged buffet style. Grab a tray and sample soups, salads, meatless main courses, baked goods, and more. Vegan and gluten-free items are available. The Table uses organic ingredients whenever possible, emphasizes whole grains, and uses maple syrup, molasses, and honey in place of refined sugar. You can also fill takeout containers if you fancy a picnic or want to stock up your fridge.

1230 Wellington St. W. ✆ **613/729-5973.** C$18 per kg. AE, MC, V. Daily 11am–9pm. Also at 261 Dalhousie St. ✆ 613/244-1100.

---

6 CHINATOWN

Somerset Street West is one of Ottawa's longest and most ethnically and economically diverse streets. Although it's common nomenclature, calling the hilly stretch between Lyon Street and Preston Street "Chinatown" is misleading, since the area is home to a broad mix of Asian and South Asian people. There are Vietnamese, Chinese, Korean, and Cambodian food outlets aplenty, and choosing just a few is difficult. I've selected a few of my favorites, but I encourage you to seek out others that catch your attention.

MODERATE

New Mee Fung ★ VIETNAMESE   Meticulous attention to detail in the composition and presentation of the dishes results in a memorable dining experience here. This small restaurant is clean, simply furnished, and casual. Lots of finger foods, dishes that require assembly (you can roll up your chicken in semitransparent rice pancakes), and chopsticks to master. Each dish on the extensive menu is coded: Just jot down the numbers on the scrap of paper the smiling server gives you and wait for a splendid feast to arrive. Many dishes feature grilled chicken, beef, and pork, and there's a good selection of soups, spring rolls, salads, and noodles. Our grilled marinated chicken was accompanied by fresh mint, basil, and lettuce; soft, paper-thin disks made from rice flour for wrapping morsels of food; glass noodles sprinkled with chopped peanuts, carrots, bean sprouts, and cucumber salad; and delicately flavored dipping sauce. Takeout is available.

350 Booth St. ✆ **613/567-8228.** Main courses C$5–C$12. MC, V. Wed–Mon 10am–10pm.

Shanghai Restaurant ★ ASIAN   Serving a mixture of Cantonese, Szechuan, and Asian dishes, Shanghai is one of the top restaurants in Ottawa's Chinatown, as well as one of the area's oldest. You'll find some familiar Canadian-Chinese dishes on the menu, but allow yourself to be tempted by spicy Thai chicken with sweet basil, ginger-teriyaki vegetable fried rice, Shanghai crispy beef, or shrimp with bok choy and roasted garlic. The coconut-curry vegetables in a spicy peanut sauce go well with a bowl of steamed rice. On Thursday evenings after 8pm the menu switches to finger foods and light snacks as a 20-something crowd moves in to listen to a DJ spin tunes until 1am. Karaoke nights are scheduled occasionally. Takeout is available.

651 Somerset St. W. (② **613/233-4001.** www.shanghaiottawa.com. Reservations recommended weekends. Main courses C$9.95–C$17. AE, MC, V. Tues–Wed 11:30am–2pm and 4:30–11pm; Thurs–Fri 11:30am–2pm and 4:30pm–1am; Sat 4:30pm–1am; Sun 4:30–11pm.

So Good ASIAN   If a restaurant were measured by choice alone, So Good would be unparalleled. Its menu is a head-spinning selection of Vietnamese, Cantonese, Szechuan, Taiwanese, and Thai, and the large number of vegetarian dishes have made it a favorite among Ottawa's socially conscious 20-somethings. Among the Szechuan specialties, the egg plant and minced pork with spicy garlic sauce caught our fancy, as did the crab meat with straw mushrooms, and the flavorful Wu Se vegetables with piquant peanut sauce. Who knows? Next time we could go in a totally different direction. After all, we still have to make it through the 13 variations on vermicelli. There is definitely something for everyone here.

717 Somerset St. W. (② **613/233-0138.** www.sogoodfood.com. Main courses C$5.50–C$17. AE, MC, V. Tues–Thurs 11:30am–9:30pm; Fri–Sat 11:30am–10pm; Sun 11:30am–9pm.

Yangtze CHINESE   Both Cantonese and Szechuan cuisine are served in this spacious dining room, which comfortably treads the line between catering to the local Chinese community and meeting the expectations of those used to more North American–style restaurants. Large, round tables will seat 8 to 10 comfortably, and a Lazy Susan in the center of the table allows everyone to help him- or herself from the communal dishes. Families and groups are welcome. Many dishes familiar to North American diners are on the menu—kung po shrimp, sweet-and-sour chicken, broccoli with scallops, beef with snow peas, chow mein, and fried rice. House specialties include chicken in black-bean sauce, pepper steak, and Imperial spareribs, which are so tasty they're habit forming. Takeout is available.

700 Somerset St. W. (② **613/236-0555.** Reservations recommended. C$12–C$16. AE, DC, MC, V. Mon–Thurs 11am–midnight; Fri 11am–1am; Sat 10am–1am; Sun 10am–midnight.

---

7 CORSO ITALIA (PRESTON ST.)

As the name Corso Italia denotes, Preston Street is the traditional heart of Ottawa's large Italian community. Most of the first- and second-generation Italian families departed the neighborhood decades ago, and while there are some landmarks like the Italian banquet hall, Sala San Marco, and a few entrenched old-school, male-only coffee shops, the street is changing quickly. I've listed some of the leading lights, which will give you an idea of the variety available here.

VERY EXPENSIVE

La Roma ★ ITALIAN   Italian doesn't get any more traditional than La Roma. Originally opened in another location in 1962, La Roma was *the* place for Italian food in the years when risotto was considered exotic in Ottawa, and it has earned its reputation as being a dependable place to enjoy Italian classics that are prepared the old-fashioned way. This is not the kind of restaurant that stacks food like edible sculptures, or employs mushroom pickers to hunt down obscure varieties. The 60-seat dining room is sophisticated and charming, and always well-appointed, thanks to the attention paid to it by interior decorator Liz Moroz. Service is impeccable. Choose from a wide variety of chicken, veal, pasta, and other Italian specialties, accompanied by Italian bread. The all-Italian wine list is impressive in both its length and variety.

430 Preston St. ✆ **613/234-8244.** www.laromaottawa.com. Reservations recommended. Main courses **111**
C$14–C$42. AE, DC, MC, V. Mon–Thurs 11:30am–2pm and 5–10pm; Fri 11:30am–2pm and 5–11pm; Sat
5–11pm; Sun 5–10pm.

MODERATE

Four Cuisine Bistro ASIAN   When a restaurant brands itself by trumpeting its four
cuisines, it may be limiting to label it "Asian," but chef-owner Minh Trang definitely
works from an Eastern base, even if many of his dishes encompass other cultures. For
example, a roasted filet of halibut is wrapped in a banana leaf and served on a bed of rice,
and pan-roasted tofu mingles with wild mushrooms and sweet potatoes. Saffron rice—
delicate and nicely flavored—is a favorite accompaniment. More traditional Western
dishes are here, as well, with a distinct focus on steak and veal. While considerably less
expensive than many restaurants with a higher profile, there is little doubt here that the
kitchen loves food and takes care in its preparation.

268 Preston St. ✆ **613/231-2888.**. Main courses C$13–C$18. AE, MC, V. Mon–Tues 5–9pm; Wed–Thurs
and Sun 11:30am–2pm and 5–9pm; Fri–Sat 11:30am–2pm and 5–10pm.

Green Papaya THAI   In a city that loves its Thai restaurants, Green Papaya garnered
a great reputation in its former cramped location on Kent Street. Now—along with a
small downtown location and another in Gatineau—it has a prime spot on the busy
corner of Preston and Gladstone, in a tall structure that looms over the street. The menu
offers classic Thai fare, with none of the contemporary twists that fusion chefs impose,
so expect a wide selection of rice and noodle dishes, and six different curries. The dishes
run from mild to very hot, but I find the kitchen errs on the side of Canadian tastes, so
if you like your food spicy you may want to discuss your preference with your server in
advance.

260 Preston St. ✆ **613/231-8424.** www.greenpapaya.ca. Main courses C$11–C$17. AE, MC, V. Mon–
Thurs 11:30am–2:30pm and 5–10pm; Fri 11:30am–2:30pm and 5–11pm; Sat 5–11pm; Sun 5–10pm.

Pub Italia (Finds) ITALIAN   What do you get when you cross an Italian restaurant
with an Irish pub? This sprawling, friendly place provides the answer. Owner Joe Cotro-
neo and his wife, Rosemary Casey McLewin, offer a bit of everything: plenty of appetizers and sandwiches for lunchtime and after-work socializing, thin-crust pizzas, nine
varieties of mussels, and pasta galore. You can choose among five types of pasta, and top
it with any of 14 sauces. I keep going back to the tomato-based sauce with spicy Italian
sausage, olives, and chiles, but for variety I also enjoy the oil-based sauce with smoked
salmon, as well as the cream sauce with Gorgonzola and leeks. The "pub" part of the
restaurant doesn't disappoint, either, offering more than 200 beers, including 36 types of
draft. If you want to mingle with the locals, this is a good place to do it. And check out
the murals on the outside walls; don't be surprised if you recognize your server among
the medieval characters portrayed there.

434¹/₂ Preston St. ✆ **613/232-2326.** www.pubitalia.ca. Main courses C$10–C$14. AE, DC, MC, V. Mon–Sat
11am–1am; Sun 5pm–midnight (2pm–midnight in summer).

Stoneface Dolly's BISTRO   In this large, open space decorated in elegant gray tones,
South African owner and chef Bob Russell treats diners like they're guests at his dinner
party, often making the rounds to chat and make menu suggestions. His menus always
include a couple of mains with Caribbean influence, such as jambalaya and jerk chicken,
and traditional Mexican fare makes a rare Ottawa appearance with a chicken breast
encrusted in sesame, topped with mole sauce, and served on dirty rice with black bean

and corn salsas. Black beans also figure prominently in a cream sauce that tops penne pasta, served with Portobello mushrooms and roasted red peppers. A small side patio allows for summertime people-watching on Corso Italia.

416 Preston St. ℂ **613/564-2222**. www.stonefacedollys.com. Main courses C$14–C$23. AE, MC, V. Mon–Fri 7:30–10:30am, 11:30am–2pm, and 5–10pm; Sat–Sun 9am–2pm and 5–10pm.

---

8 GATINEAU

Ottawa's bilingual nature makes it unique among Canadian cities outside Quebec, and so does its proximity to the sprawling city of Gatineau. The distinctive francophone culture, the presence of many senior government bureaucrats, and the luxurious Casino Lac-Leamy combine to give Gatineau more than its share of fine French-style restaurants. The area has seen a couple of high-profile failures in the past few years—most notably Café Henry Burger and Laurier-sur-Montcalm—but there are several excellent options if you want to indulge in French or Quebecois cuisine. (See chapter 11, "Side Trips from Ottawa," for two other possibilities.)

VERY EXPENSIVE

Le Baccara ★★★ FRENCH   Easily the most-honored restaurant in the Ottawa region, the 70-seat Le Baccara makes you wonder why anyone would bother stopping off in the gaming rooms of the Casino du Lac-Leamy on the way in. There's absolutely no gambling here; you are guaranteed delightful food, carefully prepared and served with utmost professionalism. Despite the steep price and quality of service, Le Baccara picks up on the easygoing atmosphere that's evident throughout the casino-hotel complex. Even with its cherry-wood paneling and rich fabrics, the restaurant is anything but stuffy; within 5 minutes of being seated the sommelier was telling me about his recent multi-stage marathon run in the Sahara. We opted for the eight-course Gastronomic Menu with our marathon man's recommendations from the restaurant's 13,000-bottle cellar. The menu changes with the season, but always features fresh local game, meat, and vegetables, as well as imaginatively prepared seafood. Whether you've just lined your pockets at the blackjack table or simply feel like splurging on a meal you'll remember from your vacation, Le Baccara offers exceptional dining experiences.

1 boulevard du Casino, Gatineau. ℂ **800/665-2274** or 819/772-6210. Main courses C$29–C$58; table d'hôte (5–8 courses) C$55–C$115; wine selection C$65–C$75. AE, DC, MC, V. Wed–Sun 5:30–11pm.

MODERATE

Le Pied de Cochon ★ FRENCH   Begin with a simple green salad, *moules marinière* (mussels with white wine), or rabbit terrine. Progress to roast leg of lamb, grilled steak with tarragon, or veal medallions with chanterelles. Complement the remainder of your bottle of wine with a fine selection of cheese. Indulge in a fine, rich, crème brûlée—and above all, linger. The decor is comfortable but unremarkable and the atmosphere is smart casual. Service is satisfyingly attentive: Your needs will be anticipated, but the intimacy—or pace—of your meal is not intruded upon. In summer, enjoy the terrace in front.

248 rue Montcalm, Gatineau (Hull sector). ℂ **819/777-5808**. www.lepieddecochon.ca. Reservations recommended. Main courses C$16–C$23; table d'hôte (3 courses) from C$29. AE, DC, MC, V. Tues–Fri 11:30am–2pm and 5:30–10pm; Sat 5:30–10pm.

7

Exploring Ottawa

Ottawa is defined by two factors: its role as Canada's capital, and its proximity to nature. As a result, there is a wealth of major attractions—such as the national museums, Parliament Buildings, and cultural festivals—and an abundance of opportunities to explore the historic Rideau Canal, bike, in-line skate, or ski in the nearby Gatineau Hills.

You could build a jampacked itinerary for each day of your vacation and still not see and do everything, so take your time to plan well and create a mix of activities that will allow you to sample the best the city has to offer.

If you're only in Ottawa for a short break, concentrate your sightseeing in and around the downtown area. You'll find that many of the major attractions are within walking distance of one another along Wellington Street and Sussex Drive, or on streets leading off these two roads. Visit www.virtualmuseum.ca for a listing

and brief description of some of Ottawa's museums and heritage attractions.

Don't forget that Ottawa is a year-round destination, despite the harsh winters. Officially recognized as the world's largest skating rink, the Ottawa portion of the Rideau Canal becomes a focal point for outdoor activities in winter, especially during Winterlude in February. Once spring comes, each week brings a new festival or cultural celebration. See chapter 3, "Planning Your Trip to Ottawa," for a list of annual events.

If this is a family vacation, keep in mind that many museums put on special programs and workshops for children and families on weekends and during school holidays (1 week in mid-Mar, the months of July and Aug, and 2 weeks surrounding Christmas and New Year's Day). Call the **Capital Infocentre** (© **800/465-1867** or 613/239-5000) for exact dates, as they vary from year to year.

1 THE TOP ATTRACTIONS

Parliament Hill ★★★ (Kids)   The dominant site in downtown Ottawa, **Parliament Hill** is the focal point for most of Canada's national celebrations, including day-long events and spectacular fireworks on July 1, Canada Day. The **Parliament Buildings,** with their grand sandstone-block construction, steeply pitched copper roofs, and multiple towers are an impressive sight. In 1860, Prince Edward (later King Edward VII) laid the cornerstone for the original buildings, which were finished in time to host the inaugural session of the first Parliament of the new Dominion of Canada in 1867. As you enter through the main gates on Wellington Street and approach the **Centre Block** with its stately central **Peace Tower,** you'll pass the Centennial Flame, lit by then–prime minister Lester B. Pearson on New Year's Eve 1966 to mark the start of Canada's centennial year. In June, July, and August, you can meet the **Royal Canadian Mounted Police** (affectionately called Mounties) on Parliament Hill. They're friendly—and love to have their photo taken.

If you're visiting the capital between mid-May and early September, your first stop on Parliament Hill should be the **Info-Tent,** where you can pick up free information on the

Canada's Government: The Basics

Canada functions as a parliamentary democracy, which means its government consists of elected representatives chosen by its citizens. Based on the British structure of federal government that was established when Canada became self-governing, the **Parliament of Canada** comprises the head of state (**Queen Elizabeth II,** who is represented by the **governor-general**), the **Senate** (the equivalent of the British House of Lords), and the **House of Commons.**

The parliamentary duties of the **governor-general** include summoning **Parliament** following each general election, announcing the current govern-ment's objectives at the beginning of each session of **Parliament** through the Speech from the Throne, and approving all bills passed by the **Senate** and the **House of Commons.** The **Senate** is made up of 105 **senators,** who represent regions and provinces. They are appointed by the **governor-general** on the advice of the **prime minister.**

The **House of Commons** has 308 seats. **Members of Parliament (MPs)** are elected to represent their constituents in each of these 308 **ridings,** or political districts, for up to 5 years. The party that wins the greatest number of seats in the House of Commons in a federal election usually forms the government, and the party's leader becomes **prime minister.**

The prime minister appoints **cabinet ministers,** who are responsible for a specific portfolio, for example, health, finance, industry, the environment, or immigration.

A parliament is made up of one or more sessions during its lifetime. Parlia-ment sits about 27 weeks of the year, from September to June. Breaks are

Hill and **free same-day tickets for tours of the Parliament Buildings.** Between Septem-ber and May, get same-day tickets from the **Visitor Welcome Centre,** at the foot of the Peace Tower. Tickets are limited, though, and there is no guarantee in the busy summer months or on weekends in spring and fall that you will get tickets for your first choice of time, or even day. Also be aware that the presence of a visiting dignitary or other special events can disrupt the normal schedule, with no prior notice. If you're visiting in summer and are adverse to lines, try to book your tour for one of the evening sessions. During the busy summer months, drop by the information tent on the lawn in front of the Parliament Buildings between 9 and 10am. You can reserve a spot on the free tour of the Centre Block for later in the day, including some evening bookings, and avoid the long lines.

Since the September 11, 2001, terrorist attacks in the United States, security has been tightened significantly on Ottawa's Parliament Hill and plans are being prepared to increase security. This may affect visitor access in the future.

Tours of the Parliament Buildings last from 20 minutes to an hour, depending on whether Parliament is in session. Allow at least 2 hours for a full tour of Parliament Hill.

The Parliament Buildings consist of 3 blocks of buildings—the **Centre Block,** with its central **Peace Tower,** and the flanking **West Block** and **East Block.** This is the heart of Canadian political life—the workplace of the House of Commons and the Senate.

scheduled to allow **senators** and **MPs** to spend time working in their regions and ridings.

The **Senate** and the **House of Commons** each meet on a regular basis to deal with issues of national concern and to debate bills (legislative proposals) that are introduced by **cabinet ministers, senators,** or **private members. Question Period** is often the liveliest part of each sitting day. During **Question Period, cabinet ministers** are held accountable for their departments' activities and also for the policies of the **government.**

To oversee the proceedings of the **Senate** and the **House of Commons,** to maintain order, and to enforce parliamentary rules and traditions, each house has a **speaker,** who sits on a ceremonial chair at one end of the chamber, with the **government** on the right and the **opposition** on the left. The **speaker of the senate** is appointed on the advice of the **prime minister.** The **speaker of the House of Commons** is a current **MP,** elected by peers.

In addition to the federal government, whose seat is Ottawa, Canada's 10 provinces and three territories elect representatives to deal with matters of provincial and territorial concern. The provinces and territories combine to make a federation in which the power is distributed between the **federal government** and the **provincial legislatures.**

When Parliament is in session, you can watch the proceedings from the public galleries in both the Senate chambers and the House of Commons. Call the National Infocentre at (C) **800/465-1867** or visit www.parl.gc.ca to view the calendar of sitting days.

When the House of Commons is sitting, you can visit the public gallery and observe the 308 elected members debating in their grand green chamber with its tall stained-glass windows. Parliament is in recess usually from late June until early September and occasionally between September and June, including the Easter and Christmas holidays. Otherwise, the House usually sits on weekdays. The 105 appointed members of the Senate sit in a stately red chamber. The West Block, containing parliamentary offices, is closed to the public. You can tour the East Block, which has four historic rooms restored for public viewing: the original governor-general's office, restored to the period of Lord Dufferin (1872–1878); the offices of Sir John A. Macdonald and Sir Georges-Étienne Cartier (the principal fathers of Confederation); and the Privy Council Chamber with anteroom.

The **Centre Block** is considered to be one of the world's best examples of Gothic revival architecture, complete with the pointed arches, prominent buttresses, and contrasting stonework that characterize the style. Free guided tours of the Centre Block, which may include the **House of Commons,** the **Senate,** the richly ornamented **Hall of Honour,** and the **Library of Parliament,** are available in English and French all year. Guides tell animated stories and interesting anecdotes about the buildings and the people who have worked there. When Parliament is in session, the tours do not visit the House of Commons or the Senate, but visitors are invited to take a seat in the public galleries

Ottawa Attractions

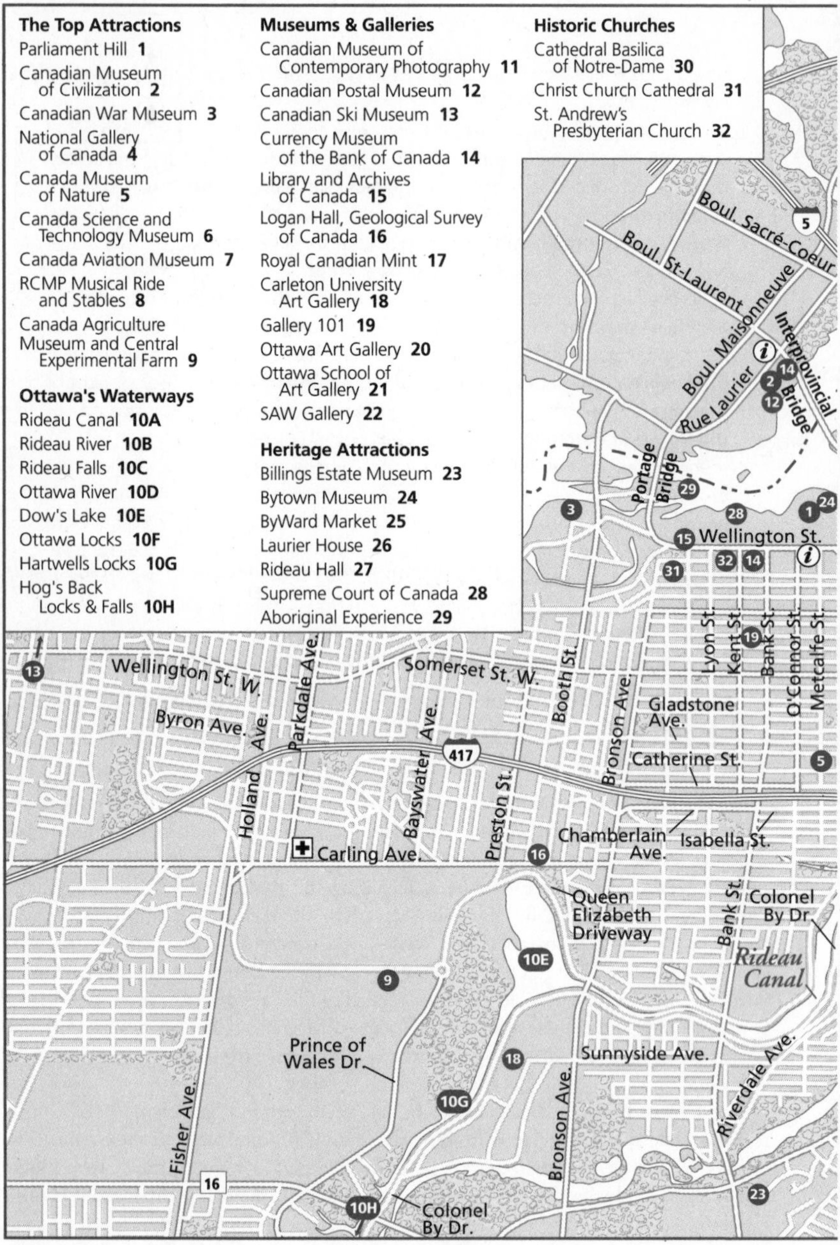

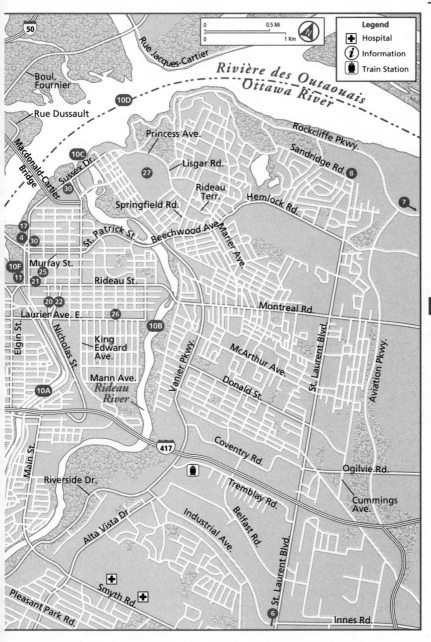

(Fun Facts   **Centre Block History**

Since 1916, the Centre Block building has been something of a work in progress. Late on a frigid February 3 that year, fire broke out in a wastepaper basket.
Within hours, the building was gutted. Only the magnificent Parliamentary
Library, a circular edifice that sits behind the main building, was saved, thanks
to the quick thinking of a clerk who closed the fireproof doors before making
his exit. The only other things saved from the inferno were a pair of ceremonial
chairs, which reportedly were dragged to a nearby cathedral by future prime
minister William Lyon Mackenzie King, then a labor consultant for the Liberal
Party. A bell, which crashed down through the devastated Victoria Tower at the
height of the fire, was salvaged from the ruins and mounted for display in later
years. Destroyed was Thomas Fuller's ornate original building, designed in
1859 and opened in 1866. In its place rose a more majestic building, designed
by the firm of Pearson & Marchand, and distinguished by its central tower—
called Victoria Tower until 1933 and then the Peace Tower thereafter.

and watch the proceedings. Centre Block tour times vary throughout the year and can
change without prior notice; call the **Capital Infocentre** at © **800/465-1867** or 613/
239-5000 for information.

The imposing 92m (302-ft.) campanile of the Peace Tower is one of the most easily
recognizable Canadian landmarks and dominates the Centre Block's facade. It houses a
53-bell carillon, a huge clock, an observation deck, and the Memorial Chamber, commemorating Canada's war dead. A 10.5m (34-ft.) bronze mast flying a Canadian flag
tops the tower. When Parliament is in session, the tower is lit. One-hour concerts of the
53-bell carillon of the Peace Tower are presented weekdays in July and August at 2pm.
From September to June, there is a 15-minute noon concert most weekdays. The elevator
in the tower is unusual; see if you can sense the 10-degree angle off vertical that the
elevator travels for the first 29m (95 ft.) of the journey. It's well worth the trip—the views
from the observation deck are marvelous in every direction. The tower closes half an hour
before the last Centre Block tour of the day.

Also in the Centre Block, the Library of Parliament is a glorious 16-sided dome hewn
from Nepean sandstone, supported outside by flying buttresses and paneled inside with
Canadian white pine. Designed in Gothic revival style, the library was opened in 1876.
Inside, a variety of textures, colors, and hand-crafted detail is evident. The floor is an
intricate parquet design of cherry, walnut, and oak. The pine paneling features thousands
of carved flowers, masks, and mythical beasts. The center of the room is dominated by a
white marble statue of a young Queen Victoria, created in 1871. In 2006, the library
reopened after extensive renovation and restoration.

Between late June and early September, you can get free same-day tickets at the Info-
Tent for a guided tour of the Parliament Hill grounds. Visitors will enjoy an introduction
to some of the historical figures who have shaped Canada's past and present. Otherwise,
you can wander around Parliament Hill and explore the monuments, grounds, and exterior of the buildings on your own with the help of a 24-page outdoor self-guiding booklet called *Discover the Hill,* available from the **Capital Infocentre** across the street from

(Fun Facts) Raising the Roof

One of the most laborious tasks of the renovation and repair of the Library of Parliament was the replacement of the copper roof. When the roofs of the Parliament Buildings are replaced, the new copper turns brown after just a couple of weeks, but it can take up to 30 years for them to take on the stately green hue. The old copper panels from the Library of Parliament have been incorporated into the interior walls of the new Canadian War Museum.

the Parliament Buildings. Stroll the grounds clockwise around the Centre Block—they're dotted with statues honoring such prominent historical figures as Queen Victoria, Sir George-Étienne Cartier, William Lyon Mackenzie King, and Sir Wilfrid Laurier. Behind the building is a promenade with sweeping views of the Ottawa River. Here too is the old Centre Block's bell, which crashed to the ground shortly after tolling midnight on the eve of the 1916 fire. At the bottom of the cliff behind Parliament Hill, a pleasant pathway leads along the river. The pathway is also accessible from the Ottawa Locks at the foot of the Rideau Canal, where it meets the Ottawa River. In July and August you may be lucky enough to meet one or more of the costumed interpreters who represent historical characters from early Confederation times and exchange a word or two with them.

One last attraction for summer visitors to the Parliament Buildings is **Sound and Light on the Hill.** Every evening between early July and early September, Canada's history unfolds and the country's spirit is revealed through music, lights, and giant images projected on the Parliament Buildings. This half-hour display of sound and light is free of charge, and limited bleacher seating is available.

Wellington St., just west of the Rideau Canal. (C) **800/465-1867** or 613/239-5000. www.parl.gc.ca/information/visitors. Free admission. Daily from 9am, but subject to change without notice; Centre Block closed Christmas Day, New Year's Day, and July 1.

Canadian Museum of Civilization ★★★   The largest of Canada's cultural institutions, the Canadian Museum of Civilization (CMC) is a combination of permanent and temporary exhibits that explore human history with special, although not exclusive, reference to Canada. Along with Parliament Hill, this is Ottawa's must-see attraction for visitors. The museum is located on the north shore of the Ottawa River in Gatineau, its stunning, award-winning architecture clearly visible from downtown Ottawa. The building's flowing curves appear to have been sculpted by the forces of nature. In fact, the building is the work of Canadian architect Douglas Cardinal, whose Native heritage is frequently reflected in his designs. Inside the museum, the impressive design continues to delight visitors as they make their way around the exhibition halls. Added attractions within the building are the Canadian Children's Museum, the Canadian Postal Museum, and the IMAX theater. You could easily spend the whole day here, especially if you take in an IMAX show, but even a cursory visit will take at least 2 hours.

You'll enter the building at street level, where you can buy your museum entrance tickets and IMAX tickets and access the Canadian Children's Museum. You can register for a 45-minute guided tour of the Grand Hall, the First Peoples Hall, or the Canada Hall for an extra C$3 per person, or just wander on your own. Before you begin your exploration of the museum, be sure to drop off coats, umbrellas, and other outdoor gear at the complimentary cloakroom and collect a stroller or wheelchair if needed. There is

How Much Do You Know About Parliament Hill?

1. How many female speakers of the House of Commons have there been?
2. How tall is the Peace Tower?
3. How was the Parliamentary Library saved during the terrible fire of 1916 that destroyed the rest of the Parliament Buildings?
4. What color is the carpet in the Senate Chamber?
5. What stands in the center of the Parliamentary Library?
6. How many bells does the carillon of the Peace Tower have?
7. When was Canada's now-familiar red-and-white flag raised for the first time on the Peace Tower?
8. Who carved the frieze in the House of Commons foyer that depicts the history of Canada. How long did it take to complete?
9. The exterior and interior of the Parliament Buildings are constructed with primarily what types of stone?
10. What images can be seen in the stained-glass windows of the House of Commons?
11. Who lit the Centennial Flame in 1967?
12. How long does it take for the copper roof panels to turn green?

ANSWERS: 1. Two. 2. 92.2m (302 ft.). 3. A quick-thinking employee closed the iron doors to prevent the fire from spreading there. 4. Red. 5. A white marble statue of Queen Victoria. 6. 53. 7. February 15, 1965. 8. Dominion Sculptor Eleanor Milne; 11 years. 9. Nepean sandstone from Ontario in the exterior and Tyndall limestone from Manitoba inside. 10. The floral emblems of Canada's provinces and territories. 11. Prime Minister Lester B. Pearson. 12. About 30 years.

underground pay parking with an inside entrance to the museum. For visitors with disabilities, there are designated bays on level 1 of the parking arcade, elevator access to all floors, and access ramps installed where necessary. Spaces are reserved for wheelchairs in the IMAX theater and in the performance/lecture theater.

From the street-level lobby, descend the escalator to the museum's showpiece—the magnificent **Grand Hall ★★**. This enormous exhibition hall features a display of more than 40 totem poles, representing the culture of the Native peoples of Canada's Pacific Northwest coast. Six Native house facades have been constructed in the hall, based on architectural styles of different coastal nations over the past 150 years. The Grand Hall also has a performance stage where storytelling sessions, demonstrations, and performances are held regularly. At the far end of the hall, a forest setting has been created in a room displaying prehistoric artifacts and articles from the Tsimshian people of British Columbia.

Set under a dramatically lit 17m-high (56-ft.) dome, **Canada Hall ★★★** takes visitors on a journey through 1,000 years of Canada's social and cultural history. The Canada Hall is a presentation of full-scale tableaux and buildings that have been constructed in the architectural style of specific historical periods using materials (solid wood beams and planking, plaster, stucco, stone, and so on) and methods in use at the time. The sights and sounds of the country's past unfold before you, beginning with the landing of the

Norsemen on Newfoundland's coast in A.D. 1000. As you move through the hall, you go west through the country and forward in time. Look below deck in a full-scale stern section of a 16th-century Basque whaling ship, see the crude process of rendering whale blubber into oil in a Labrador whaling station, and peer into a farmhouse in the St. Lawrence Valley in 18th-century New France. You'll walk into the public square of a town in New France and have the liberty of opening doors and peeking through windows into the lives of the inhabitants. Dramamuse—the museum's resident theater company—continuously reenacts daily events from Canada's past, and you may be lucky enough to meet one of the colorful historical characters who interact with the public and add a new dimension to the museum experience. Feel free to ask questions. A lumber camp shanty, a Conestoga wagon, and the main street of a small Ontario town in the Victorian era are a few more sights you'll enjoy during your exploration of Canada's heritage. **First Peoples Hall** showcases the cultural, historical, and artistic accomplishments of aboriginal peoples in Canada, and contains more than 2,000 artifacts. Various aspects of First Peoples' identity are explored, from the earliest origins to present-day contributions and challenges. Exhibits include an art gallery dedicated to contemporary aboriginal art.

In addition to the three main halls, there are several distinct exhibition spaces dedicated to short-term displays encompassing all museum disciplines—archaeology, ethnology, folk culture, and history. Call the museum to see what's on in the special exhibitions galleries, mezzanine, and salons, or just drop in and be surprised. The main exhibit during the summer of 2009 will be Mythic Creatures: Dragons, Unicorns, and Mermaids, featuring legends and fairy tales as told through ancient and modern art, theater, dance, and film.

The **Canadian Postal Museum** is housed within the Canadian Museum of Civilization and admission is included with the main museum ticket. Discover the story of postal communications from coast to coast and around the world. Interactive displays and a high-tech station teach visitors about the world of stamps. All kinds of memorabilia are on display, from toys and quilts to mailboxes and mailbags. A permanent exhibition shows the role the post has played in Canada's history and features a complete post office from Quebec. Temporary exhibits range from one introducing stamp collecting and another providing you the opportunity to design your own stamp to displays of postage stamps from around the world, with specimens from the Canadian Museum's International Philatelic Collection.

Kids absolutely love to play in the **Canadian Children's Museum** ★★. If you have children with you when you visit the Canadian Museum of Civilization, visit here first. Let the kids run around, play, and blow off steam in there, take a break for a drink and a snack or lunch (you can choose from formal dining or a cafeteria; both offer spectacular views over the Ottawa River toward the Parliament Buildings, or brown bag it in the Lunchbox), and then explore the main exhibition halls. Admission to the children's museum is included with the main entrance fee for the Canadian Museum of Civilization, although the hours may differ slightly from the main museum hours. You can visit just the children's museum if you wish, but the price will be the same.

Every exhibit is child size and the layout strongly encourages exploration. Activities and programs use real materials from the museum's collection. Visitors touch, climb, build, manipulate, move, and create. Through this highly interactive learning, children explore the world and its many cultures. For example, they can step inside a child-size Japanese family home. In the tatami (straw-matting) room, kids are invited to try the art of origami (Japanese paper folding) or write their own haiku poetry in the garden. Other adventures include exploring an Egyptian pyramid, crawling into a Bedouin tent, putting on an Indonesian shadow puppet show, sitting astride a camel, driving a Pakistani tour bus, or building a brick wall. Kids up to age 14 are the target group, but those who will get the most out of the museum (and may want to stay all day) are probably 4- to 11-year-olds. Programs, workshops, and theater performances are scheduled year-round. Call ahead to find out about upcoming special events. During the summer months, you get double the fun because the outdoor exhibition park Adventure World is open. Play chess on a giant chessboard, hop along with hopscotch, or shoot some marbles. The Artrageous Adventure exhibit area hosts visual arts activities for children. The Waterways exhibit has a boat-making yard where you can design, build, and launch your own model watercraft. Kids can climb on a log-pulling tugboat or take an imaginary tour in the floatplane.

The whole family will love the **Imax Theatre ★★**. Seven stories high and with a screen 10 times the size of a conventional movie screen, the IMAX and IMAX DOME create the feeling of being wrapped in sight and sound. To experience the full effect, a hemispheric IMAX DOME 23m (75 ft.) in diameter moves into place overhead once the audience is seated—the seats tilt back to give the audience a comfortable and clear view of the dome. Not all films use the entire screening system. Advance ticket purchase is recommended, as shows often sell out. Buy tickets in person at the museum box office (there's a discount if purchased with a museum entrance ticket). All ages admitted. Plan to arrive 20 minutes before show time, as latecomers will not be admitted.

100 Laurier St., Gatineau, QC. ✆ **800/555-5621** or 819/776-7000; 819/776-7010 for IMAX Theatre. www. civilization.ca. Admission C$10 adults, C$8 seniors and students, C$6 children, C$25 families (max. 4 people), free for museum members; free admission Thurs 4–9pm, Heritage Day (third weekend in Feb), Museums Day (mid-May), July 1, and Nov 11. IMAX tickets C$10 adults, C$8 seniors and students, C$6 children 3–12, C$25 families (max. 2 adults and 2 children). May 1–June 30 Fri–Wed 9am–6pm, Thurs 9am–9pm (children's museum till 7pm); July 1–first Tues in Sept Sat–Wed 9am–9pm, Thurs–Fri 9am–9pm; first Wed in Sept–second Tues in Oct Fri–Wed 9am–6pm, Thurs 9am–9pm (children's museum till 6pm); second Wed in Oct–Apr 30 Tues–Wed and Fri–Sun 9am–5pm, Thurs 9am–9pm (children's museum till 5pm). IMAX Theatre hours may differ from museum hours. Parking underground C$1.75 per half-hour, C$10 daily max., C$5 flat rate after 6pm; additional metered parking on adjacent street. From the Ottawa River Pkwy. or Wellington St. downtown, take the Portage Bridge to Gatineau and turn right onto rue Laurier. The museum is on the right. From the east side of the canal, take Sussex Dr. and cross the Royal Alexandra Bridge. The museum is on the immediate left as you exit the bridge.

Canadian War Museum ★★ The Canadian War Museum, which opened on May 8, 2005—the 60th anniversary of V-E (Victory in Europe) Day and the 125th anniversary of the Canadian War Museum as an institution—delivers an unforgettable visitor experience. The **permanent galleries** have made full use of leading-edge museum-design theories and techniques to bring to life Canada's role in conflicts and war, emphasizing how military events have affected Canadians at a personal, national, and international level. The story of war and its consequences is told through the stories, artifacts, and memories of ordinary Canadians, with a view to presenting the human story rather than simply a display of objects and artifacts, although there is an extensive collection of weaponry, trucks, and tanks. In addition to eight permanent exhibit galleries, which trace conflict involving Canada from the European settlement to the present, there are spaces for **special exhibitions,** an **art gallery** featuring a fine collection of **war art,** and two special halls: **Memorial Hall** and **Regeneration Hall. Memorial Hall,** with its spare interior, is designed as a sanctuary for personal remembrance. A single window has been placed so that each November 11 at precisely 11am—the time of the World War I

Tips **Online Tribute to the Fallen**

The **Canadian Virtual War Memorial** serves as an electronic tribute to the Canadians and Newfoundlanders—who only became Canadian citizens in 1949—who have lost their lives in major conflicts since 1884. The website also serves as a searchable database so people can look for men and women in their own families who have given their lives for their country. Canadians are invited to submit digital images of photos, letters, postcards, medals, and other war memorabilia. Visit **www.virtualmemorial.ca** for instructions on how to add your family's war memorabilia to the memorial.

armistice—the sun will illuminate the Tombstone of the Unknown Soldier, which originally marked the grave in France. **Regeneration Hall** is the final stop on the museum tour. It is a dramatic space flanked by expansive angled walls. The message here is hope—for the future and for remembrance of the past. "Lest we forget" and *"N'oublions jamais"* are projected on one wall in Morse code by sunlight streaming through a series of dots and dashes on the opposite wall. Still, the new museum didn't open without controversy. Some in the peace movement have complained that the displays give short shrift to alternative views of war, and portray the long-standing Canadian antiwar movement as nothing more than a byproduct of the 1960s. Calls for an expanded recognition of alternatives to armed conflict have gone unanswered, and in fact one display has been altered to assuage veterans groups who argued that Allied forces did not intentionally target civilian areas during the bombing of Germany in 1945. The museum is located at **Lebreton Flats,** a green-space area about 2km (1¼ miles) west of **Parliament Hill.** Allow 3 hours for a full tour of the museum, and be aware that children under 12 will likely tire quickly here.

1 Vimy Place, Ottawa. ℃ **800/555-5621** or 819/776-8600. www.warmuseum.ca. Admission C$10 adults, C$8 seniors and students, C$6 children 3–12, C$25 families (4 people, max. 2 adults); free admission Thurs 4–9pm, Heritage Day (third weekend in Feb), Museums Day (mid-May), July 1, and Nov 11. Early May–June 30 Fri–Wed 9am–6pm, Thurs 9am–9pm; July 1–first Mon in Sept Sat–Wed 9am–6pm, Thurs–Fri 9am–9pm; first Tues in Sept to mid-Oct Fri–Wed 9am–6pm, Thurs 9am–9pm; Mid-Oct to late April Tues–Wed and Fri–Sun 9am–5pm, Thurs 9am–9pm. Closed one week early to mid-Jan. Parking underground C$1.75 per half-hour, C$10 daily max., C$5 flat rate after 6pm; additional metered parking on adjacent street. From Wellington St. in downtown Ottawa, head west past Booth St. traffic lights until you reach Vimy Place. Turn right into the museum. There is no access to the museum when heading north on Booth St. toward Quebec.

National Gallery of Canada ★★ One of the most attractive buildings in the city, the National Gallery, designed by architect Moshe Safdie, glitters and gleams from a promontory overlooking the Ottawa River. The public entrance to the Grand Hall is along a cavernous sloped-glass concourse that offers splendid views of Parliament Hill. Ingeniously designed shafts with reflective panels maximize the amount of natural light that floods the galleries.

Regularly on display are more than 800 paintings, sculptures, and decorative works by Canadian artists, a sampling of the 10,000 works in the permanent collection. Among the highlights are a comprehensive collection of works by Tom Thomson and the Group of Seven, early Quebecois artists, and Montreal automatistes. European masters are also represented, from Corot and Turner to Chagall and Picasso, and contemporary galleries feature pop art and minimalism, plus abstract works from Canadian and American artists.

EXPLORING OTTAWA · 7 · THE TOP ATTRACTIONS

Although the Canadian collection is unparalleled, the foreign contemporary collection will likely disappoint visitors. Budget at least 2 hours of viewing time, and if you're like me, you'll want to take a break at some point to revive your senses. Advance tickets may be purchased for some exhibitions—if you particularly want to see a certain one, avoid disappointment by getting tickets ahead of time. Visit **www.national.gallery.ca** for a full calendar of events and ticket information.

Families can visit the Artissimo kiosk weekends and during school vacations, where kids ages 3 and up accompanied by an adult can create their own masterpieces. Family workshops are designed for parents and kids to learn more about art, its interpretation, and its origins. Artissimo (✆ **613/998-4888**) is a drop-in program, but registration is required for workshops and vacation activities programs. Programs are also available for guests with special needs, including practical workshops for intellectually impaired visitors and tours for visually impaired visitors.

Free guided tours of the permanent collection are held daily at 2pm. Facilities include a cafeteria, a cafe, and a gift and bookstore, the last well worth a visit. Wheelchairs are available.

380 Sussex Dr. ✆ **800/319-2787** or 613/990-1985. www.national.gallery.ca. Admission C$9 adults, C$7 seniors and students, C$4 youth 12–19, free for children under 12, C$18 families (max. 2 adults and 3 children); free admission Thurs after 5pm. Admission for special exhibitions varies. May 1–Sept 30 Fri–Wed 10am–5pm, Thurs 10am–8pm; Oct 1–end of Apr Tues–Wed and Fri–Sun 10am–5pm, Thurs 10am–8pm. Parking underground C$2.50 per half-hour, C$12 daily max.

Canadian Museum of Nature ★★ The wonders of the natural world are featured at the Canadian Museum of Nature, housed in the Victoria Memorial Museum building, which was officially recognized for its national historical significance in 2004. The architecture of the building is remarkable. Built of local sandstone, the Tudor revival design includes towers, arched windows, a crenellated roofline, magnificent stained-glass windows, and a grand central staircase.

Note: A major multiyear renovation project began in 2004. The museum is open during this period, but some exhibitions will be closed as the work progresses. New galleries were open at the end of 2006 and work is expected to be completed by June 2010. Even with the renovations, you can expect to spent at least 1½ hours here.

Parts of western Canada have yielded exceptional finds of dinosaur skeletons and the museum has some particularly good specimens. The **Talisman Energy Fossil Gallery** (Kids) on the first floor gives the popular dinosaurs an impressive new home in a setting that emphasizes environmental concerns and tells a powerful story of the dinosaurs' extinction.

Canada's mammals are featured on the second floor, many of them showcased to great effect in dioramas painted by famed Manitoba landscape artist Clarence Tillenius in the 1950s.

(Fun Facts) Too Big to Move

In order to move the eight giant mammal dioramas—one of the most-popular attractions at the museum—during renovations, technicians had to saw the fiberglass in half and reassemble it. Artists then carefully touched up the decades-old backdrops. The final work was inspected by the original artist, Clarence Tillenius, now in his 90s.

Fun Facts **Natural Law**

Following the fire that destroyed the Parliament Buildings in 1916, emergency quarters were set up for the government in the building that is now the home of the Canadian Museum of Nature. The House of Commons sat in the auditorium for 4 years, and the Senate occupied the Hall of Invertebrate Fossils (no pun intended). In 1919, the body of Sir Wilfrid Laurier lay in state in the auditorium.

The **Bird Gallery** on the fourth floor displays hundreds of species and is one of the world's largest collections of Canadian birds. This gallery is highly interactive, with touch-screen computer displays and a wild bird play area for younger children.

My last visit—in spring 2008—revealed that work on the west wing of the building is now essentially finished, and a peek through the heavy plastic lining the majestic central staircase showed work continuing apace on the eastern half of the building. Eventually, the east wing will house an extensive display on human evolution and the **Water Gallery.**

Highly entertaining and educational nature documentaries are shown in the high-definition electronic cinema. Daily shows, usually 30 to 45 minutes long, are screened in both official languages. Admission is included with the museum entrance fee.

Victoria Memorial Museum bldg., 240 McLeod St. ✆ **800/263-4433** or 613/566-4700. www.nature.ca. Admission C$5, free for children under 3, C$13 families (5 people max., 3 adults max., 1 child under 18 min.); free admission Sat 9am–noon, Museums Day (mid-May), and July 1. Admission will likely vary during renovation. Sept 5–Apr 30 Tues–Wed and Fri–Sun 9am–5pm, Thurs 9am–8pm; May 1–Sept 4 Fri–Tues 9am–6pm, Wed–Thurs 9am–8pm. Closed second week of Jan. Located at the corner of Metcalfe and McLeod sts., 1 block west of Elgin St.

Canada Science and Technology Museum ★★ Easy to overlook because it is located outside the downtown core, this excellent museum has eye-catching interactive exhibits at every turn. Plan a half-day visit here if you or your kids enjoy applied science. One of the most intriguing long-term exhibits is **Canada in Space.** Discover the story of Canada's underrated part in the exploration of space, including its significant role in the early years of satellite technology, and its ongoing contribution to global communications. A space flight simulator will take you on a virtual voyage in a six-seat cinema pod that moves to the action on the huge screen. Separate tickets at a cost of C$3 are required; it's simplest to purchase these when you arrive at the front desk. Take note of the ride time so you don't miss your trip to outer space. The **Locomotive Hall** holds four huge steam locomotives, meticulously restored and maintained. You can climb in the cabs of some of them and you can also see a caboose, business car, and old number boards, and hear sound effects that give you the feel of riding in a live locomotive. A major **exhibition on communications** is one of the largest of its kind in Canada and illustrates the history of electric and electronic communications in Canada. **Innovation Canada** celebrates great Canadian inventions. Lively, short demonstrations on various science and technology topics are held frequently during the day; ask for show times and topics when you arrive, and take in an entertaining show or two during your visit. Lots of programs and workshops are scheduled, so call ahead to see what's on. In the summer, have a picnic in Technology Park in front of the museum—kids will be fascinated taking a close-up look at the Cape North Lighthouse, radar antenna, pump jack, Convair Atlas rocket, telescope, windmill, and steam locomotive. The museum's educational-themed gift shop, located close to the main entrance, is an intriguing place to browse. The museum is fully wheelchair accessible and parking is free.

1867 St. Laurent Blvd. ☏ **866/442-4416** or 613/991-3044. www.sciencetech.technomuses.ca. Admission C$7.50 adults, C$5 seniors and students, C$3.50 children 4–14, free for children under 4, C$18 families (max. 2 adults and 3 children). Simulator ride C$3 per person. Free parking. May 1–Labor Day daily 9am–5pm; Labor Day–Apr 30 Tues–Sun 9am–5pm. From the Queensway (Hwy. 417) take the St. Laurent Blvd. South exit. Go south on St. Laurent Blvd. to Lancaster Rd. and turn left. The museum entrance is on the left.

Canada Aviation Museum ★★   One of the world's best collections of **vintage aircraft** is on display here, with the emphasis on Canada's significant role in aviation history. Whether you're young or old, you'll find something to catch your interest as you stroll through the huge exhibition hall and trace the history of aviation from its beginning to the jet age. You can come close (but not close enough to touch) to more than 50 aircraft inside the building and a number of others displayed outside in the summer months; the total number of aircraft in the collection is approximately 130. A replica of Alexander Graham Bell's Silver Dart—the first powered plane to fly in Canada—hangs from the ceiling as you enter. From that point, as you move through the museum, you'll see such famous aircraft as the Sopwith Camel, Messerschmitt, Spitfire, and Lancaster Bomber, the Beaver and Otter bush planes that helped Canada settle the North, as well as more contemporary aircraft. Video terminals dot the hall, showing short documentaries about aspects of flight. Several interactive displays designed to teach the principles of flight are simple enough for children to operate and understand. Workshops for kids are offered, ranging from 5-week midafternoon preschooler sessions to daily 2-hour sessions for kids ages 6 to 13. Entertaining demonstrations are scheduled throughout the day—on everything from understanding wind tunnels to flying a Cessna 150.

If you're looking for something a little different, try an evening program with scheduled events and dinner, or an overnight stay where you can explore the museum by flashlight and sleep under the wings of an airplane. If you are an aviation buff, or just love to fly, take advantage of a rare opportunity and splurge on a vintage aircraft flight, available from May to autumn. A 15-minute ride in an open-cockpit Waco UPF-7 biplane costs C$65 for a tour of Parliament Hill and downtown Ottawa or C$95 for a flight that also includes the Gatineau Hills. Prices are per person, based on two passengers per flight.

When you're back on terra firma, don't forget to take a turn through the Aeronautica Boutique, which stocks scale models of aircraft, books, posters, prints, toys, clothing, and kites. Free strollers and wheelchairs are available at the front entrance, plus a thoughtful addition: motorized wheelchairs for visitors with physical disabilities and seniors. There's also a library specializing in the history of aviation, with an emphasis on the Canadian experience. The library is primarily open by appointment for visitors with a special interest in aviation.

11 Aviation Pkwy. ☏ **800/463-2038** or 613/993-2010. www.aviation.technomuses.ca. Admission C$6 adults, C$5 seniors and students, C$3 children 4–15, free for children under 4; C$14 families (1 or 2 adults with children); free admission daily 4–5pm. May 1–Labor Day daily 9am–5pm; after Labor Day–April 30 Wed–Sun 10am–5pm. Closed Mon–Tues in winter except holidays and school breaks. Free parking. From downtown, travel northeast on Sussex Dr. (changes name to Rockcliffe Pkwy.) to Aviation Pkwy. Follow signs; museum is on the left.

RCMP Musical Ride Centre at Rockcliffe Stables   The Mounties are one of the most recognizable symbols of Canada throughout the world, and the police force's Musical Ride—which features mounted riders on highly trained horses—is its highest-profile

All About the Mounties

The Royal Canadian Mounted Police (RCMP) is Canada's national police force, providing a total federal policing service to all Canadians, and provincial and territorial policing to all areas except Ontario and Quebec (which operate their own independent provincial police forces). The RCMP is unique in the world because it provides policing services at the national, federal, provincial, and municipal levels. Their mission is to preserve the peace, uphold the law, and provide quality service in partnership with the communities they serve.

The idea of a mounted police force was conceived by Sir John A. Macdonald, Canada's first prime minister and minister of justice. Law enforcement officers were needed to open the western and northern frontiers of the young country for settlement and development in an orderly manner. In 1873, the North-West Mounted Police was created, inspired by the Royal Irish Constabulary and the mounted rifle units of the United States Army. A year later, approximately 275 officers and men were dispatched to northwestern Canada.

Over the years, the force expanded and developed into the present-day organization, which numbers about 22,200 employees in total. The Mounties do not, in fact, use horses for regular duties today. The last patrol on horseback was around 1936.

public element. Free tours of the training school and stables of the RCMP Musical Ride are available year-round. In the summer months, you'll find greater numbers of visitors and more frequent tour schedules. In the winter, it's advisable to call ahead and set up a time with the coordinator, although it's not essential. Tour guides are friendly and willing to answer questions about the Musical Ride or the Mounties in general. If you happen to visit on a day when the riders aren't practicing, or if the ride is away on tour across Canada (which happens often during the summer—check the Musical Ride website for an updated tour schedule), try to get tickets to one of their shows. Between May and October the ride is on tour, but there are always some Eastern Ontario venues. There's a boutique at the stables, open in the main tourist season, that stocks a variety of Mountie souvenirs.

Northeast corner of Sandridge Rd. and St. Laurent Blvd. © **613/998-8199.** www.rcmp.ca/musicalride/index_e.htm. Free admission. Donations accepted. May–Oct daily 9am–4pm; Nov–Apr Mon–Fri 10am–2pm. From downtown, follow Sussex Dr. (changes name to Rockcliffe Pkwy.) to Aviation Pkwy; follow the signs.

Canada Agriculture Museum & Central Experimental Farm ★ (Kids) One of Ottawa's unique features is the presence of a 400-hectare (988-acre) farm within its boundaries. Created in 1886 as one of five research farms across the country, the Central Experimental Farm continues to operate primarily as a scientific facility, but several parts in the northeast sector are open to the public. The **Canada Agriculture Museum,** which charges a modest entrance fee, features animal barns, special exhibits, and a chance to experience a traditional farm in action. The public can also visit the **Dominion Arboretum, Ornamental Gardens,** and **Tropical Greenhouse;** all three have free admission. The agriculture museum offers city slickers (and country bumpkins, for that matter) a chance to get up-close and personal with all things agricultural. The 2-hectare (5-acre)

Green Thumbs Up

Gardeners are well-known for their passion for touring other people's gardens, and if you're one of them, the Ottawa area has several lovely gardens open to the public. At the **Central Experimental Farm,** the **Arboretum** covers about 35 hectares (86 acres) of rolling land near the Prince of Wales Drive round-about. Open daily from sunrise to sunset, the Arboretum is a popular place for families to picnic and play in the summer. In the winter, the hills are used for tobogganing. Well over 2,400 distinct species and varieties of trees and shrubs grow here, with some dating from the 1880s. A donor tree program provides local residents and visitors with a means of contributing to the continued growth of the Arboretum, with more than 700 trees donated since 1991. The 3.2-hectare (8-acre) **Ornamental Gardens** are a must-see. They were created by the government in the late 19th century to assist European immigrant farmers to test imported flowers, shrubs, and trees in the Canadian environment. There is a perennial collection, annual garden, rose garden, sunken garden, and rock garden. The rose collection includes the Explorer series of winter-hardy roses. Some of the specimens in the hedge collection date from 1891. Approximately 100 types of iris and 125 strains of lilac are on display. The **Tropical Greenhouse,** relocated from Major's Hills Park in the 1930s, holds 500 different plants and is open daily 9am to 4pm. There is also a **Demonstration Organic Garden** adjacent to the experimental farm parking lot just off Prince of Wales Drive. The garden, maintained by volunteers, features companion planting, a perennial bed, a bee and butterfly bed, a fragrance bed, an herb bed, a rockery, fruit trees and bushes, vegetable beds that include heirloom varieties, and a composting area. **Maplelawn** is a historical Victorian walled garden located at 529 Richmond Rd. in Ottawa's west end. Dating from 1831, the garden has been preserved and rehabilitated by a volunteer group, using historical documents to aid preservation of the original design. Stroll the grounds of historic **Rideau Hall,** residence of the governor-general, and view the **Heritage Rose Garden.** The **Mackenzie King Estate,** located within beautiful **Gatineau Park,** features formal flower beds, a hidden rock garden, a collection of picturesque ruins from Canada and abroad, and forest trails. And last but not least—don't forget the magnificent displays of **tulips in mid-May** throughout the city of Ottawa.

site is a unique blend of modern working farm and museum. Several heritage buildings are on-site, including a dairy barn. The small-animal barn houses goats, sheep, pigs, and poultry. There's often something going on at the agriculture museum, whether it's a festival, a temporary exhibit, day camp, or a demonstration. If you're planning a visit, call ahead so you can catch one of the special days on the farm. Activities are planned with kids in mind and everyone from babies to seniors will enjoy meeting the animals and learning about the farm. Programs and special events focus on how science and technology meshes with modern agriculture and show visitors the processes by which Canadians get their food, textile fibers, and other agricultural products.

Admission to exhibits and animal barns C$6 adults, C$5 seniors and students, C$3 children 3–14, free for children under 3, C$13 families (max. 2 adults and 3 children, C$2 additional children, C$3 additional adults); free admission to Arboretum, Ornamental Gardens, and Tropical Greenhouse. Animal barns daily 9am–5pm except Dec 25; exhibits and barn boutique Mar 1–Oct 31 daily 9am–5pm; farm grounds daily sunrise–sunset; greenhouse daily 9am–4pm. Admission to the animal barns is free Nov 1–Feb 28, when the other exhibits are closed. Take Prince of Wales Dr. and follow the signs. The museum is just west of Prince of Wales Dr. between Carling Ave. and Baseline Rd.

2 MORE MUSEUMS & GALLERIES

MUSEUMS

Billings Estate Museum   This historical Georgian estate home, which was completed in 1829, is one of Ottawa's oldest properties. Built for Braddish and Lamira Billings, who settled on the land in 1813, the Billings estate includes several outbuildings on the 3.4-hectare (8¹/₂-acre) site and was home to five generations of the Billings family, spanning 2 centuries. Take an hour to browse the collections of family heirlooms, furnishings, tools, paintings, and documents on your own or take the brief guided tour. Hands-on activities; special events, such as antique car shows and a Mother's Day tea; and workshops are scheduled on a regular basis, and usually require an additional fee. Stroll and enjoy the lush lawns, colorful flower beds, wooded slopes, and old pathways. Enjoy tea on the lawn in the summer months, served several afternoons each week. A self-guided tour book can be purchased at the gift shop for C$5.

2100 Cabot St. ✆ **613/247-4830**. www.friendsofbillingsestatemuseum.org. Admission C$2.75 adults, C$2.25 seniors, C$1.75 children over 4, C$6.75 families, free for children 4 and under. Mid-May to Oct 31 Tues–Sun noon–5pm. Hours subject to change; call ahead.

Bytown Museum ★   Housed in Ottawa's oldest stone building (1827), which served as the commissariat during the construction of the Rideau Canal, this museum is operated by the Historical Society of Ottawa. Articles belonging to Lieutenant Colonel John By, the canal's builder and one of Ottawa's (then known as Bytown) most influential citizens, are on display. In addition, artifacts reflect the social history of local pioneer families in four period rooms and a number of changing exhibits. The rooms depict an 1850s Bytown kitchen, a French-Canadian lumber camp shanty, a Victorian parlor, and an early toy store. In 2008, the museum introduced a new audio tour that is available in six different languages and included in the price of admission. The museum is situated beside the Ottawa Locks, sandwiched between Parliament Hill and the Fairmont Château Laurier Hotel, and is worth a brief visit.

Beside Ottawa Locks. ✆ **613/234-4570**. www.bytownmuseum.com. Admission C$6 adults, C$4 seniors and students 13–18, C$3 children 5–12, free for children 4 and under, C$15 families (max. 2 adults, 3 children under 18), pay what you can June 25–Aug 27 Wed 10am–8pm. Apr to mid-May Mon–Fri 10am–2pm; mid-May to mid-Oct daily 10am–5pm (Wed till 8pm June 25–Aug 27); mid-Oct to Nov Mon–Fri 10am–2pm.

Canadian Museum of Contemporary Photography   This small museum is an affiliate of the National Gallery of Canada and the collection complements that of Canada's premier art gallery. On show is the best of documentary and art photography produced by Canada's most dynamic photographers, with exhibits changing on a regular basis. The museum also organizes traveling exhibitions and educational programs. Wheelchairs and strollers are available for visitors. The museum building is a former tunnel of the Grand Trunk Railway, and measures 166m (545 ft.) long by 17m (56 ft.) wide. The exterior blends comfortably with its historical surroundings, featuring limestone walls and stone balustrades. A glass and steel pavilion entrance on Wellington Street leads visitors down into the lobby, adjacent to the Ottawa Locks.

Note: In 2008, construction work related to the museum's underground location forced it to close for an undetermined period of time. At press time, the facility was still closed, with a reopening date yet to be announced. During the closure, the museum's holdings have been transferred to the National Art Gallery.

1 Rideau Canal. (✆) **613/990-8257.** www.cmcp.gallery.ca. Admission C$4 adults, C$3 seniors and students, C$2 children 12–19, free for children under 12, C$8 families (max. 2 adults and 3 children); free admission Thurs after 5pm. May–Oct Fri–Wed 10am–5pm, Thurs 10am–8pm; Oct–May Wed and Fri–Sun 10am–5pm, Thurs 10am–8pm. The museum is sandwiched between the Ottawa Locks and the Fairmont Château Laurier, just east of the Parliament Buildings.

Canadian Ski Museum Winter sports enthusiasts will enjoy a visit to the Canadian Ski Museum to learn about the history of skiing and how it evolved into the high-tech, high-speed sport of today. A large collection of photographs, memorabilia, and ski equipment is on display, aiming to preserve the memory of Canada's skiing history. The evolution of downhill skiing is explained, with credit for the world's first ski tow going to an enterprising Quebecker in the 1930s. Handmade wooden skis with strips of sealskin on the base to prevent back slipping are a long way from the parabolic skis of today. The Canadian Ski Museum entrance is at the side of the "Trailhead" timber frame building on the south side of Scott Street.

1960 Scott St. (✆) **613/722-3584.** www.skimuseum.ca. Free admission. Mon–Sat 9am–5pm; Sun 11am–5pm. Guided tours are available.

Currency Museum of the Bank of Canada Tracing the development of money over the past 2,500 years, the Currency Museum offers eight galleries to wander through and a spacious, light-filled atrium in the entrance hall of the center block of the Bank of Canada on Wellington Street, a couple of minutes' walk from Parliament Hill. Some unusual articles have been used as currency over the years, including teeth, grain, cattle, glass beads, shells, fish hooks, and cocoa beans. Six of the galleries are devoted to history, the seventh holds special exhibits, and the eighth showcases the most comprehensive display of Canadian numismatic (commemorative) items in the world. The collection puts particular emphasis on Canadian currency and its history. You can visit on your own or join a guided tour held twice daily in the summer months.

245 Sparks St. (✆) **613/782-8914.** www.currencymuseum.ca. Free admission. May 1–Labor Day Mon–Sat 10:30am–5pm, Sun 1–5pm; Labor Day–April 30 Tues–Sat 10:30am–5pm, Sun 1–5pm.

Library and Archives Canada Situated at the extreme west end of the downtown core, this institution merges Canada's two main historical repositories: the National Archives, founded in 1872, and the National Library, founded in 1952. With more than 60 million significant documents, oral histories, personal papers, maps, recordings, and books, it is primarily a working archive, catering to the needs of researchers and authors who must register in advance to access the collections, but the public exhibits, held on the airy ground floor, provide visitors with insights into Canada's history and culture. The building contains one of the city's best midsize concert venues, a comfortable and acoustically sophisticated auditorium that houses one of the world's most famous pianos: the late Glenn Gould's massive black Steinway. The hall is used frequently for film screenings, book launches, jazz and folk concerts, storytelling workshops, and other cultural events.

395 Wellington St. (C) **613/996-5115.** www.collectionscanada.ca. Free admission; some events require tickets and fee. Ground floor exhibition rooms Mon, Wed, and Fri 9am–4pm; Tues and Thurs 10am–5pm. Reading room daily 8am–11pm.

Logan Hall, Geological Survey of Canada   Logan Hall serves as an exhibition hall for a selection of the Geological Survey of Canada's vast collection of Canadian rocks, minerals, fossils, meteorites, and ores. Interactive displays and videos test visitors' knowledge of geology and even teach you how to pan for gold. An extensive fossil collection shows examples of bacteria, plants, and invertebrate and vertebrate animals, as well as fossils of specific historical interest. Logan Hall is named after Sir William Logan, who founded the Geological Survey of Canada in 1842 and was its first director.

601 Booth St. (C) **613/996-3919.** Free admission. Mon–Fri 8am–4pm.

Royal Canadian Mint ★   Established in 1908 to produce Canada's circulation coins, the Royal Canadian Mint is the oldest and one of the largest gold refineries in the Western Hemisphere. The mint also enjoys an excellent reputation around the world for producing high-quality coins. Since 1976, this facility has concentrated on producing numismatic (commemorative) coins. As you might expect, security is exceptionally high; double gates and watchful guards ensure that nothing valuable leaves the building. When you enter the stone "castle," you find yourself in a foyer with a set of stairs leading upward on your left and an elevator straight ahead. Both will take you to the boutique, which displays the many coins and souvenirs available for purchase in well-lit glass showcases around the room. When it's time for the tour, you're ushered into a small theater to watch a short film on a selected aspect of the mint's activities. Next your guide accompanies you to the viewing gallery, which winds its way through the factory. There is a lot to see here, and the tour guide outlines the process of manufacturing coins as you move along the corridor above the factory floor. The process is fascinating, from the rollers that transform the cast bars into flattened strips, to tubs of blanks that have been punched from the strips, to workers hand drying the blanks after washing, right to the final inspection and hand packaging of the finished coins.

320 Sussex Dr. (C) **800/276-7714** or 613/993-8990. www.mint.ca. Admission C$5 adults, C$4 seniors, C$3 children 5–17, free for children under 5, C$13 families (max. 2 adults and 4 children). Reduced admission Sat–Sun. Victoria Day (third Mon in May)–Labor Day Mon–Fri 9am–7pm, Sat–Sun 9am–5:30pm; rest of the year daily 9am–5pm. Call for reservations for guided tours.

GALLERIES

Carleton University Art Gallery   The collection here focuses on three main areas: Canadian art, particularly post-1942, when the university was founded; European art, especially prints and drawings created between the 16th and 19th centuries; and Inuit art, encompassing sculptures, textiles, drawings, and prints.

1125 Colonel By Dr., St. Patrick's Bldg., Carleton University Campus. (C) **613/520-2120.** www.carleton.ca/gallery. Free admission. Tues–Fri 10am–5pm; Sat–Sun noon–5pm.

EXPLORING OTTAWA

7

MORE MUSEUMS & GALLERIES

Gallery 101 Open since 1979, this nonprofit, artist-run center focuses on professional presentation of visual and media art from Canadian and international contemporary artists.

301½ Bank St. ✆ **613/230-2799.** www.gallery101.org. Free admission. Tues–Sat 10am–5pm.

Ottawa Art Gallery The Ottawa Art Gallery is an independent nonprofit public art gallery showing contemporary visual art from the local arts community. Programs include exhibitions, tours, and talks. The gallery is also home to the Firestone Collection of Canadian Art, a 1,600-piece private collection with numerous highlights.

Arts Court Bldg., 2 Daly Ave. ✆ **613/233-8699.** www.ottawaartgallery.ca. Admission is pay what you can. Tues–Fri 10am–5pm; Thurs 10am–8pm; Sat–Sun noon–5pm.

Ottawa School of Art Gallery The Ottawa School of Art holds courses and workshops by professional artists for all levels of students. The school gallery features work by students in addition to special exhibitions of professional artists.

35 George St. ✆ **613/241-7471.** www.artottawa.ca. Free admission. Mon–Thurs 9:30am–9pm; Fri–Sat 8:30am–4:30pm; Sun 12:30–4:30pm. Closed Sun July–Aug.

SAW Gallery Since 1973, this contemporary art center has focused on new media arts, performance visual art that reaches beyond traditional forms of expression, and art that openly declares its political and social position.

67 Nicholas St. ✆ **613/236-6181.** www.galeriesawgallery.com. Free admission. Tues–Sat 11am–6pm.

3 HERITAGE ATTRACTIONS

Ottawa has an unusually high number of designated heritage properties and districts. This is partly due to a keen interest in local architecture and history expressed by citizens and politicians. The sophisticated system of heritage planning that protects many of Ottawa's most interesting and beautiful structures is a relatively recent phenomenon, however. It began in 1975, the year that the Ontario government passed the Ontario Heritage Act, which gave power to municipal governments to designate properties of heritage significance. As a result of efforts by the Local Architectural Conservation Advisory Committee, in 1995 the City of Ottawa accepted its official policy on encouragement of heritage preservation. Approximately 3,000 properties in Ottawa are designated under the Ontario Heritage Act. About 10% of these have individual designation; the rest lie within 15 heritage conservation districts.

If you're looking to stroll through a heritage district, wander the streets in the following neighborhoods, easily accessible from downtown: ByWard Market and Lowertown (bounded by Sussex Dr., Bolton St., King Edward Ave., and Rideau St.); Sandy Hill between Waller Street, Besserer Street, Cobourg Street, and Laurier Avenue; and the Golden Triangle between Elgin Street and the Canal, Somerset Street to Argyle Avenue. Centretown (bounded by Kent St., Lisgar St., Elgin St., and Arlington Ave.), although a heritage district, is not as pleasant for walking, with a lot of street traffic and high-rise buildings on the major roads. Somerset Village, a stretch of Somerset Street between Bank and O'Connor streets, is characterized by a cluster of redbrick historical buildings. See chapter 8, "City Strolls" for two walks that will take you through some of these areas. You can also enjoy the leafy residential streets of the Glebe. Streets leading off Bank Street between the Queensway and the Rideau Canal are lined with Victorian and Edwardian

History of the ByWard Market

The ByWard Market area is the oldest part of Ottawa. Following the War of 1812, the British were looking for an alternative navigable waterway between Montreal and Kingston as a precaution against renewed hostilities with the Americans. The Rideau River was chosen, despite the fact that a canal would have to be built to bypass the Rideau Falls, the only point of contact between the Ottawa and Rideau rivers. Wrightsville was a thriving lumber town on the north shore of the Ottawa River, but a settlement was needed for canal workers on the south shore adjacent to the construction site. Accordingly, a shanty-town developed in the area between the Rideau River and the canal and came to be known as Lowertown, the heart of which is today's ByWard Market. The opening of the Rideau Centre shopping mall adjacent to the market in the early 1980s led residents and visitors to rediscover the district, and the ByWard Market is now one of the trendiest places in Ottawa for shopping, dining, and entertainment.

homes. The village of Rockcliffe Park, a residential neighborhood just northeast of Rideau Hall, has numerous gracious properties, many of which have been transformed into ambassadors' residences. If you are interested in learning more about Ottawa's heritage buildings, visit **www.heritageottawa.org**.

ATTRACTIONS

Aboriginal Experiences   On historical Victoria Island in the Ottawa River, just west of Parliament Hill, Turtle Island Tourism Company operates an award-winning aboriginal village in the summer months. Choose your "experience" package upon arrival at the site. Packages range from a 1-hour interpretive learning tour of the village at a cost of C$7 for adults and C$4 for children, to craft workshops, Native lunches, and even a 10-hour re-creation of the *voyageur* trading experience at a cost of C$136 per person, which includes two meals. Live demonstrations of traditional and contemporary Native singing, drumming, and dancing are staged daily. Listen to an ancient legend or story in an authentic tepee, enjoy traditional aboriginal foods, and visit the cultural displays. On show are tepees, birch-bark canoes, totem poles, and Cree Hunt Camps. Reservations are required for many of the scheduled events. The Trading Post craft shop stocks arts and crafts made by the local aboriginal community. You can reach Victoria Island from the Chaudière Bridge by car or via the Portage Bridge if you're walking or cycling.

Victoria Island. ℂ **877/811-3233** or 613/564-9494. www.aboriginalexperiences.com. Late June–early Sept daily 11am–5pm. Victoria Island is just west of the Parliament Buildings and lies below the Chaudière and Portage bridges.

ByWard Market ★   For many Ottawans, the heart and soul of the city is the ByWard Market. It's where they go for fresh produce early in the morning, and where they go to let their hair down late into the night. I love it at both times—particularly the smells and general bustle surrounding the open-air stalls early in the day, and the beautifully lit court-yards just east of Sussex Drive after dark. In the center of the area, 1 block east of Sussex

The Role of the Governor-General

Appointed by the queen on the advice of the Canadian prime minister, the role of the governor-general is probably one of the most complex and misunderstood in Canadian government. Because the queen is Canada's head of state, the governor-general represents her in Canada, and has the power to determine whether the government stands or falls in certain circumstances. But, on a day-to-day basis, the role is also largely ceremonial, with the governor-general symbolizing national identity, national unity, and moral leadership to Canadians and people abroad. As such, the role of governor-general is frequently criticized by antimonarchists and conservatives alike, who disparage the high cost of maintaining the office.

The choice of governor-general is quite symbolic, as well. In recent years, prime ministers have selected high-profile Canadians who reflect the country's diverse ethnic makeup. The current governor-general of Canada is Michaëlle Jean, a former broadcaster and filmmaker who was born in Haiti and came to Canada as a refugee. She is Canada's first black governor-general, and the third woman to hold the post.

Various trophies and awards, including the Stanley Cup, Grey Cup, and the Governor General's Awards in the arts, have been created by past governors-general and serve to recognize and celebrate Canadian achievements.

Drive between York and George streets, lies the ByWard Market building and the outdoor stalls of the farmers' market, where you can buy outstanding fresh local produce, flowers, and other products such as maple syrup. To complement the produce, you'll find gourmet food vendors inside the market building, as well as dozens of excellent food retailers in the district. Increasingly, the ByWard Market has also attracted independent boutiques, specializing in everything from designer clothing to high-end paper products (see chapter 8, "City Strolls" and chapter 9, "Shopping"). At night, the ByWard Market throbs with activity, due to its large concentration of bars and restaurants (see chapter 6, "Dining" and chapter 10, "Ottawa After Dark"). At night, the east end of the market tends to be dominated by college-age partiers, while the west end is home to upscale restaurants such as **Social** (p. 101), **Kinki** (p. 103), and **E18hteen** (p. 99). One exception to the rule is Murray Street, which tends to be relatively sedate all along its length and is the site of so many first-rate restaurants—including **John Taylor At Domus** (p. 100), **Navarra** (p. 100), and **Sweetgrass** (p. 101)—that it has picked up the sobriquet "Gastro Alley." Throughout the year, the ByWard Market hosts family-oriented events on weekends, including a Mother's Day celebration with special restaurant menus, an outdoor fashion show, a jazz band, and free hayrides. On the first Sunday in June, 150 vintage, classic, and high-performance cars are on display. Annual events later in the year include Bytown Days, when 19th-century Ottawa is revisited; a search for the world's biggest pumpkin; and an old-fashioned Christmas with carolers serenading visitors to the market district as they ride in horse-drawn carriages adorned with sleigh bells. The market has something for every taste.

Between Sussex Dr. and King Edward Ave., Rideau St. and St. Patrick St. www.byward-market.com. Outdoor vendors open daily 7am–6pm or later.

Laurier House   This fine Victorian residence, built in 1878, has been home to two prime ministers and is a designated National Historic Site. A tour of this home helps to put a human face on Canada's politics and history. Prior to 1896, there was no official residence provided for the prime minister. Sir Wilfrid Laurier, Canada's first francophone prime minister, was the first resident of Laurier House, purchased by the Liberal Party to house their leader. Several rooms contain furnishings and mementos of Laurier's, but the majority of the house is restored to the era of William Lyon Mackenzie King, Canada's longest-serving prime minister and the second occupant of the house. Apparently King held seances in the library, and his crystal ball is on display. The Pearson Gallery contains former prime minister Lester B. Pearson's study, which was moved here from his home in Rockcliffe Park. The gallery displays photographs and artifacts from the Pearson years, including a replica of Pearson's Nobel Peace Prize medal, which he was awarded for his role in the 1956 Arab-Israeli dispute. Wander over to Strathcona Park after visiting the museum. It's just a couple of minutes' walk east along Laurier Avenue. Stroll the pathways in summer and watch the swans glide along the Rideau River. If you have children with you, take them to the delightful playground.

335 Laurier Ave. E. *C* **613/992-8142.** www.pc.gc.ca/laurierhouse. Admission C$3.90 adults, C$3.40 seniors, C$1.90 children 6–16, free for children 5 and under. Apr to mid-May Mon–Fri 9am–5pm; mid-May to mid-Oct daily 9am–5pm; closed mid-Oct to Mar. From the Queensway, take the Nicholas St. exit (exit 118). Turn right on Laurier Ave. E. The museum is on the left.

Rideau Hall ★★   Rideau Hall has been the official residence and workplace of Canada's governor-general since 1867 and is considered to be the symbolic home of all Canadians. The public is welcome to wander the 32 hectares (79 acres) of beautiful gardens and forested areas and visit the greenhouse, and for that reason alone the place is worth a visit; the grounds are exceptional. Outdoor concerts and cricket matches are held in the summer, and there's ice skating on the pond in winter. Free guided tours of the staterooms of the residence are offered; hours vary throughout the year, although in peak tourist season in the summer there are self-guided tours every morning and guided tours in the afternoons, approximately 45 minutes long. The Governor General's Awards are presented here annually, honoring Canadians for extraordinary accomplishments, courage, and contributions to science, the arts, and humanity. Two major events are held annually for the public—the Garden Party in June or July and the Winter Celebration. The Ceremonial Guard is on duty at Rideau Hall during July and August. The first Changing of the Guard Ceremony, held in late June, features a colorful parade led by a marching band. Relief of the Sentries is a ceremony performed hourly during the summer, 9am to 5pm, and is always popular with young children. The visitor center, operating daily between May and October, has family activities, a play structure, and hands-on activities for children. The Governor General's Summer Concerts are held on the beautifully landscaped grounds. Set up your lawn chair, spread out the picnic blanket, and enjoy the sunshine and music. Wheelchairs, restrooms, and picnic tables are available at Rideau Hall.

1 Sussex Dr. *C* **800/465-6890** or 613/991-4422. www.gg.ca. Free admission to all tours and activities. Grounds daily 8am–1 hr. before sunset (subject to change without notice). From the Queensway, take the Nicholas St. exit (exit 118), turn left on Rideau St., then right on Sussex Dr. The entrance to Rideau Hall is on the right, just after crossing the Rideau River.

Supreme Court of Canada   The Supreme Court is a general court of appeal for both criminal and civil cases and is the highest court of appeal in the country. Three sessions per year, each lasting 3 months, are held between October and June. When the

The Lives and Times of Canada's PMs

As you tour around the city, you will notice public buildings, streets, and bridges named after some of Canada's most prominent past political leaders. There are plenty of places where you can learn more about the country's prime ministers and how they shaped Canada's identity, political structure, and social fabric.

If you arrive in Ottawa by air, and do not have to go through customs in Ottawa, you will be hard pressed to miss the larger-than-life bronze likenesses of **Sir John A. Macdonald,** Canada's first prime minister, and his deputy George-Étienne Cartier. They stand near the baggage carousels in the airport that is named for them. You can visit Macdonald's former office in the East Block of the Parliament Buildings. Another statue of him stands on the Hill between Centre Block and East Block. A visit to **Laurier House** at 335 Laurier Ave. E. will give you a glimpse into the lives of three prime ministers. **Sir Wilfrid Laurier** was the first prime minister to reside there. Several rooms contain items pertaining to Laurier, but the majority of the house has been restored to the era of **William Lyon Mackenzie King,** who inherited the house from the Lauriers. (British Prime Minister Sir Winston Churchill and U.S. President Franklin D. Roosevelt both visited King at this residence. King had an estate in the midst of **Gatineau Park,** which was bequeathed to the Canadian people upon his death in 1950. It's open from mid-May to mid-Oct.) Also at Laurier House is **Lester B. Pearson's** study, which was moved here from his home in Rockcliffe Park. On Parliament Hill, Laurier's statue stands at the southeast corner of East Block, King at the northwest corner of East Block, and Pearson just north of West Block. To learn more about the times of **John Diefenbaker,** take a tour of the **Diefenbunker Cold War Museum,** an underground bunker built to shelter the Canadian government in the event of nuclear attack during the period of the cold war. Diefenbaker's statue stands on the northeast corner of West Block. Finally, if you want to catch a glimpse of Canada's current head of government, keep your eyes open around the **Langevin Block** at 50 Wellington St., across from Parliament Hill. The offices of the prime minister are housed in this magnificent olive-colored sandstone building.

court is in session, it sits Monday through Friday, usually hearing two appeals a day. Law students take members of the public on free guided tours, which take about 30 minutes and are recommended for all ages. From May to August, tours are held daily on a continuing basis, and the rest of the year tours are available by prior arrangement on weekdays. The architecture of the building is impressive to behold and the grand entrance hall is magnificent. If you'd like the experience of witnessing an appeal, take a seat in the public gallery when court is in session.

301 Wellington St. ✆ **613/995-4330** or 613/995-5361 for tour reservations. www.scc-csc.gc.ca. May 1–Aug 31 daily 9am–5pm; Sept 1–Apr 30 Mon–Fri 9am–5pm.

PLACES OF WORSHIP

Christ Church Cathedral   The original church was completed in 1833. In 1872, the growing congregation required a larger church, and a new building was constructed on the site between 1872 and 1873. When the Diocese of Ottawa was formed in 1896, Christ Church became the seat of the Anglican bishop of Ottawa. The architectural style is English Gothic revival and the building's exterior has survived in its original form. Some changes have been made to the interior over the years. While not as physically impressive—or as advantageously situated—as its Catholic counterpart, the church has a rich historical past. A number of state funerals have been held here, including those of Governor-General Vincent Massey, Prime Minister John Diefenbaker, and Prime Minister Lester B. Pearson.

439 Queen St. ℭ **613/236-9149**

Notre-Dame Cathedral Basilica ★   The splendid Notre-Dame Cathedral Basilica is Ottawa's oldest church. A wooden structure was first erected on the site in 1832, and construction of the current building began in 1841. The exterior stonework has a plain, flat facade but this is offset by the magnificent French-Canadian tin steeples that house the church bells. The late-Victorian interior is typically ornate. Details include two vaulted ceilings, side galleries, extensive carved woodwork, carved altars, and 30 life-size carved figures. A 3m-high (10-ft.) wooden gilded statue of the Madonna and Child, created by Italian sculptor Cardona in 1865, stands above the apex of the front facade gable between the two steeples.

385 Sussex Dr. ℭ **613/241-7496**

St. Andrew's Presbyterian Church   St. Andrew's predates Christ Church as the oldest Protestant congregation in Ottawa, with worship held on the site since 1828. When construction of the new Christ Church began in 1872, it prompted St. Andrew's, which was also suffering from overcrowding, to build a new church on the site. Also constructed in Gothic-revival style, the new St. Andrew's was built of rock-faced gray limestone, which distinguished it from the golden sandstone of Christ Church. Then–prime minister Mackenzie King attended services at St. Andrew's. During World War II, when the Dutch royal family was in exile in Ottawa, the daughter of Queen Juliana of the Netherlands was baptized in this church.

82 Kent St. ℭ **613/232-9042**

Other downtown churches you may like to visit, which all date from the 19th century and are designated heritage properties, include St. Patrick's Basilica, 240 Kent St.; First Baptist Church, 140 Laurier Ave. W.; St. Alban the Martyr Church, 125 Daly Ave.; St. Paul's–Eastern United Church (originally St. Paul's Presbyterian Church; the United Church was not created until 1925), 90 Daly Ave.; St. Paul's Evangelical Lutheran Church, 210 Wilbrod St.; All Saints Anglican Church, 315–317 Chapel St.; and Église Ste-Anne, 528–530 Old St. Patrick St.

---

4 PARKS & WATERWAYS

URBAN GREEN SPACES

One of the first things you'll notice about Ottawa is how much green space there is within the city's core. In fact, two parks dominate the downtown area, providing terrific

(Fun Facts **Upside-Down Astrolabe**

The astrolabe (a 17th-century navigational instrument) held by the statue of Samuel de Champlain at Nepean Point was unwittingly placed upside down by sculptor Hamilton McCarthy. You can view the original astrolabe at the **Canadian Museum of Civilization** (p. 119).

sites for outdoor festivals. **Confederation Park,** on Elgin Street, is home to **Winterlude** and the **Ottawa International Jazz Festival.** There are memorials to Canadian history here, including a fountain that originally stood in Trafalgar Square in London and has been dedicated to **Lieutenant Colonel John By,** the British engineer who supervised the building of the Rideau Canal. The lieutenant colonel was a major influence in establishing Bytown, as Ottawa was formerly known. **Major's Hill Park,** Ottawa's oldest park, established in 1874, is tucked in behind the Fairmont Château Laurier. A statue of Lieutenant Colonel By stands close to the site of his house, which was destroyed by fire. This park offers outstanding views of the Parliament Buildings, the Rideau Canal, the Ottawa River, the city of Gatineau and the hills beyond, and the National Gallery of Canada. It's also a major site for many festivals and events, including the **Canadian Tulip Festival.** At the tip of the park, just north of the National Gallery of Canada, you'll find **Nepean Point.** You can share the view with a statue of **Samuel de Champlain,** who first explored the Ottawa River in 1613. The **Astrolabe Theatre,** a venue for summer concerts and events, is located here.

Hog's Back Park is situated at the point where the Rideau Canal meets the Rideau River. A refreshment pavilion, parking, and restrooms are available. Immediately south is **Mooney's Bay Park,** which has a supervised, sandy swimming beach, a playground, shade trees, a refreshment pavilion, and public restrooms. Cross-country skiing is available in the winter, on 5km (3 miles) of groomed, well-lit trails. The park is the site of the annual HOPE beach volleyball tournament (p. 33) and is adjacent to the Terry Fox Athletic Complex, which has a world-class track and field facility. A parking fee applies in the summer months. In the same vicinity, on Heron Road, west of Riverside Drive and just north of Hog's Back Park is **Vincent Massey Park,** a popular place for family celebrations and other large gatherings. Amenities include ball diamonds, horseshoe pits, a bandstand, picnic tables, fireplaces, a refreshment pavilion, playing fields, recreational pathways, drinking fountains, and public restrooms. A parking fee is charged from May to October.

SUBURBAN & RURAL GREEN SPACE

One of the best things about Ottawa is how close it is to nature. You can literally go from conservation area or ski hill to downtown in 30 minutes. Gatineau Park is a beautiful wilderness area, covering 361sq. km (139 sq. miles) in the Gatineau Hills of Quebec. The south entrance to the park is located just across the Ottawa River in the City of Gatineau, a few minutes' drive from downtown Ottawa. Hiking trails, cycling pathways, mountain-bike trails, cross-country ski trails, sandy beaches, and campgrounds are all located within the park. Your first stop should be the **Gatineau Park Visitor Centre,** at 33 Scott Rd. in Chelsea (℄ **800/465-1867** or 819/827-2020), open every day of the year. For more information on **Gatineau Park,** see chapter 11, "Side Trips from Ottawa." On the

Ontario side of the Ottawa River, the **National Capital Greenbelt** covers 200sq. km (77 sq. miles) of crescent-shaped land bordering Ottawa to the west, south, and east. A mix of forests, agricultural land, and natural areas, the greenbelt has several sectors open to the public and accessible from major highways. Moose, beavers, chipmunks, foxes, raccoons, deer, pygmy shrews, rabbits, and squirrels all call this wilderness area home. For directions to specific sites, call the Capital Infocentre (℮ **800/465-1867** or 613/239-5000). Better yet, pick up a copy of "Greenbelt All Seasons Trail Map," available at the Infocentre opposite Parliament Hill, or download it from the National Capital Commission's website at **www.canadascapital.ca**. If you're venturing into the greenbelt during bug season (May–Sept), protect yourself with insect repellent or use a bug jacket. Always respect the greenbelt rules—place all litter in the waste bins provided in parking areas, keep your dog on a leash and pick up after it, and don't walk or snowshoe on cross-country ski tracks in winter.

Perhaps the best urban adventure is the Mer Bleue Conservation Area on the southeastern edge of Ottawa, which is a unique ecological environment protected by an international treaty. The area contains a large peat bog more than 5m (16 ft.) deep and a northern boreal forest, a type of forest that is typically found much farther north. If you visit on a cool morning in the spring or fall, you may be lucky enough to witness a bluish-tinged mist hanging over the bog, which gave the area its name (mer bleue is French for "blue sea"). There are several trails crossing the area, but the easiest one to negotiate is the Mer Bleue Interpretative Trail, a walk of just over 1km (.6 mile) with a boardwalk and information panels. To reach the interpretive trail, take Innes Road to Anderson Road, then go south to Borthwick Ridge Road and follow the signs. Elsewhere in the greenbelt, during the winter you can go cross-country skiing on the trails and recreational pathways. All trails are suitable for beginner or family outings. Volunteer groups from local ski clubs machine track set some of the trails. For family tobogganing fun, visit Conroy Pit (parking lot 15, south of Hunt Club Rd. on Conroy Rd.). The hill at Conroy Pit is lit from 4 to 11pm.

OTTAWA'S WATERWAYS

Ottawa's origins are inextricably linked to its waterways—after all, it was the settlement that grew up around the canal construction site that evolved into Canada's capital city. Modern-day Ottawa enjoys the canal and river primarily for leisure and pleasure. The city's beauty is enhanced by the extensive network of parkways, pathways, and parks that follow the shores of the **Rideau and Ottawa rivers,** and the **Rideau Canal ★★★**. A National Historic Site and UNESCO World Heritage Site, the canal marked its 175th anniversary in 2007. The canal is actually a continuous chain of beautiful lakes, rivers, and canal cuts, stretching 202km (126 miles) between Ottawa and Kingston, and often described as the most scenic waterway in North America. Parks Canada has the responsibility of preserving and maintaining the canal's natural and historic features and providing a safe waterway

Kids A Great Spot for Kids

Strathcona Park **Kids** has a wonderful play area for children. The wading pool, playground, and castle ruins, complete with a slide and animal statuettes, are great fun to explore.

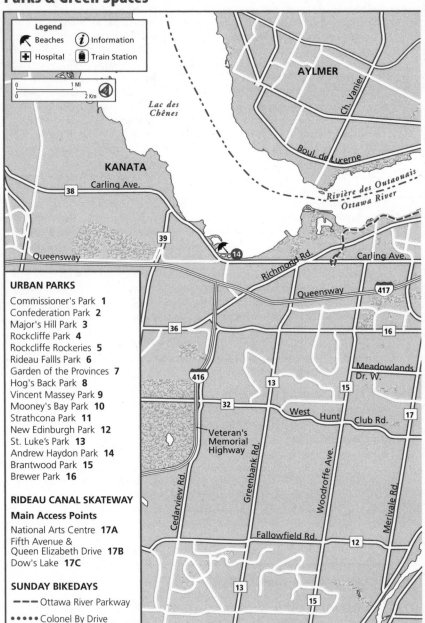

Legend

🪝 Beaches ⓘ Information

➕ Hospital 🚉 Train Station

AYLMER

Ch. Vanier

Boul. de Lucerne

Lac des Chênes

KANATA

Carling Ave.

38

Queensway

Rivière des Outaouais
Ottawa River

Richmond Rd.

Carling Ave.

39

14

Queensway

417

16

36

Meadowlands Dr. W.

416

13

15

32

17

West Hunt Club Rd.

Veteran's Memorial Highway

Greenbank Rd.

Woodroffe Ave.

Merivale Rd.

Cedarview Rd.

Fallowfield Rd.

12

13

15

EXPLORING OTTAWA

7

PARKS & WATERWAYS

URBAN PARKS

Commissioner's Park **1**
Confederation Park **2**
Major's Hill Park **3**
Rockcliffe Park **4**
Rockcliffe Rockeries **5**
Rideau Fallls Park **6**
Garden of the Provinces **7**
Hog's Back Park **8**
Vincent Massey Park **9**
Mooney's Bay Park **10**
Strathcona Park **11**
New Edinburgh Park **12**
St. Luke's Park **13**
Andrew Haydon Park **14**
Brantwood Park **15**
Brewer Park **16**

RIDEAU CANAL SKATEWAY

Main Access Points

National Arts Centre **17A**
Fifth Avenue &
Queen Elizabeth Drive **17B**
Dow's Lake **17C**

SUNDAY BIKEDAYS

– – – Ottawa River Parkway

• • • • • Colonel By Drive

141

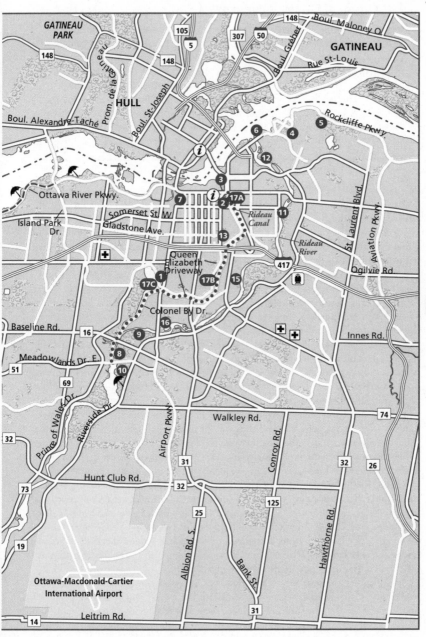

The Origin of Ottawa's Parkways & Pathways

In the 19th century, Ottawa's railways were an essential feature of the landscape. Vast networks of rail tracks crossed the city. Their existence, however, became a real challenge after World War II for the urban planners whose goal was to beautify Canada's capital while reclaiming and preserving the waterway shorelines. In 1950, work began on relocating the railway and converting old rail lines into Ottawa's parkways and pathways. Today, residents and visitors alike can enjoy the beautiful parks, pathways, and roadways of the Ottawa River shore, the Rideau Canal banks, and Dow's Lake. Most pathways are smooth asphalt on flat terrain, so they're easy to negotiate for all ages.

for boats to navigate. The canal and locks that link the lakes and rivers of the **Rideau Valley** were constructed between 1826 and 1832 to provide a secure route for the military to travel between Montreal and Kingston in the wake of the War of 1812. Lieutenant Colonel By, the British royal engineer in charge of the project, had the foresight to build the locks and canal large enough to permit commercial traffic to access the system rather than building the canal solely for military use.

There are **45 locks** manned by 24 lock stations along the main channel of the canal. The waterway rises a total of 50m (164 ft.) from Kingston on Lake Ontario to Upper Rideau Lake, then drops 83m (272 ft.) to the Ottawa River in Ottawa, ending in the 30m (98-ft.) **Rideau Falls.** In Ottawa, there are three places where you can watch the locks in action. The best spot to view one of the lock systems is in downtown Ottawa right at the point where the first locks were built. If you stand on the north side of the Plaza Bridge (between Parliament Hill and Fairmont Château Laurier) and look over the side, you'll have a wonderful view of the eight **Ottawa Locks,** which connect the canal to the Ottawa River, a drop of 24m (79 ft.). Travel time for water traffic through the locks is about 1 1/2 hours. To get down to the level of the locks, descend a stairway beside the bridge (or, if you need universal access, descend a ramp from the south side of the bridge). *Note:* If you have children with you, be extremely careful to keep them away from the sides of the locks, because there are no safety barriers next to the water.

The **Bytown Museum** is alongside the locks. Upstream along the canal, the next two locks are **Hartwells Locks,** which take about half an hour to navigate. The road entrance to the locks is off **Prince of Wales Drive** south of **Dow's Lake.** The **Central Experimental Farm** borders this section of the canal and there's an extensive network of paved and gravel bike paths. A little farther upstream are the **Hog's Back Locks,** reached by road at 795 Hog's Back Rd. An interpretive trail links the locks with Hog's Back dam. There's a bonus at Hog's Back—a **swing bridge** is part of the lock system, designed to accommodate vessels requiring a clearance greater than 2.8m (9 ft.). The bridge swings on demand except during peak traffic periods on weekdays.

In the winter, the canal freezes over and the Ottawa portion between Carleton University and Confederation Square is turned into the world's largest and most famous outdoor skating rink, the **Rideau Canal Skateway ★★★**. The season usually runs from early January to early March. For current information on ice conditions during the season, call the Skateway hot line ✆ **613/239-5234.** Heated shelters, skate and sled rentals, boot-check and skate-sharpening services, rest areas, food concessions, and toilets are located at various points along the Skateway. Main access points are by the **National Arts** **Centre, Fifth Avenue** and **Queen Elizabeth Drive,** and **Dow's Lake.**

5 ORGANIZED TOURS

ON WHEELS

Gray Line Sightseeing Tours   Ottawa is such a compact city that you don't need a bus tour to see everything, but if you like to get a perspective on things before you set out on foot, or if your time in Ottawa is limited, you can choose an open-top double-decker bus or vintage trolley bus to make a quick circuit of the key sites. Tours officially start at the corner of Sparks and Metcalfe streets, but you can step on or off the bus any time you wish at these stops: Parliament Hill, Museum of Civilization, Notre-Dame Cathedral Basilica, Rideau Hall, RCMP Rockcliffe Stables, Canada Aviation Museum, National War Museum, Royal Canadian Mint, National Gallery of Canada, ByWard Market, Rideau Canal, Dow's Lake, Central Experimental Farm, and Canadian Museum of Nature. Tours operate from May to October. Tickets are valid for 2 days and prices are reasonable—a family of four can get a 3-day, on-off-privilege ticket for C$81.

C **800/297-6422** or 613/565-5463. Call for departure locations and times. Seasonal.

ON FOOT

Aside from the tours listed here, see the walking tours described in chapter 8, "City Strolls."

Art Walk   The National Capital Commission has produced a guide, called *Street SmART,* describing seven self-guided, public-art walking tours in Ottawa and Hull. You will see statues of prominent historical figures; contemporary sculptures made of wood,

---

Ⓕun Facts   The Rideau Canal Skateway

- The Skateway is visited by more than 1 million skaters every year.
- The staff works around the clock to maintain the ice surface.
- Many residents use the Skateway to commute to work and school every day.
- The Skateway ice surface area is equivalent to 90 Olympic-size ice rinks.
- The average length of the skating season on the canal is 52 days.
- The shortest season to date was 30 days, and the longest was 90 days.
- Although a public skating surface in Winnipeg—which uses parts of the Red and Assiniboine rivers—has now claimed the title of the world's longest skating rink, the Skateway retains the title of the largest rink due to its width.
- There is a flag system for ice conditions. Green flags indicate the Skateway is open; red flags indicate the Skateway is closed.

Tips **Tiptoe Through the Tulips**

The tulip beds in Commissioners Park at the northern tip of Dow's Lake attract thousands of visitors during the Canadian Tulip Festival in May. An amazing 300,000 bulbs bloom in the park, making it the largest tulip display in the region.

stone, papier-mâché, metal, and fiberglass; war memorials; statues of Canadian heroes; totem poles; murals; and monuments. Tours vary from 35 minutes to 1 hour in length.

Street SmART available free from Capital Infocentre, 90 Wellington St. ✆ **800/465-1867.**

Confederation Boulevard Walking Tours The National Capital Commission (NCC) publishes a free 16-page guide called *Discover the Heart of the Capital* that you can use to explore more than 50 sites located along Canada's ceremonial route. "Confederation Boulevard" is a concept created by the NCC to showcase the key historical buildings and monuments in the National Capital Region. The tour can vary from 30 minutes to 6$^1/_2$ hours, depending on how much ground you want to cover.

Discover the Heart of the Capital available free from Capital Infocentre, 90 Wellington St. ✆ **800/465-1867.**

Haunted Walks Inc. ★ Follow a black-cloaked storyteller, lantern in hand, through the city streets and hear the darker side of Ottawa's history. Families are welcome on the tours (with the exception of the Naughty Ottawa Pub Tour, which, as you might expect, is for adults only). There aren't any nasty surprises or theatrical incidents on the tour— the guides prefer to tell the stories and take you to the sites of hauntings and ghost sightings, and leave the rest to your imagination. The walks take place mostly outdoors, so dress for the weather. Several tours are available, including a tour of the old Carleton County Jail (death row and the gallows are disconcertingly eerie), the Fairmont Château Laurier, and the Original Haunted Walk of Ottawa. Tours last between 1 and 2$^1/_2$ hours and the maximum distance covered is about 1.6km (1 mile). Call for information on French-language tours and Halloween tours.

Ticket booths: corner of Sparks St. and Elgin St., May–Oct daily 5–9pm; 73 Clarence St., May–Oct Tues–Sat 11am–4pm. ✆ **613/232-0344.** www.hauntedwalk.com. Tickets C$13–C$15 adults, C$11–C$13 seniors and students, C$6.50–C$8.50 children. Tours daily. Call for current schedule.

Parliament Hill Walking Tours A free 24-page booklet available from the Capital Infocentre gives a detailed description of a self-guided outdoor walking tour of Parliament Hill—and from late June to early September there is a daily guided outdoor walking tour called "In the Footsteps of Great Canadians." Same-day free tickets are available from the Info-Tent on Parliament Hill. See the "Parliament Hill" review (p. 113) for more information.

ON THE WATER

Capital Cruises Beginning in 2008, Capital Cruises began offering seasonal cruises on the Ottawa River aboard the triple-deck *Empress,* which has a capacity of more than 300. Using wireless technology, the ship offers commentary in your choice of six languages. The *Empress* has two enclosed decks and an open-air upper deck, as well as two refreshment bars and restrooms. A variety of cruises—including dinner, Sunday brunch, and themed events—are offered. Group tours are offered at 9am daily May to October; other tours depart from Jacques-Cartier Park in Gatineau and the foot of the Ottawa Locks below Parliament Hill throughout the day, beginning at 10:15am and ending at 6pm daily May–September.

Ticket kiosks: Confederation Square in Ottawa and Jacques-Cartier Park Wharf in Gatineau, open daily 8am–6pm. *©* **613/241-8811.** www.capitalcruisesottawa.com. Sightseeing cruise C$16 adults, C$14 seniors and students with ID, C$8 children 5–14, free for children under 5, C$40 families (max. 2 adults and 2 children). Seven departures daily from Jacques-Cartier Park marina in Gatineau and the Ottawa Locks. Call for departure times.

Paul's Boat Lines ★   Paul's Boat Lines cruises the Ottawa River and the Rideau Canal from May to October. The 150-passenger *Paula D* takes visitors on a 90-minute cruise of the Ottawa River, with spectacular views of the Parliament Buildings, Rideau Falls, and other sites. The *Paula D* has an open-air upper deck shaded by an awning and an enclosed lower deck with a small snack bar, tables, and chairs. On the canal, you can glide along in one of three tour boats for a 75-minute cruise that takes you past the National Arts Centre, the University of Ottawa, Lansdowne Park, Carleton University, the Central Experimental Farm, and Dow's Lake.

219 Colonnade Rd. *©* **613/225-6781** office or 613/235-8409 summer dock. www.paulsboatcruises.com. River cruise C$18 adults, C$16 seniors and students, C$10 children 5–15, free for children under 5, C$45 families (max. 2 adults and 2 children); canal cruise slightly lower rates. Four to 7 departures daily in season from Ottawa dock at the foot of the Ottawa Locks, from the Jacques-Cartier Park marina in Gatineau, and from the Conference Centre on the Rideau Canal. Call for departure times.

The Terry Fox Statue: A Symbol of Hope and Courage

Across from the Centre Block of Parliament Hill, in front of the Capital Infocentre, stands a proud memorial to a courageous young Canadian. In 1977, 18-year-old **Terry Fox** was given the devastating news that he had bone cancer and his right leg would have to be amputated 15 centimeters above the knee. After his recovery, Fox wanted to do something to give hope to people living with cancer, and he decided to run across Canada to raise money for **cancer research.** After many months of training, during which he ran more than 5,000km (3,107 miles), he dipped his artificial leg in the Atlantic Ocean on April 12, 1980, and began his **Marathon of Hope.** He traveled relentlessly through six provinces and over 5,370km (3,337 miles) before being forced to retire near Thunder Bay, Ontario. The cancer had spread to his lungs, and 10 months later, in June 1981, Fox died at the age of 22.

An annual fundraising event was established in his memory and the first **Terry Fox Run,** held at more than 760 sites across Canada and around the world in 1981, raised C$3.5 million. By 2008, the total amount of money raised in Fox's name exceeded C$400 million. Terry Fox is a true Canadian hero and has become a symbol of hope and courage not only to people living with cancer and their families and friends, but also to people everywhere.

Take Time for a Scenic Drive

Enjoy a leisurely drive along Ottawa's parkways and scenic driveways.

HEADING EAST Head east on Wellington Street past **Parliament Hill,** through Confederation Square. You'll pass the grand **Fairmont Château Laurier** on your left. Turn left at the lights (north) onto Sussex Drive. After passing the **U.S. Embassy** on your left, you'll get some great views of **Notre-Dame Cathedral Basilica** and the **National Gallery of Canada** ahead on your right and left respectively.

Continue along Sussex Drive, passing the castlelike **Royal Canadian Mint** on your left. After rounding a sweeping right-hand turn and passing the Macdonald-Cartier Bridge to Quebec, you'll encounter the **National Research Council** on your left, and, across from it, the **Lester B. Pearson Building,** headquarters of Canada's federal department of external affairs. You'll cross the Rideau River via Green Island. **Rideau Falls** is on your left. The road passes **24 Sussex Dr.,** the **residence of the prime minister,** which is not open to the public. Just ahead on your right is **Rideau Hall.** Tours of the grounds and the interior public rooms are available. Continuing, the drive becomes **Rockcliffe Parkway,** a beautiful route along the Ottawa River and through **Rockcliffe Park.** Watch for a right fork to Acacia Avenue, which leads to the **rockeries,** which are carpeted with colorful blooms in the spring. If you wish, continue along the parkway to the **RCMP Musical Ride Centre at Rockcliffe Stables** and the **Canada Aviation Museum,** or return to the parkway and head west toward downtown Ottawa.

HEADING WEST Head west on Wellington Street, past **Parliament Hill,** the **Supreme Court of Canada,** and the **Library and Archives Canada** on your right. The road opens up into the **Ottawa River Parkway,** passing the new **Canadian War Museum.** Continue through the parkland to **Island Park Drive** and turn left. This road will take you under the Queensway (Hwy. 417) and through the grounds of the **Central Experimental Farm and Arboretum.** When you reach a European-style roundabout, you have two choices. Turn **right,** taking **Prince of Wales Drive** to **Hog's Back Road.** Turn left here, by the locks and **Hog's Back Falls.** Turn left again onto **Colonel By Drive** and follow this picturesque route along the east bank of the **Rideau Canal** back downtown. If you decide to turn left (north) at the roundabout, you'll take a slightly shorter but just as pretty route back downtown along **Queen Elizabeth Driveway,** on the west bank of the **Rideau Canal.**

IN THE AIR

Hot Air Ballooning If you fancy floating in the sky at a leisurely pace with the city spread out below you and you're not afraid of heights, you might like to splurge on a trip in a hot air balloon. For many people it's a once in a lifetime experience. Prices range widely, depending on when you go and how many people are flying, but you can expect to pay a minimum of C$185 per person, and as much as C$1,000 per couple for romance-themed evening flights. There may be restrictions on the minimum age for passengers, so call ahead. Or go to a launching and just watch as the balloons are pre-pared for flight and then take off. Everyone from babies to seniors will enjoy the sight of the huge, colorful silken spheres as they gracefully rise into the sky. In the Ottawa area, the main operators are High Time Balloon Co. Inc. (© **613/521-9921**), Sundance Bal-loons (© **613/247-8277**; www.sundanceballoons.com), and Windborne Ballooning (© **613/739-7388**; www.magmacom.com/~mstevens).

Private Small Aircraft   Year-round sightseeing tours over Ottawa and Gatineau are offered by West Capital Aviation (3257 Carp Rd., Carp, west of Ottawa at Carp Airport; © **613/296-7971**). Prices vary, beginning at C$250 for a 45-minute tour.

6 OUTDOOR PURSUITS

BEACHES

Along the banks of the **Ottawa River** and the **Rideau River,** there are a number of beaches where you can cool off on a hot summer's day. Sandy shores abound, and there are usually restrooms, changing rooms, and snack bars nearby.

Supervised swimming is available at **Britannia Bay, Mooney's Bay,** and **Westboro** beaches. Beaches are open from late June until the end of August. Water quality is checked daily and beaches may occasionally be closed for the day, usually after heavy rainfall. For water-quality updates call © **613/244-5678.** You can get to **Britannia Bay,** on the Ottawa River, by following Richmond Road to Britannia Road or by traveling on the Ottawa River bike path. For **Mooney's Bay Park,** on the banks of the Rideau River, drive along Riverside Drive just north of Walkley Road, or take the Colonel By Drive bike path to Hog's Back, cross the falls east on Hog's Back Road, and then rejoin the bike path running south through the marina. You'll find **Westboro Beach** on the south shore of the Ottawa River, off the Ottawa River Parkway at Kitchissippi Lookout (west of the Champlain Bridge).

Just a short drive from the city you can visit **Baxter Conservation Area,** south of the village of Kars on Dilworth Road (© **613/489-3592**), which has a small beach on the Rideau River. The refreshing lakes of **Gatineau Park** (© **819/827-2020**) are open for public swimming from mid-June to early September. The park has five public beaches, located at Philippe, Meech, and La Pêche lakes. Lifeguards are on duty daily from 10am to 6pm; swimming in the park is prohibited at other times. Swimming is also available in **Lac Beauchamp,** at Parc du Lac Beauchamp, 745 bd. Maloney, Gatineau, PQ (© **819/669-2548**).

Kids   Cruises for Kids

If you have young children (under age 10 or so), then an Ottawa River cruise is the better choice. You can stroll around the deck or have a snack, and the open design is perfect on a hot summer's day because you can catch the cool breeze off the water. In contrast, the canal boats have a single enclosed deck and are more confined.

(Tips) **Water Safety First**

Each person should wear a life jacket while boating. If you are renting a boat, ask the rental facility to provide life jackets for everyone in your party. Be aware that Dow's Lake, the Rideau Canal, and Rideau River are unsupervised waterways and you use them at your own risk.

BOATING

If you want to spend a lazy summer afternoon drifting around in a boat, visit **Dow's Lake Pavilion,** 1001 Queen Elizabeth Dr. (© 613/232-1001). A fully operational marina at the pavilion site on Dow's Lake rents out paddleboats, canoes, kayaks, and rowboats. Dow's Lake is an artificial lake that provides a quiet place for water recreation away from the main traffic in the Rideau Canal. In **Gatineau Park,** boat rentals are available at **Philippe Lake** and **La Pêche Lake.** Call © 819/827-2020 to check opening hours for the rental booths. If you like your outdoor activities wet 'n' wild, check out the white-water rafting adventure companies listed in chapter 11, "Side Trips from Ottawa."

CYCLING & IN-LINE SKATING

Ottawa and its environs offer a comprehensive network of pathways and parkways where people can bike and in-line skate through beautiful natural scenery. In addition, there are designated bicycle lanes on a number of city streets. No wonder Ottawa has the highest per capita population of cyclists in Canada.

If you didn't bring your own equipment, **Rent-A-Bike** (on the east side of the Rideau Canal at Plaza Bridge, next to Paul's Boat Lines; © 613/241-4140; www.rentabike.ca), has all kinds of bikes, including standard hybrid bikes designed for comfortable, leisurely touring; standard light-trail mountain bikes; on-road and off-road performance bikes; and on-road tandems. You can add a two-seat trailer for infants and toddlers or a one-seat trail-a-bike for 3- to 5-year-olds to your rental bike. In-line skates are also available. Daily bike rentals start at C$9 per hour or C$23 for 4 hours, or overnight from 4pm to 10am. Escorted tours for groups of six or more are available. **Cyco's,** at 5 Hawthorne Ave. (by the canal at Pretoria Bridge; © 613/567-8180), also rents bicycles and in-line skates. You can rent mountain bikes and bike trailers in **Gatineau Park** at Philippe Lake campground general store. Rental includes helmets and locks and prices range from C$8 per hour to C$35 for a 24-hour period. **OC Transpo,** Ottawa's public transit system, has installed bike racks on more than 200 buses—most buses on routes 2, 85, 95, 96, 97, 101, 118, and 145 have racks. Each rack holds two bikes and is designed to make loading and unloading quick and easy. There's no cost to use the rack, other than regular bus fare. The program runs from spring through fall. You can also take your bike on the O-Train (enter by the door marked with the bike symbol and keep your bike in the designated area) on routes 1, 2, 4, 7, 14, 85, 95, 96, 97, 101, 118, and 145. Lock up your bike for the day at all O-Train stations and most Transitway stations. Use common sense when riding your bike or in-line skating, and be sure to follow the specific rules for cyclists. All cyclists under age 18 must wear a bicycle helmet under Ontario law. Cyclists cannot ride on the sidewalk, except where designated, and must not exceed speeds of 20kmph (12 mph) on multiuse pathways. Pass only when it is safe to do so, and use your bell or voice to let others know you're about to do so. Be considerate of other road or pathway users, and always keep to the right, whether you're skating or cycling.

If you're in the vicinity of the Rideau Centre and the ByWard Market, you can park your bike at a **supervised facility. Located at Rideau and William streets,** the facility operates daily from Victoria Day until Labor Day weekend (third Sat in May to first Mon in Sept). For maps of the pathways and more information, head to the **Capital Infocentre,** opposite Parliament Hill at 90 Wellington St. (🕐 **800/465-1867** or 613/2395000).

CROSS-COUNTRY SKIING

You're spoiled with choice for cross-country skiing in the Ottawa area. If you want to use the trails throughout the extensive **greenbelt,** consult the **"Greenbelt All Seasons Trail Map."** All trails are suitable for beginner and family outings. Many of the trails pass through wooded areas. Or go to **Mooney's Bay Cross-country Ski Centre** (2960 Riverside Dr.; 🕐 **613/247-4883**) and ski on 5km (3 miles) of groomed and well-lit trails. Classic and skate skiing are available for a mere C$2 per day or C$28 for a season's pass. Across the Ottawa River in the city of **Gatineau,** you'll find **Parc du Lac Beauchamp** at 745 boul. Maloney (🕐 **819/669-2548**). Winter activities in the park include outdoor ice skating and 15km (9 miles) of cross-country ski trails. Equipment rental is available.

For the ultimate cross-country ski experience, visit **Gatineau Park.** The park has earned a reputation as one of the best ski-trail networks in North America due to its remarkable 200km (124 miles) of trails, which are well maintained using the latest technology. The level of difficulty is marked on each trail, enabling skiers of all abilities to enjoy the meadows, valleys, and forests of the park. Both skiing styles are accommodated throughout the park, so you can glide along in classic Nordic fashion or burn up energy with the skate-skiing technique. There are eight heated shelters where you can stop to rest and refuel with a snack from your backpack. Gatineau Park ski patrollers are on watch to assist skiers in difficulty. When you arrive at the park, you can buy a day pass at any of the 16 parking lots, which give direct access to the ski trails, or at the Gatineau Park Visitor Centre (33 Scott Rd., Chelsea, QC; 🕐 **819/827-2020**), open throughout the year daily from 9am to 5pm. Daily pass prices for cross-country ski trails are C$10 for adults; C$7 for seniors, students, and youths; free for children 12 and under; and C$22 for families (2 adults and 3 teens).

Always carry a map when in wilderness areas. When you arrive at the park, pick up the **Gatineau Park official winter trail map** from the visitor center for C$5. Depicted on this highly detailed map—drawn using GIS technology—are ski trails, winter hiking trails, snowshoeing trails, huts, and shelters. Because skiing and weather conditions change frequently, Gatineau Park reviews and updates ski condition information three times daily. The trail conditions hot line (🕐 **819/827-2020**) is open 24 hours daily.

EXPLORING OTTAWA

7

OUTDOOR PURSUITS

Tips Renting Skis

Want to rent cross-country ski equipment? **Gerry & Isobel's** at 14 Scott Rd., Chelsea (🕐 **819/827-4341**), and **Greg Christie's Ski & Cycle Works** at 148 Old Chelsea Rd., Chelsea (🕐 **819/827-5340**), are close to the main entrance to **Gatineau Park.** In **Ottawa,** try **Fresh Air Experience** at 1291 Wellington St. (🕐 **877/722-3002** or 613/729-3002), or **Trailhead** at 1960 Scott St. (🕐 **613/722-4229**).

> ## (Fun Facts   Biking Around the Capital
>
> Did you know that there are more than 370km (230 miles) of major bike routes and 273km (170 miles) of minor routes in the City of Ottawa? Designated recreational pathways in the National Capital Region account for 170km (106 miles) of this total.

FISHING

Fishing with a **Quebec** provincial permit is allowed in the **Gatineau Park** lakes (Philippe Lake, Meech Lake, and La Pêche Lake). Mulvihill Lake, near the Mackenzie King Estate, has a fishing jetty designed to accommodate wheelchairs. Gatineau Park's waters are home to 40 species of fish, including trout, yellow perch, pike, and bass. Quebec fishing permits can be purchased at Canadian Tire (355 boul. de la Carrière, Gatineau; ✆ **819/ 770-7920**). To fish in **Ontario,** you need an Ontario provincial license. Ontario residents, other Canadian residents, and nonresidents all receive different licenses. **Access Ontario,** in the Rideau Centre (✆ **613/238-3630**), provides licenses as well as a list of Ottawa-area merchants that sell them. Please do not fish on Dow's Lake, since the fish stocked in this area do not respond favorably to catch and release.

GOLF

There are dozens of golf courses within an hour or so's drive of Ottawa, in both Ontario and Quebec. The varied countryside in the region provides excellent sites for courses. Most are open to the public. Greens fees vary enormously, dependent upon the season, day of the week, time of day, and other factors. Fees for 18 holes generally fall into the C$25 to C$75 range. See individual listings in chapter 11, "Side Trips from Ottawa."

HIKING

As well as checking out the pathways and trails through many of Ottawa's **city parks** and the **greenbelt** area, you might wish to explore **Gatineau Park,** the **Rideau Trail,** and parts of the **Trans Canada Trail,** particularly if you're looking for more challenging, longer routes.

The **Rideau Trail** is a cleared and marked hiking trail approximately 300km (186 miles) long that links Ottawa with the city of Kingston, on the shores of Lake Ontario. The trail path is indicated by orange triangular markers. To distinguish the two directions, Kingston-bound markers have yellow tips. The path crosses varied terrain, ranging from gentle agricultural land to the rugged Canadian Shield. The trail is designated for walking, cross-country skiing, and snowshoeing. You can pick up a comprehensive guide book with maps and a description of the trail for C$40 from the **Rideau Trail Association,** PO Box 15, Kingston, ON K7L 4V6 (✆ **613/545-0823**), or order one online at www.rideautrail.org. You'll also find the guide book at the Expedition Shoppe, 43 York St. (✆ **613/241-8397**); Mountain Equipment Co-op, 366 Richmond Rd. (✆ **613/729-2700**); Bushtukah Great Outdoor Gear, 203 Richmond Rd. (✆ **613/792-1170**); and A World of Maps, 1235 Wellington St. (✆ **613/724-6776**). Call the store of your choice before you make a special trip, as they may not always have the book on hand.

The **Trans Canada Trail** is a recreational trail currently under construction that eventually will traverse Canada from coast to coast, crossing every province and territory. In

Sunday Bikedays

In the summer, Sunday mornings present a real treat for lovers of the outdoors in Ottawa. No less than 52km (32 miles) of parkways in Ottawa and Gatineau Park are reserved exclusively for walking, running, cycling, in-line skating, and other nonmotorized recreational activities. Motor traffic is banned. In Ottawa the motor-free period runs from 9am to 1pm. In Gatineau Park, there are 30km (19 miles) of hilly roadways to hike, bike, or skate from 6 to 11am, plus one route that is designated motor-traffic-free until 1pm. **Sunday Bikedays** is sponsored by the French telecom company Alcatel-Lucent, which has a large Ottawa presence. Many local organizations provide volunteers to supervise start and end points and crossings every Sunday morning during the event.

In Ottawa, there are three motor traffic–free areas for the event, all of which are fully accessible to people with disabilities. The westbound lanes of the **Ottawa River Parkway,** located on the south side of the Ottawa River just west of downtown, has a 5.5km (3¹/₂-mile) stretch beginning at Island Park Drive and continuing to Carling Avenue. If you drive to this section, park your vehicle at the Lincoln Fields Shopping Centre at Carling Avenue. Beginning at the Laurier Bridge, you can enjoy **Colonel By Drive** as it winds along the east side of the Rideau Canal to Hog's Back Bridge, a total distance of 8km (5 miles). Park your car on one of the side streets to access Colonel By Drive. **Rockcliffe Parkway** is another choice for the Sunday morning excursion. Just east of downtown, and running along the southern shore of the Ottawa River, is an 8km (5-mile) section between the Canada Aviation Museum and St. Joseph Boulevard. Parking is available at the Canada Aviation Museum.

In **Gatineau Park,** the majority of the parkways (27km/17 miles) cover quite hilly terrain. The section north of Lac-Meech Road, accessible from parking lot 8, is recommended for families with young children.

For more information about the Sunday Bikedays program, visit the **Capital Infocentre** at 90 Wellington St. (© **800/465-1867** or 613/239-5000), or call the **Gatineau Park Visitor Centre** (© **819/827-2020**).

the Ottawa area, sections of the Trans Canada Trail can be found in Gatineau Park, Hull, the National Capital Greenbelt, and the Ottawa River Parkway. The trail is signposted with trail markers featuring the Trans Canada Trail logo. For more information, call © **800/465-3636** or visit www.tctrail.ca. For information on hiking in **Gatineau Park,** see chapter 11, "Side Trips from Ottawa."

ICE SKATING

The number-one place to skate in the nation's capital is the world-famous **Rideau Canal Skateway.** If you visit Ottawa during the skating season, you must take everyone for a glide along the canal—it's an experience not to be missed. The Skateway is the world's largest outdoor skating rink, offering almost 8km (5 miles) of continuous skating surface. The ice is usually ready in early January, and the season lasts until early March. During

The Trans Canada Trail

The **Trans Canada Trail,** currently under construction, is a recreational trail that will link Canada from coast to coast. At approximately 21,500km (13,359 miles) in length when completed, it will be the longest trail of its kind in the world.

Where practical, the trail is designated as a shared-use pathway with five core activities permitted: walking, cycling, horseback riding, cross-country skiing, and snowmobiling. Wherever possible, existing trails are used, provided they can accommodate these multiple uses. In addition, some provincial and federal park property, Crown land, abandoned railway lines, and rights of way on private land will become part of the trail.

The trail truly belongs to Canadians. Local organizations in communities across the country own, operate, and maintain their own segments, and more than 1.5 million volunteers are taking part in the project.

About 70% of the trail is already accessible, and it's expected that it will be substantially complete by late 2010. In some areas it's virtually completed, but other sections still require a significant amount of work, so you won't find a final set of maps yet. Maps of the Ontario, Quebec, and Atlantic provinces sections of the trail are available from the Trans Canada Trail website (www.tctrail.ca) for C$6 each. Eventually, maps will be produced for each region of the country.

In the Ottawa area, you'll find sections of the trail in **Gatineau Park, Hull,** the **National Capital Greenbelt,** and the **Ottawa River Parkway**—you can spot them by the trail markers with the Trans Canada Trail logo. For more information on the Trans Canada Trail, call ✆ **800/465-3636** or visit www.tctrail.ca.

the first three weekends in February, the Rideau Canal becomes the heart of **Winterlude,** Ottawa's winter festival. Skating is free. Heated shelters, skate and sled rentals, boot-check and skate-sharpening services, rest areas, food concessions, and toilets are located at various points along the Skateway. There are many access points along the canal for skating, so it's easy to get on the ice. To find out about ice conditions on the Rideau Canal, call the Skateway hot line at ✆ **613/239-5234.** For a special treat, visit the grounds of **Rideau Hall,** residence of the governor-general, and skate on the historic outdoor rink built by Lord and Lady Dufferin in 1872. The rink is open to the public on weekends from noon to 5pm and reserved for organized groups only on weekdays from noon to 8pm and weekends from 5 to 8pm. The rink opens in early January each year (weather permitting). The skating schedule may vary depending on weather conditions.

Across the Ottawa River in the city of **Gatineau,** you'll find **Parc du Lac Beauchamp.** Winter activities in the park include outdoor ice skating and cross-country skiing. For information on Lac Beauchamp call ✆ **819/669-2548.**

More than 70 outdoor skating rinks are scattered throughout the city of Ottawa. Pleasure skating, lessons, carnivals, and hockey are enthusiastically enjoyed at these sites. In **Brewer Park,** accessible from Hopewell Avenue near Bronson Avenue, there's a speed-skating oval that is open to the public, as well as two hockey rinks and a smaller ice surface.

Brantwood Park, at 120 Clegg St., has two ice surfaces. To find the outdoor rink closest to you, and to check the times for family recreational skating at indoor arenas throughout the region, call the **City of Ottawa Client Service Centre** at © 613/580-2400.

JOGGING

Jogging is an extremely popular pastime in Ottawa, as witnessed by the crowds of participants that flock annually to the National Capital Race Weekend (p. 31). For urban dwellers and visitors, the most popular running area is along the Rideau Canal—either on the sidewalks beside the waterway between the National Arts Centre and Hog's Back Falls, or on the ice surface in winter. After dark, it's advisable to use the sidewalk on the east side of the Canal, which is well lit, more public, and less obscured by shrubbery. Be aware that the sidewalks that line the canal are also used by in-line skaters and cyclists.

SWIMMING

You have a choice of riverbank beaches, municipal pools, and state-of-the-art wave pools. See "Beaches" (p. 147).

TENNIS

The following courts are open to the public—call ahead to book a court time. **Elmdale Tennis Club** is located in the Wellington West neighborhood at 184 Holland Ave. (© **613/729-3644**). The **Ottawa New Edinburgh Club** provides affordable sporting facilities for its members and the community. Seven European-style, red-clay courts and four hard courts are available. The club is located at 504 Rockcliffe Pkwy. (© **613/746-8540**). Public tennis courts can also be found at the **RA Centre,** 2451 Riverside Dr. (© **613/733-5100**). The **West Ottawa Tennis Club** is located in Britannia Park at the corner of Pinecrest Road and Carling Avenue (© **613/828-7622**). During the summer season (May 1–Sept 30), 10 clay courts and three hard courts are open. The rest of the year, play is available on six covered clay courts. Instruction for all levels is available.

7 SPECTATOR SPORTS

Ottawa has a couple of professional teams to root for, but those interested in the stars of the future can check out the variety of varsity sports at Carleton University (© **613/520-7400;** www.carleton.ca), including basketball, hockey, fencing, field hockey, golf, Nordic skiing, rowing, rugby, soccer, swimming, and water polo. The University of Ottawa (© **613/562-5700;** www.uottawa.ca) has interuniversity teams for basketball, cross country, football, hockey, rugby, soccer, skiing, swimming, and volleyball.

> **(Tips) Snow in the City**
>
> For loads of winter fun right in the city, visit **Carlington Snowpark,** at 941 Clyde Ave. ((C) **613/729-9206**). Go tubing or snowboarding and get a comfortable ride back up the hill. There are 10 slides to choose from, with night illumination and machine grooming. Hourly passes are available. Good toboggan hills can also be found at **Mooney's Bay Park** and **Vincent Massey Park.**

Ottawa Senators ★★   Experience all the excitement of National Hockey League action at Scotiabank Place, home of the Ottawa Senators. On game nights, the place rocks with loud recorded music between periods of on-ice action. Ottawa fans are among the most knowledgeable in the league. Kids will love the antics of Spartacat, the team's furry mascot. The exhibition season starts in September, and the playoffs can run as late as June. Ticket prices range from about C$14 for special promotions to about C$138, but you can visit www.capitaltickets.ca or call (C) **800/444-SENS** (7367) or 613/599-0300 to discover what's available for specific dates. I've watched games from both the top row in the arena and from just behind the players' bench, and while the experience is certainly different depending on your seat, Scotiabank Place is so well designed and steeply raked that there's really not a bad seat in the place for hockey. Scotiabank Place is located in Ottawa's far west end, and although there are 6,500 parking spots, getting to the game in a private car, and retrieving your car after the game, can be nerve-racking. OC Transpo offers five bus lines on game days (all Connexion 400 series routes); call the shuttle hot line at (C) **613/741-4390** for details. Several sports bars throughout the city also offer meal and shuttle-bus package deals on game nights. For meals, snacks, or suds at Scotiabank Place before or after the game, check out the Senate Club, Marshy's Bar-B-Q and Grill, the Penalty Box Sandwich Bar, Frank Finnigan's, Club Scotiabank, Rickard's Pub, or the Silver Seven Brew House. For all your Senators souvenirs visit Sensations, the official merchandise outlet of the Ottawa Senators Hockey Club (in the Corel Centre at gate 1).

1000 Palladium Dr. (C) **800/444-SENS** (7367) or 613/599-0300; 613/599-3267 for tickets. http://senators. nhl.com or www.capitaltickets.ca for tickets. Tickets C$14–C$138. Parking C$10. From downtown, take Hwy 417 West to Palladium Drive.

Ottawa 67's   For up-close and personal Ontario Hockey League action—featuring the NHL stars of the future—visit the Civic Centre in Lansdowne Park, home of the Ottawa 67's since their inception in—not coincidentally—1967. With a seating capacity of almost 10,000 and 47 luxury suites, it is reputed to be one of the best homes in junior hockey. On-site parking available.

1015 Bank St. (C) 613/232-6767 general information or 613/755-1166 for tickets. www.ottawa67s.com or www.ticketmaster.ca for tickets. Tickets C$14 adults, C$13 seniors and students, C$11 children 12 and under. Parking on-site C$5.

8 ESPECIALLY FOR KIDS

When traveling with children, if you can put their needs first when planning your itinerary and include activities for all ages then everyone will have a more pleasant vacation. Be sure to schedule plenty of time for relaxation (and naps, if your children are very act like adults—young children have short attention spans. When they start to wiggle and fidget, let them have half an hour to blow off steam in a playground, sit with them on a park bench and lick ice-cream cones, or take them to a movie. Here's a lineup of the best things for kids to see and do in the Ottawa area. Please don't feel restricted by these lists. The intention is to guide you to the best attractions for these age groups. No matter what their age, your kids will still enjoy visiting places not mentioned under their age group (and so will you!).

All ages   Canadian Museum of Nature, Canada Science and Technology Museum, Changing of the Guard on Parliament Hill, Canada Aviation Museum.

Ages 5 and under   Canadian Children's Museum, Canada Agriculture Museum.

Ages 6 to 9   Canadian Children's Museum, Canada Agriculture Museum, RCMP Musical Ride Centre at Rockcliffe Stables, Canadian Museum of Civilization, Rideau Canal Skateway and bikepaths, Rideau Hall grounds.

Ages 9 to 12   Canadian Museum of Civilization, Canadian War Museum, Canadian Children's Museum, Canada Agriculture Museum, RCMP Musical Ride Centre at Rockcliffe Stables, Rideau Canal Skateway and bikepaths, Changing of the Guard on Parliament Hill, Rideau Hall grounds and tour of the residence.

Teens   Canadian Museum of Civilization, Canadian War Museum, National Gallery of Canada, Parliament Hill tours, RCMP Musical Ride Centre at Rockcliffe Stables, Rideau Canal Skateway and bikepaths, ByWard Market, Diefenbunker Cold War Museum, Rideau Hall grounds and tour of the residence.

9 FOR VISITORS WITH SPECIAL INTERESTS

Animals   To see farm animals at close range and perhaps get a chance to handle small ones, or even to help milk a cow or shear a sheep, visit the **Canada Agriculture Museum.** A tour of the **RCMP Musical Ride Centre at Rockcliffe Stables** takes you right into the stables, where you can pat the horses' noses and feed them carrots. At the **Canada Museum of Nature** most of the creatures are of the preserved variety, but they are extremely well displayed.

First Nations   The **Canadian Museum of Civilization** has excellent exhibits on Native peoples and an impressive collection of giant totem poles. For a firsthand experience and the opportunity to meet First Nations people at work and play, visit Victoria Island in the summer months to experience an **aboriginal summer village** operated by Turtle Island Tourism Company, complete with tepees, canoes, storytelling, and Native foods, or the **Odawa Annual Pow Wow,** held at Ottawa Municipal Campground in late May.

Fitness   You can bike, hike, jog, walk, in-line skate, snowshoe, ski, and probably a few other things on the trails and pathways in Ottawa and Gatineau's extensive green space. Skate on the largest outdoor ice rink in the world, the **Rideau Canal Skateway.** Experience the beauty of the wilderness in **Gatineau Park.** Join in one of the annual events, such as the **Gatineau Loppet cross-country ski competition** or the **National Capital Race Weekend** that features a world-class 42km (26-mile) **marathon.**

Flight   The obvious choice here is the **Canada Aviation Museum,** where you can get close to dozens of real aircraft and sit in cockpit sections, fly a hang-glider simulator, or go up for a ride in a vintage airplane. And every Labor Day weekend (first weekend in Sept), there's the **Gatineau Hot Air Balloon Festival.** For commercial flights in small aircraft and hot air balloons, see "In the Air" (p. 146).

Ghosts   Those with nerves of steel can visit the ghost of **Watson's Mill** in Manotick or the ghost that haunts the **Ottawa International Hostel** (the site of Canada's last public hanging in this former jail). Enjoy an evening of entertainment on the **Haunted Walk of Ottawa** or check out the gravestones in **Beechwood Cemetery,** the final resting place of many famous Canadians, including politicians, writers, poets, and 12 Hockey Hall of Fame members. You'll find Beechwood Cemetery in the Vanier neighborhood of Ottawa, east of the Rideau River, bordered by Beechwood Avenue, Hemlock Road, and St. Laurent Boulevard.

History   Visit the **Canadian Museum of Civilization, Canadian War Museum, Library and Archives Canada, Billings Estate Museum, Bytown Museum, Laurier House, Rideau Hall,** and the **Diefenbunker Cold War Museum.**

The Military   The new **Canadian War Museum** is a must see. Watch the colorful **Changing of the Guard** ceremony on Parliament Hill in the summer.

Music   The **National Arts Centre** features live musical performances year-round. Popular musical artists appear at **Scotiabank Place, Centrepoint Theatre,** and the **Civic Centre.** There are dozens of live music venues as well: bars, clubs, and restaurants, some of which are listed in chapter 10, "Ottawa After Dark." Summer music festivals include the **Ottawa Chamber Music Festival, Ottawa International Jazz Festival, Ottawa Bluesfest,** and the **Ottawa Folk Festival.** Concerts are also held throughout the year at various downtown churches.

Numismatics   Visit the **Royal Canadian Mint** where you can purchase commemorative coins and take a guided tour of the factory along an enclosed walkway above all the action. Check out the **Currency Museum** in the center block of the Bank of Canada on Wellington Street.

Photography   For the most comprehensive showing of works by contemporary Canadian photographers, the **Canadian Museum of Contemporary Photography** is the place to go. The museum also runs workshops on topics related to photography. There are also some photographs exhibited in the **National Gallery of Canada.**

Philately   The **Canadian Postal Museum,** housed within the Canadian Museum of Civilization, traces the history of Canadian postal communications.

Politics/Law   In addition to the obvious **(Parliament Hill),** pay a visit to the **Supreme Court of Canada.** If you'd like to learn more about Canada's past prime ministers, see "The Lives and Times of Canada's PMs," earlier in this chapter.

Rocks and Minerals   For those with an interest in rocks, minerals, fossils, meteorites, and ores, the small museum at **Logan Hall** is a good place to spend an hour or two. The **Ecomuseum** in Gatineau (Hull sector) and the **Canada Museum of Nature** also have excellent displays of rocks and minerals, although please note that the Museum of Nature is undergoing extensive renovations and the Mineral Gallery is closed; the new Mineral Gallery is scheduled to open in 2010.

Science and Nature Best bets for the sci-and-tech crowd are the **Canada Science** **157**
and Technology Museum and the **Canadian Museum of Nature.** They'll be occupied
for hours.

Trains Train buffs will enjoy the locomotive collections at the **Canada Science and
Technology Museum** (p. 125) and the **Smiths Falls Railway Museum** (see chapter 11,
"Side Trips from Ottawa").

Visual Arts The **National Gallery of Canada** has an impressive collection of art, with
an emphasis on Canadian artists. Plan to spend several hours here if you have a passion
for art. The new **Canadian War Museum** has an extensive collection of **war art** on display. You'll also enjoy the **Canadian Museum of Contemporary Photography.** Local
galleries always have something of interest—see the listings under "More Museums &
Galleries," p. 129, and in chapter 9, "Shopping."

City Strolls

So many of Ottawa's famous land-marks, museums, and attractions are located within walking distance of one another in the downtown areas east and west of the **Rideau Canal** that you are bound to spend a fair amount of time on foot when you visit the city. The three walking tours in this section will cover most of the places of interest in the center of the city.

WALKING TOUR 1   **THE NATIONAL LANDMARKS**

START:	Fairmont Château Laurier.
FINISH:	Rideau Street and Sussex Drive.
TIME:	At least 2 hours. Depending on how long you want to linger at any of several major attractions, perhaps as long as 8 hours.
BEST TIMES:	Thursday, when the National Gallery of Canada has extended evening hours.
WORST TIMES:	Monday from October 1 to May 1, when the National Gallery of Canada is closed; anytime Parliament is sitting.

This tour follows a triangular route, takes you across provincial lines twice, and encompasses both the historical roots of Canada's capital and the seats of its legislative and judicial power. It also takes you to two of the country's most impressive—and newest—museums. If the weather is inclement, be sure to wear waterproof clothing, because you'll be crossing the Ottawa River twice.

---

❶ Fairmont Château Laurier

The granddaddy of Canada's famous rail-road hotels, the Château—as it's known throughout the city—was chosen as *the* Canadian symbol at Walt Disney World's Epcot in Florida. Some of the most important deals in the country's history have been concocted under the hotel's copper roof.

Head uphill (west) on Wellington Street. Below the bridge on your right, you'll see:

❷ The Ottawa Locks

The eight locks that connect the Rideau Canal to the Ottawa River allow boats to navigate a steep 24m (79-ft.) drop. Travel time through the locks for canal traffic is about 1¹/₂ hours.

Continue uphill to:

❸ Parliament Hill

The Peace Tower is such a powerful symbol of Canada that it's easy to overlook the fact that Parliament Hill has several components—including the Gothic Revival East Block, which contains the restored office of Sir John A. Macdonald and the magnificent Library of Parliament, as well as the relatively nondescript West Block. The Hill also has an array of statuary that depict various Canadian luminaries, so even if you're not taking the time for a full tour of the Centre Block, be sure to make a tour of the grounds. See p. 113.

From the gates of Parliament Hill, turn right and continue on Wellington Street until you're in front of:

❹ The Supreme Court of Canada

Set well back from Wellington Street, the Supreme Court building is easily overlooked. If you have an interest in jurisprudence, sit in on an appeal, but even if you're just passing by, be sure to check out

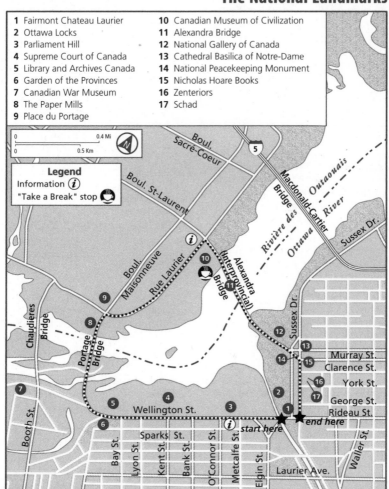

1 Fairmont Chateau Laurier	**10** Canadian Museum of Civilization
2 Ottawa Locks	**11** Alexandra Bridge
3 Parliament Hill	**12** National Gallery of Canada
4 Supreme Court of Canada	**13** Cathedral Basilica of Notre-Dame
5 Library and Archives Canada	**14** National Peacekeeping Monument
6 Garden of the Provinces	**15** Nicholas Hoare Books
7 Canadian War Museum	**16** Zenteriors
8 The Paper Mills	**17** Schad
9 Place du Portage	

Legend
Information ⓘ
"Take a Break" stop ☕

CITY STROLLS

8

THE NATIONAL LANDMARKS

the stunning architecture of the grand entrance hall. See p. 135.

Continue west on Wellington Street. On your right is:

❺ Library and Archives Canada

Most of the building is a working archives and open by appointment only, but public exhibits can be viewed on the ground floor. If you have a classical music fan in the family, be sure to check out Glenn Gould's famous black Steinway CD 318, located in the public area. See p. 130.

On the opposite side of Wellington Street, you'll see:

❻ The Garden of the Provinces

Commemorating the union of Canada's provinces and territories, this small park has two fountains and displays the flags, coats of arms, and floral emblems of the various parts of the country.

Ahead of you is:

❼ The Canadian War Museum

It's a bit of a hike out of the way to get to Canada's newest national museum, but this angle allows you to appreciate a different aspect of the building's unique design. Though the grass-covered roof makes it seem to merge into the landscape when seen from the southern approach, from here the eastern end of the museum rises like a church steeple. See p. 122.

Follow the curve of Wellington Street onto the Portage Bridge and cross the Ottawa River into the province of Quebec. To your left and right, you can see:

❽ The Paper Mills

Paper is one of the reasons Ottawa exists. Along with timber, wood pulp was the fuel of the area's economy until the late 19th century. On both the left and right sides of the Quebec end of the Portage Bridge you can still see the mills of E.B. Eddy, which turned out paper products and wooden matches here for decades. Taken over by Domtar in 1998, the mills are scheduled for closure and discussions are underway to determine the future of these heritage buildings.

At the end of the Portage Bridge, follow the sidewalk right onto rue Laurier. On the opposite side of rue Laurier is:

❾ Place du Portage

Consisting of four "phases," these monolithic buildings were constructed in the '70s to house a large percentage of the federal public service employees who work in the capital. Dozens of buildings in the old city of Hull were razed, and thousands of civil servants had to adjust to commuting across the Ottawa River.

Continue east on rue Laurier to:

❿ The Canadian Museum of Civilization

The undulating walls of Douglas Cardinal's building have become a national landmark, and the museum's collection takes the visitor from the country's aboriginal roots to contemporary times. The

Children's Museum is especially well done. Even if you don't have time for a full tour, stop and enjoy this marvelous piece of modern architecture. See p. 119.

> ☕ **TAKE A BREAK**
> The Canadian Museum of Civilization offers several options: the **Lunch Box** for light snacks, a cafeteria with a terrific view of Ottawa, and the **Café du Musée** (✆ **819/776-7009**), a fine dining restaurant for which reservations are recommended.

As you leave the museum, turn right onto rue Laurier and then right again onto:

⓫ The Interprovincial Bridge

Also known as the Alexandra Bridge, this structure isn't particularly attractive, but it does offer some spectacular views of the Parliament Buildings and the Canadian Museum of Civilization. As you cross, take a moment to imagine how this area must have appeared to explorer Samuel de Champlain's men as they paddled up the Ottawa River for the first time. At the top of the summit to your left you can see Champlain holding his astrolabe aloft. (If you look closely, you'll see that he's holding it upside down, the sculptor's error.)

Continue walking east until you reach:

⓬ The National Gallery of Canada

The Quebec side of the river has Cardinal's serpentine museum, the Ontario side has Moshe Safdie's crystal jewel box. The gallery's collection of contemporary works is spotty, but this is the best place to get a feel for the roots of Canadian art—from First Nations pieces to the Group of Seven. See p. 123.

From the gallery, cross Sussex Drive at St. Patrick Street and turn right at:

⓭ Notre-Dame Cathedral Basilica

Ottawa's oldest church has impressive spires and spectacular woodwork throughout its interior. Enter through the small door to the right of the main entrance. See p. 137.

⑭ The National Peacekeeping Monument

Before Canada took a more aggressive stance in countries like Afghanistan and Bosnia, the nation played important peacekeeping roles in Cyprus, Haiti, and the Middle East. This monument, which has dominated the square since 1992, recognizes Canada's contributions to global peace.

Continue south on Sussex Drive, where you can browse at:

⑮ Nicholas Hoare Books

If I were rich, I'd have a library that looks like this bookstore at 419 Sussex Dr. (© 613/562-2665), with honey-colored floor-to-ceiling shelves filled with beautiful

books. If you're lucky, and it's chilly outside, you might score one of the prime seats at the rear of the store near the fireplace. A rare independent bookstore in Ottawa, this shop has a great selection of architectural texts and books on language.

⑯ Zenteriors

If you love Japanese culture, Sam and Yumiko Toma's shop, at 459 Sussex Dr. (© 613/241-0699) will definitely have something to catch your eye.

⑰ Schad

Stocking popular international clothing brands like Betsey Johnson and Kookaï, **Schad**, at 527 Sussex Dr. (© 613/236-4111), is well established with Ottawa's young scene makers.

WALKING TOUR 2	CENTRETOWN & THE UNIVERSITY OF OTTAWA

START:	Confederation Square.
FINISH:	York and Dalhousie streets.
TIME:	2 to 4 hours.
BEST TIMES:	Weekdays in early September, when the University of Ottawa campus is buzzing with activity.
WORST TIMES:	Evenings or weekends from November to March, Christmas and Winterlude excepted.

Covering the city's core on both sides of the Rideau Canal, this tour has a bit of everything: two somber memorials, one of Canada's oldest universities, the heart of Ottawa's gay neighborhood, and even a castle.

---

① The National War Memorial

An iconic national symbol, the National War Memorial was designed by Englishman Vernon March, following an international competition in 1925. Built to commemorate the 60,000 Canadians killed in World War I, the monument was, ironically, not finished until just 4 months before the outbreak of World War II. In 2000, a second tomblike monument—designed by Dominion Sculptor Maurice Joanisse (Canada's official sculptor)—was unveiled at the foot of the cenotaph in honor of 116,000 Canadian war dead.

Cross Elgin Street and head west on Sparks Street.

② Sparks Street Mall

Once a busy east-west thoroughfare, in the early '60s, Sparks Street was just the second street in North America to be converted into a pedestrian walkway. It hasn't always been a success (the street is bereft of pedestrians after dark, and many merchants have fled the area) but the fountains and sidewalk cafes make it a pleasant place to wander on summer afternoons.

At Bank Street, turn left onto:

❸ Bank Street Promenade

As its name suggests, Bank Street was the heart of Ottawa's financial district in its early years. Today, it continues to be a busy commercial hub, with a wide mix of retail outlets and restaurants.

Continue south on Bank Street 9 blocks to Somerset Street and turn left into:

❹ Somerset Street Village

Characterized by a dozen of the city's most attractive Victorian buildings, Somerset Street West between Bank and O'Connor streets is one of Ottawa's oldest commercial districts and the heart of the gay neighborhood. Trees, five-globe streetlamps, and redbrick sidewalks were added in an extensive renovation program in the mid-1980s.

At Metcalfe Street, turn right and continue 7 blocks to:

❺ The Canadian Museum of Nature

David Ewart's 1910 Victoria Memorial Museum building is one of Ottawa's treasures, and a renovation project to restore it to its full glory is scheduled to be completed in 2010. Even with parts of the building under wraps and covered with scaffolding, you can visit newly restored galleries featuring dinosaurs and fossils, and Canada's mammals and birds. See p. 124.

From the museum, head east a very short block on McLeod Street to Elgin Street and then left 2 more short blocks to:

> **TAKE A BREAK**
> You won't find any "vertical food" at the **Elgin Street Diner** (p. 98). Leave that fancy stuff to the cafes and bistros on the ByWard Market; this is the place to come if you want simple food, done well. If you crave a protein hit, make sure you have one of their signature poutine dishes. Don't know what poutine is? Just ask.

Head north on Elgin Street to Lewis Street and to:

❻ St. Luke's Park

Surrounded by a fine assortment of vintage redbrick houses, tiny St. Luke's Park has become the focal point for the continuing issue of violence against women in contemporary society. A monument featuring a number of small stone obelisks commemorates Ottawa area women who have been murdered by men, and a vigil is held here each December to remember the 14 women killed in the 1989 Montreal Massacre.

Exit the park at its east side and walk east on Gilmour Street a block to MacDonald Street. Turn left and enjoy the heritage homes along MacDonald Street for 2 blocks to Somerset Street. Turn right, cross the Queen Elizabeth Driveway, and then cross the Rideau Canal on:

❼ The Corktown Footbridge

Opened in 2006, this bowed bridge over the Rideau Canal offers sweeping views to both north and south. The perspective out toward the turrets of Fairmont Château Laurier with the Gatineau Hills in the background is especially good and has quickly become a favorite with photographers.

At the east end of the bridge, take the short staircase on your right and head to the traffic lights ahead. Once across Colonel By Drive, head under the OC Transpo bridge and enter the campus of:

❽ The University of Ottawa

Canada's oldest bilingual university, the school was founded by the Oblate fathers in 1848 as the College of Bytown. Today, the university has 33,000 students in 10 faculties, and is a leading research institution in such areas as technology and law. In addition to the campus's main buildings, the university occupies a number of heritage homes in the area.

Zigzag through the campus on a series of small streets named Jean-Jacques Lussier, Université, Louis-Pasteur, and Thomas-More to King Edward Avenue. Turn left and walk down the steep hill to Rideau Street. On your left you'll see:

1 National War Memorial
2 Sparks Street Mall
3 Bank Street Promenade
4 Somerset Street Village
5 Canadian Museum of Nature
6 St. Luke's Park
7 Corktown Footbridge
8 University of Ottawa
9 Ottawa Little Theatre
10 King Edward Avenue
11 Cundell Stables

| 0 | | 0.4 Mi |
| 0 | | 0.5 Km |

Legend
Information ⓘ
"Take a Break" stop

⑨ The Ottawa Little Theatre

Founded in 1913, this is Canada's oldest amateur theater company, and has featured budding Ottawa entertainers like comedian Rich Little. The theater has twice been destroyed by fire. The current 510-seat auditorium was built in 1970, and is the venue for eight plays each year.

Cross Rideau Street to the north end of:

⑩ King Edward Avenue

Now a fairly mundane four-lane road, King Edward Avenue played a key role in the early plan for Ottawa to become the North American equivalent of Paris. The boulevard had a canopy of trees, and fine Ottawa ladies and gentlemen promenaded here on Sunday afternoons. Today, the busy street is a reminder that urban progress sometimes isn't all it's cracked up to be.

Follow King Edward Avenue for another 2 blocks, to York Street, cross to the north sidewalk, and go left on York to no. 113 and:

⑪ The Cundell Stables

Ottawa hasn't had a horse-pulled bread or milk wagon since the late '50s, but Cundell Stables (© 613/241-8054) is a reminder of the ByWard Market's past, when horsepower ruled. Today, the business survives on carriage rentals and sleigh rides.

WALKING TOUR 3	THE BYWARD MARKET, LOWERTOWN & SANDY HILL

START:	ByWard Market building.
FINISH:	Rideau and Nicholas streets.
TIME:	2 to 3 hours.
BEST TIMES:	Early weekend mornings, when the ByWard Market is busiest.
WORST TIMES:	Late afternoons on weekdays, when some of the streets can be congested.

This walk takes you through some of Ottawa's oldest neighborhoods, includes several historic sites, and shows you how the city continues to evolve. Even a decade ago, parts of this tour—Cathcart Street and the northern part of Dalhousie Street—were areas where Ottawans would never send visitors. Now, every part of Lowertown has been rejuvenated, and young families and businesspeople are moving into gentrified areas that used to be derelict. Earlier changes—including, perhaps surprisingly, the fall of the Soviet empire and the end of capital punishment in Canada—also play a role in this tour that covers the eastern part of the downtown core.

Begin at:

❶ 55 ByWard Market Square

The main ByWard Market building dominates the area and bustles inside and out with activity. Inside, you'll find a range of international crafts and foods; outside, the building is lined on its west side with fruit and vegetable stalls, representing the best produce from around the region.

Follow ByWard Market Square to the north side of Clarence Street and turn left. Follow Clarence Street to the Blackthorn Café and the entrance to:

❷ The Tin House Court

King Edward Avenue may have fallen victim to short-sighted redevelopment since the era when Prime Minister Wilfrid Laurier dreamed of Ottawa as the Paris of the North, but the Tin House Court still keeps his dream alive. Highlighted by artist Art Price's reimagined house facade, the cobblestone courtyard is one of my favorite places in Canada. Make a point to return after dark, when the artistic lighting makes it shine like a jewel.

Exit the Tin House Court at its north end onto Murray Street and turn left. Turn right at Sussex Drive and walk north to:

❸ Cathcart Street

Definitely not the prettiest street in Ottawa, Cathcart nevertheless shows the city's working-class roots to best advantage. On one side, small frame houses are the kind of dwellings favored by Ottawans at the beginning of the 20th century, while the other side is dominated by the Élisabeth Bruyère Health Centre—once Bytown's first hospital, now the home of the Family Health Faculty of the University of Ottawa. Farther east, Cathcart opens up with Bingham Park, providing views of the rear of the Lester B. Pearson Building, the headquarters of Canada's Department of Foreign Affairs.

Follow Cathcart Street east a block to Dalhousie Street and turn right. Take some time to browse at:

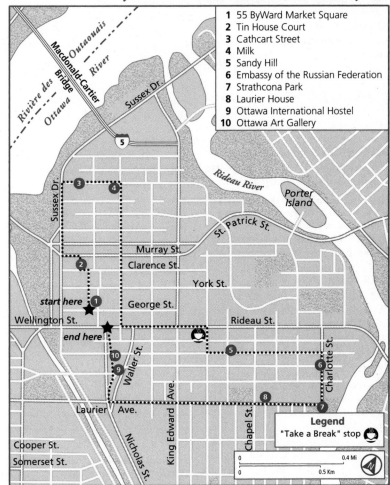

1 55 ByWard Market Square
2 Tin House Court
3 Cathcart Street
4 Milk
5 Sandy Hill
6 Embassy of the Russian Federation
7 Strathcona Park
8 Laurier House
9 Ottawa International Hostel
10 Ottawa Art Gallery

Legend

 "Take a Break" stop

0   0.4 Mi
0   0.5 Km

CITY STROLLS

8

THE BYWARD MARKET, LOWERTOWN & SANDY HILL

❹ Milk

Selected as Ottawa's women's boutique by the readers of *Ottawa Xpress* in 2007, **Milk**, 234 Dalhousie St. (✆ **613/789-6455**), is an unpretentious shop that specializes in innovative fashion by designers like Blend-She, Dace, Drifter, and Golddigga.

Continue south on Dalhousie Street to the south side of Rideau Street and turn left to:

TAKE A BREAK
Heads of state, rock stars, Teamsters—they've all enjoyed the forthright service and Jewish comfort food at **Nate's,** 316 Rideau St. (✆ **613/789-9191**). A mainstay of lower Rideau for decades, this deli serves terrific blintzes, latkes, and chopped liver, but try the smoked meat eggrolls—a house specialty.

Continue east on Rideau Street, turn right on Nelson Street for 2 blocks and then left on Daly Street, a typical residential street of:

❺ Sandy Hill

Once the expansive estate of Louis-Théodore Besserer, this became Ottawa's wealthiest neighborhood after the University of Ottawa parceled it off to the city's lumber barons and senior bureaucrats. As the wealthier residents moved farther east to Rockcliffe Village, the area became more middle class, but many of the foreign embassies and ambassadorial residences remained. Today, the population hovers at around 15,000.

Continue east on Daly Street to Charlotte Street and turn right. Across Charlotte Street at the corner of Wilbrod Street you'll see:

❻ The Embassy of the Russian Federation

It was from this building, in 1945, that Soviet cipher clerk Igor Gouzenko smuggled documents that some say launched the cold war. Decades later, when embassy officials welcomed peace marchers in for tea, it signaled the arrival of glasnost and the beginning of the end of the Soviet empire.

Adjacent to the embassy, at the southern end of Charlotte Street, is:

❼ Strathcona Park

Flanked on the east by the Rideau River and on the west by some of the city's oldest mansions, this well-landscaped park can seem like an urban oasis from a much earlier time. Africans from the nearby embassies and high commissions love to play soccer here, and kids frolic on the castle ruins and in the wading pool. In the summer, the Odyssey Theatre Company stages plays in the park.

Head west on Laurier Avenue East to:

❽ Laurier House

Overshadowed by larger and more centrally located national museums, Laurier House is one of Canada's quirkier historic sites. Both Wilfrid Laurier and William Lyon Mackenzie King—two of the country's most colorful, and influential, prime ministers—lived here, and the museum also contains a restored version of Prime Minister Lester B. Pearson's study, including a replica of his Nobel Peace Prize. It was in this house that King communed with mystics—and, his diaries hinted, prostitutes—in efforts to determine how Canada should conduct itself during World War II. His crystal ball is one of the artifacts on display. See p. 135.

Keep walking west on Laurier Avenue East to Nicholas Street on your right. Follow Nicholas Street under the Mackenzie King Bridge to:

❾ Ottawa International Hostel

The site of Canada's last public hanging, this was the county jail until 1972, when it was converted—with only minor alterations—to a youth hostel. My oldest daughter worked as a desk clerk here for one summer, and supports claims that the building is haunted. Is it the ghost of Patrick Whelan, who was hanged here for the murder of Member of Parliament Thomas D'Arcy McGee? Feel free to ask, if you encounter him. See p. 82.

Just north of the hostel on Nicholas Street, you'll see:

❿ The Ottawa Art Gallery

Once a provincial courthouse, the building at the corner of Nicholas and Daly streets is now an artist's co-op, housing the Ottawa Gallery, the SAW video co-op, and studio space for a variety of visual artists and musicians.

Continue north on Nicholas Street to Rideau Street.

Shopping

As recently as 20 years ago, Ottawans looking for the latest fashions, unique gifts, or the best bargains headed east to Montreal, west to Toronto, or south to the factory outlets of Vermont and New Hampshire.

Although you still won't find Gucci, Chanel, Prada, or Ralph Lauren stores in the capital, the city has a good selection of medium-size outlets for most national chains; a large number of locally owned, one-of-a-kind retailers; and a variety of stores geared to the tourist trade.

1 THE SHOPPING SCENE

The vast majority of Ottawans live in the city's suburbs, so shopping malls and clusters of big-box retailers such as Wal-Mart, Home Depot, and Canadian Tire dominate the outlying areas along the main arterial routes like Hwy. 417 and Bank Street. Fortunately for visitors, the downtown core and major urban neighborhoods are home to a growing number of unique stores, including a variety of small art galleries and boutique-style fashion retailers.

Ottawa's proximity to the Gatineau Hills, Algonquin Park, and the northern reaches of the Ottawa River has spurred the growth of outfitters—most of which are concentrated in the Westboro neighborhood (p. 63)—and other types of outdoor stores. The city also has more than the usual number of kitchenware outlets, and, in keeping with its role as national capital, a good share of Canadian craft and souvenir shops.

Most stores in Ottawa are open Monday through Saturday from 9:30 or 10am to 6pm, and many have extended hours on Thursday and Friday. Sunday hours are generally from noon to 5pm, although some malls open at 11am, while some independent stores are closed. You should call ahead if you have a specific destination in mind. During December, many stores, and most malls, stay open in the evenings throughout the week.

Sales taxes add a hefty chunk to your bill. The provincial sales tax in Ontario is 8% for most items—two exceptions are basic groceries and children's clothing, which are exempt. The federal Goods and Services Tax (GST) is 5%.

Almost every establishment accepts MasterCard and Visa, and a growing number take American Express. Many retailers accept U.S. cash, especially in the downtown core. Rarely will you find a retailer that does not have an Interac terminal for direct debit transactions.

2 GREAT SHOPPING AREAS

Bank Street Promenade

You'll discover 15 blocks of stores and services in this area, beginning at Wellington Street in the heart of downtown and stretching south to Gladstone Avenue. About 500 businesses operate on this stretch of Bank Street, ranging from small, locally owned retailers, bargain stores, and souvenir shops to restaurants, bars, and cafes. The streetscape and street life takes on a much funkier aspect at its southern end—particularly near Somerset and MacLaren streets—but it's safe as big cities go, even in the evening hours.

Beechwood Avenue

Marking the boundary between tony New Edinburgh to the north and traditionally working-class Vanier to the south, Beechwood Avenue is a comfortable mix of the two, with a variety of craft and nature shops, bakeries, and cafes that draw a rich cross section of locals.

ByWard Market ★★★

More than 100 boutiques jostle for position with restaurants, pubs, services, and food retailers in the warren of side streets and century-old squares that make up the vibrant ByWard Market area, bordered by Sussex Drive, Cathcart Street, King Edward Avenue, and Rideau Street. Head for this district to be entertained, excited, and delighted by what's on offer and by the impressive collection of 19th-century architecture. The ByWard Market building, located on the original site where farmers and loggers met to carry out their business in the 1800s, was restored in 1998 and now houses gourmet food shops and the wares of local and regional artisans. Excellent-quality local fruit, vegetables, flowers, and other farm products are available at outdoor stalls surrounding the market building between April and October. Cheese shops, butcher shops, bakeries, and other food retailers complete the mix. Don't miss the northern end of Dalhousie Street between Murray and Cathcart streets, which is a burgeoning area for funky boutiques and cafes, and the various squares that are situated between George, York, Clarence, and Murray streets.

The Glebe ★★

The 13 blocks of Bank Street between Isabella Street in the north and Holmwood Avenue in the south serve the shopping needs of Ottawa's Glebe residents and are home to many of the city's most interesting shops. From Arbour Environment Shoppe, which specializes in hemp goods, to World Mosaic, with its exceptional selection of kitchen and bathroom tile, the neighborhood teems with shopping opportunities. The small urban oases, Brown's Inlet, and Central Park, are tucked a couple of blocks west of Bank Street, north of Queen Elizabeth Drive and offer a relaxing break. For winter strolling, take refuge in the atrium at Fifth Avenue Court.

Ottawa South ★★

The section of Bank Street between the Rideau Canal and the Rideau River—about 10 compact blocks that run sharply downhill from north to south—serves as an annex to the Glebe and is home to many of the city's antiques dealers. There are also a number of good pubs and cafes to fuel you as you shop.

Sparks Street Mall

Canada's oldest permanent pedestrian shopping street, Sparks Street Mall runs between Elgin and Lyon streets, one block south of Parliament Hill. Although it's busy during the working day because of the many office blocks that surround it, Sparks Street can seem deserted on evenings and weekends. In summer, restaurants set up patio tables and chairs.

SHOPPING

9

GREAT SHOPPING AREAS

Wellington Street West ★

Not to be confused with Wellington Street in the downtown core, which runs in front of the Parliament Buildings and the Supreme Court, Wellington Street West is actually a continuation of Somerset Street West in the stretch between Parkdale Avenue and Island Park Drive. To confuse things even more, the thoroughfare's name changes to Richmond Road at Western Avenue. There's an interesting mix here, with fine-dining restaurants, neighborhood cafes, interior decorating retailers, and antiques, collectibles, and second-hand shops, as well as the vibrant Parkdale Market, and a couple of old-school taverns. This is an area in rapid transition, with new shops popping up every month or so.

Westboro Village ★★

Until the 1980s, it was a brave retailer who opened for business in Westboro; the area was a veritable death valley for shopping. One of the oldest independently incorporated municipalities in the pre-Ottawa Bytown era, Westboro—centered around Richmond Road between Island Park Drive and Roosevelt Avenue—was popular with returning World War II veterans, who flocked to the area's reasonably priced houses. Today, Westboro is one of the city's hottest real estate markets, and shops and cafes have been sprouting like mushrooms. Spurred by the success of the locally owned outfitter Trailhead, Westboro now has Canada's largest concentration of outdoor stores, including one of Mountain Equipment Co-operative's flagship outlets. It's also a great place for family shopping, due to the presence of toy stores, a skateboard shop, several child-friendly restaurants, and a pet specialty store.

---

3 MALLS & SHOPPING CENTERS

Ottawa has one major mall—the Rideau Centre, discussed below. Downtown, several smaller, upscale indoor malls serve office workers and tourists alike, although their opening hours tend to reflect a 9-to-5 mentality. **L'Esplanade Laurier,** at the corner of Bank Street and Laurier Avenue, features women's fashions, gift shops, banking, and postal services. At the corner of Sparks and Bank streets, **240 Sparks Shopping Centre** has a large food court and is anchored by Holt Renfrew, which stocks designer-label men's and women's clothing and stays open until 7:30pm on Thursday and Friday; Sunday hours are noon to 5pm. **World Exchange Plaza,** at the corner of Metcalfe and Albert streets, combines movie theaters, services, and a food court catering to the office crowd.

Rideau Centre   In the heart of downtown, with direct access from the Ottawa Congress Centre and the Westin Hotel, the four-level Rideau Centre has more than 170 stores, including services, restaurants, and cinemas. The mall is open Monday–Friday 9:30am to 9pm, Saturday until 6pm, and Sunday 11am to 5pm. You'll find a selection of jewelers, leather goods stores, and good-quality casual clothing. This mall is an excellent bet for gifts and souvenirs—Mastermark Pewter, Ottawa Souvenirs & Gifts, Swarovski, and WIX are all worth a look. Free stroller and wheelchair rental and a nursing room are available. 50 Rideau St. ✆ **613/236-6565.** www.rideaucentre.net.

ANTIQUES & COLLECTIBLES

There are a number of fine antiques dealers and a host of collectibles shops in the city, but if you want to hit a few places in a single neighborhood, head south on Bank Street to Ottawa's very own antiques alley.

Architectural Antiques ★　Specializing in vintage lighting, this Westboro store is a treasure trove of vintage finishings and fixtures. They also do custom design work. 356 Richmond Rd. ✆ 613/722-1510.

Bloomsbury & Co Antiques　With interests that include antique and period furniture, silver, prints, china, pottery, and decorative items, this store at the corner of Bank and Sunnyside is always on the lookout for antique and period pieces to add to its inventory. 1090 Bank St. ✆ 613/730-1926.

Champagne dit Lambert Antiques　This high-end antiques dealer specializes in fine furniture, particularly mahogany, and also silver completion, china, and decorative items. They have a strong reputation in the city for their attractive window displays. An annex known as "the Warehouse" stocks teak furniture and other objects for young urban collectors. 1130 Bank St. ✆ 613/730-1181.

Logan Antiques　The specialties here run to Art Deco, art glass, and pottery, as well as estate jewelry. Open daily 10:30am to 5 pm. 1097 Bank St. ✆ 613/730-8943.

Ottawa Antique Market　In the heart of Ottawa South, more than 40 antiques dealers display their wares in this indoor market daily 10am to 6pm. 1179A Bank St. ✆ 613/730-6000.

Yardley's Antiques　On dry days, you'll see the pavement in front of this shop crammed with articles for sale. There's something for everyone here. Antiques rub shoulders with country pine furniture, old light fixtures, and pop memorabilia. 1240 Bank St. ✆ 613/739-9580.

ART

Artésol Gallery　Opened in 2005, this gallery is dedicated to showcasing the work of up-and-coming Cuban artists, and frequently hosts solo exhibits. 279 Dalhousie St. ✆ 613/789-0874. www.artesolgallery.com.

Cambridge Design Gallery　The latest addition to the burgeoning Wellington West neighborhood, this gallery features a mixture of local, Canadian, and international artists, and also offers a range of consultation and artistic design services. 1282C Wellington St. ✆ 613/232-2787. www.cambridgedesigngallery.com.

Cube Gallery (Finds)　One of several contemporary galleries that have opened in predominately residential neighborhoods—in this case, Wellington West—Cube features new exhibits monthly. Located in a former soda-bottling plant, the gallery has a larger-than-average display area, making it the ideal venue to view big works. The gallery also frequently hosts cultural events and has quickly become a hub for Ottawa's young boho community. 7 Hamilton Ave. N. ✆ 613/728-1750. www.cubegallery.ca.

Galerie d'Art Vincent　This gallery, located in the elegant Edwardian Fairmont Château Laurier Hotel, features Canadian historical and contemporary art, including exquisite, unique sculptures; 20th-century Canadian paintings; and original Inuit carvings and prints. 1 Rideau St. (inside Château Laurier Hotel). ✆ **613/241-1144. www.inuitfinearts.com.**

Parkdale Gallery   Opened by artist James Robinson in 2006, the Parkdale Gallery reflects his passion for growing a broad, well-networked arts community within the solidly working-class Hintonburg neighborhood. In addition to special shows, the gallery features about 100 works by a dozen or so painters and sculptors. 229 Armstrong St. ✆ **613/614-4308. www.parkdalegallery.com.**

Snapdragon Gallery   The front window display of this Glebe shop is a work of art in itself, featuring a variety of pieces by both emerging and established Canadian artists. Step inside and you'll find jewelry, ceramics, glass, wood, leather goods, Inuit sculpture, and copper etchings. 791 Bank St. ✆ **613/233-1296.**

The Snow Goose Limited   This fine arts and crafts shop specializes in Canadian, Inuit, and Native works from the Arctic and the West Coast in every price range. You'll find clothing, sculptures, prints, masks, pottery, quill boxes, totems, leather goods, and jewelry. It is located on the Sparks Street Mall close to the Parliament Buildings. 83 Sparks St. ✆ **613/232-2213. www.snowgoose.ca.**

Wallack Galleries   One of Ottawa's most established galleries, Wallack has an extensive selection of contemporary paintings and sculptures, and frequently features the work of renowned Ottawa-based photographer Jennifer Dickson. 203 Bank St. ✆ **613/235-4339.**

AUDIO & ELECTRONICS
The Audio Shop   A standby in the Glebe for many years, this store handles brands ranging from Bose to Panasonic. 685 Bank St. ✆ **613/233-1201.**

Bleeker Stereo & TV   While big-box electronics outlets have slowly knocked off much of the independent competition, this family-owned business continues to thrive, featuring a broad array of small and large entertainment equipment, and appliances. 1400 Clyde Ave. ✆ **613/225-5191.**

BOOKS
Books on Beechwood   This independent store carries general fiction and nonfiction. The emphasis is on literary fiction rather than pulp. It also has a large children's and young adult section, a number of British and military history books, and a small but select mystery section. 35 Beechwood Ave. ✆ **613/742-5030.**

Chapters   Gaining a presence on city street corners as well as participating in big-box suburban commercial sprawl, Chapters has become a familiar name and favored destination for Canadian shoppers. There are five locations to choose from in the Ottawa area, offering an array of books and magazines. Larger stores carry CDs and a growing selection of giftware. 47 Rideau St. ✆ **613/241-0073.** 2735 Iris St. ✆ 613/596-3003. 2210 Bank St. ✆ 613/521-9199. 400 Earl Grey Dr. ✆ **613/271-7553.** 2401 CityPark Dr. ✆ 613/744-5175.

Collected Works (Finds)   This independent store stocks general fiction and nonfiction, with an emphasis on literary fiction and children's books. It offers a cozy browsing atmosphere, augmented with comfy chairs and a small coffee bar and frequently offers in-store readings by authors. 1242 Wellington St. ✆ **613/722-1265. www.collected-works.com.**

Indigo   After assuming control of the Chapters chain, Indigo maintained some of its own bright, attractive stores in selected cities. The Ottawa outlet has a particularly large magazine section, as well as the usual selection of books and gifts. 125 RioCan Ave. ✆ **613/843-0045.**

Leishman Books Ltd. This independent store carries general fiction and nonfiction and French-as-a-second-language books. There's a large children's section at the back of the store. Westgate Shopping Centre. ✆ 613/722-8313.

Librairie du Soleil This new location of Librairie du Soleil lives up to its name—the sun streams into the interior. Come here for the most impressive selection of French-language books in Ottawa. A good choice of French/English dictionaries is on hand. Calendars, TinTin memorabilia, and other nonbook items are also available. The staff is a bilingual. 33 George St. ✆ 613/241-6999.

Mother Tongue Books ★ The focus here is on women's lives and issues, with a large number of works on feminism, health, and lesbian literature. The store is an excellent source of information about alternative events in Ottawa. 1067 Bank St. ✆ 613/730-2346.

Nicholas Hoare ★ Specializing in British authors and publishers, this shop also offers a comprehensive children's section and excellent choices in Canadian fiction. The atmosphere is restful and the background music soothing. Floor-to-ceiling bookshelves line the walls and elegant library ladders glide on rails to allow access to the top shelves. Enjoy literature, popular fiction, art books, hardcover coffee table books, travel books, and cookbooks. 419 Sussex Dr. ✆ 613/562-2665.

Octopus Books (Finds) Before its gentrification, the Glebe was a hotbed of leftist politics, and Octopus Books was often a focal point of socialist dialogue and debate. The focus of the store remains on books that encourage analytical thinking about the economic, political, and social world. Many of the recommended texts for social and political science courses at Carleton University and the University of Ottawa are stocked here. Canadian and international fiction are also featured prominently on the shelves. 116 Third Ave. ✆ 613/233-2589. www.octopusbooks.org.

Patrick McGahern Books Inc. A delightful collection of used and rare books—Canadiana, Arctica, voyages and travel, medicine, Irish history and literature, and more—line the shelves here. Ladders are available to access those tempting titles just out of reach. A must to include on a stroll in the Glebe. 783 Bank St. ✆ 613/230-2275.

Perfect Books An independent bookseller carrying general fiction and nonfiction, Perfect Books has a strong literary fiction section, plus a sizable one on politics and current events. Higher-end cookbooks are also stocked. 258A Elgin St. ✆ 613/231-6468.

Prime Crime Books As you will have deduced, this bookstore specializes in crime and mystery fiction. Frequented by local authors and mystery fans. 891 Bank St. ✆ 613/238-2583.

Singing Pebble Books ★ (Finds) Those with an interest in and passion for subjects leaning toward the esoteric will find themselves at home here. Metaphysics, Eastern and Western spirituality, alternative health and healing, women's studies, psychology, and philosophy are some of the subjects featured. 202A Main St. ✆ 613/230-9165. www.singing pebblebooks.ca.

Sunnyside Bookshop Consciousness raising and alternative spirituality are the main topics of interest here, and the stock runs to tarot cards, New Age CDs, and books on Native studies. 113 Murray St. ✆ 613/241-0943.

CAMERAS

Canadian Camera Service Centre This place sells and repairs all makes of cameras. It also stocks lenses, binoculars, projectors, and photographic equipment and offers 1-hour photo service and free estimates on repairs. 250 Albert St. ✆ 613/238-4892.

Ginn Photographic ★★ This locally owned store sells and rents new and used photographic equipment and supplies, plus darkroom equipment and supplies. It also provides digital equipment sales and service and imaging services, including black-and-white photofinishing. The Ginn family's depth of experience and their knowledgeable staff make this a favorite with local professionals and photographic artists. 433 Bank St. ✆ 613/567-4686. www.ginnphoto.on.ca.

CHINA, SILVER & GLASS

McIntosh & Watts Established in 1906, McIntosh & Watts deals in fine china, crystal, flatware, and giftware. Bayshore Shopping Centre. ✆ **613/828-9174.** Place d'Orléans Shopping Centre. ✆ 613/834-8442. Kanata Signature Centre. ✆ 613/591-7702. Rideau Centre. ✆ 613/560-5311. Holly Lane Superstore. ✆ 613/523-7240.

CRAFTS

Lewiscraft Lewiscraft offers lots of materials and supplies for artistically inclined kids and grown-ups, plus a knowledgeable and helpful staff. Place d'Orléans. ✆ **613/834-9039.**

Michael's Arts and Crafts Taking up the big-box challenge of trying to carry everything under one roof, Michael's has aisle upon aisle of shelves simply groaning with arts and crafts supplies for the home crafter and decorator, including kid-friendly supplies and seasonal decorations for every major annual festival. Especially good hunting ground at Easter, Halloween, and Christmas. 2685 Iris St. ✆ **613/726-7211.** 4220 Innes Rd. ✆ 613/590-1813. 2210 Bank St. ✆ 613/521-3717.

Sassy Bead Company (**Kids**) Browse the colorful jars, trays, and boxes filled with beads of every description. Make your selection, then sit at a table and create your own jewelry right in the shop. Creative staff is on hand 7 days a week to help with design and assembly. There's also a good selection of unique ready-made items. Workshops and kids' birthday parties are available. The Bank Street location carries a line of Sassy clothing for teens and women. 757 Bank St. ✆ **613/567-7886.** 11 William St. ✆ 613/562-2812.

DEPARTMENT STORES

The Bay Established in the Canadian North more than 300 years ago as a fur-trading post known as the Hudson's Bay Company, the Bay carries standard department-store collections of fashions and housewares. Sales and promotions are frequent and merchandise is good quality. The Bay occupies an anchor spot at four large Ottawa area malls—Bayshore Shopping Centre, Place d'Orléans Shopping Centre, Rideau Centre, and St. Laurent Shopping Centre.

Sears Canada Offering a comprehensive range of consumer goods, Sears anchors Carlingwood Shopping Centre, Rideau Centre, and St. Laurent Shopping Centre. Like the Bay, Sears offers sales and promotions on an ongoing basis.

DISCOUNT SHOPPING

Act II Fashions With two west-end locations, Act II specializes in women's designer label clothing on consignment. 471 Hazeldean Rd. ✆ **613/831-8386.** 3500 Fallowfield Rd. ✆ 613/843-9549.

Clothes Encounters of a Second Time The store's close proximity to the upscale neighborhoods of New Edinburgh and Rockcliffe give it an edge when it comes to scooping up barely used designer wear. 67 Beechwood St. ✆ **613/741-7887.**

The Clothes Secret   The stock consistently includes plenty of brand-name labels, and new arrivals are set apart to make browsing easy. 1136 Bank St. ✆ **613/730-9039.**

Consignment World   Small household items abound at this hip store for bargain hunters. 1500 Bank St. ✆ **613/739-1500.**

HUSH ReSale Clothing   The racks here are conveniently organized by size, and the store offers a "special item" search service. 395 Richmond Rd. ✆ **613/724-4874.**

Value Village   Quickly becoming as much a national icon as Tim Horton's, Value Village—the Canadian arm of Savers—always offers an eclectic mix of clothing, books, toys, furniture, and appliances. 1824 Bank St. ✆ **613/526-5551.** 1221 Cyrville Rd. ✆ **613/749-4977.** 1375 Clyde Ave. ✆ **613/288-1390.**

EYEWEAR

Jack Winter Opticians   When Jim Veitch took over the store from its namesake, the stock included a large selection of vintage glasses from the '40s and '50s. Since the change in ownership, the store has attracted musicians, actors, and other assorted scene makers who enjoy cat's-eye frames and other retro looks. 237 Elgin St. ✆ **613/232-2408.**

FASHION, CHILDREN'S

Glebe Side Kids   If you don't want to dress your kids in the same gear as your friends and neighbors, step into Glebe Side Kids for designer clothing in eye-catching colors and styles. You'll find casual and dressy clothing for boys and girls in sizes from infants to teens. Lines include Bleu and Deux Par Deux from Quebec and imports from Germany and France. The clothing is high quality—with prices to match. 793 Bank St. ✆ **613/235-6552.**

Tickled Pink   This effervescent collection features lines from three Ottawa designers. The clothes have bright, intense colors, practical styling, and fun patterns. Also available are Yummy Mummy maternity wear from Toronto; locally made sheepskin hats, gloves, and slippers; and dress-up clothes (fairies, ballerinas, princesses). 55 ByWard Market. ✆ **613/562-8350.**

West End Kids   Tired of mall wear? Head here for top-quality upscale clothing for infants to teens. Labels include Mexx, Columbia, Tommy Hilfiger, Deux Par Deux, and Fresh Produce. 373 Richmond Rd. ✆ **613/722-8947.**

FASHION, MEN'S

Buckland's Fine Clothing   Buckland's offers clothing and accessories for well-heeled clients. Top brand names and designer labels include Tommy Hilfiger, Arnold Brant, and Cambridge Suits. 722 Bank St. ✆ **613/238-2020.**

E.R. Fisher Ltd.   This family-owned business has been an Ottawa institution since 1905 and offers custom-made shirts, tailored to measure, and formal-wear service. Lines include Cambridge, Coppeley, Jack Victor, Samuelsohn, Swiss Army, Cutter & Buck, and Cline. 199 Richmond Rd. ✆ **613/829-8313.**

Harry Rosen   Pay a visit to this upper-end men's clothiers for top-quality service and the finest in menswear designers. Choose from Hugo Boss, Brioni, Versace, and others. Rideau Centre. ✆ **613/230-7232.**

Morgante Menswear   This store carries fine clothing from formal wear rental to casual and sportswear, with lines by Canali, Jeans Couture, Versace, and Hugo Boss. Professional tailoring available, and alterations while you wait. 141 Sparks St. ✆ **613/234-2232.**

Anik Boutique   This high-end women's fashion retailer carries top lines including Boss, Versace, Marc Cain, AJ Armani, and Ferre. 334 Cumberland St. ℂ 613/241-2444.

Eclection   Exclusively stocking Canadian designers, Eclection has fascinating and unusual women's separates and accessories. Jewelry, hats, and scarves are also available. Check out the line of medieval-style street clothing, like tunics with bell sleeves. 55 ByWard Market. ℂ 613/789-7288.

Richard Robinson ★   This exciting Ottawa-based fashion designer—who made his name with his eye-popping dresses for local socialite Marlen Cowpland—has a ready-to-wear collection available at the boutique next to the Richard Robinson Academy of Fashion Design. 447 Sussex Dr. ℂ 613/241-5233.

Sable Classics   Sable offers women's fashions and accessories, with an emphasis on dresses and sportswear. One of the featured designers is Canadian Linda Lundstrom. 206 Sparks St. ℂ 613/233-8384.

Shepherd's   Canadian, American, and European designers are featured at this local boutique, including lines by Helen Kaminski and Linda Lundstrom. Good selection of accessories, including jewelry, handbags, belts, and purses. Bayshore Shopping Centre. ℂ 613/596-0070. Rideau Centre. ℂ 613/563-7666.

Trustfund   The decor here reflects a kitchy retrocollegiate sensibility, but the clothing is very current, catering to sophisticated, young adults. The stock includes a mix of new designers and recognizable brands, including Velvet, Free People, Citizens of Humanity, Splendid, and Brown Sound. 493 Sussex Dr. ℂ 613/562-0999. www.trustfundboutique.com.

Workshop   Opened in 2005, Workshop features a mix of women's clothing and hand-crafted products with the emphasis on local designers. If you're in the market for something funky and unique, this is a good place to look. As the name suggests, the store also features frequent workshops on sewing, knitting, and design. 242¹/₂ Dalhousie St. ℂ 613/789-5534. www.workshopboutique.ca.

FOOD

Bell Pastry & Delicatessen   As well as servicing the catering needs of the telephone company and nearby law offices, Bell Pastry & Delicatessen offers a wide range of packaged and fresh foods, including many European specialties. Place Bell Canada, 160 Elgin St. ℂ 613/238-1010.

Boushey's Fruit Market   One of Ottawa's oldest family businesses, Boushey's is an institution on Elgin Street, meeting the demands of the adjacent neighborhoods and the late-night revelers on the busy bar strip. "Fruit" only begins to hint at the array of food-stuffs available here, including specialties such as caviar. 348 Elgin St. ℂ 613/236-4482.

La Bottega Nicastro Fine Food Shop   The Nicastro family has been specializing in fine Italian foods for decades, and their ByWard Market location is packed with shoppers on weekends. 64 George St. ℂ 613/789-7575.

Laura Secord   This chocolatier has been a Canadian favorite for more than 85 years. The chocolates and truffles are delicious. Try the white chocolate almond bark and the butterscotch lollipops. 85 Bank St. ℂ 613/232-6830. Billings Bridge Plaza. ℂ 613/737-5695. Place d'Orléans Shopping Centre. ℂ 613/837-7546. Rideau Centre. ℂ 613/230-2576. St. Laurent Shopping Centre. ℂ 613/741-5040.

Ottawa Bagelshop & Deli ★★★ (Finds) You won't find better bagels than those that come out of the wood-burning oven here. A humble bagel shop has grown into a sprawling food emporium that features dozens of varieties of olive oil, mustard, and other condiments, as well as a small restaurant and coffee bar. An extensive selection of candies includes Rogers' chocolates from Victoria, BC, and the cakes are some of the best in the city. 1321 Wellington St. ✆ 613/722-8753.

Rocky Mountain Chocolate Factory This British Columbia–based company has lots of goodies—chocolate (of course!), cookies, fudge, candy apples, and other sweet treats. Located inside the ByWard Market building at the south end. 55 ByWard Market. ✆ 613/241-1091.

Sugar Mountain (Kids) Kids love this place. Adults are also known to be frequent visitors. The walls are lined with clear plastic bins at the right height for scooping the most outrageous colors and flavors of sugar-loaded confections into loot bags. Islands of boxed and wrapped candy and chocolates fill the two-level store. Looking for retro candy? This is the place. 71 William St. ✆ 613/789-8428. 286 Elgin St. ✆ 613/230-8886. 753 Bank St. ✆ 613/234-7776.

GIFTS/SOUVENIRS

Burapa Asian Perspective This store offers an intriguing collection of home accessories, personal wear (silk, pashmina, and cashmere), jewelry, old-teak furniture, and gift items from Thailand, Nepal, Burma, Laos, and Vietnam. 91 Murray St. ✆ 613/789-0759.

Canada's Four Corners Fine crafts and quality Canadian souvenirs share space with a gallery of framed and matted prints. 93 Sparks St. ✆ 613/233-2322. www.canadasfour corners.com.

Giraffe African Arts Giraffe offers authentic art from Africa, including handmade masks, statues, fabric wall hangings, jewelry, ebony, soapstone, musical instruments, and pottery that represent traditional and contemporary art forms. 19 Clarence St. ✆ 613/562-0284.

Mon Cadeau Next door to the delicious Ma Cuisine, Mon Cadeau specializes in unique, personal gift items. 261 Dalhousie St. ✆ 613/241-4438.

O'Shea's Market Ireland Family owned and operated for more than 25 years, O'Shea's is packed with goods imported from the Emerald Isle, as well as a selection of items from Scotland. Popular items include Celtic jewelry and woolen goods—especially sweaters, cardigans, blankets, and throws. Hundreds of family crests and coats of arms are on hand. 91 Sparks St. ✆ 613/235-5141. www.osheasmarketireland.com.

Ottawa Souvenirs and Gifts Browse the selection of T-shirts, sweatshirts, mugs, plaques, spoons, and maple syrup products. Rideau Centre. ✆ 613/233-0468.

The Snow Goose This Canadian arts and crafts shop specializes in Inuit and Native works in every price range. You'll find clothing, sculptures, prints, masks, dreamcatchers, soapstone carvings, totems, and jewelry. 83 Sparks St. ✆ 613/232-2213.

3 Trees Specializing in spiritual items from faraway lands, 3 Trees is a browser's heaven. Imported spiritual tools from Nepal, India, and Thailand include bowls, statues, meditation cushions, candles, incense, and chimes. Imported clothing, jewelry, gifts, and home decor accessories are available too. 202 Main St. ✆ 613/230-0304.

HEALTH & BEAUTY

Holtz Spa   Open since 1985, in conjunction with the Santé Thai fusion restaurant, the Holtz Spa offers a full range of therapeutic treatments, including glycolic peals, massage, reflexology, oxygen therapy, and cellulite treatments. Located in the heart of the downtown core, the upscale facility offers a couples Romance Package for C$485. 45 Rideau St. ℂ 613/241-7770. www.holtzspa.ca.

Le Nordik Nature Spa   A 10-minute drive north of Ottawa, Le Nordik offers a full Scandinavian relaxation regime, including baths, and Swedish, California, and hot stone massage. Nestled into the rocky Gatineau Hills, the spa emphasizes its proximity to nature and has a gorgeous, natural outdoor pool area. Prices are reasonable, and the facility is geared toward couples and groups. 16 Nordik Rd., Chelsea, Quebec. ℂ 819/827-1111. www.lenordik.com.

York Street Spa   Situated in one of the ByWard Market's vintage stone buildings, this full-service Aveda spa offers facials, body treatments, manicures, pedicures, and makeup. Highlighted by burnished wood, warm colors and rich leather treatment chairs, this spa is a feast for the senses. 11 York St. ℂ 613/562-2121. www.yorkstreetspa.com.

HOBBIES

Birder's Corner   If birding is your thing, check out this store's selection of foreign and domestic bird guides and gifts for fellow enthusiasts. 101-2 Beechwood Ave. ℂ 613/741-0945.

Dynamic Hobbies (Kids)   Model enthusiasts will love the radio-controlled model cars, airplanes, helicopters, and boats; the on-site indoor and outdoor tracks, and the 45m (148-ft.) slot-car track. 21 Concourse Gate, Unit 6. ℂ 613/225-9634.

Hobby House   This store offers a wide variety of hobby supplies, including plastic model kits, model trains and accessories, military and aviation books, modelers' tools and supplies, rockets, kites, die-cast models, wooden ship kits, and puzzles. 80 Montreal Rd. ℂ 613/749-5245.

Lee Valley Tools   A pioneer in mail-order and online shopping, Ottawa-based Lee Valley Tools has fans far and wide among gardeners and woodworkers. The headquarters store is the place where you can feast on their tools, hardware, and accessories firsthand, and trade tips with the knowledgeable staff. 900 Morrison Dr. ℂ 613/596-9202. www.leevalley.com.

HOME DECOR

Belle de Provence   This store is deliciously French in its merchandise and atmosphere. It offers exquisite toiletries, linens, books, and items for the home. A delightful shop. 80 George St. ℂ 613/789-2552.

La Cache   La Cache features beautiful classic floral linens for dining rooms and bedrooms. 763 Bank St. ℂ 613/233-0412.

My First Apartment   Opened in 2005, My First Apartment merges contemporary style with affordability. The selection ranges from bedding to retro kitchen appliances. 255 Bank St. ℂ 613/234-0646. www.myfirstapartment.ca.

Ten Thousand Villages   For 60 years, this nonprofit project of the Mennonite Church has specialized in fairly traded goods, including design items like silk throw pillows from Vietnam and bone-handled salad servers from Kenya. 371 Richmond Rd. ℂ 613/759-4701. 1170 Bank St. ℂ 613/736-0401.

Zone   From funky chrome knickknacks to functional desk lighting, the offerings in this Quebec-based chain never fail to capture my imagination. 471 Sussex Dr. ✆ **613/562-2755.** www.zonemaison.com.

JEWELRY

Birks   Founded in 1879, Birks is a respected Canadian jewelry retailer. It carries a wide range of silver, crystal, and china as well as top-quality jewelry. Popular for engagement rings. Bayshore Shopping Centre. ✆ **613/829-7692.** Rideau Centre. ✆ **613/236-3641.**

Davidson's   Serving customers from their Glebe store since 1939, Davidson's is a full-service jeweler, offering design, repairs, appraisals, and gem prints. The store carries Canadian diamonds, Fabergé, Lladró, Movado, and other top brands. 790 Bank St. ✆ **613/234-4136.**

Howard   This family-owned downtown business specializes in jewelry design, and there's an artist on staff. The diamond-ring collection features platinum, 18K-gold, and 14K-gold settings. Wristwatches by Tag Heuer, Gucci, Da Vinci, and Rolex are also offered. Repairs and appraisals available. 200 Sparks St. ✆ **613/238-3300.** www.howards.ca.

Jubilee Fine Jewellers   Owned by a family of jewelers who left war-torn Uganda, Jubilee features Lazare and government-certified Canadian Polar Bear diamonds and Mikimoto pearls, as well as Montblanc pens, and timepieces by Rolex, Cartier, Omega, and Baume & Mercier. Rideau Centre. ✆ **613/238-1886.** St-Laurent Shopping Centre. ✆ **613/747-1797.** Bayshore Shopping Centre. ✆ **613/596-3070.** Carlingwood Shopping Centre. ✆ **613/728-6134.**

La Maison d'Or   In the Place d'Orléans Shopping Centre, this jeweler specializes in diamonds from around the world, including from Canada. Rings can be custom designed, then set right in the studio. La Maison d'Or also buys and sells estate and antique jewelry. Place d'Orléans Shopping Centre. ✆ **613/837-1001.**

KITCHENWARE

C.A. Paradis   The southernmost store in Ottawa South, C.A. Paradis has some very classy merchandise. If a chef craves it, this place probably has it. Check out their cellaring equipment, tasting supplies, and Reidel stemware too. 1314 Bank St. ✆ **613/731-2866.**

Domus   It's a real dilemma—do you eat first in the delectable Domus restaurant (see chapter 6, "Dining") and shop afterward in the kitchen store, or vice versa? Both are outstanding. Enjoy. 85 Murray St. ✆ **613/241-6410.**

Glebe Emporium   You're bound to see something you just can't resist owning yourself or buying as a gift for someone else. In addition to a wide selection of kitchen gadgets, dinnerware, and table linens, the store carries cookbooks and has an entire floor of Canadian-made Paderno cookware, including factory seconds at terrific discounts. 724 Bank St. ✆ **613/233-3474.**

Grace In The Kitchen   Do residents of Ottawa South do anything but cook? It seems unlikely, and this place only adds to the obsession with Wüsthof knives, SAECO and Krups coffeemakers, Le Creuset cookware, and Cuisinart and KitchenAid appliances. 1167 Bank St. ✆ **613/521-4818.** www.graceinthekitchen.com.

J. D. Adam Kitchen Co.   Walk slowly around this compact Glebe shop so that you don't miss anything. Space is at a premium here, but the store makes good use of every inch. There is great merchandise and a helpful staff. You'll find a great selection of Emile

Henry oven- and tableware from France, insulated travel mugs, and wooden kitchen tools by artist Tom Littledeer. 795 Bank St. ✆ 613/235-8714.

Ma Cuisine   Spacious and gracious, Ma Cuisine has chic dinnerware, a good selection of glassware, pans, gadgets, cookbooks, linens, and lots more. The staff is courteous and welcoming. 269 Dalhousie St. ✆ 613/789-9225.

LEATHER & FURS

Dworkins   Established in 1901, Dworkins features furs, shearlings, and leather garments, and provides remodeling, repair, and cleaning services. Designer labels include Louis Féraud, Dominic Bellisimo, and Zuki. 256 Rideau St. ✆ 613/241-4213.

Gregory's Leather & Suede Fashions   For more than 30 years, Gregory's has provided custom-designed leatherware. Leather repair is also a specialty. 458 Rideau St. ✆ 613/789-4734. www.gregorysleather.com.

Ottawa Leather Goods   A longtime fixture on the Sparks Street Mall, this store features a wide range of leather goods, including over-the-shoulder bags designed to reduce back strain. 179 Sparks St. ✆ 613/232-4656.

Pat Flesher Furs   In business since 1929, this store offers mink, beaver, fox, raccoon, sable, and other furs. Its specialty is its "three-pound coat." 437 Cooper St. ✆ 613/237-1700.

LINGERIE

Brachic   Specialties include European lines such as Rigby & Peller, as well as sports bras from Shock Absorber. The staff also specializes in fitting cup sizes C to J. 433 Richmond Rd. ✆ 613/321-0401.

Marianne's (Finds)   Marianne's understands that no two women are built alike, so it specializes in fitting bras, ranging from size AA to 52H. The store also carries a range of swimwear. Westgate Shopping Centre. ✆ 613/722-6614.

MAGAZINES/NEWSPAPERS

Britton's ★   A Glebe institution for many years, the store disappeared for a while, but is now back in two locations. A great place to meet the locals and to find an exceptional selection of cigars from Cuba and other countries. 846 Bank St. ✆ 613/237-6116. 352 Richmond Rd. ✆ 613/729-0551.

Globe Mags & Cigars   Located in the heart of the ByWard Market, this store stocks more than 2,000 periodicals and a good selection of maps. 57 William St. ✆ 613/241-7274.

Mags & Fags   The punning title gives you an idea of the spirit of this place. A lively landmark on the Elgin Street bar-and-restaurant strip, Mags & Fags carries titles you won't find elsewhere. The store is open every day except Christmas. 254 Elgin St. ✆ 613/233-9651.

MAPS

A World of Maps   Situated where else but at the geographical center of Ottawa, A World of Maps is both a retailer and a mail-order company. It is a regional distributor for all Canadian government maps and charts produced by the Canada Map Office. Topographical, aeronautical, nautical, international, and world maps; atlases; globes; travel books; and other map-related items are available here. 1235 Wellington St. ✆ 800/214-8524 or 613/724-6776. www.worldofmaps.com.

ByWard Farmers' Market ★★   The quality of the produce is outstanding at this thriving outdoor farmers' market, with about 200 vendors. The market is open daily 7am to 6pm, but is at its peak from May to October. In spring and early summer, flower stalls abound. Lots of family-oriented events are scheduled on weekends throughout the year. ByWard Market Square and William Street.

Ottawa Famers' Market   Introduced in 2007, this twice-weekly (Thurs and Sun) market is restricted to local producers who grow or raise their own fruit, vegetables, meat, and fowl, as well as craftspeople. Open between early May and late October, the market includes more than 100 vendors. Landsdowne Park, 1015 Bank St. ✆ **613/239-4955.** www. ottawafarmersmarket.ca.

Ottawa Organic Farmers' Market   For fresh market produce grown without pesticides or other chemicals, head down to the Ottawa Organic Farmers' Market on a Saturday, year-round between 10am and 2pm. Ecole Parsifal Waldorf School, Bank St. at Heron Rd. (behind the Canadian Tire store). ✆ **613/256-4150.** www.oofmarket.ca.

Parkdale Farmers' Market   This small, open-air farmers' market, with about 20 vendors, offers fresh, high-quality produce and operates between April and December, daily 7am to 6pm. Parkdale Ave., north of Wellington St. ✆ **613/244-4410.**

MUSIC

Larger shopping malls each have at least one store specializing in CDs and DVDs, although they tend to limit their selection to mainstream bestsellers and charge full price. The two big chain stores in the Ottawa area are **HMV Canada** and **Music World.** The alternative is to hunt down independent or used music stores—they carry new as well as used CDs and DVDs, with lower prices than the malls. Some also deal in cassette tapes and vinyl records.

Birdman Sound   The best music stores are always run by music fans, and this small store proves the rule. This is the place for hard-to-find roots- and rock-oriented independent releases and collectors' items. 593B Bank St. ✆ **613/233-0999.** www.birdmansound.com.

Compact Music   Brothers James and Ian Boyd have been dealing records for decades, and their store reflects their devotion to rock, blues, and folk music. 134 Bank St. ✆ **613/233-7626.** 785A Bank St. ✆ **613/233-8922.**

The Leading Note   Classical music fans often complain that music stores give them short shrift, instead favoring pop music. This small store, which also offers sheet music, music books, and accessories, fills the void. 370 Elgin St. ✆ **613/569-7888.** www.leadingnote. com.

The Turning Point ★   Two floors of used music will keep music fans occupied for hours. A wide range of genres, including rock, blues, jazz, hip-hop, dance, classical, pop, folk, world, and more. They are a buy-sell-trade enterprise, so the selection is always changing. Used DVD, vinyl, and CD prices are low. Owners Tom and Dan Gamble are knowledgeable and passionate about music. 411 Cooper St. ✆ **613/230-4586.** www.turning pointmusic.ca.

Vertigo   This store has a huge selection of vinyl records and new and used CDs. Collectors and music buffs will enjoy browsing the music accessories, which include headphones, record players, and collector sets. Special orders are accepted. 193 Rideau St. ✆ **613/241-1011.**

MUSICAL INSTRUMENTS

Ottawa Folklore Centre ★ (Finds)   This store repairs, buys, sells, consigns, trades, rents, and appraises just about any instrument you can think of—from guitars to amps, banjos, fiddles, Celtic harps, mandolins, recorders, folk flutes, hand drums, autoharps, accordions, and dulcimers. Like all good music stores, it encourages customers to try the equipment. 1111 Bank St. © 613/730-2887. www.ottawafolklore.com.

OUTDOOR GEAR

Bushtukah Great Outdoor Gear   This store has an excellent stock of tents, camping gear, sleeping bags, and other assorted outdoor equipment. The staff is also very knowledge-able about marathon running. 203 Richmond Rd. © 613/792-1170. www.bushtukah.com.

The Expedition Shoppe   Coffee lovers have Starbucks; travelers have the Expedi-tion Shoppe. From quick-dry, no-iron clothing with style to travel accessories of every variety, this is a travelers' haven. The staff is well-informed, and loves to trade travel tales. 369 Richmond Rd. © 613/722-0166. 43 York St. © 613/241-8397. www.expeditionshoppe.com.

Irving Rivers   An Ottawa institution—part discount store, part outfitter—Irving Rivers is the place to go for boots, hats, rainwear, and inexpensive camping gear. 24 ByWard Market St. © 613/241-1415. www.irvingrivers.com.

Mountain Equipment Co-op (MEC)   Created in 1971, and still run as a member-owned co-operative (you'll need to purchase a $5 membership in order to buy anything), MEC is now a Canadian icon. Whether you're an ice-climbing fanatic or just a weekend cyclist, you'll find something that meets your needs. The staff's knowledge about outdoor recreation is unsurpassed. 366 Richmond Rd. © 613/729-2700. www.mec.ca.

The Scout Shop Camping Centre   You can't miss the huge totem pole on the front lawn. Housed in the Scouts Canada Headquarters building, the Scout Shop has lots of practical, neat, and useful camping accessories, plus books, Scout uniforms, and small toys. 1345 Baseline Rd. © 613/224-0139.

Trailhead   This is the store that started the outfitting craze in Ottawa, and its lodge-style headquarters remains a mecca for those planning outdoor excursions. Trailhead specializes in renting canoes, kayaks, and tents, but also carries a wide selection of cloth-ing and accessories. 1960 Scott St. © 613/722-4229. www.trailhead.ca.

PET SPECIALTIES

Bark & Fitz   If you have a pampered pooch at home, or on the road with you, this store is a must. Whether you're in the market for innovative, "battle-tested" toys, a fleecy hoodie for Fido, or organic doggie treats, Bark & Fitz likely has it. Dogs never had it so good. 354 Richmond Rd. © 613/792-3711. www.barkandfitz.com.

SEX TOYS

The Adult Fun Superstore   This is a bright, welcoming store where fun is empha-sized, whether you're looking for an outrageous Halloween costume, or something more intimate. A favorite with women shoppers. 1565 St. Laurent Blvd. © 613/741-7200. www.adultfun.ca.

Venus Envy   Their motto is "designed for women and those who love them," which just about says it all. The stock includes a wide array of books, alternative health prod-ucts, safe sex supplies, and sensual bath and body products. 320 Lisgar St. © 613/789-4646. www.venusenvy.ca.

Craig Armstrong Shoes   In business since 1934, this store stocks names like Bostonian, Clarks, Nine West, and David Tate, and has several Ottawa locations. 240 Sparks St. ✆ **613/230-7840.** www.armstrongshoes.com.

Dack's   Dack's has been supplying high-quality men's footwear to customers in the Ottawa area since 1834. 240 Sparks St. ✆ **613/233-4377.**

Letellier   Specializing in walking and comfort shoes, Letellier is an established shoe retailer in Ottawa, serving customers since 1897. It offers a large selection of widths and sizes in both men's and women's footwear, with lines from Clarks, Rockport, Ecco, Mephisto, Timberland, and more. 146 Rideau St. ✆ **613/241-6557.** www.letelliershoes.ca.

Sports 4   This athletic and casual footwear specialist carries brand-name footwear, including New Balance, Birkenstock, Nike, Reebok, and more. A large range of widths and sizes is available. 149 Bank St. ✆ **613/234-6562.**

SPORTS EQUIPMENT & CLOTHING

Cyco's   Specializing in rental and sales of in-line skates, ice skates, bikes, and clothing and accessories for both sports, this store also sells used sports equipment. Next-day turnaround on most repairs. 5 Hawthorne Ave. (beside Rideau Canal) ✆ **613/567-8180.**

Figure 8 and Hockey One Skate Specialists   Whether you're skating in competitions or just gliding along the canal, Figure 8 has a skate for you. It offers new, used, and rental skates, as well as expert sharpening and skate mounting, and hockey-skate blade replacement. 380 Industrial Ave. ✆ **613/731-4007.** www.figure8.ca.

Fresh Air Experience   This is the store for bicycles (mountain, hybrid, road, and children's), cross-country skis, and specialty clothing. 1291 Wellington St. ✆ **613/729-3002.** www.freshairexp.com.

Tommy & Lefebvre   One of the city's best-known sporting goods retailers, in business since 1958, Tommy & Lefebvre has an excellent range of goods for adults and children at several locations throughout the region. Ski, board, bike, golf, in-line skates, and more. It arranges lift tickets and transportation for area ski resorts. 464 Bank St. ✆ **613/236-9731.** 2206 Carling Ave. ✆ **613/828-4550.** 250 Centrum Blvd. ✆ **613/265-3499.** Terry Fox Dr. ✆ **613/271-8524.**

STATIONERY

Paper Papier   A peek inside this little store will reward you with the discovery of unusual and inspiring gift wrap, pens, greeting cards, stationery, journals, and other paper-related items. 18 Clarence St. ✆ **613/241-1212.**

The Papery   This store sells delicate, pretty, and funky things made of paper—cards, wrapping paper, ribbons, invitations, stationery, journals, albums, as well as pens. During the holiday season, check out their elegant Christmas crackers, remarkable gift wrap, and exquisite table-top angels. 850 Bank St. ✆ **613/230-1313.**

TOYS

Lost Marbles   Grown-ups and kids alike will find this store fascinating. Where else would you find a plush moray eel, a build-your-own set of shark's jaws, a table with human legs, or 16 different kinds of dice? 315 Richmond Rd. ✆ **613/722-1469.** 809 Bank St. ✆ **613/594-3325.** 55½ William St. ✆ **613/244-3363.**

Mrs. Tiggywinkles   This store stocks a variety of educational and high-quality toys and games for infants to teens. It's a great place to browse. There's a two-floor emporium in the Glebe, a large store in Westboro, and several mall locations. 809 Bank St. ☎ **613/234-3836**. 313 Richmond Rd. ☎ **613/761-6055**.

Playvalue Toys   This is a full-line dealer for Little Tikes, Step 2, Brio, Playmobil, Lego, and other quality toys. 1501 Carling Ave. ☎ **613/722-0175**.

Scholar's Choice Retail Store   This store carries educational and high-quality toys for infants and up, as well as elementary teachers' resources. 1001 Daze St. ☎ **613/260-8444**. 2121 Carling Ave. ☎ **613/729-5665**.

TRAVEL GOODS

Capital City Luggage   Capital City carries luggage, garment bags, computer bags, trunks, travel accessories, and briefcases and repairs handles, zippers, and locks. 1337 Wellington St. ☎ **613/725-3313**.

Ottawa Leather Goods   This store offers travel accessories, luggage, business cases, handbags, and small leather goods. There is a repair shop on premises. 179 Sparks St. ☎ **613/232-4656**.

VIDEO & DVDS

Two major video stores in the Ottawa area are **Blockbuster Video** and **Rogers Video,** both with more than a dozen locations. DVD and VHS movies and games are available for sale and rental. Rental requires membership. Check out "Music," on p. 180, for listings for used and new DVDs at discount prices. You'll also find DVDs for sale at **Music World** and **HMV Canada;** both stores are found in major malls.

Glebe Video International   Foreign, independent, and hard-to-find videos and DVDs are the specialty of this store. Movies from the world's major film festivals are available here. 779 Bank St., 2nd floor. ☎ **613/237-6252**.

VINTAGE CLOTHING

Orange Vintage Clothing   Owner Sylvie Poitevin has been collecting clothes for decades, and her basement shop—open weekends 11am to 5 pm—is packed with treasures. 145 York St. ☎ **613/731-5550**.

Ragtime Vintage Clothing   Ragtime has been around so long that some of the vintage stuff on display was still on the fashion runways when the store opened. The selection of vintage suits, which the store also rents, is particularly good. 43 Flora St. ☎ **613/233-6940**.

Young Jane's   One of a handful of independent stores that have sprung up along the north end of Dalhousie Street, Young Jane's is a tiny space that features vintage clothing, accessories, and shoes. 203 Dalhousie St. ☎ **613/794-6452**.

WINE & SPIRITS

Most of Ontario's wine, some beer, and all spirits are purchased through the provincial government–owned **Liquor Control Board of Ontario** retail stores. There are locations all over the city. The **LCBO's flagship retail store** is downtown at 275 Rideau St. (☎ **613/789-5226**). This large store has two floors of products from around the world, as well as an extensive **vintages** section with a wide range of wines, cognacs, and single-malt whiskys. Wine accessories are available, and seminars and tastings are regularly

184 scheduled. Individual winery boutiques are also licensed to sell wine, and can frequently be found in malls anchored by a Loblaws Superstore. You can't buy alcoholic beverages in grocery or convenience stores in Ontario, but if you cross the Ottawa River into Quebec, you can buy beer and wine at corner stores (called *dépanneurs*) and grocery stores, although the selection is far better at the provincial government–owned **Société des alcools du Québec (SAQ)** outlets. In Ontario, beer is also available at the Beer Store, a provincially owned and operated business with about 20 locations in Ottawa. Opening hours vary by individual store. You must be 19 to purchase beer, wine, or alcohol in Ontario; in Quebec, the minimum age is 18.

10

Ottawa After Dark

Ottawa has many things going for it, but a dynamic, year-round cultural scene and thriving nightlife are not among them. True, the city has seen an upswing in high-end restaurants, and there have always been bars that cater to students from the three main postsecondary schools, but Ottawa will never be mistaken for Toronto, Vancouver, or San Francisco. The city has turned out its share of famous performers—among them Rich Little, Paul Anka, Dan Ackroyd, Alanis Morissette, and Kathleen Edwards—but it has been more of a launching pad than a showcase for their talents; all of them rose to fame after they left town. Fortunately, the fact that the city is the national capital means government money subsidizes some major cultural institutions and annual festivals that might not otherwise exist without more grassroots arts infrastructure.

Most of the after-dark action is centered around the ByWard Market, although Hull (now the Hull sector of Gatineau) has long held the reputation as the city where Ottawans go to play at night. Today, most of that action happens at the **Casino du Lac-Leamy.**

FINDING OUT WHAT'S ON For current live music, theater, and film—particularly aimed at young audiences—your best bet for finding out what's happening and where is to pick up a copy of ***Ottawa Xpress,*** a free publication distributed each Thursday, or read it online at www.ottawa xpress.ca. ***Where Ottawa/Gatineau,*** a free monthly tourist guide listing entertainment,

shopping, and dining, is available at hotels and stores in the city. ***Voir*** is a French-language weekly arts and entertainment paper that lists some venues and events in Gatineau as well as Ottawa.

Visiting families should keep an eye out for ***Capital Parent,*** a free monthly newspaper that's available at 400 outlets. The ***Ottawa Citizen*** has a comprehensive Arts section on Friday with an emphasis on films and a special Going Out section on Saturday, which lists upcoming live entertainment events.

GETTING TICKETS Tickets to events at the **National Arts Centre** and most other live venues are sold at the on-site box offices or through **Ticketmaster** (✆ 613/755-1166 sports line; ✆ 613/755-1111 other events; www.ticketmaster.ca). You can also visit the Ticketmaster box office at 112 Kent St. A competing service, **Capital Tickets** (✆ 877/788-3267 or 613/599-3267; www.capitaltickets.ca) handles tickets for events at **Scotiabank Place** and some major festivals. Also see the individual listings in this chapter.

SPECIAL EVENTS Ottawa occasionally hosts large sports and entertainment events, so check with the Ottawa Tourism and Convention Authority (www.ottawatourism.ca) or the National Capital Infocentre, 40 Elgin St., Ottawa ON, K1P 1C7 (✆ 800/465-1867 or 613/239-5000; www.canadas capital.gc.ca) for special events scheduled during your visit. Another source is the **Council for the Arts in Ottawa** (CAO; ✆ 613/569-1387; www.arts-ottawa.on.ca).

1 THE PERFORMING ARTS

Because Ottawa serves two masters—the Canadian population as the national capital and the local citizens of the City of Ottawa—the arts and entertainment field includes a major federal arts presence as well as a local arts community. For an in-depth look at the local arts scene, drop in to **Arts Court** at 2 Daly Ave. (✆ **613/564-7240**), Ottawa's center for performing, visual, media, and literary arts.

FESTIVALS

One huge advantage to being the national capital is the funding and infrastructure that various levels of government offer to "animate" the city. Festival organizers of every stripe have taken advantage over the years, with the result that barely a week goes by in the summer that one festival or another isn't on the go.

Cisco Ottawa Bluesfest   Although it still has the word *blues* in its name—and continues to book a large slate of blues, soul, and gospel acts each July—Bluesfest also regularly features mainstream popular music acts like Sting, the Black-Eyed Peas, and Snoop Dogg. Headliners are usually announced by the end of April each year. Lebreton Flats. ✆ **866/258-3748** or 613/247-1188. www.ottawabluesfest.ca.

Festival Franco-Ontarien   One of the largest celebrations of French culture in North America presents a variety of musical and theatrical performances to entertain all ages. Festival Plaza. ✆ **613/321-0102**. www.ffo.ca.

International Student Animation Festival of Ottawa   Alternating with the Ottawa International Animation Festival in odd-numbered years, this event is devoted to students and first-time animators. Competitions, workshops, recruiting, and a trade fair are part of the event, which is held at various venues around the city. ✆ **613/232-8769**. www.awn.com/ottawa.

International Youth Orchestra Festival   Held in Ottawa in odd-numbered years, the festival offers concerts, broadcasts, demonstrations, and a gala mass concert. Call the Capital Infocentre for more information. ✆ **800/465-1867**.

Magnetic North Theatre Festival   Staged at the National Arts Centre, Canada's national festival of contemporary English-language theater is held in odd-numbered years. ✆ **866/850-2787** or 613/947-7000. www.magneticnorthfestival.ca.

Ottawa Folk Festival   This 3-day gathering celebrates Canada's rich folk traditions with music, dance, storytelling, and crafts. Some of the world's finest acoustic musicians, including Steve Earle and Emmylou Harris, have performed on the main stage. Lakeside Gardens and other venues. ✆ **613/230-8234**. www.ottawafolk.org.

Ottawa Fringe Festival   Each June, this festival features a wide range of exciting and vibrant theater, dance, music, visual arts, video, and film on six stages in the heart of Ottawa's downtown. More than 70 companies stage more than 300 shows. ✆ **613/232-6162**. www.ottawafringe.com.

Ottawa International Animation Festival   Held in even-numbered years at various venues, this is North America's largest animation festival, featuring showcase screenings of new animated films from around the world and discussions of the art form. ✆ **613/232-8769**. www.awn.com/ottawa.

The Ottawa International Chamber Music Festival The world's largest chamber music festival showcases the finest musicians in some of the most beautiful churches in downtown Ottawa over 2 weeks in late July and early August. ℭ 613/234-8008. www.chamberfest.com.

Ottawa International Children's Festival This event brings the best of live theatrical arts to children at sites in and around the Canada Science and Technology Museum, 1867 St. Laurent Blvd. Families will enjoy music, theater, crafts, and other kids' entertainment. Other performing arts events for children are staged throughout the year at various local venues. ℭ 613/241-0999. www.ottawachildrensfestival.ca.

Ottawa International Writers Festival Held at Library and Archives Canada, 395 Wellington St, each spring and fall, this is a celebration of the finest new and established writing from Canadian and international creators. Highlights include authors reading from their newly published or forthcoming works, and panel discussions. ℭ 613/562-1243. www.writersfestival.org.

TD Canada Trust Ottawa International Jazz Festival Founded in 1981, this 10-day festival features international headliners and local musicians in both indoor and outdoor venues from noon until well after midnight. Confederation Park and other venues. ℭ 888/226-4495 or 613/241-2633. www.ottawajazzfestival.com.

UniSong More than 400 members of youth and children's choirs from across Canada perform 4 days of concerts at the National Arts Centre, 53 Elgin St., and other venues. Enjoy a full program of Canadian music and celebrations, including a massed performance featuring all the performers on Canada Day. ℭ 613/234-3360. www.abc.ca.

MAJOR PERFORMANCE VENUES

Centrepointe Theatre Featuring a unique blend of community and professional programming, Centrepointe Theatre is home to the productions of many community groups. Four places are reserved for guests in wheelchairs on the orchestra level, and you can make special arrangements to accommodate larger groups. An audio-loop system for the hearing impaired is also available. To arrange for special seating, please specify your needs to the box-office attendant when purchasing tickets. Parking is free. The theater is one block from the OC Transpo Baseline Station. Ben Franklin Place, 101 Centrepointe Dr. ℭ 866/752-5231 or 613/580-2700. www.centrepointetheatre.com.

Maison de la culture de Gatineau The 841-seat Odyssée Hall is located here. Patrons enjoy francophone theater, music, comedy, and dance performances. 855 de la Gappe Blvd., Gatineau. ℭ 819/243-2525. www.maisondelaculture.ca.

National Arts Centre (NAC) Situated in the core of the city across from Confederation Square and Parliament Hill, the NAC is one of the largest performing-arts complexes in Canada. Three performance halls are housed within the unique multilevel structure. **Southam Hall,** the largest of the three performing halls with more than 2,300 seats, hosts Broadway musicals, ballets, operas, musical acts, lectures, ceremonies, films, orchestral music, and other entertainment and corporate events. Megamusicals such as *Phantom of the Opera* and *Les Misérables* have been staged in Southam Hall. **The Theatre,** with just under 900 seats—ideal for plays, musicals, seminars, conferences, films, chamber music, and other musical events—also presents numerous Stratford Festival productions. **The Studio** is a versatile venue that has a capacity of 250 to 300 depending on the seating arrangement. **The Fourth Stage** is a multipurpose performance space for community programming, including dance, music, storytelling, choral singing, and theater.

The Fourth Stage can accommodate various stage configurations and seats up to 150. The NAC is fully accessible to guests with disabilities and provides special tickets for patrons in wheelchairs. Underground parking is available; parking entrances are located on Elgin Street (at the corner of Slater St.) and on Albert Street. 53 Elgin St. ✆ **613/947-7000.** www.nac-cna.ca. For tickets visit the NAC box office or call Ticketmaster at ✆ 613/755-1111.

Ottawa Civic Centre This 10,000-seat facility hosts numerous events annually, including family entertainment and midsize rock concerts. 1015 Bank St. ✆ **613/580-2429.**

Scotiabank Place This 19,153-seat, multipurpose sports and entertainment complex hosts various events from Bruce Springsteen to monster truck races. OC Transpo (✆ **613/741-4390**) provides direct bus service from Transitway stations across the city to all Senators games and most other events. Free parking is provided at five Park & Ride lots. For sports and concert tickets call CapitalTickets at ✆ **613/599-3267** or visit the box office (Gate 1). 1000 Palladium Dr. ✆ **613/599-0100.** www.scotiabankplace.com.

Théâtre du Casino du Lac-Leamy This state-of-the-art theater has been designed as an intimate space despite the 1,001 seating capacity. Opened in 2001, the theater is part of the Casino du Lac-Leamy complex. The entrance is separate from the casino to allow theater patrons of all ages to enjoy performances that range from musicals to Cuban bands to rock acts from the '70s and '80s. 1 du Casino Blvd., Gatineau (Hull sector). ✆ **819/772-2100.** www.casino-du-lac-leamy.com.

CLASSICAL MUSIC, CHORAL MUSIC & OPERA

As the presence of the world's largest chamber music festival suggests, Ottawa has an extensive and active classical music scene, featuring a number of well-established ensembles and presenters.

Cantata Singers of Ottawa One of the region's most popular choirs, the Cantata Singers perform regularly with the NAC Orchestra and also have their own annual concert series at various venues around the city. ✆ **613/798-7113.** www.cantatasingersottawa.ca.

NAC Orchestra ★★ Offering more than 100 performances a year, this vibrant, classical-size orchestra draws accolades at home and abroad. Its profile increased significantly in 1998, when violin virtuoso Pinchas Zukerman took over as the fifth conductor in the orchestra's history. In 2006, he signed a new, multiyear contract. The NAC Orchestra performs with Opera Lyra Ottawa and frequently accompanies ballets, including regular performances in Ottawa by Canada's three major ballet companies—the National Ballet of Canada, the Royal Winnipeg Ballet, and Les Grands Ballets Canadiens de Montréal. The Pops Series combines popular songs and light classical music, often featuring world-renowned soloists. NACO Young Peoples Concerts are directed to 7- to 11-year-olds and feature music, storytelling, animation, and audience participation. Performing at the NAC, 53 Elgin St. ✆ **613/947-7000.** For tickets visit the box office or call Ticketmaster at ✆ 613/755-1111.

Opera Lyra Ottawa Ottawa's resident opera company performs at the NAC, staging four operas between September and April. Recent main-stage productions include Mozart's *Le Nozze di Figaro* and Tchaikovsky's *Eugene Onegin*. Performing at various venues, including the NAC. For tickets call Opera Lyra Office at ✆ **613/233-9200** or Ticketmaster at 613/755-1111. www.operalyra.ca.

Ottawa Chamber Music Society Concert Series Some of Canada's most accomplished chamber music artists perform in downtown Ottawa churches from September to March. A 2-week summer festival is also held. Performing at various locations. ℭ **613/234-8008.** www.chamberfest.com.

Ottawa Choral Society This 100-voice symphonic chorus performs major works from every period of the choral repertoire. They perform regularly with the NAC Orchestra, Ottawa Symphony Orchestra, and various other ensembles. ℭ **613/725-2560.** www.ottawachoralsociety.com.

Ottawa Symphony Orchestra With 90 musicians, the Ottawa Symphony Orchestra is the National Capital Region's largest orchestra. A series of five concerts is held at the NAC from September to May, featuring the music of the 19th and early 20th centuries. Performing at the NAC, 53 Elgin St. ℭ **613/231-7802.** www.ottawasymphony.com.

Thirteen Strings One of Canada's foremost chamber music ensembles, Thirteen Strings has an annual subscription series of six concerts at St. Andrew's Presbyterian Church in Ottawa and performs a wide range of music for strings from the 15th to the 20th centuries. Performing at St. Andrew's Presbyterian Church, 82 Kent St. ℭ **613/738-7888.** www.thirteenstrings.ca.

DANCE

Ottawa has a strong history of local dance, and, thanks to the presence of the **National Arts Centre (NAC),** ongoing exposure to many of the world's leading companies. Throughout the year, the NAC hosts a variety of dance performances, ranging from classical ballet to contemporary dance. Guest dance companies include Les Grands Ballets Canadiens de Montréal, the Alvin Ailey American Dance Theatre, LaLaLa Human Steps, Toronto Dance Theatre, Iceland Dance Company, Ballet British Columbia, Brazilian Dance Theater, National Ballet of Canada, and the Royal Winnipeg Ballet. For information call ℭ **613/947-7000** or visit www.nac-cna.ca.

Of the local companies, none has a better reputation than **Le Groupe Dance Lab,** ★, which focuses on the process of creating dance rather than the production of finished choreography. The group holds interactive public presentations of works in progress each season. For information call ℭ **613/235-1492** or visit www.legroupe.org.

Les Petits Ballets is a nonprofit organization that develops youth ballet talent. Professional guest dancers and young local talent share the stage in full-length ballets, including *The Little Mermaid* and *Cinderella.* Performances are held twice yearly at Centrepointe Theatre. For information call ℭ **613/580-2700. Anjali** (Anne-Marie Gaston) is a classically trained East Indian dancer, choreographer, teacher, lecturer, and photographer. Performances consist of East Indian temple dances and innovative, contemporary choreography based on traditional forms. Recitals are performed against a backdrop of images of temples, goddesses, and remote corners of Bhutan and the Himalayas. Call ℭ **613/745-1368** for the performance schedule and venues.

THEATER

The presence of the **National Arts Centre (NAC)** and its resident English and French theater companies dominates the local dramatic arts scene. The **NAC English Theatre** develops, produces, and presents an English-language theater program locally, as well as coproducing plays with theater companies in other Canadian centers. The season consists of a five-play **Mainstage** series; a four-play alternative **Studio** series; special presentations; family, youth, and education activities; and a new play development program. The plays that make up the season range from the classics to new Canadian works. The **Family Theatre Series** presents three plays, with matinee and evening performances on weekends. **NAC French Theatre** features a variety of French-language productions, including performances for children ages 4 to 11. For more information call ✆ **613/947-7000** or visit www.nac-cna.ca.

Ottawa's other full-time, professional theater company, the **Great Canadian Theatre Company** ★★, has been providing bold, innovative, and thought-provoking theater for more than a quarter of a century. Featuring predominantly Canadian playwrights and local actors, the season runs from September to March. In 2007, the company moved into a new environmentally friendly, multipurpose theater complex—the Irving Greenberg Theatre Centre—at 1233 Wellington St. W. For more information call ✆ **613/236-5196** or visit www.gctc.ca.

Founded in 1990, **A Company of Fools** aims to make Shakespeare entertaining and accessible. Initially, the troupe rehearsed and acted out Shakespearean scenes on the street. Audiences respond to their unique brand of high-energy performance, classical text, and modern slapstick. Successful shows include performances at the Ottawa Fringe Festival and "Shakespeare Under the Stars," featuring scenes, sonnets, and songs beneath the night sky in various parks in the Ottawa region. For more information call ✆ **613/863-7529** or visit www.fools.ca.

Odyssey Theatre is a professional summer company that is noted for its imaginative use of masks, dancelike movement, and original music. Its open-air productions are based on Italian Renaissance street theater, known as *commedia dell'arte*. Odyssey specializes in productions of classic comic texts and original works. For 5 weeks in late summer, they perform in Strathcona Park on the banks of the Rideau River, close to downtown Ottawa. For youth and family audiences, the troupe also stages 1-hour versions of the summer production, with demonstrations and a question-and-answer period. For more information, call ✆ **613/232-8407** or visit www.odysseytheatre.ca.

The **Orpheus Musical Theatre Society** has been entertaining Ottawa audiences with musical performances since 1906. The company performs three fully staged musical shows per season. Recent shows include *Crazy for You, Damn Yankees,* and *Oliver!* For more information call ✆ **613/580-2700.**

Operating out of the Ron Maslin Playhouse in Ottawa's far west end, **Kanata Theatre** has staged more than 110 productions since 1968. Their focus is broad, covering works by playwrights like Tennessee Williams to lesser-known contemporary artists. For more information, call ✆ **613/831-4435** or visit www.kanatatheatre.com.

Since 1913, **Ottawa Little Theatre** has been producing popular, mainstream theater in Ottawa. The company stages eight productions between September through May. Productions range from comedies to dramas, mysteries, farces, and musicals, and include the works of William Shakespeare, Agatha Christie, and Neil Simon. For more information call ✆ **613/233-8948** or visit www.o-l-t.com.

The **Savoy Society of Ottawa** is an organization of people who share a common interest in performing the comic operas of Gilbert and Sullivan. The society staged its first production, *The Pirates of Penzance,* in 1976 and now presents one play annually, running seven public performances (including a Sun matinee). For more information call ✆ **613/825-5855** or visit www.savoysociety.org.

A new company, **Suzart Productions** is a nonprofit group that specializes in family entertainment. Operating out of Centrepointe Theatre, Suzart has staged works including *The Music Man* and *My Fair Lady.* For more information call ✆ **613/721-9790.**

The **Tara Players** stage classic, modern, and contemporary dramas and comedies from and about Ireland and written by playwrights of Irish heritage. Three productions are

2 THE CLUB & LIVE-MUSIC SCENE

Dance clubs, bars, and live entertainment venues are, by their nature, constantly in flux. Your best bet for finding out what's happening, and where, is to pick up a copy of *Ottawa Xpress,* a free publication distributed each Thursday. The ***Ottawa Citizen*** publishes a hefty Arts section on Friday and a special section, Going Out, on Saturday. *Voir* is a French-language weekly arts and entertainment paper that lists some venues and events in Gatineau as well as Ottawa.

DANCE CLUBS & LOUNGES

Mercury Lounge   Targeting a professional clientele, this lounge's prices are a little higher and the crowd's a little older. It has been described as a 21st-century soul club. This is a place to dance or listen to the music as you sip martinis on red velvet couches. The musical mix includes electronica, funk, soul, Latin, and world rhythms. 56 ByWard Market Sq. (upstairs). © **613/789-5324.**

MTL & Co.   MLT is a chic two-floor club featuring martinis and wine by the glass. House, world beat, soul, jazz, hip-hop—there's something different each evening, Wednesday through Sunday. 47–49 William St. © **613/241-6314.**

COMEDY CLUBS

Absolute Pub   From Wednesday to Saturday nights, the Absolute Pub features Absolute Comedy. Prices range from C$5 to C$12. The pub offers food, pool, shuffleboard, and sports TV. 412 Preston St. © **613/233-8000.** www.absolutecomedy.ca.

Yuk Yuk's   Stand-up comedians are featured in this club, part of a successful Canadian chain, which has a bar and restaurant service. Shows are Wednesday to Saturday evenings and last about 2 hours. Admission is C$6 for new-talent night on Wednesday; other evenings generally C$17 to C$25. 88 Albert St. © **613/236-5233.** www.yukyuks.com.

LIVE MUSIC

It is the era of the DJ, the sports bar, and the high-end martini place. Consequently, Ottawa's popular music scene has seen better times, and likely will again. These things tend to go in cycles, and clubs come and go. A good example of these trends is **Barrymore's Music Hall,** 323 Bank St. (© **613/233-0307**). In its heyday, it regularly featured top-name performers, and became somewhat legendary for playing host to the likes of U2 and Tina Turner just before they hit the big time. The place changed hands again in 2008, and the new owners plan to return it to its former glory as a top-line showcase bar for up-and-coming rock artists.

Supplanting Barrymore's somewhat as the city's main venue for live music is **Capital Music Hall,** 128 York St. (© **613/719-0934**), which features rock, punk, and hip-hop artists who are on the international tour circuit.

Zaphod Beeblebrox, 27 York St. (© **613/562-1010**), is another club that has suffered somewhat from changing musical tastes, and the shifting economics of the music business, yet it continues to feature live acts on a regular basis.

Some of the most interesting independent acts on the road, particularly American roots and folk musicians, perform at the **Blacksheep Inn,** 753 Riverside Dr., Wakefield, QC (✆ **819/459-3228**), which is located in a picturesque village on the Gatineau River, a 20-minute drive from downtown Ottawa. Still a working-class tavern by day, the Blacksheep gained a higher profile when it became the launching pad for singer-songwriter Kathleen Edwards, who still performs here between world tours.

One genre of music that has always thrived in Ottawa is blues, and although it, too, has fallen on hard times, it continues to rule at the **Rainbow Bistro,** 76 Murray St. (✆ **613/241-5123**). An oddly shaped room (patrons must climb a staircase beside the stage to access the restrooms), the Rainbow has hosted the biggest names in the business, and helped launch the careers of Ottawa musicians like Sue Foley. Live music is featured 7 nights a week.

Café Paradiso, 199 Bank St. (✆ **613/565-0657**), features local acts on weekends, and occasionally books New York City–based jazz musicians like saxophonist Dave Liebman and singer Sheila Jordan.

Many pubs and bars throughout Ottawa feature local solo performers or duets—mainly folk or Celtic musicians, but also the occasional jazz performer—on weekend evenings. Check the entertainment listings for these bookings as the performers tend to shift between venues fairly regularly.

3 THE BAR SCENE

With three postsecondary institutions and Parliament Hill, you *know* Ottawa must have its share of drinking establishments. In fact, there are now so many bars in the ByWard Market/Lowertown area that the city council has twice issued a moratorium on new liquor licenses there. Elgin Street is also chockablock with bars, and you can find one on almost every block in the Glebe and Ottawa South, too. The trick, as always, is finding the *right* bar. In Ottawa, it's usually a good idea to avoid any bar with a name that sounds like a double entendre or a tawdry pickup line—this is a three-college town, after all. Usually, that means staying away from the area of the ByWard Market east of William Street, especially on York Street, and from Elgin Street south of Somerset Street West (with the exception of the Manx and a couple of others). The recommendations here attempt to cover all the bases, including places where the only wines sold are either house red or white, and some where martinis come in every color of the rainbow.

DOWNTOWN EAST OF THE CANAL

Earl of Sussex Located right on the tourist track, the Earl of Sussex is an English-style pub, with wing chairs, a fireplace, and a dartboard. The atmosphere is friendly and cozy, as tourists mix with regulars and businesspeople. There are more than 30 beers on tap, including European and domestic. The sunny rear patio is popular in warm weather. 431 Sussex Dr. ✆ 613/562-5544.

E18hteen In a heritage building at 18 York St., this is a bar and restaurant (p. 99) that looks like it was patterned after one on *Sex and the City.* Martini madness is on Saturday; Friday features jazz and acid jazz; and Saturday is retro soul. The 25-plus crowd dresses up. If you want to sample several wines from their extensive selection, order a cluster of four 2-ounce glasses. 18 York St. ✆ **613/684-0444.**

Empire Grill   Trendy and upscale, the Empire Grill has a wide variety of cocktails and an extensive wine list. Outdoor patio in summer, live jazz some nights, DJs after 10pm other nights. 47 Clarence St. ✆ **613/241-1343.**

Foundation   Also a decent restaurant (p. 100), Foundation has a large, sunken bar area with swarms of young, beautiful people on weekends. If design-heavy contemporary surroundings and electronica music are your thing, you'll love it here. 18B York St. ✆ **613/562-9331.**

The Irish Village   In the heart of the ByWard Market, four distinct pubs have come together to make a small "Irish village." The first, the **Heart & Crown,** opened in 1992. A few years later the **Snug Pub** was added with a fireplace and cozy corners for small groups. **Mother McGintey's** and **Roisin Dubh** (the Black Rose) are the most recent additions. All have a good range of beer. Live Celtic music is offered at Heart & Crown and Mother McGintey's several nights a week. Favorite pub fare is served, including fish 'n' chips. 67 Clarence St. ✆ **613/562-0674.**

Métropolitain Brasserie & Restaurant   A newcomer in 2006, this sprawling, Parisian-style bar is located on the ground floor of the city's hottest condominium, and it just oozes style. From the zinc-covered bar to the great jazz that's always playing, this place really does have a European feel to it, but it has yet to catch on with many people. The bar features a wide selection of cocktails and a better-than-average choice of single malts. 700 Sussex Dr. ✆ **613/562-1160.**

Patty Boland's Irish Pub & Carvery   This is a spacious meeting place, with two floors of dark wood and brass. Pub fare is available. Two fireplaces warm your toes in winter, and two patios offer alfresco sipping in summer—one out front for people-watching, and a quieter one at the back for conversation. 101 Clarence St. ✆ **613/789-7822.**

Social   There's a bit of everything at this popular upscale evening destination. A fusion of French and Mediterranean cuisine is served in the restaurant (p. 101). At night, enjoy jazz or blues. On weekends, a DJ revs up the music. 537 Sussex Dr. ✆ **613/789-7355.**

DOWNTOWN WEST OF THE CANAL

ARC Lounge   The lounge bar at ARC The.Hotel (p. 75) is sleek, minimalist, and sophisticated. Try their signature martini, the Arctini. An upscale destination. 140 Slater St. in ARC The.Hotel. ✆ **613/238-2888.**

D'Arcy McGee's Irish Pub   Housed in a heritage building at the corner of Sparks and Elgin streets, D'Arcy McGee's has an authentically Irish interior (it was actually designed and handcrafted in Ireland and imported). The crowd includes a smattering of politicians, their assistants, lawyers, and tourists. Live Celtic, Maritime, and folk music is featured. The patio has a great view over Confederation Square, with the Fairmont Château Laurier in the background. 44 Sparks St. ✆ **613/230-4433.**

Hooley's   A cavernous room that bills itself as "a maritime pub," Hooley's pumps the Alexander Keith's out to college-age kids who miss Halifax and points east. If you're after a riotous good time, this is the place to find it. 292 Elgin St. ✆ **613/231-3888.**

Hy's   Also a popular steakhouse in the old-school style, this is the place to go if you want to rub shoulders with the city's—and Canada's—movers and shakers. Frequented by federal cabinet ministers, lobbyists, and high-profile journalists, the elegant, wood-and-brass cocktail bar had a recent makeover and glows with the golden patina of success. 170 Queen St. ✆ **613/234-4545.**

For Beer Lovers

True beer connoisseurs always appreciate a pint of the best, and Ottawa has dozens of British-style pubs and North American–type bars where you can sample brews from Britain, Ireland, Germany, Belgium, and, of course, Canada.

There are several local **microbreweries** to keep an eye out for in Ottawa-area restaurants and pubs. Specializing in all-natural beers, **Beau's** exploded onto the scene in 2008, winning the award as the Best Brewery in Ontario and landing the plum sponsorship of the Ottawa International Jazz Festival. Its Lug-Tread Lagered Ale can be found on tap at a number of local bars and restaurants. The **Scotch Irish Brewing Co.** in Fitzroy Harbour produces a British-style bitter called Session Ale and an Irish-style porter, Black Irish. **Heritage Brewing Ltd.** in Carleton Place brews Heritage Premium Lager and a traditional dark ale

If you want to sample the homemade draft of a **brew pub,** here are a couple to try. The **Clocktower Brew Pub** at 575 Bank St. ((C) **613/233-7849**) features an ever-changing selection of seasonal brews, listed on a chalkboard menu. Two of the most popular are Bytown Brown, a heavy, dark beer to accompany a pub meal on a winter's night, and Indian Summer Ale, which is perfect in a pitcher on the large summer patio. **Master's Brew Pub & Brasserie,** 330 Queen St. ((C) **613/594-3688**), brews a variety of lagers and ales on site. Decor is Art Deco and it's generally open Monday to Friday, early to late, to serve local office workers and downtown hotel patrons.

OTTAWA AFTER DARK

10

THE BAR SCENE

Lieutenant's Pump   In the heart of the Elgin Street bar district, this large pub draws a big crowd. There are more than a dozen beers on tap, including Montreal microbrews. 361 Elgin St. (C) 613/238-2949.

The Manx   This British-style pub has a mix of younger and older clientele. With its impressive selection of Scotch—more than 50 single malts, plus 10 Irish whiskeys—the pub occasionally holds Scotch tastings. Provides wall space for local artists. 370 Elgin St. (C) 613/231-2070.

Royal Oak   You'll bump into Royal Oaks all over town—downtown, east end, west end, the Glebe; there are 10 in total. The original pub, dating from 1980, is at 318 Bank St., where the crowd tends to reflect whatever band is headlining at Barrymore's Music Hall across the street. All locations have a good selection of British and Irish beers on draft. 318 Bank St. (C) 613/236-0190.

THE GLEBE & OTTAWA SOUTH

The Arrow & Loon   This comfortable neighborhood watering hole is filled with regulars. Ontario and Quebec microbrews are featured. Try a draft sampler—four 5-ounce glasses of different locally crafted beers for C$5. 99 Fifth Ave. (C) 613/237-0448.

The Barley Mow   Cask-conditioned ales and about 18 microbrews and imported beers on tap, plus an extensive selection of single-malt Scotch, earns this pub a nod from beer and whiskey lovers. 1060 Bank St. (C) 613/730-1279.

4 THE GAY & LESBIAN SCENE

Social life and entertainment for the gay and lesbian community in Ottawa is clustered around Bank Street in the vicinity of Frank Street, Somerset Street West, and Lisgar Street. There are also a couple of venues in the ByWard Market district. A free monthly paper, **Capital Xtra,** serves the gay and lesbian community, and has extensive entertainment listings. You can find it at vendor boxes throughout the downtown core.

Cell Block For those that like an edge to their entertainment, this place draws Ottawa's leather and denim crowd. Part of the **Centretown Pub,** which is located in a three-story Victorian house, the Cell Block is comfortable and friendly and frequented by regulars, mostly men. It has been described as a "gay Cheers." 340 Somerset St. W. ✆ 613/594-0233.

Edge A young crowd favors this dance club with four separate bars. 212 Sparks St. No phone.

Heaven This large, three-story nightclub is fashioned after the clubs in New York City and Miami. 400A Dalhousie St. ✆ 613/482-9898.

Helsinki This popular club draws a mixed crowd of gays and straights, and features drag shows on Wednesday. 15 George St. ✆ 613/241-2868. www.helsinki.ca.

Le Pub The rooftop patio is popular when the weather is nice, and drag shows are featured on Friday. 175 Promenade du Portage, Gatineau. ✆ 819/771-8810.

Lookout This bar attracts a diverse crowd of gays, lesbians, and straights of all ages. The balcony is popular in the summer. On DJ nights, tables are moved back to make room for dancing. Latin music is featured on Sunday. 41 York St. (upstairs). ✆ 613/789-1624. www.thelookoutbar.com.

Shanghai Restaurant One of Ottawa's older, family-run Chinese restaurants, Shanghai is now a hotbed of gay and lesbian activity thanks to the gay sons of the original owners. 651 Somerset St. W. ✆ 613/233-4001.

Swizzles Bar & Grill Events and entertainment includes karaoke nights, open-mic poetry and prose readings, all male go-go shows, and movie nights. Bar food is served from lunch to midnight. 246B Queen St. ✆ 613/232-4200.

5 FILM

Film lovers in Ottawa are well served, thanks to an excellent repertory cinema, the **Bytowne Cinema;** the presence of one of the world's few IMAX/OMNIMAX screens; and the **Canadian Film Institute.** Ironically, visitors staying downtown will have a difficult time finding a first-run release from a major Hollywood distributor because most of the screens have moved to the suburbs. If you're staying downtown, you'll find small multiplex theaters at the **Rideau Centre** (p. 169) and the **World Trade Center,** 130 Slater St.

HIGH-TECH CINEMA
IMAX Theatre The technology of IMAX plus a giant OMNIMAX dome gives you the sense of being wrapped in sights and sounds. At seven stories high, the IMAX screen is amazing enough, but the real adventure begins when the 23m (75-ft.) hemispheric

dome moves into place overhead once the audience is seated. Not all films use the entire screening system. This theater is busy, so buy your tickets in advance and plan to arrive 20 minutes before show time—latecomers will not be admitted. All ages are welcome. New IMAX films—often with a nature, travel, or space theme—are usually featured, but older favorites like the extreme sports showcase, *Extreme,* and the concert film of the Rolling Stones, *Rolling Stones at the Max,* return on occasion. Canadian Museum of Civilization, 100 Laurier St., Gatineau. ✆ **819/776-7010** for show times. For tickets visit the museum box office or call Ticketmaster at ✆ 613/755-1111.

REPERTORY CINEMAS

Bytowne Cinema ★★   Ottawa's premier independent cinema takes film very seriously, and treats its audiences—most of whom hold memberships—well. Some years ago it took over this large, well-equipped theater, and has since installed comfortable seating. Its snack bar, which features popcorn with real butter, is consistently voted the best in Ottawa by readers of *Ottawa Xpress.* Independently released films, festival winners, and European films are featured for multiday runs. Two to four movies are screened every day, with the lineup changing every few days. 325 Rideau St. ✆ **613/789-3456.** www.bytowne.ca.

Canadian Film Institute Cinema   The Canadian Film Institute presents a regular public program of contemporary, historical, and international cinema in the auditorium of Library and Archives Canada. Festivals and special events are held. If you have an interest or expertise in the art of cinematography, check out their calendar of events. All screenings in the Library and Archives Canada auditorium, 395 Wellington St. ✆ **613/232-6727.** www.cfi-icf.ca.

Mayfair Theatre   Screening a mixture of recent releases and older films, the Mayfair changes its bill almost daily. Two films are run every night, and most evenings feature two movies for the price of one. Pick up the monthly printed calendar at the theater, or check the website for the schedule. 1074 Bank St. ✆ **613/730-3403.** www.mayfair-movie.com.

OTTAWA AFTER DARK

10

GAMING

6 GAMING

Casino du Lac-Leamy   The extensive facilities of Casino du Lac-Leamy have continued to grow since the complex opened in 1996 on the shores of Lac-Leamy (Leamy Lake). Open daily 9am to 4am, this huge entertainment and gaming destination can accommodate 6,100 visitors at a time and puts the emphasis on glitz and fun. Unlike many casinos, the gaming room is designed to let in natural light—and remind you that there's a real world outside—and the extensive use of falling water creates a soothing atmosphere. There are 2,400 gaming spaces, including 1,900 slot machines and more than 60 gaming tables, featuring just about any game you care to play. The Texas Hold'em poker room seats 120 and features electronic play rather than dealers and cards. The interior of the gaming area is vast. The following customer services are free: self-parking, admission, and coat check. The casino has been designed to accommodate guests with physical disabilities. Smoking lounges with high-performance ventilation systems are provided; smoking is prohibited in all other areas. Approximately two-thirds of the gaming area is nonsmoking. A dress code is imposed, but don't feel that you need to tux up like James Bond to fit in. For more detail on the dress code, visit the website at www.casino-du-lac-leamy.com and click "Practical Information." Four dining areas

Tips **Gambling Should Be Fun, Not Obsessive**

Many people enjoy playing games of chance for entertainment. But for a minority of people, gambling becomes a real problem and they find themselves unable to control the amount of money they spend. Information on dealing with a gambling problem can be obtained by calling (*) **800/461-0140** in Quebec or (*) **888/230-3505** in Ontario.

and two bars are on-site. **Le Baccara** (p. 112) is an elegant fine-dining restaurant that has established a remarkable reputation for its cuisine. **Banco** offers a choice of buffet-style or a-la-carte dining. **La Fondue Royale** has live entertainment on Friday and Saturday evenings. For a quick snack, drop in to **Le Café.** A forest of tropical plants fills **Le 777 Bar.** Offering a selection of more than 70 imported beers, **La Marina** features a saltwater aquarium, an outside patio, and panoramic views over Lac de la Carrière, the focal point of which is a 60m-high (197-ft.) fountain. 1 boul. du Casino, Gatineau (Hull sector), QC. (*) **800/665-2274** or 819/772-2100. Free admission, self-parking, and coat check. Admittance restricted to adults age 18 and over.

Rideau Carleton Raceway & Slots   Less than a 10-minute drive south of the airport, this gaming complex features more than 1,200 slot machines and live harness racing. Open daily 9am to 3am, facilities include a dining room, sports bar, outdoor patio, and three grandstand lounges. Take the Airport Parkway to Lester Road, travel east to Albion Road, and head south. You'll see Rideau Carleton Raceway & Slots on your left, between Leitrim Road and Mitch Owens Road. 4837 Albion Rd. Ottawa. (*) **613/822-2211.** Free admission and parking. Admittance restricted to adults age 19 and over.

Side Trips from Ottawa

Defined by both its historical context and its abundant natural features, the Ottawa region offers many options for exploring either facet.

One of Ottawa's appeals is the number of outdoor recreational opportunities—from bungee jumping to white-water rafting—that you can pursue without having to shift your home base from the city itself. Though the peaks of the Gatineau Hills cannot compete with the Laurentians north of Montreal, let alone the mountains of British Columbia or Colorado, the cross-country skiing is

excellent, and the downhill facilities are well established and well-appointed if you want to spend a day, or evening, on the slopes.

The region also has a number of excellent golf courses, including several first-class facilities that have been built since the high-tech boom brought new businesses into the area in the 1990s.

And, if all that's not enough, how about a visit to a genuine cold war hydrogen-bomb shelter?

1 THE OUTAOUAIS REGION OF QUEBEC

Immediately north of Ottawa—just cross the Ottawa River and you're there—the Outaouais is a large, diverse region that encompasses the urban sprawl of **Gatineau;** small, rustic villages like **Chelsea** and **Wakefield;** and rugged wilderness. The area has a mixed relationship to Ottawa. Since World War II, Gatineau (or the discrete cities of Aylmer, Hull, and Gatineau as they were then) has been Ottawa's late-night playground, the site of rowdy nightclubs, discos, and bars—courtesy of Quebec's more liberal drinking laws (the drinking age in Quebec is 18; in the rest of Canada, including Ottawa, it's 19). More recently, Gatineau has become the site of large-scale federal government installations, such as the Place du Portage office complex, the Canadian Museum of Civilization, and the climate-controlled warehouse of Library and Archives Canada, and an area where housing is less expensive than in Ontario. The region has also been a popular spot for summer cottagers and artists, who have turned Wakefield and other communities into interesting enclaves. Go a bit farther north, into the areas around Low and Kazabazua, and you can find rural francophones whose lifestyles remain relatively untouched by their proximity to the nation's capital.

Just as the year 2001 heralded a new beginning for the city of Ottawa as it experienced amalgamation of a dozen local municipalities, expanding its geographical area as well as its population, 2002 ushered in the new city of Gatineau. Comprising the cities of Hull and Gatineau plus the neighboring communities of Aylmer, Buckingham, and Masson-Angers, the new city has a population of almost 230,000. While visiting Quebec you may come across references to the various sectors that have preserved their original names. Hence, an address in the old city of Hull is often referred to as being in "Gatineau (Hull sector)," or "Gatineau (*secteur de Hull*)."

(Tips) Walk in the Steps of the Early Canadians

Seek out the Indian Portage Trail at Little Chaudière Rapids in **Brébeuf Park.** To reach the park, take boulevard Alexandre-Taché, turn left onto rue Coallier, opposite the south entrance to Gatineau Park, then continue to **Brébeuf Park.** At the eastern end of the park, where the trail continues beside the river, you will find the old portage route that was used by First Nations peoples, fur traders, and explorers. A statue of Saint Jean de Brébeuf stands as a memorial to this 17th-century French missionary. Look for the rock steps used by the *voyageurs* as they transported their goods and equipment by land to circumvent the rapids.

ESSENTIALS

Visitor Information For visitor information on the Outaouais region of Quebec, visit the Association touristique de l'Outaouais, 103 Laurier St., Gatineau, QC J8X 3V8 (*©* **800/265-7822** or 819/778-2222; www.outaouais-tourism.ca). The office is open mid-June to Labor Day (first Mon in Sept) Monday to Friday 8:30am to 8pm and Saturday to Sunday 9am to 7pm. The rest of the year, it's open Monday to Friday 8:30am to 5pm and weekends 9am to 4pm. The building is wheelchair accessible and there is free parking on the west side. The easiest way to reach the tourist office from Ottawa is to walk or drive across the Alexandra Bridge, which leads off Sussex Drive just east of the Parliament Buildings and west of the National Gallery. You'll see the office facing you as you come to the end of the bridge.

URBAN EXPERIENCES

Gatineau (Hull Sector) On the shores of the Ottawa River next to the Canadian Museum of Civilization, **Jacques-Cartier Park** has beautiful pathways for strolling or cycling. The small stone house at the western end of the park was built by Philemon Wright, the founder of Hull, in the late 1830s. At the opposite end of the park you'll find an information booth, La Maison du Vélo, where you can obtain information on recreational pathways in the Outaouais region. Jacques-Cartier Park offers spectacular views of the Ottawa skyline. Annual events include Winterlude (*Bal de Neige*) activities, and a fireworks display on Canada Day. **Lake Leamy Park** (*Parc du Lac-Leamy*) is bordered by Lake Leamy, the Gatineau River, and the Ottawa River. Vehicular access is via boulevard Fournier. The park offers a supervised beach, a refreshment pavilion, restrooms, and picnic tables. For park information, call *©* **800/465-1867.**

The **Casino du Lac-Leamy** (1 boulevard du Casino; *©* **800/665-2274** or 819/772-2100; www.casino-du-lac-leamy.com) is picturesquely situated between Lac de la Carrière and Lac-Leamy. A sweeping tree-lined drive leads to ample parking in front of the main entrance. Once inside, you enter a different world. Unlike the prototypical Las Vegas casino, this gaming area features lofty ceilings, thousands of tropical plants, soothing waterfalls and reflecting pools, and an abundance of natural cherry wood. There is no shortage of glass to allow natural light to penetrate and remind you that there's a world outside. Sixty gaming tables offer popular gambling games, including blackjack, baccarat, roulette, various types of poker, including an electronic version of Texas Hold'em. There's also a 20-seat Keno lounge, Royal Ascot Electronic Track Horse Racing, and more than 1,900 slot machines. Open 24 hours a day, the casino offers free

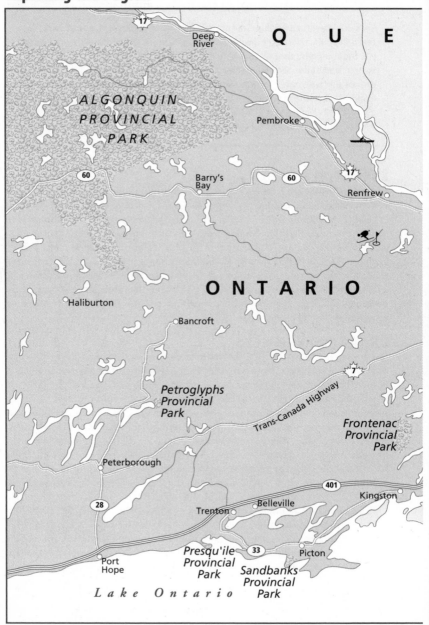

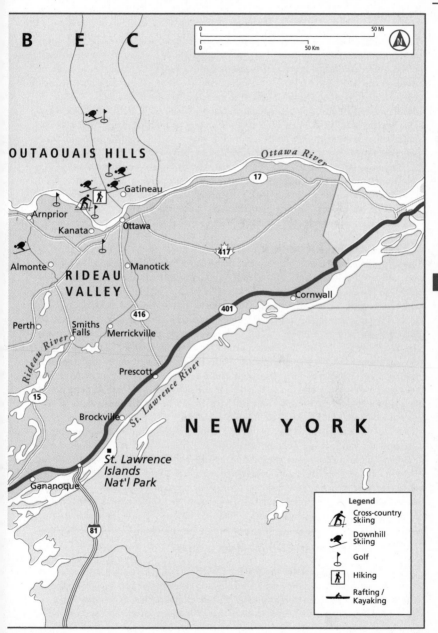

Legend

Cross-country Skiing

Downhill Skiing

Golf

Hiking

Rafting / Kayaking

admission, but is restricted to persons 18 and over. There are five restaurants, including the award-winning fine-dining restaurant Le Baccara (p. 112), and two bars. See chapter 10, "Ottawa After Dark," for more information.

Gatineau (Gatineau Sector)   The old city of Gatineau, across from the Hull sector on the east side of the Gatineau River, was created in 1975 with the merger of seven smaller communities. Its population numbered around 105,000 until the new city of Gatineau was established. Like other communities in Quebec, Gatineau reflects its citizens' love of outdoor and cultural activities, so recreational facilities abound. Gatineau's **Municipal Arts Centre,** 855 boulevard de la Gappe, Gatineau (© **819/243-2305;** www.ville.gatineau.qc.ca/mcg), features entertainment ranging from children's theater to jazz concerts throughout the year. Every year on Labor Day weekend the **Gatineau Hot Air Balloon Festival** (www.balloongatineau.com) draws large crowds. Rue Jacques-Cartier has numerous sidewalk cafes that offer a great view of Ottawa and the Ottawa River. **Lac-Beauchamp Park** is a large urban park where you can swim, picnic, canoe, bike, skate, and cross-country ski. For park information call © **819/669-2548.** For more information on the city of Gatineau, contact Outaouais Tourism, 103 Laurier St., Gatineau (Hull sector), QC (© **800/265-7822** or 819/778-2222).

GATINEAU PARK ★★★

Just a 15-minute drive from downtown Ottawa lies a beautifully preserved wilderness park. Within the 361sq. km (139 sq. miles) of **Gatineau Park,** there are 200km (124 miles) of cross-country ski trails and 165km (103 miles) of hiking and biking trails. The park's landscape is carved from the Canadian Shield, and the exposed rocks, dating back to the Precambrian era, are among the oldest exposed rocks on Earth. More than 50 glacial lakes are scattered throughout the park. The forested areas consist mainly of maple and oak; spruce, white pine, and eastern hemlock cover only about 3% of the park's land. The large number of rare plant and animal species has stimulated many scientific research projects. Gatineau Park is open year-round and has something to offer in every season. Vehicle access fees are in effect in certain areas of the park during the peak summer period of mid-June to early September. Your first stop should be the **Gatineau Park Visitor Centre,** 33 Scott Rd., Chelsea, QC (© **800/465-1867** or 819/827-2020), open every day of the year except Christmas. It's a great source for park maps and information on special events and festivals. The knowledgeable and friendly staff is available to answer questions and help you to plan your visit. The village of **Chelsea,** lying roughly halfway between Hull and Wakefield and close to Gatineau Park Visitor Centre, has several restaurants serving French cuisine. Lakes in the park are home to **40 species of fish,** including trout, yellow perch, pike, and bass, which are all popular sportfishing catches.

 What Should I Do If I Meet a Bear?

Black bears make their home in Gatineau Park. If you happen to see a bear on a trail, calmly back away from it while maintaining visual contact. Make loud noises and keep your distance. Never try to feed a bear or approach it, as you may make the bear feel threatened. Keep well away from a mother and her cubs, and never position yourself between them. Never try to outrun, outswim, or outclimb a bear; the animal may interpret your actions as a sign of weakness.

Tips **Looking for a Smooth Ride?**

Because of its topography, the park's network of bike paths requires cyclists to be in good physical condition and experienced in cycling on challenging terrain. If you're looking for a leisurely cycle ride, you will find the relatively flat and smooth surface of the bikeways in the city of Ottawa easier and more enjoyable. You might also consider cycling in the park on Sunday mornings in the summer, when the main roadways are closed to motorized traffic.

Around 2,000 **white-tailed deer** also live in the park. They are most likely to be observed feeding in early morning or late afternoon, close to La Pêche Lake and Philippe Lake, or in open fields and alongside roads. In the far northwest corner of the park live one or two **timber wolf packs.** You are unlikely to see them because they avoid contact with humans, but you might be lucky enough to hear them howl. A wolf pack howls in a drawn-out, harmonious chorus, which is distinguishable from the short, high-pitched bark of a coyote pack. When you're on the trails, keep an eye out for **black bear** tracks on muddy sections of the trail and around **beaver** ponds. If you're unfamiliar with animal tracks, drop in to the visitor center before your hike and ask the staff for information. Also watch for claw marks on the trunks of trees—black bears love to climb.

Along the Gatineau Parkway are numerous beaver ponds where you can observe these busy, furry creatures in action, especially at dawn and dusk. Other wildlife that make the park their home include the **bobcat, Canada lynx, wolverine, mink,** and **otter.** If you enjoy bird-watching, you're in for a treat. The waterways, fields, forests, wetlands, and rocky escarpments provide vital food and shelter for about **230 species of birds.** A brochure listing dozens of species and hints for when and where to observe the park's feathered friends is available from the visitor center. **Grass snakes, turtles, frogs, toads, bull frogs, tree frogs, salamanders,** and **newts** are also native park inhabitants.

Gatineau Park has three **campgrounds,** each offering a different outdoor experience. Philippe Lake is the largest campground, with 250 wooded campsites. Sandy beaches, a convenience store, and plenty of water taps and restrooms contribute to a comfortable vacation. If you don't mind fewer modern conveniences in exchange for being a little closer to the wilderness, try Taylor Lake, which offers rustic tent camping with only 33 sites, all close to the lake. If you want still more of a back-to-nature adventure, La Pêche Lake has canoe-in camping available at 35 individual sites in a dozen wooded areas around the lake. For all three sites, call ℂ **866/456-3016** or 819/456-3016 to make campsite reservations. Sites are C$30 per night and there is a reservation fee of C$7.50. To arrange boat and mountain-bike rentals at Philippe Lake and La Pêche Lake, call ℂ **819/456-3016.** Note that alcoholic beverages are not allowed in the campgrounds or elsewhere in the park. Pets are not allowed in campgrounds, picnic areas, or on beaches, although dogs on a leash are permitted on hiking trails.

If you are traveling in a group of at least six and prefer not to camp, the park offers a cabin at Brown Lake for C$15 per person per night. For reservations, call ℂ **819/456-3016.** The cabin is equipped with bunk beds for 16, a refrigerator, stove, electric heater, and woodstove.

Glide along the peaceful waters of Gatineau Park's lakes in a **canoe.** Launch your own craft at the McCloskey Boat Launch on Meech Lake. Philippe Lake has a boat launch·

and **rowboat, kayak,** and **pedal boat rentals.** La Pêche Lake offers canoe and rowboat rentals in addition to a boat launch facility. Rental fees, which include two paddles and two life jackets, are C$12 per hour, C$36 for 4 hours, and C$40 per 24-hour period. The 24-hour rate is for campers only.

If you prefer to explore the park **by bike,** you can purchase a detailed trail map at the visitor center to help you plan your route on the network of trails and paved bikeways in the park. The length and variety of mountain-bike trails are excellent. Trails are open from May 15 to November 30. The sport is restricted to 90km (56 miles) of designated trails to protect the natural environment; you may not use cross-country ski trails for winter biking. Mountain bikes are available for rental at the Philippe Lake campground general store. Rentals include a helmet and lock.

The park boasts 165km (103 miles) of **hiking trails,** including about 90km (56 miles) of shared-use trails (walkers and mountain bikers), with the remainder set aside exclusively for hiking. Some of the shorter trails feature interpretation panels and are suitable for wheelchair and stroller access. If you are considering hiking one of the longer trails, make sure you are sufficiently prepared, with appropriate clothing, food, water, and sturdy, comfortable footwear. The Gatineau Park Visitor Centre has an excellent map available (1:25,000 scale) for C$5; it is strongly recommended for hikers and mountain bikers. If you enter the park at the south entrance, off boulevard Alexandre-Taché in Gatineau (Hull sector), the first short trail you'll find is **Des Fées Lake,** a 1.5km (1-mile) trail around a small lake; the trail should take about an hour to walk leisurely. A little farther along the Gatineau Parkway, **Hickory Trail** is just under 1km (.5 mile) long, and takes about 20 minutes to walk. This trail is ideal if you need stroller or wheelchair access. A picnic area and interpretive panels provide diversion along the pathway. As you drive deeper into the park, you'll pass **Pink Lake.** This site is exceptionally beautiful in the fall, when the many deciduous trees turn to red, orange, and yellow against a background of dark green firs. Pink Lake (it's green, by the way, not pink) is unusual because it is one of only a dozen or so meromictic lakes in Canada (see "Unique Waters," below). There is a 2.5km (1.6-mile) trail around the lake, which takes about 1¹/₂ hours to walk.

If you're looking for panoramic vistas, try one of the trails leading to the top of the **Eardley Escarpment.** A steep 2.5km (1.6-mile) path called **King Mountain Trail** rewards hikers with a wonderful view of the Ottawa Valley. Farther into the park, the **Champlain Trail,** 1.3km (.8 mile) long, has interpretive panels explaining how the site has evolved since the time of the last glaciers. From the **Champlain Lookout,** the valley view sweeps majestically for many miles. To reach the picturesque **Luskville Falls Trail,** travel west on boulevard Alexandre-Taché past the main south entrance to Gatineau Park, and continue west on Hwy. 148 to Luskville. Follow signs for Luskville Falls, where you'll find a parking lot and picnic site. The 5km (3-mile) trail—a steep 300m (984-ft.) vertical rise from base to summit—leads to the top of the Eardley Escarpment, where you will be rewarded with a sweeping view of the Ottawa Valley.

> ⟮**Fun Facts**⟯   **Unique Waters**
>
> A meromictic lake is an unusual body of water where there is no circulation between the different layers of water. It typically has a green color and is home to saltwater fish that have adapted to freshwater conditions. There are often sedimentary deposits dating back 10,000 years and prehistoric bacteria in its depths.

A Prime Minister's Retreat

Perhaps the most distinctive attraction in Gatineau Park is the **Mackenzie King Estate.** The summer residence of William Lyon Mackenzie King, Canada's longest-serving prime minister, was bequeathed to the Canadian people upon his death in 1950. You can visit the restored cottages on the property and stroll through the gardens, which include formal flower beds, a hidden rock garden, and a collection of picturesque ruins from as far away as England. A tearoom on the premises serves light refreshments. The estate is open mid-May to mid-October, weekdays 11am to 5pm, weekends and holidays 11am to 6pm. Admission is C$8 per car per day. For general information call ✆ **800/465-1867** or 819/827-2020.

The park offers **five public beaches** with lifeguard supervision, located at Philippe, Meech, and La Pêche lakes. The sandy beaches, which are all popular with families, are open mid-June to mid-September daily from 10am to 6pm. Swimming is prohibited in the beach areas outside these times, and at all times elsewhere in the park. The beaches have an access fee of C$9 per car.

Gatineau Park has lots to offer **winter visitors.** An extensive network of **cross-country ski trails** and special trails for **hiking, snowshoeing,** and **kick sledding** will keep you active outdoors. Rent snowshoes at the visitor center for C$5 per hour or C$15 per day. Children's snowshoes are C$3 per hour or C$10 per day. You can rent cross-country ski equipment from a number of outfitters close to the main entrance of the park. See chapter 7, "Exploring Ottawa," for details. The park has earned a reputation as having one of the best ski-trail networks in North America because of its remarkable 200km (124 miles) of trails, which are well maintained using the latest technology. Both classic Nordic-style cross-country skiing and the more energetic skate skiing are accommodated. The park provides eight heated shelters. Ski patrollers travel the area, ready to assist skiers in difficulty. When you arrive at the park, you can buy a day pass for the trails at any of the 16 parking lots that give direct access to the trails, or at the visitor center. If you don't have a map, your first stop should be the visitor center to buy the official winter trail map for C$5. An extremely accurate winter trail map has been produced using GIS (Geographic Information Systems) technology, which includes contour lines, magnetic north orientation, and exact representation of the trails. The map can be downloaded from the Gatineau Park section of www.canadascapital.gc.ca or purchased at either the visitor center or at the Capital Infocenter, 90 Wellington St., Ottawa. Because skiing and weather conditions change frequently, Gatineau Park reviews and updates ski information three times daily. A ski-condition report can be obtained by calling ✆ **819/827-2020,** or see the Gatineau Park section of www.canadascapital.gc.ca.

SPECIAL EVENTS IN GATINEAU PARK

Other events may be scheduled in addition to the ones listed below, and dates may change from year to year. For more information, contact the **Gatineau Park Visitor Centre,** 33 Scott Rd., Chelsea, QC (✆ **819/827-2020**).

The park celebrates winter with **Ski-Fest,** a weekend ski festival, which includes ski lessons for beginners and activities for the whole family.

FEBRUARY

The annual **Gatineau Loppet** is Canada's largest cross-country skiing event. Races are offered for all ability levels and every member of the family—there's even a 2km (1.25-mile) race for children under age 12.

MAY

The **Mackenzie King Estate** opens for the summer season.

The **Canadian Tulip Festival** is celebrated at the Mackenzie King Estate.

Sunday Bikedays begin for the season.

JULY

Canada Day celebrations take place at the Mackenzie King Estate.

The Mackenzie King Estate hosts its annual **Estate in Bloom** event.

Learn about conservation and the natural and historic heritage of Gatineau Park on **Parks Day.**

SEPTEMBER/OCTOBER

Fall Rhapsody, a celebration of nature's autumn colors, takes place in the park. Ride the Camp Fortune chairlift to view the fall colors, participate in orienteering events, or enjoy an autumn menu at the Mackenzie King Estate's tearoom.

SKIING/WATER SLIDES

Camp Fortune In the heart of Gatineau Park, just 15 minutes from downtown Ottawa, Camp Fortune has 20 runs, a snowboarding park, and a designated children's area. This resort has numerous lifts, including several quad chairs. The greatest vertical rise is 180m (591 ft.). Camp Fortune's ski school and racing programs enjoy a good reputation. Mountain biking is offered in summer.

300 chemin Dunlop, Chelsea, QC. ✆ **888/283-1717** or 819/827-1717. www.campfortune.com. Take Hwy. 5 north to exit 12, chemin Old Chelsea. Travel west on Meech Lake Road and turn left into Camp Fortune.

Edelweiss With a vertical rise of 200m (656 ft.), Edelweiss offers 18 runs served by four lifts. The tubing park has 11 trails and one lift. A ski bus runs on weekends and holidays; call the resort for details. In Edelweiss Valley, you can also swoosh down the hills in the summer months at Le Grand Splash Water Park. This family water park features 5 water slides, a children's pool, a lounge pool, and an enormous 15m (49-ft.) hot tub. Picnic areas and tennis courts are also on-site. Edelweiss is about a half-hour drive from Ottawa.

538 chemin Edelweiss, Wakefield, QC. ✆ **819/459-2328.** www.mssi.ca. Take Hwy. 5 north to Rte. 105 toward Wakefield. Take Rte. 366 east (chemin Edelweiss) to the ski hill.

Mont Cascades This resort, with a vertical rise of 160m (525 ft.), offers plenty of activities in winter and summer. For skiers and snowboarders, there are four lifts and 19 runs, with illuminated night skiing on 12 of those. Lessons and equipment rental are available. The water park has something for everyone. There's an area for kids under 121 centimeters (4 feet) tall, with water sprays, five small slides, and a wading pool. For older and braver kids, there's a tunnel slide, a four-lane racing slide, a large slide that several people can slip down together in a raft, and other innovative ways to get wet while having fun. For lunch, visit the restaurant or bring your own and munch at a picnic table in the shade. Mont Cascades is about a half-hour drive from Ottawa.

448 chemin Mont-Cascades, Cantley, QC. 𝓒 **888/282-2722** or 819/827-0301. www.montcascades.ca. To get there from Ottawa, take the Macdonald-Cartier Bridge across the Ottawa River, then take Hwy. 50 east. Take the first exit, which is boulevard Archambault. Turn right onto Hwy. 307. Turn left on chemin Mont-Cascades, and proceed 7km (4¹/₃ miles) to Mont-Cascades.

Mont Ste-Marie This resort has the highest vertical in the Outaouais region, at more than 381m (1,250 ft.). Two peaks and two high-speed chairlifts give beginners and experienced skiers a choice of 24 runs in total. The resort boasts one of the longest beginner trails in western Quebec and a terrain park filled with boxes, rails, and tabletops. Rentals and lessons are available. A ski bus operates from Ottawa; call for details. Mont Ste-Marie is about a 1-hour drive from Ottawa.

76 chemin de la Montagne, R.R. 1, Lac Ste-Marie, QC. 𝓒 **800/567-1256** or 819/467-5200. www.mont-stemarie.com. Take Hwy. 5 north through Hull and join Hwy. 105 north. Stay on Hwy. 105 until you see the signs for Mont Ste-Marie.

Ski Vorlage This resort, with a vertical rise of 152m (499 ft.), offers a choice of 15 runs including a terrain park, with 12 runs illuminated for night skiing. Try tubing—fly down the slope on an inflatable doughnut and get towed back up the hill. Ski Vorlage promotes itself as a family ski area and extends a special welcome to families and kids. Nonskiers might like to spend a couple of hours in the shops and restaurants of nearby Wakefield. Vorlage is about 25 minutes from Ottawa by car.

65 Burnside Rd., Wakefield, QC. 𝓒 **877/867-5243** or 819/459-2301. www.skivorlage.com. Follow Hwy. 5 north to Hwy. 105 north and turn right into Wakefield. Turn onto Burnside Road and follow the signs to Vorlage.

OTHER ACTIVITIES

Great Canadian Bungee An acquired taste, to be sure, bungee jumping isn't everyone's idea of fun. But, if you love a thrill, free falling at the end of a rope into a 60m-deep (197-ft.) limestone quarry above a spring-fed lagoon of deepest aqua blue will provide a particularly vivid memory of your trip. If you don't want to take part in the madness, you can enjoy the barbecue and picnic facilities, play and swim at the supervised beach area, rent a pedal boat or kayak, and be entertained by all those crazy dudes who are willing to pay C$90 for the biggest adrenaline rush of all time. Note that there are no age restrictions, but those under 18 must have a signed parental-consent form and jumpers must weigh between 36 and 181 kilograms (79–400 pounds). Another thrill ride—the RIPRIDE is a 310m (1,017-ft.) cable slide that accelerates as you travel along its length, at an average speed of 85kmph (53 mph). The weight limit for the RIPRIDE is 90 kilograms (198 pounds). The fee is C$31. Reservations are a must for all rides.

Morrison's Quarry, Wakefield, QC. 𝓒 **877/828-8170** or 819/459-3714. www.bungee.ca. Bungee jump C$90; RIPRIDE C$31. Reservations required. Call for operating hours.

LaFlèche Adventure This attraction combines an aerial adventure park—consisting of an impressive 82 bridges suspended from the tops of trees in the forests of the Laurentians—and a large network of white marble caves. Wannabe Tarzans must be at least 1.3m (4 ft.) tall for the two junior sections of the aerial adventure. The remaining four park sections are restricted to visitors with a minimum height of 1.5m (5 ft.). A general tour of the caves is suitable for all ages and takes about 1¹/₂ hours. More adventurous souls can follow an experienced guide on a 3-hour tour of narrow spaces and galleries. The temperature inside the caves remains steady all year round, between 3° and 7°C (37°–45°F). Wear sturdy walking shoes and warm clothing. Guides will provide you with a hard hat and a headlamp for both tours, as well as with the extra equipment needed for the caving adventure tour. Above ground, enjoy the snowshoeing trails in winter and picnic areas and nature trails in summer. Reservations are required for cave tours.

255 route Principale, Val-des-Monts, QC. ☏ **877/457-4033** or 819/457-4033. www.aventurelafleche.ca. Package (caverns, aerial park, and winter snowshoeing) C$42 adults, C$34 junior (13–17), C$32 children (5–12), C$133 families (2 adults and 2 children). Reservations required. Call for operating hours. Take Hwy. 50 north through Gatineau (Hull sector), exit on Hwy. 307 north, and travel to Val-des-Monts. It's about a half-hour drive from Ottawa.

WHERE TO DINE

Les Fougères ★★ QUEBECOIS A bright, welcoming room with a gorgeous outdoor terrace, Les Fougères regularly draws Ottawans who enjoy fine dining. It's worth the drive in every way. Like many forward-looking chefs in the region, Charles Part and Jennifer Warren-Part are helping to redefine Canadian cuisine by using fresh local ingredients and combinations that you won't find anywhere else in the world. Game and fish are regular features, as are local goat cheese, fiddleheads, and wild mushrooms. A four-course table d'hôte menu is C$45 or C$74 with the sommelier's choice of wine. A weekend brunch, served until 3pm, is extremely popular.

783 Rte. 105, Chelsea, QC. ☏ **819/827-8942**. www.fougeres.ca. Reservations recommended. Main courses C$29–C$34. MC, V. Mon–Fri 11am–9:30pm; Sat–Sun 10am–9:30pm.

L'Orée du Bois ★ FRENCH Chef Guy Blain grows his own herbs; smokes fish, poultry, and meat on the premises; and even makes chocolate. Open since 1978 in a century-old farmhouse, the restaurant has earned its reputation as one of the best in eastern Quebec by using fresh local ingredients, and combining traditional French cooking with New World flair. Scallops nestle in puff pastry, spiced with a delicious coriander, ginger, and lime sauce, and braised rabbit is flavored with a delicate balance of black peppercorns and blueberries. The table d'hôte menu starts at C$34 and offers many options for substitution.

15 chemin Kingsmere, Chelsea, QC. ☏ **819/827-0332**. www.oreeduboisrestaurant.com. Reservations recommended. Main courses C$17–C$23. MC, V. Tues–Sat 5:30–10pm (year-round); Sun 5:30–10pm May–Oct.

2 THE RIDEAU VALLEY

The **Rideau Valley** lies southwest of Ottawa, following the path of the **Rideau Canal.** The canal is actually a continuous chain of beautiful lakes, rivers, and canal cuts, stretching a distance of 202km (126 miles) between Ottawa and Kingston, and often described as the most scenic waterway in North America. One of nine historical canals in Canada, the **Rideau Canal Waterway** has been designated a **National Historic Site** and was named a UNESCO World Heritage Site to mark its 175th anniversary in 2007. Parks Canada has the responsibility of preserving and maintaining the canal's natural and historical features and providing a safe waterway for navigation. You can explore the region by boat; drive along the country roads that wind their way through the towns and villages along the waterway; or hike a portion of the **Rideau Trail,** a cleared and marked footpath about 300km (186 miles) long that meanders between Ottawa and Kingston.

Many of the towns in the Rideau Valley became thriving retail centers as a result of the canal and the highways that followed its course. In the 20th century, many continued to flourish as a result of the farms around them, and several—particularly **Manotick,**

Rideau Canal by Numbers

• Number of locks in the main channel	45
• Number of lock stations	24
• Length of canal (Ottawa to Kingston)	202km (126 miles)
• Length of man-made canal cuts	19km (12 miles)
• Minimum available water depth	1.5m (5 ft.)
• Size of locks	41m by 10m (135 ft. by 33 ft.)
• Travel time by boat, one-way	3 to 5 days

Merrickville, and **Smiths Falls**—have continued in good health due to a combination of baby boomers who enjoy the rural lifestyle and visitors who want to sample some of the region's heritage.

ESSENTIALS

GETTING THERE   From Ottawa, take either Prince of Wales Drive (Hwy. 73) or Riverside Drive (Hwy. 19) south. Manotick is about 40 minutes from downtown, while Merrickville and Smiths Falls are about 30 minutes and 40 minutes, respectively, beyond that. The most scenic route south of Manotick follows the course of the canal, including Hwy. 13 to Kars, then Hwy. 5 to Becketts Landing, and Hwy. 2 to Merrickville. From Merrickville, take Hwy. 43 to Smiths Falls.

VISITOR INFORMATION   The most comprehensive source of information on the area is the Rideau Heritage Route's website, **www.rideauheritageroute.ca**, which has links to many other sites for various attractions and extensive listings for shopping, dining, accommodations, and historical destinations. Real Ontario, the tourist information association that manages the Rideau Heritage Route, can be contacted at ✆ **613/269-2777.**

RIDEAU CANAL & LOCKS

The canal and locks that link the lakes and rivers of the **Rideau Valley** were constructed between 1826 and 1832 to provide a safe route for the military between Montreal and Kingston in the wake of the War of 1812. Lieutenant Colonel John By, the British engineer in charge of the project, had the foresight to build the locks and canal large enough to permit commercial traffic to access the system, rather than building the canal solely for military use. As things turned out, the inhabitants of North America decided to live peaceably. The canal became a main transportation and trade route, and communities along the canal grew and thrived. With the introduction of railroads in the mid–19th century, the commercial traffic subsided and the canal gradually became a tourist destination due to its beauty and tranquility. The locks have operated continuously since they first opened. See chapter 7, "Exploring Ottawa," for more details on the canal and locks located within the city of Ottawa.

MANOTICK

Manotick is a quiet village about 24km (15 miles) south of Ottawa on the banks of the **Rideau River.** The original settlement grew around a water-powered grist mill, now

(Fun Facts   **The Ghost in the Mill**

Watson's Mill is reputedly haunted. There have been ghostly sightings of a tall, fair-haired young woman, believed to be the wife of Joseph Currier, one of the original mill owners. During a visit to the mill in 1861, the young bride's long skirts were accidentally caught in a revolving turbine shaft. She was thrown against a nearby support pillar and died instantly.

known as **Watson's Mill,** on the west side of the river. The village expanded around the original buildings, which date from the mid-1800s, and now includes residences on Long Island, a 3.5km-long (2-mile) island in the river, and an area on the east side of the river. Dickinson Square, in the heart of the village, is a good spot for strolling and visiting local shops. Wander across the dam and feed the ducks on the millpond. **Watson's Mill** is open to visitors in the summer. Every second Sunday afternoon from mid-June to October the mill swings into operation, grinding wheat to make flour. You can wander through the five-story historic stone building or take a guided tour. The mill is open from early May to June 1, Wednesday to Sunday, 10am to 4pm; from June 2 to Labor Day, daily 10am to 4pm; and during September, Monday to Friday, 10am to 4pm and Saturday to Sunday 10am to 2pm. Call © **613/692-2500** for more information.

In recent years, Manotick's beautiful setting and proximity to Ottawa have attracted a number of wealthy residents. Consequently, the community has one of the country's highest per-capita income rankings, and a large array of huge showcase homes, particularly south of town on River Road.

One of the best places to watch the world go by in the summer is the riverside deck of **Kelly's Landing** pub and restaurant, 1980 River Rd. (© **613/692-1243**).

MERRICKVILLE

The picturesque village of Merrickville—selected as Canada's most beautiful in 1998—is a popular tourist destination, especially in the summer months when the streets are decorated with flowers, and in December when merchants contribute toward creating an old-fashioned Christmas feel. Founded in 1793 by William Merrick, the village was originally a large industrial center on the Rideau River with a number of woolen mills, sawmills, and gristmills. Today, more than 100 heritage properties have been faithfully restored. The original blockhouse, overlooking the locks, is now a small museum. Dozens of professional artists make their home in the vicinity of Merrickville, and their wares—ranging from paintings to leather crafts, wood carvings, pottery, and other creations—are available in boutiques and shops in the village. Be sure to check out **Kevin Gray Glass Blowing,** 635 St. Lawrence St. (© **613/269-7979**), to watch glass blowers at work; **Rowland Leather,** 159 St. Lawrence St. (© **613/269-3151**), for buttery soft bags by designer Michael Rowland; and **Hucklebuck's,** 108 St. Lawrence St. (© **613/269-2513**), for unique bird feeders and garden accessories.

If you work up a hunger or thirst, stop into the **Goose and Gridiron English Country Pub,** 317 St. Lawrence St. (© **613/269-2094**), which features 13 brands of beer on tap and has a cozy fireplace, or the charming **Sam Jakes Inn,** 118 Main St. E., (© **800/567-4667** or 613/269-3711).

SMITHS FALLS

The town of Smiths Falls, established in the mid-1800s, was built around the heart of the Rideau Canal. Three small museums in town chronicle the history of the canal, the railroads, and the pioneers who settled in this district. Check operating hours before visiting, since two of them are open by appointment only during the winter months. Of the three towns, Smiths Falls has the most to offer in terms of formal tours, and you could easily spend a full morning or afternoon here—especially if you have kids in tow.

Smiths Falls Railway Museum of Eastern Ontario (Kids) Railroad buffs will enjoy a visit to this museum, housed in a former Canadian Northern Railway Station built in 1914. Railway artifacts on display include express train and passenger train memorabilia, archives, track tools, and old photographs and prints. Kids will love the full-size steam and diesel locomotives, passenger coaches, and cabooses.

90 William St., Smiths Falls, ON. ✆ **613/283-5696.** www.sfrmeo.ca. Admission C$5 adults, C$3 seniors and students, C$2 children 3–11. Mid-May to June 30 Wed–Sun 10am–4:30pm; July 1 to first Mon in Sept daily 10am–4:30pm.

Rideau Canal Museum This museum has many hands-on displays for visitors to explore. You can operate a working lock model or test your skill as a canal skipper as you maneuver a model boat. Climb up to the lookout to get a panoramic view of the Rideau Canal and the town of Smiths Falls. Artifacts and historical displays share five floors with high-tech touch-screen computers and laserdisc minitheaters. A guided tour of the Smiths Falls Combined Locks is available daily June to August or by request. The outdoor walking tour is about an hour and includes the modern hydraulic lock system and the original three-lift manual system built by Lieutenant Colonel John By in 1829.

34 Beckwith St. S., Smiths Falls, ON. ✆ **613/284-0505.** www.rideau-info.com/museum. Admission indoor exhibits: C$4 adults, C$3.50 seniors, C$2.50 children 7–18, free for children 6 and under; locks and lockmaster's house are an additional fee: C$3 adults, C$2 children and seniors. Mid-Oct to mid-May by appointment; mid-May to mid-Oct daily 10am–4:30pm.

Heritage House Museum Adjacent to the Rideau Canal, Old Slys Lockstation, and a Victorian landscaped picnic area, this house has been restored to the time of Confederation (1867). Seven period rooms are featured, reflecting the lifestyle of a wealthy mill owner. Special programs, tours, and events are scheduled throughout the year.

Old Slys Rd. (off Hwy. 43), Smiths Falls, ON. ✆ **613/283-8560.** www.smithsfalls.ca/heritagehouse. Admission C$4 adults, C$3.50 seniors, C$2.50 children 6–18, free for children 6 and under; C$13 families (4 max.). Early Jan–early May Mon–Fri 10:30am–4:30pm; early May–late Dec daily 10:30am–4:30pm.

WHERE TO DINE

Black Dog Bistro BISTRO Restaurateur Dot Janz made her name by providing informal-yet-creative dining experiences with her Red Dot Restaurant in rural Osgoode. The two-story Black Dog Bistro on historic Manotick's main street provides a more upscale setting, but the mood remains warm and welcoming. It's not unusual to see off-duty corporate executives rubbing elbows with tradesmen at the small bar, which offers a modest wine list and some nice touches like locally brewed Beau's organic beer on tap. Bistro fare like steak and sweet potato fries, grilled salmon, and linguini with scallops, shrimp, and mussels in a lobster sauce are mainstays. I've returned time and again to the adobo ribs, which are nicely smoky and dry in the Memphis style I prefer. Also welcome is a substantial "mids" menu that allows you to combine smaller plates—including a tasty grilled chicken burger with cranberry mayonnaise and a Black Angus striploin burger—with an appetizer like orange-ginger scallops or shrimp sautéed in Lemoncello and served with rice noodles. Between the friendly locals that crowd the place and the satellite radio blues station that's piped in, the main floor can get loud; solace can be found upstairs or on the spacious patio.

5540 Main St., Manotick. ℓ **613/692-3779.** www.blackdogbistro.ca. Main courses C$17–C$24. AE, MC, V. Mon–Sat 11:30am–10:30pm.

The branch restaurant ★ (Value) ORGANIC   Chef Bruce Enloe grew up in Texas and earned his restaurant spurs in California. Along with spouse Nicole LeBlanc and partners Brent and Jennifer Kelaher, he is spearheading a growing local produce-and-music movement in the Ottawa region. The restaurant—a high room from the 1880s with a pressed-tin ceiling and plenty of charm—balances a diverse array of musicians and a small menu of locally sourced specialties that would easily fit in at any far-trendier—and more expensive—restaurant in Ottawa. The menu changes frequently, reflecting what's in season and available, but you can count on exceptional soups and what one of my carnivorous friends swears is the best liver he's ever tasted. Served in an organic beer-based butter sauce with onions and roasted potatoes, the liver is pan-seared pork liver from Pickle Patch Farms. Another standby is wild-caught jumbo shrimp served with seasonal vegetables and sandwiched between phyllo flatbread—the Thai seasoning tweaked to your liking on a five-point scale. I find organic wines a little thin, and Enloe's choices have yet to convince me otherwise, but that's a small concession when this much attention is paid to detail and this much passion is evident in the food, atmosphere, and service.

15 Clothier St. E., Kemptville. ℓ **613/258-3737.** www.thebranchrestaurant.ca. Main courses C$12–C$32. AE, MC, V. Tues–Sat 11:30am–2pm and 5–9:30pm; Sun 2–8pm.

3 ON THE LINKS

There are literally dozens of public golf courses within an hour's drive of Ottawa—to say nothing of some fine private courses. A few suggestions are listed below, but there are many more excellent courses to visit. Check out **www.ottawagolf.com** or **www.golfeogo.ca** for more comprehensive listings.

Amberwood Village   This is a nine-hole, par-66 course in a quiet suburban setting about a half-hour from Ottawa. Take Hwy. 417 (Queensway) west; exit at the Carp Road/Stittsville exit. Turn left onto Carp Road for approximately 2km (1¼ miles). Turn left onto Hazeldean Road, then right onto Springbrook Drive until you reach Amberwood. 54 Springbrook Dr., Stittsville, ON. ℓ **613/836-2581.**

Calabogie Highlands Resort and Golf Club   Rated in the top 50 golf courses in Ontario, this resort features an 18-hole championship course and a 9-hole lake-view course ideally suited for beginners. Accommodations, a practice range, an outdoor pool, and tennis are available. Take Hwy. 417 (Queensway) west past Arnprior. Turn left on Hwy. 508 to Calabogie (about 23km/14 miles). Turn left onto Hwy. 511, then right onto Barryvale Road. The resort is about an hour's drive from Ottawa. 981 Barryvale Rd., Calabogie, ON. ℓ **613/752-2171.**

Capital Golf Centre   Situated in the south end of the city next to the greenbelt, this 18-hole course is exclusively par 3, with the longest hole at 202 yards. The layout deliberately omits water and sand hazards as a benefit to beginning golfers, and it is an affordable place to learn and practice. More experienced golfers can play the course to sharpen up their short game. There's also a championship miniature golf course with holes ranging from 25 to 65 feet, and three practice ranges for all types of play—drives, short irons, bunkers, and chipping. Lessons are available. It is located 4km (2¹/₂ miles) south of Hunt Club Road on Bank Street. 3798 Bank St., Ottawa. ✆ 613/521-2612.

Champlain Golf Club Just 10 minutes from downtown Ottawa, this 18-hole championship course was established in 1929. There's a great practice center here where all levels of players can improve their game. Facilities include a driving range, two chipping greens, three practice sand traps, and two putting greens. Lessons, a pro shop, and refreshments are available. Cross the Champlain Bridge over the Ottawa River to Gatineau (Hull sector) and turn left on Hwy. 148 (boul. Alexander Taché/chemin d'Aylmer). A mere 1.3km (³/₄ mile) along on your right you'll find the golf club. 1145 chemin d'Aylmer, Gatineau (Aylmer sector), QC. ✆ 819/777-0449.

Château Cartier A luxurious golf and conference resort, situated on 62 hectares (153 acres) on the north shore of the Ottawa River, Château Cartier is just a short drive from Ottawa. See chapter 5, "Where to Stay," for details on this beautiful property. Cross the Champlain Bridge over the Ottawa River to Gatineau and turn left on Hwy. 148 (boul. Alexander Taché/chemin d'Aylmer). After a couple of minutes' drive, the resort will be on your left-hand side. 1170 chemin d'Aylmer, Gatineau (Aylmer sector) QC. ✆ 819/777-8870.

Eagle Creek Golf Course Eagle Creek public course is a challenging 18-hole championship course designed by U.S. Open winner Ken Venturi with the aim of rewarding precision over power. The course has been rated as one of the top ten courses in Ontario. The Eagle Creek Classic Tournament has been held for several years here as part of the Canadian Professional Golf Tour. The course was a *Golf Digest* 4-star award winner from 1996 to 2001. Take Hwy. 417 (Queensway) west and exit at March Road/Kanata/Eagleson Road. Travel north on March Road for about 8km (5 miles), then turn right onto Dunrobin Road for 10km (6 miles). Turn right onto Vances Sideroad for around 3km (2 miles). Turn left onto Greenland Road. About 1.5km (1 mile) along, turn left onto Ventor Boulevard. A few meters along the boulevard, you'll find the club. 109 Royal Troon Lane, Dunrobin, ON. ✆ 888/556-7651 or 613/832-0728. www.clublink.ca.

Mont-Cascades Golf Club One of the most scenic golf courses in the Ottawa area, this semiprivate golf club has a mature championship course, clubhouse, and outdoor deck overlooking the Gatineau River and Gatineau Hills. To get to Mont-Cascades from Ottawa, take the Macdonald-Cartier Bridge to Hull, then take Hwy. 50 east. Take the first exit, which is boulevard Archambault. Turn right onto Hwy. 307. Turn left on chemin Mont-Cascades, and proceed 7km (4¹/₃ miles) to Mont Cascades. It's about a half-hour drive from Ottawa. 448 chemin Mont-Cascades, Cantley, QC. ✆ 819/459-2980. www. golf.montcascades.com.

Mont Ste-Marie This classic mountain course set in the rolling contours of the Gatineau Hills has a challenging layout. A driving range, power carts, locker room, golf boutique, and bar/restaurant are available at this public course. To reach Mont Ste-Marie, take Hwy. 5 north through Hull and join Hwy. 105 north. Stay on Hwy. 105 until you see the signs for Mont Ste-Marie, a driving time of about 1 hour from Ottawa. 76 chemin de la Montagne, R.R. 1, Lac Ste-Marie, QC. ✆ 800/567-1256 or 819/467-3111. www.montste marie.com.

Pine View Municipal Golf Course Play a choice of two 18-hole courses here—one championship and one executive—at this City of Ottawa–owned public golf course. Locals have voted this course a favorite in past years. Take Hwy. 417 (Queensway) east, and continue on Hwy. 174 when the highway splits in two (don't take 417 toward Montreal at exit 113). Exit Hwy. 174 at Blair Road. Turn left onto Blair Road for 400m (1,312 ft.) to the course. 1471 Blair Rd., Ottawa. ☎ **613/746-4653.**

4 ON THE RIVER

One of the most popular white-water rafting and kayaking rivers in Canada, the Ottawa River has everything for the white-water enthusiast—dozens of islands, rapids, waterfalls, sandy beaches, and dramatic rock formations. An hour or two northwest of Ottawa, a number of white-water tour operators have established businesses that allow novices and families to enjoy running the rapids just as much as experienced extreme-sports participants do. Keep a lookout for one of the newest thrills, riverboarding. Equipped with a board, wetsuit, life jacket, helmet, and fins, riverboarders ride the rapids lying prone on their board. They read the direction of the current and point the board where they want to go using their arms as paddles and their flippers as rudders.

Esprit Rafting   Offering day trips and longer-stay outdoor adventure packages, Esprit Rafting operates on the Ottawa River about 1¹/₂ hours by road from Ottawa; the company can arrange transportation between Ottawa and the rafting site. They offer a wide range of adventure packages, including white-water rafting, white-water canoeing, white-water kayaking, and riverboarding. You can add horseback riding, mountain biking, or a bungee jump to your package. Esprit offers a great family white-water experience. In the morning, the family (children must be age 7 or older) rafts together with the assistance of an experienced guide. In the afternoon, children under age 12 take part in supervised shore activities while parents and children over age 12 take a more adventurous trip through the rapids. The day trip meets at a rendezvous point along the highway; get directions when you call to make your reservation. Overnight accommodations can be arranged at Esprit's private 2-hectare (5-acre) peninsula on the Upper Ottawa River, where camping facilities (tent and sleeping bag rental) and a hostel provide places to sleep. There is a lodge serving meals, and activities include kayaking, canoeing, volleyball, and mountain biking.

☎ **800/596-7238** or 819/683-3241. www.espritrafting.com. Seasonal (after the spring thaw until late fall); call for operating schedule.

Owl Rafting   Owl Rafting operates on the Ottawa River near Forester's Falls, between Renfrew and Pembroke off Hwy. 17. Paddle your own course with a guide if you wish, and choose everything from chicken runs to a champion challenge. Two-person inflatable kayaks are available. Owl Rafting also offers a half-day family float trip that takes you more than 6km (3³/₄ miles) along the river, through white water and calm pools. They return you to base on a gentle cruising raft (with chairs and a barbecue lunch on board). Passengers must weigh a minimum of 22 kilograms (49 pounds). Trips run on weekdays, and life jackets and helmets are provided. No paddling is required—just hold on and enjoy riding waves up to 1m (3 ft.) in height. Overnight accommodations (2 nights camping and 5 meals provided) are available. Reservations are required.

Summer: 40 Owl Lane, Forester's Falls, ON K0J 1V0. ☎ **800/461-7238** or 613/646-2263. Winter: 39 First Ave., Ottawa, ON K1S 2G1. ☎ **613/238-7238.** www.owl-mkc.ca.

River Run Whitewater Resort   River Run, just a 90-minute drive northwest of Ottawa, is a 56-hectare (138-acre) riverfront resort on the Ottawa River. Experiences range from gentle family rafting rides to aggressive sport-boat programs, and everyone on

Under the Ground

Once you've explored air, land, and water, what do you do next? Go underground, of course. The **Diefenbunker Cold War Museum** is definitely one of a kind.

At this museum, you can visit an underground bunker built during the cold war and designed to shelter officials of the Canadian government in the event of a nuclear attack. This is a rare opportunity to glimpse a somber and alarming period in recent world history, when precautions were taken against the threat of nuclear war. The huge four-story bunker—named for cold war–era prime minister John Diefenbaker—is buried deep under a farmer's field and designed to house more than 500 people and enough supplies for a month.

The guided walking tour takes about 1½ to 2 hours, and many of the guides used to work in the Diefenbunker before it was decommissioned in 1994. During the tour, you will see the blast tunnel and massive blast doors, the CBC radio studio, the Bank of Canada vault that was designed to hold Canada's gold reserves, the war cabinet room, the decontamination unit, a detailed model of the bunker, a 1-megaton hydrogen "practice bomb," a reconstruction of a family fallout shelter, and lots more.

To get to the Diefenbunker from Ottawa, follow Hwy. 417 (the Queensway) west, take the Carp-Stittsville exit, and bear right onto Carp Road. Travel about 8km (5 miles) into the village of Carp. Watch for signs on the left indicating the entrance to the Diefenbunker.

3911 Carp Rd., Carp, ON. ✆ **800/409-1965** or 613/839-0007. www.diefen bunker.ca. Admission C$14 adults, C$13 seniors and students, C$6 children 6–17, free for children 5 and under. Guided tours July 1—Labor Day daily at 11am, noon, 1pm, 2pm, and 3pm; early September—June 30 Mon–Fri at 2pm, Sat–Sun at 11am, 1pm, and 2pm. Reservations required.

board gets involved—you get to paddle on this one. There's also a complete range of outdoor recreational activities at the resort. Packages with overnight accommodations (everything from camping to rustic cabins to luxury inn rooms) can be arranged, including raft 'n' golf and raft 'n' spa packages.

PO Box 179, Beachburg, ON K0J 1C0. ✆ **800/267-8504** reservations or 613/646-2501 information. www. riverrunners.com. Seasonal (after the spring thaw until late fall); call for operating schedule.

Wilderness Tours Wilderness Tours is a 266-hectare (657-acre) resort and adventure destination on the banks of the Ottawa River. Paddle a small, sporty six-person raft with a guide, or take a family raft trip geared toward families with children between the ages of 7 and 12. Raft trips include professional guides and a post-trip video and barbecue. A variety of vacation packages are available, for short and long stays. Packages include meals, scenic camping or cabin rental, use of the resort facilities, and a supervised children's program in the evenings.

PO Box 89, Beachburg, ON K0J 1C0. ✆ **800/267-9166** or 613/646-2291. www.wildernesstours.com. Seasonal (after the spring thaw until late fall); call for operating schedule.

Appendix: Fast Facts, Toll-Free Numbers & Websites

1 FAST FACTS: OTTAWA

AMERICAN EXPRESS For card member services, including traveler's checks and lost or stolen cards, call © **800/869-3016** or 363/393-1111 collect (only if your card is lost or stolen). There is an American Express Travel Agency, which provides travel and financial services, at 220 Laurier Ave. W. ((© **613/563-0231**).

AREA CODES The telephone area code for Ottawa is 613; for Gatineau and surrounding areas it's 819. The area codes must be used for all local calls, although there is no charge for calls between Ottawa and Gatineau.

ATM NETWORKS/CASHPOINTS See "Money & Costs," p. 44.

AUTOMOBILE ORGANIZATIONS Motor clubs will supply maps, suggested routes, guidebooks, accident and bail-bond insurance, and emergency road service. The **Canadian Automobile Association (CAA)** is the major auto club in Canada. If you belong to a motor club in your home country, inquire about CAA reciprocity before you leave. You may be able to join CAA even if you're not a member of a reciprocal club; to inquire, call CAA (© **800/267-8713;** www.caa.ca). CAA is actually an organization of regional motor clubs, and the branch representing northern and eastern Ontario is located in Ottawa at 1224 Wellington St. CAA has a

nationwide emergency road service telephone number ((© **800/CAA-HELP**). In the Ottawa area, the CAA's emergency telephone number is © **613/820-1400**.

BUSINESS HOURS Most **stores** are open Monday to Saturday from 9:30 or 10am to 6pm, and many have extended hours one or more evenings. Sunday opening hours are generally from noon to 5pm, although some stores open at 11am and others are closed all day. **Banks** generally open at 9:30am and close by 4pm, with extended hours one or more evenings; some are open Saturday. **Restaurants** open at 11 or 11:30am for lunch and at 5pm for dinner, although many in the ByWard Market district stay open all day. Some **museums** are closed Monday from October to April; some also close Tuesday in the winter months. Many stay open on Thursday until 8 or 9pm.

CAR RENTALS See "Toll-Free Numbers & Websites," p. 222.

DRINKING LAWS You must be **19 years of age or older** to consume or purchase alcohol in Ontario. Bars and retail stores are strict about enforcing the law and will ask for proof of age if they consider it necessary. The **Liquor Control Board of Ontario (LCBO)** sells wine, spirits, and beer. Their flagship retail store, at 275 Rideau St. (© **613/789-5226**), has two floors of products from around the world, as well as a vintages section with a wide selection of high-quality products. Wine accessories are also available, and the LCBO regularly schedules seminars and tastings. This store is well worth a visit. Ontario wines are available at individual winery outlets. Beer is also available at the Beer Store, with about 20 locations in the Ottawa area.

Across the Ottawa River **in Quebec the drinking age is 18.** Quebec has traditionally had more liberal liquor laws than Ontario, and while hard liquor and imported wine is sold through provincially controlled outlets run by the **Société des alcools du Québec (SAQ),** beer and less-expensive domestic wines can be purchased at convenience and grocery stores.

DRIVING RULES   See "Getting There & Getting Around," p. 36.

ELECTRICITY   Like the United States, Canada uses 110 to 120 volts AC (60 cycles), compared to 220 to 240 volts AC (50 cycles) in most of Europe, Australia, and New Zealand. Downward converters that change 220–240 volts to 110–120 volts are difficult to find in North America, so bring one with you.

EMBASSIES & HIGH COMMISSIONS As the nation's capital, Ottawa is the home to embassies and high commissions representing almost every country in the world. If your country isn't listed below, call for directory information in Ottawa (© 613/ 555-1212) or check **www.ottawakiosk. com/embass.html**.

The embassy of the **United States** is at 490 Sussex Dr., Ottawa, ON K1N 1G8 (© 613/238-5335; http://ottawa.us embassy.gov).

The high commission of **Australia** is at 50 O'Connor St., Ste. 710, Ottawa, ON K1P 6L2 (© 613/236-0841; www.ahc ottawa.org).

The embassy of **Ireland** is at 130 Albert St., Ste. 1105, Ottawa, ON K1P 5G4 (© 613/233-6281).

The high commission of **New Zealand** is at 99 Bank St., Ste. 727, Ottawa, ON K1P 6G3 (© 613/238-5991; www.nz embassy.com).

The high commission of the **United Kingdom** is at 80 Elgin St., Ottawa, ON K1G 5K7 (© 613/237-1530; www. britainincanada.org).

EMERGENCIES   Call © 911 emergency services for fire, police, or ambulance. For Poison Control, call © 800/267-1373 or 613/737-1100.

GASOLINE (PETROL)   At press time, in Canada, the cost of gasoline (also known as gas, but never petrol), is abnormally high. Regular-grade gasoline is averaging about C$1.20 per liter (0.26 U.S. gallons) but has climbed as high as C$1.32 per liter. Taxes are already included in the printed price. Fill-up locations are known as gas or service stations and can be found throughout downtown Ottawa. While most stations in the center of the city close by 10pm, 24-hour stations can be found east of the core on Montreal Road, or to the south on Woodroffe Avenue.

HOLIDAYS   Banks, government offices, post offices, and many stores, restaurants, and museums are closed on the following legal national holidays: January 1 (New Year's Day), the third Monday in May (Victoria Day), July 1 (Canada Day), the first Monday in August (Civic Holiday), the first Monday in September (Labor Day), the second Monday in October (Thanksgiving Day), November 11 (Remembrance Day), and December 25 (Christmas).

HOSPITALS   The **Children's Hospital of Eastern Ontario (CHEO),** 401 Smyth Rd. (© 613/737-7600), is a pediatric teaching hospital affiliated with the University of Ottawa that services a broad geographical area, including Eastern Ontario and Western Quebec. The hospital has an emergency department. For adult care, the **Ottawa Hospital** is a large multicampus academic health sciences center with emergency departments at two sites: the **Civic** campus at 1053 Carling Ave. (✆ **613/761-4621**), and the **General** campus at 501 Smyth Rd. (✆ **613/737-8000**). Ontario emergency rooms are extremely busy and wait times for non-urgent cases are typically several hours.

HOT LINES Counselors trained to deal with sexual assault can be reached 24 hours a day at ✆ **613/562-2333.** The Ottawa & Region Distress Centre can be reached at ✆ **613/238-3311.** Kids or teens in distress can call ✆ **800/668-6868** for help.

INSURANCE **Medical Insurance** Although it's not required of travelers, health insurance is highly recommended. Most health insurance policies cover you if you get sick away from home—but check your coverage before you leave.

International visitors to Canada should note that, although each of the country's provinces and territories provide free health care, this social medicine policy does not extend to foreign visitors. Even for Canadian citizens, long waiting lines at emergency wards are now commonplace, and it is next to impossible to gain access to a general practitioner—either in or out of a hospital. Good policies will cover the costs of an accident, repatriation, or death. Canadian travel insurance companies such as **Blue Cross** (✆ **866/732-2583**; www.useblue.com), **Manulife Financial** (✆ **800/268-3763**; www.manulife.ca), and **RBC Insurance** (✆ 800/565-3129; www.rbcinsurance.com) can provide a starting point to compare policies and answer questions about coverage.

If you're ever hospitalized more than 241km (150 miles) from home, **Medjet Assist** (✆ **800/527-7478**; www.medjetassistance.com) will pick you up and fly you to the hospital of your choice in a medically equipped and staffed aircraft 24 hours day, 7 days a week. Annual memberships are US$225 individual, US$350 family; you can also purchase short-term memberships, starting at US$85 for 7-day coverage.

Canadians who are traveling to Ottawa from outside the province of Ontario should check with their provincial health plan offices or call **Health Canada** (✆ **866/225-0709**; www.hc-sc.gc.ca) to find out the extent of their coverage and what documentation and receipts they must take home in case they are treated in Ontario.

Travelers from the U.K. should carry their European Health Insurance Card (EHIC; ✆ **0845/606-2030**; www.ehic.org.uk), which replaced the E111 form as proof of entitlement to free/reduced cost medical treatment abroad. Note, however, that the EHIC only covers "necessary medical treatment," and for repatriation costs, lost money, baggage, or cancellation, travel insurance from a reputable company should always be sought (www.travelinsuranceweb.com).

Travel Insurance The cost of travel insurance varies widely, depending on your destination, the cost and length of your trip, your age and health, and the type of trip you're taking, but expect to pay between 5% and 8% of the vacation itself. You can get estimates from various providers through **InsureMyTrip.com.** Enter your trip cost and dates, your age, and other information, for prices from more than a dozen companies.

U.K. citizens and their families who make more than one trip abroad per year may find an annual travel insurance policy works out cheaper. Check **www.moneysupermarket.com**, which compares prices across a wide range of providers for single- and multitrip policies.

Most big travel agents offer their own insurance and will probably try to sell you their package when you book a holiday. Think before you sign. **Britain's Consumers' Association** recommends that you insist on seeing the policy and reading the fine print before buying travel insurance. The **Association of British Insurers**

(☎ 020/7600-3333; www.abi.org.uk) gives advice by phone and publishes *Holiday Insurance,* a free guide to policy provisions and prices. You might also shop around for better deals: Try **Columbus Direct** (☎ 0870/033-9988; www.columbusdirect.net).

Trip Cancellation Insurance Trip-cancellation insurance will help retrieve your money if you have to back out of a trip or depart early, or if your travel supplier goes bankrupt. Trip cancellation traditionally covers such events as sickness, natural disasters, and government-issued travel advisories. The latest news in trip-cancellation insurance is the availability of **"any-reason"** cancellation coverage—which costs more but covers cancellations made for any reason. You won't get back 100% of your prepaid trip cost, but you'll be refunded a substantial portion. **TravelSafe** (☎ 888/885-7233; www.travelsafe.com) offers both types of coverage. Expedia also offers any-reason cancellation coverage for its air-hotel packages. For details, contact one of the following recommended insurers: **Access America** (☎ 866/807-3982; www.accessamerica.com); **Travel Guard International** (☎ 800/826-4919; www.travelguard.com); **Travel Insured International** (☎ 800/243-3174; www.travelinsured.com); and **Travelex Insurance Services** (☎ 888/457-4602; www.travelex-insurance.com).

INTERNET ACCESS See "Staying Connected," p. 56.

LAUNDROMATS Most hotels provide same-day laundry and dry-cleaning services or have coin-operated laundry facilities.

LEGAL AID If you are "pulled over" for a minor infraction (such as speeding), never attempt to pay the fine directly to a police officer; this could be construed as attempted bribery, a much more serious crime. Pay fines by mail, or directly into the hands of the clerk of the court. If accused of a more serious offense, say and

do nothing before consulting a lawyer. In Canada, the burden is on the Crown (the province or the country) to prove a person's guilt beyond a reasonable doubt, and everyone has the right to remain silent, whether he or she is suspected of a crime or actually arrested. Once arrested, it is customary that you will be permitted to contact a lawyer or family member. International visitors should call your embassy or consulate immediately, or ask a family member to do so.

LOST & FOUND Be sure to tell all of your credit card companies the minute you discover your wallet has been lost or stolen and file a report at the nearest police precinct. Your credit card company or insurer may require a police report number or record of the loss. Most credit card companies have an emergency toll-free number to call if your card is lost or stolen; they may be able to wire you a cash advance immediately or deliver an emergency credit card in a day or two. Visa's Canadian emergency number is ☎ 800/847-2911 or 410/581-9994. American Express cardholders and traveler's check holders should call ☎ 800/668-2639. MasterCard holders should call ☎ 800/307-7309 or 636/722-7111. For other credit cards, call the toll-free number directory at ☎ 800/555-1212.

If you need emergency cash over the weekend when all banks and American Express offices are closed, you can have money wired to you via **Western Union** (☎ 800/325-6000; www.westernunion.com).

MAIL Mailing letters and postcards within Canada costs C$.52. Postage for letters and postcards to the United States costs C$.96, and overseas C$1.60.

MAPS Maps of Ottawa are readily available in convenience stores and bookstores, as well as at the **Capital Infocentre,** 90 Wellington St. (☎ 800/465-1867 or 613/239-5000). For a good selection of maps and travel guides, visit **A World of Maps,** 1235 Wellington St. W. (*©* **800/214-8524** or 613/724-6776).

MEASUREMENTS See the chart on the inside front cover of this book for details on converting metric measurements to nonmetric equivalents.

MEDICAL CONDITIONS If you have a medical condition that requires **syringe-administered medications,** carry a valid signed prescription from your physician; syringes in carry-on baggage will be inspected. Insulin in any form should have the proper pharmaceutical documentation. If you have a disease that requires treatment with **narcotics,** you should also carry documented proof with you—smuggling narcotics aboard a plane carries severe penalties in Canada.

NEWSPAPERS & MAGAZINES The daily newspapers are the *Ottawa Citizen,* the *Ottawa Sun,* and *Le Droit,* Ottawa's French-language newspaper. Keep an eye out for *Capital Parent,* a local free publication that advertises family-friendly events. *Where Ottawa* is a free monthly guide to shopping, dining, entertainment, and other tourist information. You can find it at most hotels and at some restaurants and retail stores. *Ottawa Magazine* and *Ottawa Life* are city monthlies. Arts and entertainment newspapers include the English-language *Xpress* and the French-language *Voir.* Gays and lesbians should check out *Capital Xtra!* For a great variety of international publications, visit **Mags and Fags,** at 254 Elgin St. (*©* **613/233-9651**), or **Planet News,** at 143 Sparks St. (*©* **613/232-5500**).

PASSPORTS The websites listed below provide downloadable passport applications as well as the current fees for processing applications.

For Residents of the United States U.S. citizens must apply in person at one of more than 9,000 passport facilities across

the country. A complete list and application details can be found at www.travel.state.gov/passport. Allow plenty of time before your trip to apply for a passport; processing normally takes 4 to 6 weeks (3 weeks for expedited service) but can take longer during busy periods (especially spring). And keep in mind that if you need a passport in a hurry, you'll pay a higher processing fee.

For Residents of Australia You can pick up an application from your local post office or any branch of Passports Australia, but you must schedule an interview at the passport office to present your application materials. Call the **Australian Passport Information Service** at *©* **131-232,** or visit the government website at www.passports.gov.au.

For Residents of Ireland You can apply for a 10-year passport at the **Passport Office,** Setanta Centre, Molesworth Street, Dublin 2 (*©* **01/671-1633;** www.irlgov.ie/iveagh). Those under age 18 and over 65 must apply for a 3-year passport. You can also apply at 1A South Mall, Cork (*©* **21/494-4700**) or at most main post offices.

For Residents of New Zealand You can pick up a passport application at any New Zealand Passports Office or download it from their website. Contact the **Passports Office** at *©* **0800/225-050** in New Zealand or 04/474-8100, or visit www.passports.govt.nz.

For Residents of the United Kingdom To pick up an application for a standard 10-year passport (5-yr. passport for children under 16), visit your nearest passport office, major post office, or travel agency or contact the **United Kingdom Passport Service** at *©* **0870/521-0410** or visit its website at www.ukpa.gov.uk.

POLICE In a life-threatening emergency or to report a crime in progress or a traffic accident that involves injuries or a vehicle that cannot be driven, call ☏ **911.** For other emergencies (a serious crime or a break and enter) call ☏ **613/230-6211.** For all other inquiries, call ☏ **613/236-1222.**

SMOKING Ontario has among the most stringent nonsmoking legislation in the world. Smoking is prohibited in any enclosed, public place in Ottawa, and within several meters (or yards) of most public buildings. There is no smoking in any restaurants or bars, and smoking is only permitted in designated rooms in hotels.

TAXES The national Goods and Services Tax (GST) is 5%. The provincial retail sales tax (PST) is 8% on most goods; certain purchases, such as groceries and children's clothing, are exempt from provincial sales tax. The accommodations tax is 5%.

TELEPHONES See "Staying Connected," p. 56.

TELEGRAPH, TELEX & FAX **Telegraph and telex services** are provided primarily by **Western Union** (☏ **800/325-6000;** www.westernunion.com). You can telegraph (wire) money, or have it telegraphed to you, very quickly over the Western Union system, but this service can cost as much as 15% to 20% of the amount sent.

Most hotels have **fax machines** available for guest use (be sure to ask about the charge to use it). Many hotel rooms are wired for guests' fax machines. A less-expensive way to send and receive faxes may be at stores such as **Staples.**

TIME Canada is divided into **six time zones:** Newfoundland Standard Time (NST), Atlantic Standard Time (AST), Eastern Standard Time (EST), Central Standard Time (CST), Mountain Standard Time (MST), and Pacific Standard Time (PST). For example, when it's 9am in Vancouver (PST), it's 10am in Calgary (MST), 11am in Winnipeg (CST), noon in Ottawa (EST), 1pm in Halifax (AST),

1:30pm in St. John's (NST), 5pm in London (GMT), and 2am the next day in Sydney.

Daylight saving time is in effect from 1am on the second Sunday in March to 1am on the first Sunday in November, except in Saskatchewan. Daylight saving time moves the clock 1 hour ahead of standard time.

TIPPING Tips are a very important part of certain workers' income, and gratuities are the standard way of showing appreciation for services provided. (Tipping is certainly not compulsory if the service is poor!) In hotels, tip **bellhops** at least C$1 per bag (C$2–C$3 if you have a lot of luggage) and tip the **chamber staff** C$1 to C$2 per day (more if you've left a disaster area for him or her to clean up). Tip the **doorman** or **concierge** only if he or she has provided you with some specific service (for example, calling a cab for you or obtaining difficult-to-get theater tickets). Tip the **valet-parking attendant** C$1 every time you get your car.

In restaurants, bars, and nightclubs, tip **service staff** 15% to 20% of the check, tip **bartenders** 10% to 15%, tip **checkroom attendants** C$1 per garment, and tip **valet-parking attendants** C$1 per vehicle.

As for other service personnel, tip **cab drivers** 15% of the fare; tip **skycaps** at airports at least C$1 per bag (C$2–C$3 if you have a lot of luggage); and tip **hairdressers** and **barbers** 15% to 20%.

TOILETS You won't find public toilets or "restrooms" on the streets in most Canadian cities but they can be found in hotel lobbies, bars, restaurants, museums, department stores, railway and bus stations, and service stations. Large hotels and fast-food restaurants are often the best bet for clean facilities. Restaurants and bars in resorts or heavily visited areas may reserve their restrooms for patrons.

VISAS See "Entry Requirements," p. 26.

MAJOR CANADIAN AIRLINES

(*flies internationally as well)

Air Canada*
© 888/247-2262 (in U.S. and Canada)
© 0871/220-1111 (in U.K.)
www.aircanada.com

Porter Airlines*
© 866/619-8622 (in U.S. and Canada)
www.flyporter.com

WestJet*
© 800/538-5696 (in U.S. and Canada)
www.westjet.com

MAJOR U.S. AIRLINES

(*flies internationally as well)

American Airlines*
© 800/433-7300 (in U.S. and Canada)
© 020/7365-0777 (in U.K.)
www.aa.com

Continental Airlines*
© 800/523-3273 (in U.S. and Canada)
© 084/5607-6760 (in U.K.)
www.continental.com

Delta Air Lines*
© 800/221-1212 (in U.S. and Canada)
© 084/5600-0950 (in U.K.)
www.delta.com

JetBlue Airways
© 800/538-2583 (in U.S. and Canada)
© 080/1365-2525 (in U.K.)
www.jetblue.com

Northwest Airlines
© 800/225-2525 (in U.S. and Canada)
© 870/0507-4074 (in U.K.)
www.flynaa.com

United Airlines*
© 800/864-8331 (in U.S. and Canada)
© 084/5844-4777 in U.K.
www.united.com

US Airways*
© 800/428-4322 (in U.S. and Canada)
© 084/5600-3300 (in U.K.)
www.usairways.com

MAJOR INTERNATIONAL AIRLINES

Aeroméxico
© 800/237-6639 (in U.S. and Canada)
© 020/7801-6234 (in U.K.,
   information only)
www.aeromexico.com

Air France
© 800/237-2747 (in U.S.)
© 800/375-8723 (in U.S. and Canada)
© 087/0142-4343 (in U.K.)
www.airfrance.com

Air India
© 800/223-7776 (in U.S. and Canada)
© 91 22 2279 6666 (in India)
© 020/8560-9996 (in U.K.)
www.airindia.com

Air New Zealand
© 800/262-1234 (in U.S.)
© 800/663-5494 (in Canada)
© 0800/028-4149 (in U.K.)
www.airnewzealand.com

Alitalia
© 800/223-5730 (in U.S.)
© 800/361-8336 (in Canada)
© 087/0608-6003 (in U.K.)
www.alitalia.com

American Airlines
© 800/433-7300 (in U.S. and Canada)
© 020/7365-0777 (in U.K.)
www.aa.com

British Airways
© 800/247-9297 (in U.S. and Canada)
© 087/0850-9850 (in U.K.)
www.british-airways.com

Continental Airlines
© 800/523-3273 (in U.S. or Canada)
© 084/5607-6760 (in U.K.)
www.continental.com

Delta Air Lines
© 800/221-1212 (in U.S. and Canada)
© 084/5600-0950 (in U.K.)
www.delta.com

EgyptAir
© 212/581-5600 (in U.S.)
© 416/960-2441 (in Canada)
© 020/7734-2343 (in U.K.)
© 09/007-0000 (in Egypt)
www.egyptair.com

El Al Airlines
© 972/3977-1111 (outside Israel)
© *2250 (from any phone in Israel)
www.elal.co.il

Emirates Airlines
© 800/777-3999 (in U.S. and Canada)
© 087/0243-2222 (in U.K.)
www.emirates.com

Finnair
© 800/950-5000 (in U.S. and Canada)
© 087/0241-4411 (in U.K.)
www.finnair.com

Iberia Airlines
© 800/722-4642 (in U.S. and Canada)
© 087/0609-0500 (in U.K.)
www.iberia.com

Lufthansa
© 800/399-5838 (in U.S.)
© 800/563-5954 (in Canada)
© 087/0837-7747 (in U.K.)
www.lufthansa.com

Swiss Air
© 877/359-7947 (in U.S. and Canada)
© 084/5601-0956 (in U.K.)
www.swiss.com

United Airlines*
© 800/864-8331 (in U.S. and Canada)
© 084/5844-4777 (in U.K.)
www.united.com

US Airways*
© 800/428-4322 (in U.S. and Canada)
© 084/5600-3300 (in U.K.)
www.usairways.com

Virgin Atlantic Airways
© 800/821-5438 (in U.S. and Canada)
© 087/0574-7747 (in U.K.)
www.virgin-atlantic.com

BUDGET AIRLINES

Aegean Airlines
© 210/626-1000 (in U.S., Canada, and U.K.)
www.aegeanair.com

Aer Lingus
© 800/474-7424 (in U.S. and Canada)
© 087/0876-5000 (in U.K.)
www.aerlingus.com

CAR RENTAL AGENCIES

Avis
- 📞 800/331-1212 (in U.S. and Canada)
- 📞 084/4581-8181 (in U.K.)
- www.avis.com

Budget
- 📞 800/527-0700 (in U.S.)
- 📞 800/268-8900 (in Canada)
- 📞 087/0156-5656 (in U.K.)
- www.budget.com

Dollar
- 📞 800/800-4000 (in U.S.)
- 📞 800/848-8268 (in Canada)
- 📞 080/8234-7524 (in U.K.)
- www.dollar.com

Enterprise
- 📞 800/261-7331 (in U.S.)
- 📞 514/355-4028 (in Canada)
- 📞 012/9360-9090 (in U.K.)
- www.enterprise.com

Hertz
- 📞 800/645-3131 (in U.S. and Canada)
- 📞 800/654-3001 (for international reservations)
- www.hertz.com

National
- 📞 800/CAR-RENT (227-7368)
- www.nationalcar.com

Rent-A-Wreck
- 📞 800/535-1391
- www.rentawreck.com

Thrifty
- 📞 800/367-2277 (in U.S. and Canada)
- 📞 918/669-2168 (international)
- www.thrifty.com

MAJOR HOTEL & MOTEL CHAINS

Best Western International
- 📞 800/780-7234 (in U.S. and Canada)
- 📞 0800/393-130 (in U.K.)
- www.bestwestern.com

Courtyard by Marriott
- 📞 888/236-2427 (in U.S. and Canada)
- 📞 0800/221-222 (in U.K.)
- www.marriott.com/courtyard

Crowne Plaza Hotels
- 📞 888/303-1746
- www.ichotelsgroup.com/crowneplaza

Days Inn
- 📞 800/329-7466 (in U.S. and Canada)
- 📞 0800/280-400 (in U.K.)
- www.daysinn.com

Embassy Suites
- 📞 800/EMBASSY (362-2779)
- http://embassysuites1.hilton.com

Hampton Inn
- 📞 800/HAMPTON (426-4766)
- http://hamptoninn1.hilton.com

Hilton Hotels
- 📞 800/HILTONS (445-8667) (in U.S. and Canada)
- 📞 087/0590-9090 (in U.K.)
- www.hilton.com

Holiday Inn
- 📞 800/315-2621 (in U.S. and Canada)
- 📞 0800/405-060 (in U.K.)
- www.holidayinn.com

Howard Johnson
- 📞 800/446-4656 (in U.S. and Canada)
- www.hojo.com

Hyatt
- 📞 888/591-1234 (in U.S. and Canada)
- 📞 084/5888-1234 (in U.K.)
- www.hyatt.com

InterContinental Hotels & Resorts
- 📞 800/424-6835 (in U.S. and Canada)
- 📞 0800/1800-1800 (in U.K.)
- www.ichotelsgroup.com

Marriott
☎ 877/236-2427 (in U.S. and Canada)
☎ 0800/221-222 (in U.K.)
www.marriott.com

Quality
☎ 877/424-6423 (in U.S. and Canada)
☎ 0800/444-444 (in U.K.)
www.qualityinn.com

Radisson Hotels & Resorts
☎ 888/201-1718 (in U.S. and Canada)
☎ 0800/374-411 (in U.K.)
www.radisson.com

Ramada Worldwide
☎ 888/2-RAMADA (272-6232)
  (in U.S. and Canada)
☎ 080/8100-0783 (in U.K.)
www.ramada.com

Residence Inn by Marriott
☎ 800/331-3131 (in U.S. and Canada)
☎ 0800/221-222 (in U.K.)
www.marriott.com/residenceinn

Sheraton Hotels & Resorts
☎ 800/325-3535 (in U.S.)
☎ 800/543-4300 (in Canada)
☎ 0800/3253-5353 (in U.K.)
www.starwoodhotels.com/sheraton

Travelodge
☎ 800/578-7878
www.travelodge.com

Westin Hotels & Resorts
☎ 800-937-8461 (in U.S. and Canada)
☎ 0800/3259-5959 (in U.K.)
www.starwoodhotels.com/westin

INDEX

See also Accommodations and Restaurant indexes, below.

ACCOMMODATIONS

Restaurants

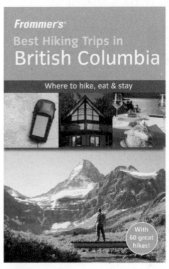
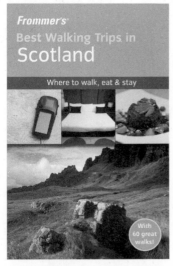

Discover Canada with Frommer's®!

All the up-to-date, practical information and candid insider advice you need for the perfect vacation in Canada!

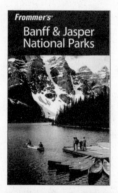

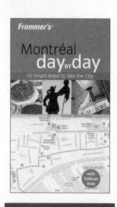

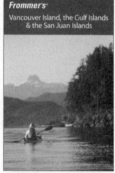

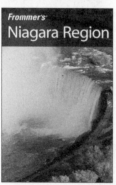

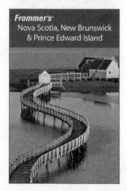

Explore over 3,500 destinations.

Frommers.com makes it easy.

Find a destination. ✓ Book a trip. ✓ Get hot travel deals.
uy a guidebook. ✓ Enter to win vacations. ✓ Listen to podcasts. ✓ Check out
he latest travel news. ✓ Share trip photos and memories. ✓ And much more.

Frommers.com